psychology and contemporary problems

psychology and contemporary problems

NORMAN W. HEIMSTRA
University of South Dakota

ARTHUR L. McDONALD
Montana State University

BROOKS/COLE PUBLISHING COMPANY
MONTEREY, CALIFORNIA

A Division of Wadsworth Publishing Company, Inc.

ISBN: 0-8185-0067-0
L.C. Catalog Card No: 72-90321
Printed in the United States of America
1 2 3 4 5 6 7 8 9 10—77 76 75 74 73

This book was edited by Anne Phillips and designed by Jane Mitchell, with technical illustrations by John Foster. It was typeset by Continental Data Graphics, Culver City, California, and printed and bound by Kingsport Press, Kingsport, Tennessee.

preface

More and more psychologists are now viewing their research efforts in terms of the contributions they can make to the solving of real-world problems. The range and magnitude of these problems are vast; psychologists are now involved in areas that, only a few years ago, would have seemed far removed from the realm of psychological inquiry.

The primary aim of this book, then, is to expose the reader to as broad a spectrum of problem areas as possible, while still presenting a reasonably detailed description of a particular area, the research approaches utilized by investigators "tackling" the problem, and the important concepts and findings in the problem area. A number of specific studies are cited in order to illustrate research approaches—not to present an "encyclopedia" of facts for the reader to digest. An effort has been made to summarize, in general terms, the current status of research in a given problem area and to appraise the contributions made by psychologists who are attempting to solve the problem.

Since the problem areas in which psychologists now work are so diverse, an author attempting to write a moderate-sized textbook dealing with psychology and real-world problems is confronted with the difficult decision about what should be included in the book and what should be omitted. Because of the available data, it is tempting to deal heavily with the more "traditional" areas in which psychologists have been working for a number of years. Thus topics such as mental health, industrial psychology, and educational psychology are certainly appropriate "problem" areas about which a great deal could be written. However, psychologists in increasing numbers are becoming involved in a variety of other problem areas of more recent interest—problem areas such as those of the environment, transportation, overcrowding, aggression and violence, and drugs and alcohol.

In this book, we have attempted to emphasize these newer areas, even though, in some cases, they are so new that there is a paucity of research data dealing with them. These subjects have been included because of the interest psychologists have shown in the area and because psychologists will probably be making important contributions to the solution of the problems. Environmental psychology is an example of this type situation.

A background in psychology is not necessary to understand this book. Research and research findings are discussed in such a fashion that the reader does not have to understand statistics and experimental design in order to understand the implications of the research.

There are a number of individuals who, in one way or another, contributed substantially to this book. We wish to thank reviewers Gordon E. Anderson, C. A. Dawson, Jr., Franklin F. Gould, Edward L. Walker, and Robert D. Williams for their comments and suggestions concerning the manuscript, many of which have been incorporated in the final version of the text. A number of people at the Brooks/Cole Publishing Company provided valuable assistance at all stages of the development of the book—Terry Hendrix and Bonnie Fitzwater during the writing and review stages and Anne Phillips and Vena Dyer during the production stages. Finally, a very special debt of gratitude is owed to Mrs. Velda Kilstrom for the many hours spent typing the manuscript and for her help in so many other ways during the writing of the book.

Norman W. Heimstra

Arthur L. McDonald

contents

psychology and
contemporary
problems

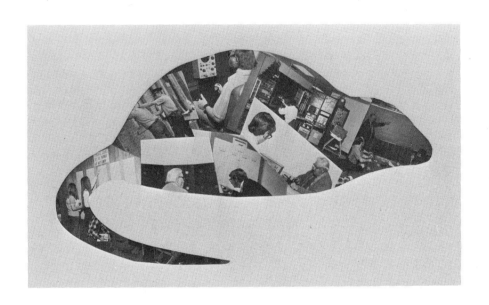

chapter

1

Introduction

Research is the major activity of many psychologists as they attempt to answer a tremendous range of questions. Some psychologists feel that their research should add to the general knowledge that exists about behavior; they are not concerned about whether the information they gather will be used to solve any practical problems. This type of research is called *basic* or *pure*. However, an increasing number of investigators have been directing their research toward solving practical, real-world problems. This kind of research is called *applied*.

There are strong advocates of both types of research in psychology, but there appears to be a growing realization that it is not a question of one or the other; rather, both kinds are necessary if psychology is to advance as a science. This book is concerned with the research that psychologists have conducted and are conducting in an effort to solve some of the pressing real-world problems that currently exist; however, much of this research is possible only because of the foundation of psychological knowledge that basic research has built over the years. Similarly, much of the applied research discussed in this book may contribute to the basic foundation of behavior theory.

WHY THE TREND TOWARD PRACTICAL RESEARCH?

Psychology is not alone in its increased emphasis on applied research. This is also the case with many other fields that, only a few years ago, were primarily concerned with basic research. What are some of the reasons for this change in emphasis?

In the first place, large segments of society no longer accept these problems as inevitable and as something over which they have no control. Consider, for example, the environment. Once it became reasonably clear to the public that this was indeed a serious problem, there was a widespread reaction ranging from expressions by individual citizens—newspaper articles, talks on television, and so forth—through "environmental sit-ins," all the way to violent demonstrations. The public demanded that something be done about these problems.

As this demand has increased in recent years, the scientific community has been required to re-evaluate its role in society and readjust. Scientists have made the adjustment not only because they are sensitive to problems of society and recognize that they can contribute to the solution of these problems but also because research requires money. The government agencies that fund much of this country's scientific research have in recent years been committing increasing proportions of their research budgets to projects that deal with the problems and issues confronting society. Thus scientists from every field are concerning themselves with real-world problems.

As part of this changing emphasis in research, members of each particular scientific group are often asked to answer this question: What has your discipline contributed to the solution of the problems and issues confronting society, what is it doing now, and what can it do? This book is concerned with the answers that members of one particular discipline—*psychology*—might have concerning certain of these problems.

WHAT ARE THE PROBLEMS?

We have indicated that the real-world problems that psychologists and researchers from many other disciplines are concerned with range from those that threaten our whole society to those that are inconvenient for a few members of society. Thus if we were to ask a number of individuals to prepare a list of what they considered problems, the lists would not only be long but would vary considerably. On the other hand, many problem areas would appear on virtually all of the lists. For example, everyone is concerned with the increase in aggression and violence demonstrated by individuals and groups within our society. Each year we receive reports that there have been significant increases in the crime rate; in many cities it is unsafe to walk the streets at night. In addition, we are constantly reminded that our environment is being jeopardized and that if drastic steps are not taken in the near future it may as pollution, congested highways, over 50,000 deaths per year from highway crashes, and many more. So although many human-factors psychologists are concerned with the man-machine relationships involved in operating vehicles, others are active in the larger problems that have developed in the public transportation system.

The need for psychologists in the human-factors area has increased steadily in recent years. If we compare the complexity of the machine systems that exist today with those existing just a few years ago, it is apparent that there is even more need for paying attention to the human factors in these systems. However, the range and sophistication of the human-factors activities has increased and there are now human-factors experts involved in problem areas such as mass transportation, environmental misuse, and mass housing as well as in the design and administration of hospitals, in the educational systems, in automation, and in numerous other areas. Indeed, instead of being an expert in man-machine relationships, a human-factors psychologist has now become an expert in man-environment relationships.

When we deal with problems of man in unusual environments, the hazards of the environment, and several other areas, we will frequently be discussing work of human-factors psychologists. In Chapter 7, which is concerned with problems encountered when we attempt to "fit the job to the man," the more traditional human-factors activities—that is, those involving the design of equipment to better accommodate the human operator—will be taken up in some detail.

Industrial Psychology

As pointed out earlier in this chapter, most individuals spend a large part of their lives in a "working environment" of one kind or another. Many people are satisfied with their jobs and do not view their working environment as giving rise to any serious problems, but many other individuals are dissatisfied with their jobs. As a matter of fact, so many are dissatisfied that the problem of worker-job relationships is viewed by some as a serious problem in our society. Researchers in the field of industrial psychology are actively engaged in attempting to solve certain of the problems associated with worker-job relationships. The role of the industrial psychologist is nicely summarized by Schultz (1970) who states:

Psychologists are actively involved in selecting the right man for the right job, in matching the characteristics and requirements of both for optimal satisfaction and performance level. Once a man is selected for a job, the psychologists' contributions become even more important. The worker must be trained to perform the job efficiently and safely. The foremen and supervisors who guide him must be aware of and sensitive to the many factors affecting both the worker and his job. The psychological and physical work environment must be designed to produce not only efficient performance but also motivation, reward, and job satisfaction. The worker's performance must be fairly and objectively evaluated periodically to provide an equitable basis for job advancement. If the company and the worker are to prosper, the manufactured product must be advertised and packaged, promoted and sold. In all of these activities—from worker selection to product promotion—psychologists make major contributions. In most corporations today, psychologists are actively working to design the best relationship between a man and his job [p. 1].

Social Psychology

Unlike human-factors psychology and industrial psychology, social psychology did not develop in response to real-world problems. However, in recent years numerous social psychologists have become interested in these problems and are beginning to attempt to study them in hopes of arriving at some solutions. Trained to study the behavior of individuals in groups and to deal with the manner in which groups influence the individual's behavior, social psychologists are starting to make progress in studying such problem areas as violence and aggression, racial tensions, and discrimination, and are arriving at answers to some of the questions about how intergroup conflict may best be reduced or eliminated. It is quite possible that social psychology may eventually have a significant impact on many of the most serious problems that confront us today.

Psychology in Education

Because the educational system of this country is so vast and complex, nearly everyone is involved in the educational system in one way or another. There are many who feel that this system does not function as it should and that the problems associated with it are of major concern to society. Many of these problems are directly related to lack of adequate financing, but there are others associated with the educational process itself and it is this kind of problem that psychologists attempt to deal with.

Since the educational process involves so many different facets, the research of psychologists in numerous areas is often applicable to the problems encountered in the educational system. Research dealing with learning and motivation is particularly relevant, as is that dealing with problem solving, intelligence, personality and personality development, tests and measurement, interpersonal relationships, and other areas of psychology.

Much of the research in recent years has dealt with the development and evaluation of new techniques to be used in the educational system. Considerable effort has been directed at the design, implementation, and evaluation of innovative techniques such as programmed and computer-assisted instruction. Similarly, increased attention has been given to improving instructional methods and approaches for use with culturally deprived children, children with various types of handicaps, and children with backgrounds that for various reasons may make them less able to benefit from standard instruction than other children. There are many other areas of education in which psychologists are actively studying particular problems, and many of the improvements in the educational system that have taken place in recent years can be directly attributed to the work of psychologists.

Clinical and Counseling Psychology

A major problem area, which has a considerable impact on society, is mental health. Psychologists have, of course, been active in this area for many years, and much of what we know about the treatment and prevention of mental disorders is due to the research of these psychologists. There are currently a large number of psychologists who are attempting to deal with this problem area and, although their efforts have had only limited success, new approaches and techniques that are being developed show considerable promise. Although we will not deal with the mental-health problem to any great extent in this book, we will consider some of the special problem areas in mental health that have been receiving increased attention in recent years.

Legal Psychology

Under the rather broad label of "legal psychology" we find psychologists involved in a wide range of activities, attempting to define the personal factors associated with criminal behavior as well as the environmental factors. They are interested in the psychological aspects of rehabilitation, the treatment of young offenders, the application of psychological principles to correction, the prevention of new crime, and so forth. Many psychologists in this area must also be well versed in courtroom procedures since they are frequently called on as expert witnesses. Because of the significant increase in crime and the recognition that psychologists can help in this area, a number of psychologists have entered this field in recent years.

We could go on for a number of pages describing other areas of psychology that have been or are now becoming involved in research dealing with practical problems and issues. Virtually all of our societal systems have created problems of one type or another and, in many cases, psychologists are working to solve these problems with varying degrees of success. However, the areas of psychology we have discussed are those in which psychologists have made (or have the potential to make) significant contributions to the solving of real-world problems. Although the research discussed in this book is from many areas of psychology—some we have not described—much of the research that we will talk about has been conducted by investigators in these areas.

THE SCOPE OF THE TEXT

When you looked at the table of contents for this book, you probably wondered why certain topics were included and why others, which you may consider major problem areas, were not included. Obviously, the amount of material that can be covered in a book of this size is limited, and we were forced to select from the virtually hundreds of areas that could appropriately be discussed. The general areas included, however, represent important problem areas—areas in which psychologists have been quite active. For example, most would agree that the problems associated with man and his "living" and "working" environments are of considerable significance. The specific topics selected for discussion in each of the problem areas were chosen as being most illustrative of the problem itself and the approaches researchers used to attack the problem.

The primary goal of this book is to acquaint the reader with the role that psychology plays in attempting to solve some of the problems confronting society, but there is also a secondary aim. It is hoped that on completion of this book you will have a better understanding of how the science of psychology deals with problems—that is, an understanding of the methods employed by psychologists in attempting to solve problems. Therefore, whenever appropriate, a brief discussion is included of the approach of the researchers in attacking problems, pitfalls that are encountered, and other approaches that might have been more fruitful.

We stress that the nature and magnitude of any existing problem is such that no single scientific discipline is likely to provide the solution to the problem, and, when a solution is achieved, it will be due to the contributions of researchers from a variety of disciplines. Sometimes the investigators work with small, carefully delineated aspects of a problem area, whereas other times they attempt to tackle a much greater part of the problem. For example, in the problem area of alcoholism, some investigators are engaged in studies dealing with genetic predispositions toward alcoholism, others are concerned with establishing and evaluating vast treatment programs, and still others are attempting to devise methods of getting the alcoholic driver off the road. Even though their approach to the problem and their views about the type of research that will contribute most to the solution may be quite different, all are concerned with the problem that alcoholism presents to our society. This is true for all of the problem areas we will discuss—investigators have varying opinions and techniques, but they are all working to solve society's problems.

part 1

MAN AND HIS LIVING ENVIRONMENT

Many psychologists are becoming concerned with the way the environment influences man's behavior and, in turn, the way man's behavior affects his environment. This has led to the emergence of a new applied field called *environmental psychology*. Several areas of research in this new field as well as the methodological problems encountered are discussed in Chapter 2. Psychologists are also interested in using psychological principles to design environments that are more adequate for man; some of the problems of environmental design are considered in Chapter 3.

Man must frequently perform in environments that, for various reasons, are considered unusual. Examples include those encountered in space, under water, where excessive stimulation is present, and where there is inadequate stimulation. Man's performance in unusual environments is discussed in Chapter 4. Chapter 5 is concerned with some of the research conducted by psychologists who are interested in attempting to reduce hazards of the environment that result in accidents. As you will see in Chapter 5, accidents are one of the major health hazards, and the development of effective countermeasures against accidents involves researchers from many disciplines, including psychology.

chapter 2

Environmental Psychology

When we attempt to consider our "total" environment, it quickly becomes apparent that we are dealing with a broad and ill-defined composite of interacting features that influence us in a number of ways. Frequently, when psychologists refer to "environment," they have in mind a specific aspect of the total environment such as the home, family, social groups, and so forth. However, we are involved daily with many other features of the total environment, such as buildings and their related facilities, the community in which we live, transportation systems, and so forth. We can label these as belonging to the *built environment* in order to contrast them with the *natural environment,* which also forms an important part of the total picture. All of the numerous features of the total environment may have an impact, either good or bad, on our daily life.

Because of their impact on behavior, there are numerous features of the total living environment that are of interest to psychologists. Many areas that come under the heading of "total environment" have been investigated by researchers for a number of years. For example, there is a considerable amount of research dealing with man and the environment in which he works. In Part 2, man and his working environment will be discussed in detail. Similarly, transportation systems have been well researched and will be discussed in later chapters. There are many other aspects of the total environment that have

Photo courtesy of Travel Division, South Dakota Dept. of Highways, Pierre, S. D.

been studied by psychologists, although many of them possibly did not label their studies as "environmental" research.

Currently, there is a growing interest in the area of environmental psychology. Kaplan (1972, p. 141) points out: "As man drifts toward overpopulation and environmental decline, it is incumbent on us as psychologists to try to figure out what lies behind these disastrous tendencies." In recent years a number of graduate schools have initiated new programs concerned with the study of the human organism and its effects on the environment as well as the converse relationship. In fact, there are several schools at the present time offering graduate degrees in environmental psychology. Most of these programs are new and, as with any scientific discipline in its embryo stage, the definition of the subject matter is not precise. In 1970, Proshansky, Ittelson, and Rivlin defined environmental psychology as the study of human behavior in relation to the man-ordered and man-defined environment. Although they do not consider their statement an adequate definition of environmental psychology, they feel it does serve to describe the direction the new subfield is taking. In other words, the environmental psychologist is concerned with the natural environment as it is influenced by human behavior and the ways in which the environment influences behavior. The importance of man's effect on the environment is quite obvious when problems such as air pollution, housing-development design, highway construction, water pollution, noise pollution, strip mining, lumbering, and even traditional agricultural production are considered.

Although numerous of the physical sciences have concerned themselves in the past with specific "environmental" problems (such as cloud seeding by meteorologists, cumulative pesticide toxins by fish and wildlife management, freshwater supply sources by microbiologists, and so forth), the separate study of environmental science is just beginning. The study of the environmental sciences has stemmed from the rather arrogant attitude of Western culture toward its natural resources. The basic philosophy in the winning of the West has been to exploit the environmental resources and hope that some mysterious process will heal the wounds and cleanse the refuse produced by this exploitation. What man has done to his environment in the past, is doing in the present, and may do in the future has frightened a large number of people. These people, in ever-increasing numbers, have put pressure on politicians and scientists to find ways of studying the problems in an effort to understand and eventually alleviate the situation. It becomes clear, then, that the impetus for the environmental sciences in general, and environmental psychology in particular, has arisen because of social pressures. Environmental problems then become and should not be separated from social problems.

16

Psychologists working in almost every specialty are beginning to question their particular activities in relation to the possible effects their research might have on the environment as well as to take into account the contribution of the existing environment on their research. In this chapter we shall explore some of the areas in which psychologists are seeking answers to the numerous environmental-behavioral interactions. Our interest will be primarily with problems of the "natural" environment. In the next chapter, some of the questions concerning the "built" environment will be taken up.

ENVIRONMENTAL PSYCHOLOGY— WHAT IS IT?

Regardless of how we attempt to define and describe environmental psychology, the basic assumption underlying this new discipline is that human behavior is a potent factor in shaping the physical environment and, conversely, human behavior is profoundly shaped by the physical environment. Obviously, based on this assumption, the subject matter that could be included under the label of environmental psychology is practically limitless. Consequently, the definition of its subject matter is far from precise; what one psychologist thinks of as being appropriate to environmental psychology may not seem so to another psychologist. However, we will utilize the relationships presented by Wohlwill (1970) as a framework for describing the field and for presenting some of the research in this area.

Some Behavior-Environment Interrelationships

Wohlwill (1970, p. 304) suggests that three forms of interrelationships between behavior and the physical environment can be distinguished. First, behavior always occurs in some particular environmental context. *The environment will impose major restrictions on the range of behaviors that can occur within it.* For example, a child growing up in a city will have different constraints imposed on his behavior from those imposed on a child growing up in a small town.

This particular facet of the behavior-environment relationship has received a considerable amount of attention. Thus much of the research in "ecological" psychology, although often not placing a clear-cut emphasis on the physical environment, is relevant. Similarly, the research dealing with the effects

17

of crowding on animal behavior (which we will discuss in some detail later), also applies. Some of the investigations that have attempted to study the human-factors aspects of architecture are also relevant to this particular behavior-environment relationship. Actually, a complete review of the psychological literature would permit the retrieval of a great deal of information that is applicable and would bear directly on contemporary environmental issues.

The second form of relationship suggested by Wohlwill involves *the qualities of the environment that may exert generalized effects on broader response systems of the individual.* This aspect of the environment includes overcrowding, climate, under- or over-stimulation, and so forth. He further points out, however, that in spite of the apparent importance of these qualities of the environment, they are the least studied and the least known. Although this area is beginning to attract researchers, there is very little in the way of substantive research at present. This will be apparent when the problem of overcrowding in cities is considered later.

Third, we find that *behavior may be brought about and directed at certain characteristics of the physical environment.* As Wohlwill points out:

Individuals give evidence of more or less strongly defined attitudes, values, beliefs, and affective responses relating to the environment . . . They develop diverse forms of adjustment and adaptation to environmental conditions. They exhibit temporary and permanent responses of approach and avoidance or escape from given environmental situations, ranging all the way from recreation and tourism to migration . . . [p. 304].

This third area is perhaps the most urgent in terms of current environmental problems. Under this type of relationship, Wohlwill considers three more specific facets and discusses some of the research, or lack of research, in these areas. (1) He considers environment as a source of affect (emotion) and attitudes and asks (p. 305) "What accounts for the remarkable power of the physical environment to elicit affect, ranging from pleasure and excitement to aversion and boredom, and to become the object of pervasive attitudes varying from identification and loyalty to detachment or outright hostility?"

(2) The approach and avoidance responses are determined by environmental attributes. The environment not only arouses strong affective reactions and attitudes but also serves as an object of approach or avoidance behavior. Why do people move from the inner city to the suburbs or vice versa? What influences residential choice and migration? What factors are involved in vacationing and tourism? What characteristics of an area make it attractive to the tourist? Conversely, what do overuse, population, man-made features, and so forth do in terms of attraction of a vacation spot?

18

(3) The question of adaptation to environmental qualities due to prolonged exposure must be considered. For example, we know virtually nothing about the long-term behavioral effects of continued exposure to many of the features of the physical environment that are now being encountered (noise, traffic, pollution and so forth). How does a person adapt to these characteristics of the physical environment? What are the limitations?

Wohlwill has presented a thought-provoking analysis of the problem areas of environmental psychology, and, if you are interested in this area, we suggest you read the original article.

METHODOLOGICAL CONSIDERATIONS IN ENVIRONMENTAL PSYCHOLOGY

In conducting his research, a psychologist makes use of a number of different methods or approaches. For example, in some studies the investigator may simply observe the behavior of a person and record what he sees. In other instances, he may interview the individuals that he is interested in, or he may design a study where he administers one or more tests to various groups. Often, however, the research involves the use of the basic *experimental method.*

The Experimental Method

The experimental method in psychology has, as its central point, the concept of experimental control—that is, the situation in which the behavior occurs must be directly controlled by the experimenter. To understand the process of experimental control, it is necessary to understand three key terms related to the process: *dependent variable, independent variable,* and *nuisance variable.*

The dependent variable in an experiment is some quantifiable response on the part of the organism being studied. The response may be motor, verbal, or physiological. The independent variables are those aspects of the experimental situation whose effects on the dependent variable we are attempting to assess. For example, suppose we are interested in the ability of a radar operator to detect weak and infrequent signals on his radar scope. The dependent variable, in this case, would probably be the number of missed signals in a given period of time (although we could also record the number of false responses, the time taken to respond after a signal appeared, and the force of the response, as well as other potential responses). We are also interested in various factors that might have an effect on the radar operator's performance.

Thus we may be concerned with the effects that the intensity or frequency of the signal will have on the number of missed signals (the dependent variable in our study). Signal intensity and signal frequency are the independent variables. These are systematically varied (increased and decreased), and measures of the dependent variable are taken at each value of the independent variables. We might find that few signals are missed (dependent variable) at a high signal intensity (independent variable), whereas many more signals are missed at a low signal intensity.

In addition to the independent variables, there are other aspects of the experimental situation that may affect the dependent variable. For example, the lighting in the room may have an effect on the subject's performance. If the room were brighter during the experimental condition where the signal intensity was lowest, we would not know whether more signals were missed because of the signal intensity or because of the lighting in the room. To avoid this situation, nuisance variables—variables whose effects on the dependent variable we are not interested in—are either eliminated or are held constant throughout the experiment.

In a study such as that described, it is a rather straightforward procedure to determine what effect the independent variables (signal intensity or frequency) might have on the dependent variable (number of missed signals). Now let us consider a hypothetical study that begins to present some of the kinds of problems that an environmental psychologist frequently encounters in attempting to design an investigation. For example, suppose we are interested in answering this question: "What are the effects of varying wind velocities on the performance of construction workers building a superhighway?" We are immediately faced with problems of control of the many variables included in the real world. We do not have control of the wind velocity; we may only record the velocity of the wind at the time we obtain our measures. We do not have control of the composition of the air including dust, construction particles, and other debris. Again, we can only measure this property as it occurs. We cannot control the temperature, humidity, or direction of the wind; we may only record what is there. In addition, every road is constructed in differing areas ranging from high peaks in the Rocky Mountains to flat cornfields in Iowa to endless miles of desert in the Southwest. (As a matter of fact, the general environmental setting does seem to play a role in the tolerance of workers to "put up with" rather adverse conditions if, for example, that setting is in the Big Horn Mountains of Wyoming compared with the rather tedious and uncomfortable settings in the Mohave Desert.) It becomes quite clear that our control of the independent variable and our ability to handle the extraneous variables is quite different from the case in our laboratory study.

Measuring the dependent variable is another problem. Again, in the real-life situation with the behavior setting in the natural environment, we are faced with an extremely complex measurement problem. It is always tempting to take a single quantitative variable, which, in our particular study, might be the number of cubic yards of dirt moved from one place to another. Another variable might be the amount of roadbed finished in a given time period. Still a third variable might be the number of loads of dirt hauled by a particular operator during a given time period. Unfortunately, this is still not the entire picture, since the equipment operator must be concerned not only with the number of yards of dirt moved but also with the accuracy of where the dirt is placed (a skilled operator must place the right amount of dirt within very precise limits to conform to the design of the roadbed). Selection of dependent variables, then, may be a difficult task.

Our road-construction example, although not typical of the studies that environmental psychologists have been conducting, serves to illustrate some of the methodological problems that are encountered. You may have noted, however, that even though the situation is much more complex, both the environmental psychologist and the basic researcher in the laboratory are still concerned with independent and dependent variables and the effects that the former have on the latter. Let us consider the problem of independent and dependent variables in environmental research in more detail.

Independent and Dependent Variables in Environmental Psychology

We have stated that environmental psychology is based on the assumption that human behavior shapes and is shaped by the physical environment. Environmental influences, then, can be investigated by treating human behavior as the dependent variable and the environmental factors as the independent variables. Since it is also assumed that man's behavior shapes the environment, then research can also be conducted where aspects of man's behavior are considered the independent variables and some characteristics of the environment the dependent variables.

Obviously, since certain features of the environment might have an effect on almost any kind of behavior, the behavior selected as a dependent variable in environmental psychology studies could include just about anything in a person's behavioral repertoire. However, McCormick (1970, p. 574) has suggested a list of possible dependent variables that might be utilized in environmental studies. Thus the environmental variables (the independent variables in this case) could be considered in terms of how they affect (1) performance of various

21

activities, (2) physical convenience, (3) convenient mobility, (4) physical welfare, (5) physical comfort, (6) emotional health and welfare, (7) personal space, (8) social interaction, (9) aesthetic values and preferences, (10) fulfillment of personal values, and (11) financial considerations.

McCormick (1970, p. 575) also categorizes the features of the total environment (the independent variables) that might have an effect on one or more of the dependent variables he suggests. He includes such categories as (1) building design characteristics, (2) physical environment, (3) ambient environment such as illumination, noise control, and so on, (4) the community, and (5) transportation facilities. One could, of course, add to both of McCormick's lists. However, his lists serve to illustrate the many different kinds of variables that must be taken into consideration by the environmental psychologist.

Some Other Methodological Problems

As we pointed out earlier, the physical environment has a remarkable power to elicit affective reactions in people, ranging from pleasure to aversion and from excitement to boredom. This response to the environment is of interest to psychologists but presents some unique problems in researching. It involves measuring, in some fashion, a person's comprehension of his physical environment and his reaction to it.

In discussing the comprehension of the physical environment, Craik (1970) uses the term *environmental display* to represent a unit of the physical environment. The environmental display may be a room, building, urban scene, or a forest glade. Craik suggests that when an environmental psychologist sets out to study the comprehension of an environmental display, he must take several issues into account. First he must decide how to present the environmental display to the observers. This may involve direct presentation or may be by means of representations such as sketches, pictures, and television.

Second, and most important, the psychologist must decide what behavioral response of the observer he will elicit and record. These responses can, of course, be quite diverse. Some impressions that the observers have of the environmental display can be expressed in everyday language. Other procedures make an assumption that many of the observers' reactions to the display are subtle and are not easily communicated in everyday language. There are a variety of ways of obtaining these subtle responses, usually by "teasing" them out by means of different types of rating scales, adjective checklists, and psychological tests.

Another issue that the environmental psychologist must take into account in studying the comprehension of environmental displays is the nature of the observers themselves. The kind of observer selected will obviously depend on the purpose of the study. Often the researcher is interested in special groups and will select these for his investigation. Thus one researcher may be working with college graduates and another with slum dwellers.

Affective reactions are important considerations in environmental research. Research dealing with affective responses to environmental displays is common in environmental psychology. The affective responses and the attitudes of the population toward their environment have become potent political considerations in recent years and have served as activating forces behind much of the current push toward a better environment.

ENVIRONMENT-BEHAVIOR INTERRELATIONSHIPS

The three types of environment-behavior relationships that Wohlwill (1970) suggested are (1) a relationship where the environment imposes major restrictions on the range of behavior that can take place within it, (2) a relationship where certain qualities associated with a particular environment may have a general effect on broader attributes of the behavior and personality of the individual, and (3) a relationship where environmental stimulation must be considered a motivating force.

We will not be able to discuss all of the possible implications of these relationships in terms of the environmental variables that might be involved and the behavioral variables that may be modified. Consequently, we will consider only a representative study or two in each of these areas.

The Physical Environment and Patterns of Behavior

There is a considerable amount of research in this particular area of environment-behavior relationships. Ecological approaches are utilized by a number of investigators. Thus the famous studies by Barker (1965) dealing with the observation of behavior of children in their natural environment is an example of an ecological approach to understanding this kind of environment-behavior relationship.

There are also some studies dealing with behavior that occurs in designed environments—buildings, rooms within buildings, wards in hospitals, and so forth. The approaches used in these investigations differ, but often the researcher is interested in determining the effects of specific environmental variables on certain aspects of behavior. Thus the independent variable might be the alteration of some room or complex of rooms, and the dependent variable might be the types of activities engaged in by the people using the room(s) (where the people might tend to congregate, what kinds of people might use the rooms, and so forth).

A study by Ittelson (1967) is a good example of research done in a designed environment. In a series of studies in psychiatric wards, Ittelson obtained a great deal of information about activities of the patients—where they tended to group together in the wards, and so forth. One of the wards studied had a room that was rarely used by patients or staff because it was not furnished adequately, was very hot, and had no draperies. However, there was a certain amount of isolated pacing, staring, talking to oneself, and so on in this room. When the room was remodeled, the behavioral consequences included a marked increase in social activities and the elimination of the isolated behavior. However, the location of the isolated behavior had merely shifted and now occurred in an entry corridor. Because the design of the studies had been such that baseline data were obtained before the room was renovated, Ittelson was able to pinpoint accurately the impact of the environmental change on the activity of the people occupying the ward.

Other studies dealing with the effects of environmental variables of a "built-in" nature on behavior have been conducted in nurseries, university dormitories, libraries, museums, and public housing projects.

As we have indicated, there are a number of different kinds of investigations that are relevant to the environment-behavior relationship where the environment poses major restrictions on some aspects of behavior. Currently a great deal of interest is being expressed concerning the effects of population density on behavior, so we will take a more detailed look at this particular area.

Population Density and Animal Behavior

We will rarely discuss animal studies in this book, and with good reason. All too frequently it is difficult to generalize from the laboratory to the real world when human subjects are involved, and it is even more difficult when animal subjects are employed. Since this book is aimed at calling attention to what psychologists are doing in an attempt to solve some of the real-world problems, there will not be much reason to talk about animal research. In this chapter, however, we will make an exception because there is so little data involving the effects of overcrowding on human behavior. As Calhoun (1970, p. 116) suggests, "In the end we can justify our experimental studies of animal populations only on the ground that insights from them will assist us in guiding the destinies of populations in more natural settings, whether they be other animals or of man himself." The several animal studies that are discussed here were selected because of their possible implications for other species, including man, in other situations.

Calhoun's Study. In a frequently cited study, Calhoun (1962) partitioned a 10 × 14 foot room into four pens (see Figure 2-1). Each pen was a complete dwelling unit for rats and included a drinking fountain, a food hopper, and an elevated artificial burrow that was reached by a winding staircase. The pens were separated by electrified partitions that had ramps built

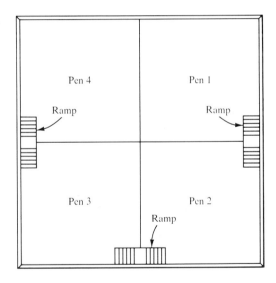

FIGURE 2-1. A top view of a pen arrangement such as that used by Calhoun to study overcrowding in rats. Each pen contained food hoppers, water bottles, and living quarters. Note that ramps connect all pens but 1 and 4.

over them so that the rats could get from one pen to another. However, there were only three ramps; there was no ramp between pens 1 and 4, which made them end pens. Pens 2 and 3 were reached by two ramps each, whereas pens 1 and 4 were reached by only one ramp each. In Calhoun's study, the behavior of the rats could be observed from a window in the ceiling of the room. Several experiments, each of which lasted for a considerable period of time, were conducted in this room. Although the experiments were started with varying numbers of rats (32 and 56), populations were held constant at 80 rats (this was done by removing excess infants and leaving only enough young rats to replace the older ones that died).

Because of the number of ramps leading to pens 2 and 3 and for other reasons, these pens tended to favor a higher population density than pens 1 and 4. The female members of the population gradually distributed themselves about equally in the four pens, but the male population was concentrated overwhelmingly in the two middle pens. The end pens each contained a dominant male who would tolerate a few other males provided they respected his dominancy.

Soon, bizarre behavior began to develop, particularly among the animals in the crowded middle pens. The females in the densely populated pens became less adept at building adequate nests and finally quit building them altogether. They no longer transported their litters from one place to another but simply dropped their pups at different places on the floor of the pen. These females were stressed in a number of ways, particularly during heat, when they were continually pursued by a pack of males. Among these females there was a very high rate of mortality from disorders during pregnancy and parturition.

Calhoun points out that the aggressive, dominant males were the most normal in the populations, but even they exhibited abnormal behavior on occasion. They would go berserk, attacking females, juveniles, and less active males, frequently biting their tails, which is very unusual behavior for rats. Nondominant males became homosexuals, or pansexuals, and could not discriminate between appropriate and inappropriate sex partners. They attempted to copulate with other males, with females that were not in heat, and with juvenile rats. Although frequently attacked by the dominant males, they rarely fought back.

There were two other types of males observed. Some were completely passive and moved through the pens like somnambulists. They ignored all other rats, which, in turn, ignored them. They appeared healthy (fat, sleek, with no scars), but their social disorientation was nearly complete. Probably the strangest of all the rats were those that Calhoun labeled the "probers."

These rats, which were hyperactive, always lived in the middle cages. They were also hypersexual, continually on the alert for the estrous female. If they could not find one in their own pen, they would lie in wait for one on the top of the ramp leading to another pen. They were also homosexual and some turned cannibalistic.

We have briefly summarized a fascinating research project. The interested reader is urged to read the original study, which is reported in *Scientific American* (February 1962, Vol. 206, No. 2, pp. 139–148). Certainly studies of this type, which indicate that social pressures will result in drastic behavior changes in animals, must be considered in terms of their possible implications for other species of animals—including man.

Self-Limiting Populations.   It has been known for many years that the population size of many mammalian species is self-limiting. In other words, once the population reaches a certain density it tends to stabilize, regardless of the available food supply. For example, a rodent population in a particular area may level off at some number even if there is shelter, space, and food for many more. This has been of interest to a number of researchers, and several theories have been advanced as to the reason for the self-limiting nature of some animal populations.

One explanation is that after a certain population density is reached, the social pressures are such that the animals are subjected to a severe stress; the stress will cause physiological changes such as increased adrenal gland weight, which reduces gonadal activity and, consequently, reproduction. A number of studies have verified this.

In an early investigation, Christian and Davis (1956) systematically studied rat populations in 21 city blocks in Baltimore. Since rats seldom cross streets, each block was essentially an independent population. Each block was categorized as belonging to one of five successive stages of a population cycle: low-stationary, low-increasing, high-increasing, high-stationary, and decreasing. The investigators trapped animals in each of the blocks, killed them, and carefully weighed their adrenal glands. Numerous studies have shown that adrenal gland weight is correlated with stress—that is, the more the stress, the larger the adrenal gland. Beginning with the low-increasing stage, an increase in adrenal size was found for the successive stages. The results strongly suggest a progressive increase in stress with increasing population density. Since adequate food was available, it was concluded that social rather than biological factors were responsible for the stress.

Findings similar to those of Christian and Davis have been obtained in a number of laboratory studies. For example, in one study Christian (1955) placed weanling male mice in groups of 1, 4, 6, 8, 16, and 32 for one week. At the end of a one-week period, the mice were killed and the adrenal glands weighed. The weights were progressively heavier for each larger group, with the exception of the largest group (32 mice). Actually, the reduction in adrenal weight for this group probably indicated an even more severe stress, since after a certain stress point is reached the adrenal glands will atrophy.

Many other studies with essentially similar results could be cited. These studies have involved both laboratory and natural environments. It appears that with a number of species of animals, when the population density reaches a certain level, social stresses build up that result in a reduction in population. This is accomplished through the physical reactions to stress that result in a reduction in gonadal activity and, therefore, a reduction in reproductive behavior. Along with the physical changes, we have also seen that there may be some striking behavioral changes that come about as a result of overcrowding. Although we cannot be certain what implications findings of this sort have for man, they do stimulate thought and further research.

Generalized Effects of the Physical Environment

The second environment-behavior relationship Wohlwill (1970) discusses is the generalized effect certain qualities of the environment (such as crowding, over- or understimulation, climate, and so forth) may have on behavior and personality. This particular relationship is the least studied, although it has obvious implications.

There is a growing interest in the effects of crowding on human behavior, and a little research has been conducted (this topic will be taken up in more detail in a later chapter). Similarly, some work has been done dealing with the comprehension of climatic conditions by occupants of particular areas. For example, Kates (1963) investigated the comprehension of flood-hazard conditions by occupants of flood plains. For a number of the sites that Kates selected for study, extensive records of past floodings were available, and he considered the relative frequency of flooding a key environmental variable. He obtained some interesting information about how the inhabitants of these flood plains viewed the occurrence of floods, their notions about protective devices, their expectations about future floods, and so forth. He related these views to the frequency of floodings. Kates found that there was a general adaptive relationship between the relative frequency with which a site is flooded and the expectations of the inhabitants regarding future floodings. However, he found that individuals have a difficult time predicting future events based on their past experience. Thus, of the inhabitants of one site, where over 57 percent had experienced floods previously, only 36 percent expected future floods and 52 percent declared they did not expect future floods. Some of the inhabitants considered floods to be repetitive and orderly phenomena, which would occur regardless of their actions; others felt that new protective measures would prevent future floods or that the particular configuration of circumstances that had led to a flood in the past would never occur again.

Somewhat similar studies have been conducted with occupants of semi-arid regions, where there is characteristically a low level of moisture. In general, however, this particular environment-behavior relationship remains to be studied.

Motivational Aspects of Environmental Stimulation

In many ways, behavior is instigated by and directed at particular attributes and characteristics of the physical environment. In other words, the physical environment can motivate behavior. In this regard, the physical environment can serve as a source of affect and attitudes. There are also attributes of the environment that will result in approach and avoidance responses on the part of persons.

The Environment as a Source of Affect and Attitudes. The power of the physical environment to arouse affective states in individuals is apparent in numerous ways. For instance, there are many of us who get quite angry when we see a polluted stream or a mountain glade littered with empty beer cans. Also, there are many of us who derive a great deal of pleasure from observing some kinds of environmental displays that we find appealing. We have attitudes about certain aspects of the environment. As we shall see, these attitudes are complex and are based on a number of interacting factors.

Measuring affective reations.   There are several ways we can evaluate the affective reaction of an individual to a particular environmental feature. We pointed out earlier that an environmental display (such as a building, stream, or glade) can be presented to an observer in any of a variety of ways. The observer's reaction to the display can also be measured in several different ways.

For example, one method of measuring a person's response to a particular environmental display is to have him describe the mood that the display brings about in him. A person's mood can be measured by means of several types of tests, the most popular being an adjective checklist (Nowlis, 1965). This test consists of a number of adjectives describing mood factors such as anxiety, fatigue, concentration, and so forth, and a person is asked to rate each of the adjectives on the basis of how he feels at the moment. The person rates himself on a four-point scale. In other words, for the adjective *relaxed*, he decides that he definitely feels relaxed at the moment, he feels slightly relaxed, he cannot decide, or he definitely does not feel relaxed at the moment. He indicates his decision on a checklist and then goes on to another adjective. Analysis of the data obtained gives the experimenter a comprehensive picture of the observer's mood. By giving the mood-adjective checklist before and after the presentation of an environmental display and determining the amount of mood change, the experimenter can obtain some idea as to the effects the display had on the particular affective state of an individual that we call *mood*.

In an unpublished study conducted by one of the authors (Heimstra), observers viewed films that showed various scenes of environmental devastation. The mood-adjective checklist was administered before and after the films. However, subjects shown "neutral" films did not demonstrate change in as many of the mood factors or as much change when it did occur.

Noise pollution attitudes.   There has been a considerable amount of research regarding attitudes toward various aspects of the environment. Particular attention has been paid in recent years to the attitudes people hold regarding pollution, overpopulation, and other pressing environmental issues that have developed because of increased technology, population growth, and urbanization. In order to illustrate the problems that confront investigators in this area, let us consider attitudes toward one form of pollution—*noise pollution.*

Listeners' attitudes toward noise pollution have been studied under a number of different conditions. For example, many investigations have been conducted in California and in several other urbanized areas regarding attitudes toward traffic noise. Much of the research has also dealt with attitudes toward

FIGURE 2-2. This environmental display will elicit negative feelings in most observers. Until attitudes toward the environment are modified, environmental displays of this type will be common.

aircraft noise. In the United States particular interest has been directed toward the problems of sonic booms, whereas in Europe more of the research has been aimed at determining attitudes toward commercial overflights and airport traffic. Attitudes toward aircraft noise can become highly emotional, as was demonstrated during the SST controversy in Congress; much of the opposition to the SST appeared to be based on the noise pollution aspects.

In conducting studies dealing with attitudes toward noise, researchers attempt to measure attitudes in several ways. The easiest method is probably interviewing. It is important that the researcher asks for opinions rather than waiting for complaints to be written or phoned in to an appropriate agency; most people will not take this step, but they will be willing to express their sentiments to an interviewer. An additional precaution is necessary, however. When soliciting opinions about a specific subject, the investigator must be able to determine whether or not the topic is really *bothering* the person he interviews.

For example, if an interviewer asks a number of people about air and water pollution, he will probably find that everyone agrees that these ecological mistakes should be remedied. This does *not* mean that everyone surveyed was bothered by the problems, but only that when asked they agreed that the problem ought to be solved. However, a number of sophisticated techniques have been developed for measuring attitudes and are becoming more common in environmental research.

Regardless of the method used to determine attitudes toward noise (or other types of pollution), it is apparent that the attitudes are not simple and are determined by a complex interaction of factors. In summarizing some of the findings of attitude surveys concerned with aircraft noise, Kryter (1970) states that:

> ... three factors which had a statistically significant bearing on the responses of citizens around military bases were (a) fear of aircraft crashes, (b) feelings regarding the considerateness of air base officials and pilots for the comfort and safety of the citizens, and (c) feelings of importance of the air base. These sociological studies showed that individuals who deemed the air base to be important and considerate and also expressed little fear about aircraft crashes would show the same complaint potential for about four times the noise exposure per day as those individuals who were fearful and had negative feelings about the air base and its importance [p. 387].

Problems of attitude measurement.   The problems that a psychologist encounters when attempting to measure attitudes toward particular features of the environment are numerous. A rather striking example of the effect attitude can have on tolerance for adverse environmental conditions can be gleaned from the authors' personal experience. A few years back we contracted a guide and outfitter for an extended fishing trip into the Grand Tetons of Wyoming. In an effort to acclimate to the higher altitude and cooler temperature, we arrived at the point of departure a day early. Our guide, who also worked as a carpenter when not acting as a guide, was working on a house when we arrived. During that afternoon a small storm came up with moderate winds and a little rain. The man, in his role as a carpenter, packed up his tools and came home immediately, commenting that it was much too miserable to work in that kind of weather. On the second day of the pack trip a severe storm came up with rain, hail, and more than moderate winds. However, the same person in his role as a guide never issued a word of complaint. Although this is a rather extreme example, it illustrates why the environmental psychologist must take into account the importance of the relationship of attitudes to the behavior setting. A psychologist measuring the guide's attitude toward the natural environment when he was building a house or on a pack trip would probably have obtained quite dissimilar results.

Studies of attitudes toward noise and other forms of pollution are complicated by other factors. Environmental scientists and conservationists in general have had a long, frustrating history of trying to quantify and measure the effect of environmental pollution on the general well-being of man. For example, if we consider the pollution of a freshwater stream from the standpoint of a microbiologist, it is a relatively easy task to identify and quantify the various components contributing to that pollution. On the other hand, the psychological components of the effect of that same pollution are more difficult to measure and quantify.

One of the questions environmental psychologists are being asked is "Is it possible to measure the quality of the environment?" In other words, if on the one hand the pollution of the stream kills the fish, is the environment still "acceptable"? What is a good fishing stream worth to the human population? What makes a "good" wilderness area? In the final analysis, perhaps a "good" wilderness area does what a wilderness area should do. But what should it do? Any answer will be a qualitative subjective judgment made by an observer interested in the question. Along with the requirements of a "good" or "acceptable" natural environment from a physiological point of view, there are numerous other demands on our natural resources that must be taken into account in any of the decisions affecting these resources that belong to the public. For example, most of our public lands include not only timber but rich mineral deposits. In addition, these lands are very often in demand for agricultural purposes. This sets up a very difficult situation in which the conservationist, who believes that a natural environment is important to preserve for primarily psychological arguments, is faced with the quantitative arguments from various other interested industries. What relative weight should be given to the economic impact on a community provided by opening a new strip mine as opposed to the loss of aesthetic appeal of the countryside if the strip-mining operation is allowed? Not only, then, does the particular environmental setting have an effect on behavior, but the quality of the environment must also be taken into account.

Approach and Avoidance Responses.　As indicated previously, there are a number of questions of interest to psychologists when the physical environment is thought of as an object of approach or avoidance on the part of an individual. Questions of residential choice, migration, and so forth are of considerable interest. Similarly, the motivations and attitudes of the millions of people who move through the environment on vacations is important. As Wohlwill (1970) points out in regard to vacationing and tourism, these short-term activities may be important in regard to the person's adaptation to and tolerance of his permanent environmental circumstance. Obviously, the effects of this kind of behavior are also felt on the areas that are visited.

In the past few years there has been an increase in interest by psychologists in exploring some of the motivational factors influencing people to get away from the city and get back to nature. This movement is evidenced by the large numbers of people visiting the remote parts of our National Park system. The psychological dynamics involved are indeed challenging to all psychologists. For example, what motivates urban dwellers in a large city on the East Coast to load up family and camping gear and drive most of the way across the United States to visit a semi-wilderness area such as Yellowstone National Park? Certainly numerous explanations and reasons come to mind. Perhaps it is the need to get away—away from the cement and asphalt of the city, from the continuous exhaust odor, from the continual barrage of noise, from the constant perceptual stimuli of flashing lights, neon signs, and other man-made technologies, or from pressures generated by constant exposure to large numbers of people. Another hypothesis is that man is basically an organism evolved in a natural environment and thus becomes uncomfortable when forced to live continuously in an unnatural environmental setting. He understandably finds a trip to a National Park or wilderness area refreshing in comparison with his technological existence.

Although many of the above reasons are plausible explanations for the motivation behind the extensive use of National Parks and wilderness areas, there has been too little psychological research so far to draw any firm conclusions. To psychologists concerned with the motivations of human behavior, it is obvious that any one of the indicated pressures would be sufficient cause for a trip back to the natural environment. On the other hand, as psychologists we are also aware that individuals have varying levels of tolerance for pressure in the differing sensory modalities. As a consequence, it is extremely difficult to determine just what motivational factors are operating in any given situation.

For administrative and other reasons, it has become essential that the officials responsible for the operation of our National Parks have some idea as to the attitudes and motivations of the ever-increasing numbers of visitors to the parks. Some research in this area has been conducted. For example, several years ago McDonald was involved in such a study in the Yellowstone National Park in Wyoming (McDonald and Clark, 1968).

This particular study was designed to obtain information in several different areas of interest. Of primary interest to the National Park Service was an evaluation of what they call their interpretive program—a program consisting of extensive visitor centers, wayside exhibits, campfire talks, nature walks, and general information provided by park rangers. A second purpose of the study was to determine what kind of expectations, attitudes, and backgrounds park visitors had.

Information was obtained by means of several types of questionnaires that were administered at different points in the park. The primary data collection points were at park gates, where incoming and outgoing visitors were administered the questionnaires. A total of 2,763 interviews were conducted. In addition to the data dealing with the effectiveness of the park's interpretive program, a general "profile" of the park visitor could be drawn from the data. For example, consider the partial breakdown of occupations shown in Table 2-1. Note that, although there are fluctuations across the summer, teachers and students comprise a fairly large segment of the visitor population. Although the table does not reflect all of the 57 different occupations identified, an interesting aspect of the profile is apparent: the level of education of the park visitor is much higher than is found in the general population. Thus 68% of the visitors interviewed had gone to school beyond the high school level. These findings are similar to those reported by Gilligan (1962), who found that about 80% of all visitors to certain wilderness areas had a college education and that 27% of these had even had some postgraduate training.

There were some other interesting findings. For example, 47% of the visitors had been to the park at least once previously. Frustration and ill will toward the park administration was indicated by a number of the visitors when leaving the park because the demand for camping facilities far exceeded the supply. The predominant attitude expressed by the visitors concerning their reason for coming to the park was to get close to nature. This would seem to indicate that for a substantial number of people there is a need to get away from a highly technological existence and participate in

TABLE 2-1. **Percentages of visitors' occupations by month.**

Occupation	June	July	August
Teacher	7.88	6.07	7.97
Student	5.76	2.80	7.97
Labor	6.97	7.48	5.18
Engineers	5.45	6.54	7.17
Business	9.09	9.81	8.37
Military-government	5.76	3.74	7.17
Agriculture	3.33	3.27	5.18
Retired	6.67	5.14	4.38

FIGURE 2-3. Although millions of visitors drive long distances to visit National Parks and Forests, the motivations underlying their visits are still not clearly understood.

a natural environment that provides clean air, mountain streams, clear lakes, wildlife, and so forth, as well as large areas of unpopulated space, few man-made sounds, and the opportunity to see and participate in an environment not yet exploited by man. However, much more research is required before we will understand why people find some aspects of the physical environment attractive and wish to avoid other features.

Adaptation to Environmental Features. In considering the motivational force of environmental stimulation, we have briefly discussed the environment as a source of affect and attitudes and as having attributes that bring about approach and avoidance responses. As the final facet of this particular environment-behavior interrelationship (that is, the motivational aspects of the environment), Wohlwill (1970) also considers adaptation to environmental qualities due to prolonged exposure to these qualities.

Although there is a good deal of information available about man's ability to adapt to various situations, much of this information has come from laboratory studies. Thus we know a considerable amount about visual, olfactory, and other sensory adaptation processes, " . . . but we know very little as yet concerning the long-term *behavioral* effects of exposure to the visual and auditory stimulus world (and perhaps olfactory and thermal world as well) of our urban ghettos, of center-city or urban freeway traffic conditions at rush hour, or life in the immediate vicinity, for example, of a jetport or industrial plant" (Wohlwill, 1970, pp. 307–308).

We do know, of course, that man has remarkable ability to adapt both behaviorally and biologically to a wide variety of environmental conditions (discussed in Chapter 4). The majority of us do not have to adapt to weightlessness or extended periods of living under water; nevertheless, there are many such practical questions that environmental psychologists must concern themselves with regarding adaptation processes involved in situations that are encountered in everyday "real world" living.

CONCLUSION

In this chapter we have only touched on the range of problems that are currently of interest to environmental psychologists. However, as we have indicated, this is a new field and there are actually relatively few psychologists who are active in this area. It has become apparent, though, that concern for the physical environment has emerged as a new focal point for public issues, and interest in the environment will undoubtedly increase as technology, urbanization, and the population explosion have more dramatic consequences on the physical environment. What role the psychologist can play in helping to solve the many complex problems that have arisen and will continue to arise remains to be seen.

chapter
3

Problems in
Environmental Design

In the previous chapter our primary concern was with the way environmental features can affect human behavior. However, as we acquire knowledge about the behavioral effects of physical environment (particularly the built or designed environments), this knowledge, in turn, should aid us in making design decisions about the environment. Once we have studied the behavior patterns that are developed because of particular features, the environment can be "designed" to either accommodate these behavior patterns (if they happen to be desirable), or to eliminate them (if they are not desirable). Osmond (1957) has coined the terms *sociofugal* and *sociopetal* in order to describe spatial arrangements in buildings that either encourage or discourage social interaction in the building. In one situation, such as a psychiatric ward, it might be desirable to achieve sociopetal conditions (maximum social interaction) whereas in another situation, such as a library, sociofugal conditions (minimum social interaction) might be desired.

The idea that various facets of the environment can be designed in order to modify behavior has some interesting implications. Craik (1970, p. 37) states: "Using environmental design to achieve socially valued outcomes places it among the standard behavior modification techniques, next to hypnosis, psychotherapy, education, persuasion, and brainwashing, and raises the question: what leverage does the environmental designer possess to influence behavior?"

Photo courtesy of Travel Division, South Dakota Dept. of Highways, Pierre, S. D.

Of course the idea of designing certain aspects of the physical environment so as to modify human behavior is not new. For a number of years psychologists have studied the effects of selected environmental variables (such as illumination, temperature, space, and ventilation) on human performance. Applying their findings, they have modified the environment in order to enhance performance. On the other hand, their studies have typically been rather restricted, with very specific features of the environment involved. When attempts have been made to study more globally distinct environmental settings (such as housing quality, overall architectural design, and "urban atmosphere"), relatively few environment-behavior linkages have been identified.

The psychologist who is interested in environmental design, then, is confronted with several problems. In the first place, there is very little data available concerning the effects of the environment on behavior. These kinds of data are required before the psychologist can begin to think in terms of designing the environment in such a fashion that it may modify behavior. In addition, the investigator has all of the problems of dependent and independent variables as well as the other methodological problems discussed in the previous chapter. In spite of the drawbacks, there is interest in the environment-behavior relationship. In this chapter we will be concerned with some of the advances that have been made in recent years.

THE DESIGN OF BUILDINGS

In the previous chapter, we discussed a number of dependent variables that could be used in the evaluation of any given designed environment. These variables, suggested by McCormick (1970), included such categories as performance of activities, physical convenience, physical comfort, personal space, and so forth. The features of the environment (independent variables) that might have an effect on these dependent variables included building design considerations, physical environment, ambient environment, and several others.

Ideally, if we had a great deal more data available and knew how to use them, we could design a building that was based on a consideration of all of the dependent variables that were listed. The design of the building would insure maximum performance of activities, maximum physical convenience, maximum personal space, ideal social interactions (whether sociofugal or sociopetal), maximum aesthetic value, and so on. Perhaps at some future date it will be possible for the building planners to incorporate all of these considerations into their design; at present it is not feasible for a number of reasons.

Therefore, although planners of buildings recognize that the environments they design may have behavioral effects, they are confronted with several problems when they attempt to take behavior into account in their planning. In the first place, the sort of data they need for this type of planning has often not been available. However, Ward and Grant (1970) suggest that:

Another and greater problem has been that the designer has not known what sort of data he needed in the first place, let alone whether or not it existed. A third problem, the greatest of all, is that if the designer has known what sort of data would be useful and if, as has increasingly been the case in recent years, the data has been found to be available, the designer has not known how to incorporate it into his decision-making processes [p. 2].

Typically, an architect will try to find out as much as he can about the people who will use the environment he is designing. However, as Craik (1970, p. 22) points out: "...skepticism is increasing concerning the ability of any client to report reliably what really goes on in any specific environments, a skepticism fed by growing awareness of the paucity of ecologically valid knowledge of environments such as psychiatric wards, households, dormitories and high schools." Craik then goes on to ask whether an individual, such as a hospital administrator, can actually act as the spokesman for all user-clients involved in hospital design. The answer is probably no. The question, then, is: where does the designer get this type of information? One source is environmental case studies.

Environmental Case Studies

There are a number of approaches used in environmental case studies. Basically they involve the description of behavior in some particular environmental setting of interest to the investigator. Obviously this may include the natural environment; studies of this kind have been and are currently being undertaken. By means of different techniques, behavior in various designed environments can also be studied and related to certain aspects and features of the environment.

How does one study the behavior of the users of a building? Again, the techniques will vary considerably depending on the nature of the particular behavior that is of interest and the characteristics of the building that is to be designed. For example, the psychologist might be interested in *what* kind of behavior takes place, *when* it takes place, and *where* (locational behavior) it takes place. The method employed might be designed to obtain information about one or all of these aspects.

Bechtel (1967) was interested in studying the locational behavior of visitors to a large room in an art museum. He developed an instrument called the hodometer (from the Greek *hodos,* meaning pathway), consisting of a number of electric switchmats placed on the floor of the room. Essentially the floor could be visualized as looking like a large checkerboard, with each one-foot square containing a sensitive electric switch. The switchmats were covered with a carpet, and electric counters in an adjacent room were activated when people walked or stood on them. With this device, the investigators were able to analyze the locational behavior in the room in terms of the total number of locations occupied by an individual and the frequency of his presence at each location.

This counting technique was also employed in a study concerned with the effects of room color on movements of visitors to the gallery (Srivastava and Peel, 1968). Although there has been speculation about the effect the color of a room might have on its occupants, there is little in the way of empirical evidence to prove it has any effect. This study is one of the few that does demonstrate that color has an effect on behavior.

Srivastava and Peel (1968) utilized the hodometer to study the movements of subjects in the art gallery under two conditions. One room was painted light beige and had a corresponding rug. The second room was painted dark brown and again had a matching rug. It was found that subjects in the brown room took more steps, covered nearly twice as much area, and spent less time than those in the beige room. In this situation it would appear that the color of the room had an effect on the behavior of the subjects.

Other devices are currently being used that will automatically track and record the locational behavior of large numbers of people in a common area. Data of this sort are of interest to the planners of buildings meant to serve similar purposes. For example, a designer of another art museum would probably find Bechtel's data of considerable interest. Similarly, studies of behavior patterns of students in high-rise dormitories should be of interest to architects commissioned to design this kind of building. Thus the findings of one study, which showed that students spent more time studying in bed than at the desks that were provided, might have some design implications.

Researchers conducting environmental case studies are often surprised at their findings. For example, Langdon (1966) pointed out that the design of public-housing kitchens in England was based on the assumption that they are primarily places for working and washing. However, study has shown that there is a vast range of family activities that take place in the kitchen, ranging from children completing their homework to mending a flat cycle tire. A U. S. study concerned with what impoverished families wanted in the way of housing found that very few of the people wanted a dining room. Rather, they wanted a kitchen large enough to eat in.

There have been a number of other studies along these lines. Data have been collected concerning private dwellings, public buildings, office buildings, and dormitories and union buildings on college campuses. The dependent variables have included a wide range of behavior measures—social interaction, efficiency, movement, and affective measures—and independent variables have involved various physical characteristics of the buildings—room size, number of windows, color, and structural characteristics.

Although it is difficult to draw any conclusions from the data available, it would appear that manipulation of the areas in which people work and live may very well have effects on their behavior. Data of this kind are beginning to become available, but there is still the question of how to incorporate the data into design decisions.

Actually, the studies concerned with the *what, when,* and *where* of behavior in designed environments are relatively straightforward. Various methods can be utilized to study what activities are engaged in, when these activities take place, and where. Often the experimental design of this type of study leaves much to be desired, but there are practical considerations limiting the "neatness" of the design. For example, suppose an investigator was interested in determining the effects of room size on some aspect of behavior. Ideally, a number of rooms of differing size would be constructed, with all other variables—light, sound, windows, heating, and so on—held constant. The investigator could then study behavior in these rooms and feel reasonably confident that any differences were due to room size. However, no one has constructed a building just for this kind of research as yet, and it is not likely to be done, at least not in the immediate future.

There are a number of less tangible aspects of behavior that may be influenced by the designed environment. In the previous chapter we discussed the effects of environmental features on emotions and attitudes. Buildings can have much the same effect.

Psychological Aspects of Buildings

What kinds of reactions do people have toward buildings? How can we measure these reactions? What features of buildings or rooms arouse these reactions? These and other questions are of interest to investigators concerned with psychological aspects of buildings.

Some of the methods used to evaluate environment-behavior relationships are also appropriate for studying the reactions of individuals to characteristics of rooms and buildings. For instance, subjects can be presented with an "environmental display" directly or indirectly, and their responses to the display can be recorded by means of descriptive responses, adjective checklists, or other means.

One method used to study the response of persons to buildings is the *semantic differential,* developed by Osgood and coworkers (1957). With this technique a person is presented with a pair of opposing adjectives such as pleasant-unpleasant, comfortable-uncomfortable, and friendly-unfriendly. The individual is asked to make a judgment about something on a scale with the opposing words at opposite ends. For example, consider the semantic differential scale shown in Figure 3-1. In this case the persons whose reactions to a room in a building are desired might be asked to view the room and complete the scale. If each position on the scale from left to right was numbered one to seven, then the individual might judge the room as a three on the pleasant-unpleasant scale and a five on the comfortable-uncomfortable scale. Typically, a variety of such scales would be included and the judgments could be averaged in order to obtain the reactions of a number of people to the particular room. This technique has been used by Canter (1968), who identified a number of different reactions of people to buildings. The primary ones Canter identified were pleasantness, comfort, friendliness, and coherence.

Craik (1970) describes an unpublished study by Kasmar and Vidulich (1968) that involved the development of an Environmental Description Scale. These investigators had students envision two rooms they liked and two they did not like and then list adjectives describing the rooms. In addition, other environmental dimensions were obtained from architectural journals; students were also asked to list adjectives for these. By means of statistical analysis, the researchers compiled a list of bipolar adjectives (much like those described above for the semantic differential). Further analysis showed that the Environmental Description Scale was sensitive and reliable.

Room

Pleasant	___ :	___ :	_X_ :	___ :	___ :	___ :	___ : Unpleasant
Comfortable	___ :	___ :	___ :	___ :	_X_ :	___ :	___ : Uncomfortable
Friendly	___ :	___ :	___ :	_X_ :	___ :	___ :	___ : Unfriendly

FIGURE 3-1. Three scales from a semantic differential. Typically, the subject would fill out a number of similar scales.

What Causes the Reactions? There seems to be little question that people do react to various aspects of a room or a building, but these reactions are frequently in the form of a general response or "feeling." The particular stimulus configuration (aspect) of the room or building that causes a feeling may be difficult to isolate and define. Undoubtedly, there are a number of factors that could be proved important in causing particular reactions. For instance, if a room is hot, cold, noisy, or poorly illuminated, some predictable reactions will be obtained. However, there are many other factors that are probably also important but are not as easily recognized. For example, what is the significance of the *form* of a building in determining a reaction to it, or the *scale*, or the *proportion*, or the *light* and *color*? Although there is relatively little research in this area, it is apparent that people react differently to many characteristics of the designed environment.

Conclusion

We have just touched on an area that is beginning to attract more and more interest. There is an increasing tendency for architects and psychologists to work together, incorporating data from the behavioral sciences into environmental design. Schools of architecture are beginning to add psychologists to their staffs. In the new Ph.D. program in architecture at the University of California, one of the four major options is behavioral science applications to design (Ward and Grant, 1970). A number of psychologists now identify themselves as "architectural psychologists." In the next decade, this promises to be one of the most exciting areas of applied psychology.

PSYCHOLOGICAL ASPECTS OF COMMUNITIES

There are a number of different ways to look at a city. A city can be thought of as a system consisting of a variety of subsystems, such as transportation, administration, law enforcement, and physical facilities. It can be viewed as fitting some kind of pattern based on certain of its features. Depending on whether one is a legislator, traffic engineer, city planner, or psychologist, communities can be discussed and described from many points of view.

How does a psychologist look at a city? Once again the dependent variables discussed by McCormick (1970) are appropriate. Similarly, we could use some of the same procedures employed to investigate reactions and attitudes toward environmental displays. However, there have been several rather unique approaches to studying the psychological aspects of communities, and we will limit our discussion to them.

The Image of a City

People often refer to the "urban atmosphere." Many individuals seek it, even at some financial sacrifice. There has been some interest on the part of psychologists to find out exactly what "urban atmosphere" is and to isolate and define the factors that cause it.

Obviously, the look, or physical layout, of a city will have an effect on its atmosphere; some would argue that the look of Paris or London or New York can be equated with their atmospheres. There are undoubtedly many visual components of a city that contribute and are therefore of interest to anyone who is concerned with urban atmosphere.

For example, the tempo or pace of a city contributes to its atmosphere. A visitor to a city is immediately impressed with the apparent hectic quality of the life. This may be an erroneous impression (empirical data are lacking), but it is certainly part of the atmosphere. Similarly, the density of the population, the types of people represented in the population, and the attitude and behavior of the people toward each other and toward visitors all contribute. It is a complex interaction of the inhabitants' characteristics and the city's characteristics that forms the "urban atmosphere."

This interaction is not easy to measure and quantify. In the first place, a person's impression of a city will be determined by some of his own characteristics, as well as those of the city. Milgram (1970) points out that there are three factors, apart from the actual atmosphere of the city, that will affect a person's response to it. First, a person's impression of a particular city will depend on his standard of comparison. A Parisian visiting New York may think of that city as being hectic and frenetic. However, a native of Tokyo may think of New York as a relatively leisurely city. Second, perception of a city is affected by the status of the perceiver—tourist, a newcomer to the city, an oldtimer, or someone returning after a number of years. Third, a visitor will bring to a city some preconceived views and expectations about the city. Sometimes they are accurate and sometimes they are not, but these preconceptions will help determine the visitor's perception of the city. These "personal" factors make it difficult to study the impression a city creates.

An interesting approach to studying the image of a city was developed by Lynch (1960). In individual interviews, natives of several cities were requested to:

46

(1) Tell what comes to mind when they think about their particular city and to give a broad description of it.
(2) Draw a quick map of the central area of the city as though they were making a quick sketch for a stranger to show him the location of some point.
(3) Give a thorough description of their trip from home to work. They were also asked to do the same for an imaginary trip along some route given by the interviewer. Their emotional reactions to the trips were requested along with the physical description.
(4) Give what they thought were the distinctive elements of the central areas of the cities.

    With a technique such as this, it is possible to determine what kind of an image urban natives have of their particular communities. When asked to tell what comes to mind when they think about their city and to give a broad description of it, many kinds of responses are possible. Some individuals may describe overcrowding, slums, pollution, characteristics of certain buildings that they find attractive or repellent, the design of streets and interchanges, and so forth. Some characteristics such as certain buildings, parks, and city squares may be viewed in a favorable light by many of the inhabitants whereas other characteristics may be almost uniformly disliked. Some characteristics would result in strong images; other characteristics of the city might be noticed by only a few individuals. When the information from a number of interviews is combined, the investigator will have a fairly comprehensive view of the occupants' image of the city. Based on his studies of Boston, Los Angeles, and Jersey City, Lynch (1960) was able to relate the images of the cities to corresponding features of the urban form and to offer some principles for designing future urban environments.

    Another technique for obtaining "impressions" of physical characteristics of an urban environment involves taking photographs at a number of points in a city and determining what proportion of a sample of the city's residents can identify the locale shown in each of the photographs. With similar procedures, opportunities exist for a number of different kinds of investigations concerning how images of a city are formed. For example, how do these images develop? Studies with children might reveal some interesting findings. Do the perceptions of a city differ as a result of membership in different cultural subgroups? Studies dealing with the acquisition of an image could be conducted by testing newcomers to a city and then retesting them periodically over a long period of time. The possibility exists for a variety of comparative studies making use of many cities, both in the United States and in a number of foreign countries.

Various investigators have been very interested in the techniques described for studying the urban atmosphere, but an extensive battery of other methods is also required. Before psychologists can make truly meaningful "inputs" into the urban-design process, a great deal more is going to have to be known about how the community affects the behavior of its inhabitants and what characteristics of the community can be modified to bring about a more desirable form of behavior. The "urban atmosphere" may appeal to many residents, but it does not to many more. Because economic considerations may force more and more people into living in urban areas, an important future role of psychologists may be to help design the urban environment so that it has an appeal to a much broader range of people.

THE DESIGN OF TRANSPORTATION SYSTEMS

There are few, if any, features of the "built" environment that have more influence on our behavior than those aspects designed to move people and goods—that is, the transportation systems. Virtually all that we have said previously about environment and behavior can be directed specifically at transportation systems. These systems and their component subsystems are capable of eliciting strong affective reactions ranging from anger to happiness. Similarly, there are features of these systems that bring about strong avoidance responses and equally strong approach responses. Everyone has attitudes, both positive and negative, about transportation systems.

Much of this type of research has been sponsored by organizations interested in selling a particular system. However, there has also been a great deal of transportation research conducted—research dealing with such factors as safety, training and licensing of operators, safe and efficient traffic flow, human-factors aspects of vehicles and aircraft, and so forth. In later chapters, research dealing with the human components of the transportation systems will be considered in detail. At present, we will be concerned with some of the newer concepts of transportation systems for which the science of human behavior can provide some guidelines for design decisions.

Characteristics of Transportation Systems

As Hulbert and Burg (1970) point out, the human-factors research conducted on transportation systems has tended to focus on rather specific interests with minimal attention directed at interactions and overlaps. They further point out that characteristics of the transportation systems tend to encourage specialization because of their sheer magnitude. Hulbert (1968) has remarked that it is difficult to think of any other system where two major constituents (the vehicles and the roads) are designed and developed by two different groups of engineers, completely isolated from each other. Hulbert and Burg go on to point out that it is a system with virtually no operating instructions or training provided for the users of the system and that the operational responsibility of the system is shared by two additional groups (traffic engineers and law enforcement personnel) who have nothing to say about the initial design of the system. There are a number of other characteristics of the transportation systems that make them unique among the systems we encounter as part of our designed environment.

The purpose of a transportation system, typically, is the conveyance of persons and material from one physical location to another. This purpose is modified somewhat by the secondary, but important, requirements of safety, convenience, and efficiency of operation. New concepts in transportation systems are being developed that will enhance all of these aspects. Along with the engineers, psychologists are helping design these systems, and the behavioral sciences will have made significant contributions to some of the systems that may be commonplace in the not-too-distant future. Let us briefly consider some of the new concepts in transportation that are now being developed.

New Concepts in Transportation System Design

There will be many major problems associated with the increased population density; one of the most significant problems will be the increase in total number of motor vehicles and the vehicle miles traveled. This can be expected to make our already chaotic traffic system even worse.

Currently a considerable amount of thought and research is being directed at future transportation systems that will help reduce the traffic problems, substantially increase traffic flow rates, and dramatically reduce the number of highway accidents and fatalities. Some of these ideas have to do with the development of high-speed, efficient public transportation systems, which will help reduce the "overload" on the private systems. New types of vehicles will be developed. For example, there is already a great deal of interest in the *surface-effect* vehicle for land and sea use, which will maneuver on a cushion of air. With the development of new vehicles of this type, as well as others, it is probable that completely new human operator problems will also develop.

Many other new concepts are being developed. It is recognized that, along with the engineering aspects, the impact of these systems on man's behavior must be taken into account. Psychologists are involved in the design decisions being made.

Much of the current thinking in the area of future transportation systems has to do with automatic vehicle guidance and control. Basically, the concept of automatic vehicle guidance and control involves placing much of the nation's highway system under almost complete electronic control. Fenton (1970), in an interesting overview of the "state of the art" in highway automation, suggests a roadway complex consisting of both automated and nonautomated roads. The primary highways would be equipped for automation whereas rural roads and many urban streets would not be. A vehicle would enter the automated system at a special entrance point, undergo a rapid automatic check-out, and the driver would indicate his destination. Assuming that the vehicle passed the check-out, it would move to an entrance ramp and would then be merged, automatically, into the traffic stream. The vehicle would be automatically controlled until the preselected exit was reached; it would then be guided onto an exit ramp and control would be returned to the driver. As Fenton (1970) points out:

One can expect two primary benefits from this system, greatly increased lane capacity at high speeds, and a reduction in the number of highway accidents. Estimates of the former range up to 800 percent and would depend, of course, on the chosen system design. The expectation of fewer accidents arises from both the rapid reaction time and consistency of an electronic system in comparison with a driver [p. 153].

Needless to say, the physical characteristics required of such a system are highly complex, and the details of the proposed characteristics are beyond the scope of our discussion. However, we can discuss in general terms what some of the requirements of a system of this type would be. Among a number of requirements would be those involved with maintaining automatic longitudinal control—that is, control of velocity and distance between vehicles on the highway; automatic lateral control, which refers to the position of the vehicle on the roadway relative to the edge of the road; and automatic merging control for merging vehicles into a traffic stream. Although there are a number of other requirements, these appear to be the most critical. Undoubtedly, control of the system will be through elaborate centrally located computers with individual units in each vehicle.

In order to illustrate some of the thinking that has taken place concerning certain aspects of the automatic control of vehicles, let us briefly consider one of the requirements listed above—that of automatic lateral control. As indicated, lateral control refers to the placement of the vehicle on the highway in terms of the edge of the road or in relation to the center line of the roadway— that is, the location of the vehicle in regard to some roadway reference.

As Fenton (1970, p. 157) points out, the design of the automatic lateral control system requires three main parts: (1) a suitable roadway reference for guidance purposes, (2) suitable sensors that will determine the position of the vehicle relative to the reference, and (3) suitable steering control.

Several types of roadway references have been suggested. For example, a painted stripe on the highway that could be sensed by photoelectric cells located on the vehicle has been considered. Similarly, a ferrous material buried in the roadway that could be sensed by detectors on the vehicle has also been suggested. Possibly the most tested type of reference, however, consists of a single cable buried in the center of a controlled road lane. The cable has an electric current running through it that induces a voltage in each of two devices located on either side of the vehicle. The difference between these two induced voltages is used to determine the location of the vehicle in relation to the center line (the cable). With all of these devices, as well as several others that have not been mentioned, the information from the sensors serves as an input to the steering control subsystem, which is automatically activated.

What about longitudinal control? In order to accomplish it, one must have the means for measuring the headway and relative velocity between cars in a traffic stream. There are a variety of ways one can obtain a continuous measure of headway and relative velocity. Some thought has been given to

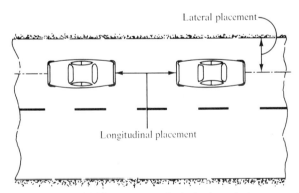

FIGURE 3-2. In an automated highway system, both the lateral placement of a vehicle, which is the car's distance from the edge of the road or the center line, and the longitudinal placement, which determines the distance between cars, will have to be automatically controlled.

radar techniques, light beams, and gamma radiation. Thus a vehicle might be equipped with a "projector" of some sort, and when a vehicle ahead of it comes into the beam being projected, this information is relayed back to the car with the projector, and corrective action is automatically taken by the computer. Other methods of measuring headway have also been proposed. However, Fenton points out that efforts to develop a satisfactory, inexpensive, and reliable measuring device have not been successful, and he suggests this area as a prime one for research.

We are, of course, a long way from the implementation of an automatic vehicle control and guidance system. There are a number of interesting implications of a system of this sort, however, other than those associated with traffic flow. For example, what sort of psychological implications are involved with a system such as this? To many individuals, the car is a great deal more than just a means of getting from one place to another, and driving the car may serve as a source of recreation and pleasure. How are these people going to react to being "plugged into the system" and losing another small part of the control that they have over their own activities? One can imagine many other sorts of problems. For example, what sort of behavior might we expect if the central computer that controls the traffic in a major sector of the country should suddenly become inoperative, as computers have a habit of doing? Questions such as this are going to have to be considered as the system develops.

Currently, psychologists are active in various projects that will contribute to the development of this system. It is recognized that a system such as this will have to be introduced in overlapping stages. The first stage involves the installation and use of various driver aids so that drivers can be more effective decision-makers. Psychologists have been working in this particular area for some time. A second stage will involve the gradual introduction of various automatic control subsystems that will allow for at least partial automatic control. This is currently being undertaken. The third phase would include the transition to complete automatic vehicle control. However, as Fenton (1970, p. 160) remarks: " . . . a tremendous amount of effort in both research and development will be required before a satisfactory automatic system is in operation. This effort must involve not only vehicle control studies, but also an intensive investigation of the present driver-vehicle complex, as the knowledge gained will be necessary for the proper specification and introduction of the control system components." In the area of research dealing with the driver-vehicle interface, the contributions of psychologists will be particularly valuable.

chapter
4

Man in Unusual
Environments

Simply stated, an unusual environment differs in some significant way from the environment to which one has become adapted. Thus if we were abruptly transplanted from Southern California to the Arctic, it would be an unusual environment for us but not the native who has lived in the Arctic for all his life.

Bevan (1967) points out that an environment may be unusual in one or more of several respects. "First of all, an environment may be unusual in that the dominant dimensions may differ qualitatively from those that typically characterize the organism's habitat" (p. 393). For example, man is primarily a visual animal. If he is placed in a situation in which orientation and adaptation are dependent to a major degree on kinesthetic or auditory stimulation, he is in an unusual environment. As Bevan further points out, however, "examination of unusual environments will undoubtedly reveal that environments that are truly qualitatively different are rare indeed."

Typically, the unusual environment represents a different level or complexity of stimulation than is encountered in the "usual" situation. For example, there is a normal level of sound to which we are accustomed. A situation in which virtually all sound is eliminated is unusual; so is the environment in another situation in which the noise level is extreme. Similarly, man normally functions in an environment that involves some gravitational forces acting on his body. However, when man is in outer space, there is zero gravity, which,

Photo courtesy of Travel Division, South Dakota Dept. of Highways, Pierre, S. D.

of course, is unusual. During the launch and re-entry of the space craft, the opposite extreme holds true, and there are excessive gravitational forces acting on the astronauts. The primary characteristic, then, of unusual environments is that the level of stimulation is either more or less intense than that which usually characterizes the stimulus situation to which man is exposed.

In many of the applied settings where psychologists are concerned with unusual environments, the stimulation is too intense rather than below the level to which man is accustomed. For example, there is seldom a case in which the noise level in a system is so low that it might affect behavior. In contrast, the noise level in many systems is so high that it might adversely affect behavior. The same is true for vibration. However, there are also situations in which stimulus deprivation may be a problem, such as in long periods of confinement or isolation; considerable research has been conducted in this area in recent years.

In this chapter we will deal with only a few of the many unusual environments that man encounters. In some instances, our emphasis will be not so much on the unusual environment itself as on the kinds of research that psychologists have conducted in attempting to simulate this situation so it could be studied under controlled conditions. As you will see, studying the behavior of man in unusual environments has presented researchers with some rather unique problems that are not encountered in most other areas of research.

RESEARCH APPROACHES

The psychologist who is interested in studying behavior in unusual environments must often conduct his research in laboratories. Frequently, these studies will involve elaborate simulation techniques that attempt to duplicate the real-world unusual environment as closely as possible. In many instances it would be desirable to investigate the behavioral effects of the unusual environment in the actual situation, but this may not be feasible for a number of reasons. In the first place, sometimes the actual environment is not available for use in the study. For example, it was necessary for research to be conducted on the effects of reduced gravity on behavior prior to the initial space shots in order to have some idea what problems would confront the astronauts in their first flights. And, even though much more information is now available from the actual flights, the opportunities for gathering quantitative data during these space flights are limited by operational requirements. For the same reasons, elaborate simulators were designed to study the effects of lunar gravity on performance before man actually set foot on the moon. Similarly, it has been necessary to study the effects of long periods of confinement on behavior before the astronauts made extended trips to determine whether this would be an important factor in space flight.

Sometimes the effects of unusual environments are studied in the laboratory rather than in the actual situation because of the potential hazard to the subject in the unusual environment. In this kind of investigation, steps can be taken to protect the subject—steps that could not be taken in the "real world." Also, lack of experimental control in the actual situations can be overcome in laboratory studies. For these and other reasons, much of the research on unusual environments and behavior has taken place in laboratory settings.

One disadvantage of laboratory research is that it is often hard to accurately apply to the actual environmental situation. This problem appears to be particularly relevant to unusual-environments research. For example, a review of the literature dealing with the problems of weightlessness published prior to obtaining actual empirical data from the space flights reveals a considerable range of "findings" concerning what weightlessness was expected to do to work performance and other aspects of behavior. However, many of the findings concerning the unusual effects of weightlessness did not materialize. On the other hand, space walks have demonstrated that human performance capability is considerably different from that on earth: tasks performed under weightless conditions are significantly more difficult. Terrestrial studies using a variety of simulation techniques have also demonstrated this finding.

Not all research on unusual environments, of course, is carried on in a laboratory. In many instances the environment itself is such that investigations can be effectively conducted in the actual setting, which then becomes a laboratory. We will discuss several studies of this type in this chapter.

Variables in Unusual-Environment Research

Obviously, there are a variety of independent variables that are associated with unusual-environment research; the particular independent variables selected will be decided by the environmental conditions. If the researcher is interested in the effects of noise on performance, noise will be the independent variable and the investigator may manipulate it in a number of ways (intensity, intermittency, types of noise, and so forth). Similarly, if the researcher is concerned with vibration, he will expose the subject to different conditions of vibration. Isolation, reduced gravity, or immersion in water can all serve as independent variables.

Although the independent variables are determined to a large extent by the nature of the unusual environment involved, the dependent variables selected range from gross measures of work output to various physiological responses. Frequently, the dependent variable involves some measure of psychomotor performance, such as tracking, reaction time, coordination tests, and steadiness. Sometimes cognitive tests, such as problem solving, concept formation, or conditioning and learning, have been used as dependent variables. Various perceptual tests including sensory thresholds, flicker fusion (the point at which a subject perceives an intermittently flashing light as a steady one), perceptual retention, and other types of perceptual tasks have also been used as dependent variables. A number of pages could be devoted to a brief description of the variety of dependent variables that have been utilized in unusual-environment studies. However, the important consideration from the experimenter's point of view is to select dependent variables that are relevant to performance in the practical situation.

Along with the behavioral measures, many studies also take various psychophysiological measures. Since it is often assumed that an unusual environment is also a stressful environment, researchers have been interested in obtaining measures that would reflect the stress of the situation. There are a number of psychophysiological indices that have been used, including skin resistance (which has been used as a measure of emotional arousal), heart rate, blood pressure, and respiration. These indices, as well as several others, have been shown in some studies to correlate with the stress that is associated with a particular environment. However, in other studies no relationship has been found. Some researchers still utilize individual psychophysiological measures, but most now employ batteries of these measures. This approach permits a more reliable evaluation of the psychophysiological response of a person to the unusual environment.

REDUCED-GRAVITY RESEARCH

You have probably seen the televised presentations of astronauts moving about on the surface of the moon. You are probably also aware of the tremendous technological advancements that were required in order to achieve this feat. Major breakthroughs were necessary in numerous scientific disciplines before the first successful Apollo mission was accomplished; these breakthroughs have been well publicized. However, less is known by the public about the research of many psychologists and others who, for some time before the first manned space flights, were concerned with the effects of partial and zero gravity on man's performance.

Simulation of reduced gravity has been an area of increasing concern
as researchers attempt to improve the methods of predicting the performance
of man in space and on extraterrestrial surfaces. This research was necessary
in order to prepare for the first space missions; even after man has spent some
time on the lunar surface, additional simulation research is still required to
determine the most effective use of man on the moon for scientific and operational activities. When missions are planned, it is necessary for the decision-
makers to have some idea about whether or not their plans are realistic in
terms of the astronaut's capabilities. In making these plans, they must rely
to a considerable extent on data from reduced-gravity simulation studies. Although some data are now available from actual missions, the prohibitive costs
and inherent dangers associated with experiments conducted during space
flights and on the moon's surface require that most reduced-gravity data be
obtained by means of simulation techniques.

Simulation Techniques

Three general types of simulation techniques have been developed in
order to study man's performance capabilities in reduced- and zero-gravity
situations. One type of simulation technique involves cable suspension systems
of one kind or another, which will suspend the major parts of the body either
completely (to simulate weightlessness) or partially (to simulate reduced-gravity
situations such as those encountered on the lunar surface). One example of
this type of simulation technique is shown in Figure 4-1. The particular lunar-
gravity simulator illustrated was developed by Case Western Reserve University
under a contract with NASA. This system permits the subject to remain in
the vertical position with approximately five-sixths (simulated lunar environment) of his weight supported by the constant-force motors. Therefore, as he
walks, moves his arms, and so on, all movements are "assisted" by the suspension
system so that they require only 1/6 the effort that would normally be needed.
In other words, the effort required to move is as though gravity had been
reduced to a level similar to that on the moon's surface. Various versions of
the cable-suspension system simulators have been used in a number of different
reduced-gravity studies.

Weightlessness can be studied in an aircraft under certain conditions.
The pilot dives to build up speed and then climbs and flies a parabolic arc.
This "ballistic" trajectory flown by the plane (shown in Figure 4-2) essentially

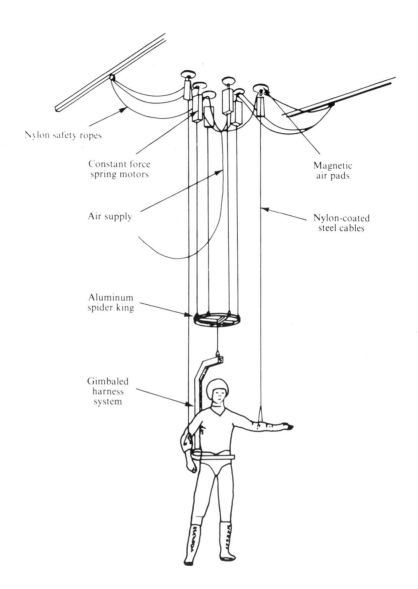

Nylon safety ropes

Constant force
spring motors

Magnetic
air pads

Air supply

Nylon-coated
steel cables

Aluminum
spider king

Gimbaled
harness
system

FIGURE 4-1. One method of simulating lunar-gravity conditions. By means of various cable and motor systems, the subject can remain in a vertical position with about five-sixths of his weight supported by the system. (From Amos A. Spady, Jr., Prototype of a new lunar-gravity simulator for astronaut mobility studies. In *Human Factors*, 1969, **11**(5), 411–450. Reprinted by permission of the Human Factors Society.)

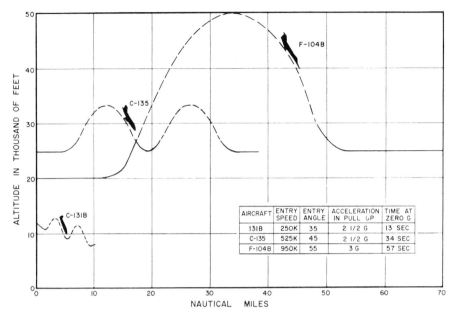

FIGURE 4-2. Several parabolic flight maneuvers, which produce zero gravity. (From M. J. Moran, Reduced-gravity human factors research with aircraft. In *Human Factors*, 1969, 11(5), 463–472. Reprinted by permission of the Human Factors Society.)

places the aircraft and its occupants in a controlled state of free fall. Since the occupants are enclosed by the aircraft, they do not experience a sense of falling—only the experience of weightlessness for a half minute or so. By repeating this maneuver, during a given flight a number of cumulative minutes of weightlessness can be experienced.

This method has several disadvantages. One, it is expensive. Also, a high percentage of the subjects tested become nauseated. In addition, the periods of weightlessness are rather short, and many experiments are such that these short intervals are not sufficient to accomplish a great deal. The advantage, however, is that the subject is not constrained in any way by cables, nor is there a liquid-imposed drag as is the case in the liquid-immersion simulation techniques.

In order to achieve the long periods of reduced gravity that are typical of extra-vehicular (EVA) tasks required of astronauts, water immersion at neutral buoyancy has been shown to be a useful simulation technique. The pressure-suited subject can move around under water unencumbered by cables and can do so for long periods of time. The immersion technique has been an effective method for studying the astronaut's capability to execute extra-vehicular work procedures.

The three general simulation techniques we have mentioned—mechanical simulation, parabolic flight, and neutral buoyancy—have been utilized in a wide range of investigations. Most of the studies have been designed to answer some specific question that is of concern to those responsible for planning the activities of the astronauts on a future mission. Studies of this kind leave many questions unanswered, but they have provided a data source for those responsible for development of space-hardware systems and space-mission planning.

A Lunar Simulation Study. There are a number of factors that have an effect on man's performance in the lunar environment. These include the effects of lunar gravity, the effects of reduced atmospheric pressure, space suit encumbrances, and the effects the confinement of the trip may have on his behavior. Generally, in research concerning lunar-environment effects on performance, a single-factor approach (one variable is investigated and the others are excluded) has been utilized. Although these studies have provided useful data, Seminara and Shavelson (1969) felt that the best assessment of the lunar astronaut's performance capabilities would be obtained from a study that combined these various lunar environmental effects. Since the Seminara and Shavelson study is somewhat unique because of its approach, we will consider it in some detail.

Seminara and Shavelson's (1969) program, called Lunar Surface Exploration Simulation (LUSEX), involved a complex simulation system with a number of elements or subsystems. The basic elements consisted of a 1/6 gravity suspension system, a large rectangular space-environment chamber measuring 18 × 18 × 36 feet, an associated chamber airlock measuring 10 × 10 × 10 feet, a model of the lunar surface, realistic mock-ups of lunar vehicles and scientific exploration equipment, and various performance-testing apparatus.

The airlock was designed to represent a lunar shelter. The large environmental chamber, which could be depressurized to represent up to 100,000 feet altitude, was designed to simulate the lunar extra-vehicular environment. The mock-up of the lunar vehicle and scientific equipment was located in the environmental chamber. The simulated lunar shelter provided waste management, sleeping, personal hygiene, food preparation, recreation, exercise, and storage provisions as well as behavioral-testing apparatus.

The basic design of the study called for extensive training of four subjects (who had met rigid educational and physical standards) before they took part in the five-day "space flight." In this training, subjects performed in "shirt sleeves" so that the data could be used later as comparison or base-line data when the subjects performed in the space-suit, reduced-gravity, and altitude conditions of the lunar chamber. The four subjects were confined for five days in the simulated lunar shelter. During the fourth and fifth days, two subjects each made two simulated sorties outside the shelter (that is, outside the airlock into the lunar-environment chamber). These sorties were made at 1/6 gravity under pressurized space suit conditions at chamber altitudes of 18,000 and 100,000 feet. The subjects were required to perform several basic maintenance tasks, such as bolt torquing, connector mating, and nut threading. They worked on each task separately, tightening the bolts to a specified level, mating and disconnecting push-pull connectors, and threading and removing nuts on protruding bolts. Time to perform each task was used as the measure of performance. The subjects also performed on several control tasks, which involved the manipulation of several kinds of controls.

After the performance times on the three maintenance tasks were averaged, the comparison between the simulated lunar working conditions and earth working conditions showed a 202% increase in performance time for the lunar work. On the control tasks, the average of the three tasks showed an 89.7% increase in performance time under the simulated lunar working conditions when compared with the "shirt sleeve" earth working conditions.

In this study, then, the interactive effects of lunar gravity, reduced pressure, shelter confinement, and suit encumbrances were examined. Seminara and Shavelson (1969) were able to conclude that these combined effects will considerably degrade performance and that control and maintenance tasks will have to be performed at a significantly slower rate in the lunar environment. Their conclusions have been validated by the astronauts who have attempted to perform similar tasks on the lunar surface.

There is a great deal more that could be said about reduced-gravity simulation and research in this area. Many of the studies have been extremely interesting and have presented the researchers with a number of challenges. If you are interested in pursuing this topic further, a special issue of *Human Factors* (1969, Vol. 11, No. 5) deals with all the various techniques utilized in reduced-gravity simulation and with research conducted in these techniques.

MAN UNDER WATER

Although we read and hear a great deal about the unusual environments that man encounters in space and on the lunar surface, we hear little about an equally unusual and adverse environment that covers a large part of the earth's surface—that is, the water environment. Because of the increasing need for the natural resources of the oceans and general scientific curiosity, interest in studying these bodies of water has increased greatly in recent years. Along with many other kinds of research, studies dealing with man's ability to live and function under water have also been conducted.

One of the first questions that researchers attempted to answer was whether it was feasible for man to survive under water for long periods of time. Several projects aimed at answering this question were carried out. Typical of these were the SEALAB programs of the U. S. Navy.

The SEALAB project had multiple purposes and contained a wide variety of studies in nearly every branch of marine science, technology, engineering, medicine, and human behavior. SEALAB I demonstrated that men not only could survive but also could function in an apparently normal manner during an 11-day period of living in a submerged habitat at nearly 200 feet while breathing an oxygen-helium-nitrogen gas mixture.

SEALAB II was designed to further study the operation of placing and maintaining men in a submerged habitat. One of the major purposes of the project was to evaluate the diver's ability to do useful work in the open sea while commuting to and from the SEALAB.

SEALAB II is a non-propelled craft, much like a miniature submarine, that can be placed on the ocean floor. It serves as an underwater habitat for as many as 10 divers for prolonged periods of time. In a study reported by Bowen and associates (1966), the SEALAB was located in 205 feet of water off the California coast. Their study, concerned with human performance, was part of a joint program in which physiological and social-personality data were also obtained. The purpose of the human performance study was (1) to examine the effects of the environment and the conditions of diving on the performance of divers, (2) to study the work capability of divers operating from a submerged habitat, and (3) to extract preliminary conclusions on tool and equipment design for future underwater work.

Prior to the submersion, the divers were available for training and gathering of base-line data on the psychomotor tests that were to be used under water. Data were obtained on land and also during a 15-foot dive in a clear lake. In the actual study, three teams of ten divers each followed one another; each team occupied the SEALAB II for 15 days. Testing took place outside the SEALAB during some of the sorties made by the divers. Compared to performance on dry land or in the shallow water condition, performance on the psychomotor tasks showed considerable deterioration. Many divers found that they reacted much more slowly. The general pattern of the results suggested that simple, short-term tasks suffered least and the complex tasks suffered the most.

It should be emphasized that the psychomotor testing was only one small aspect of the SEALAB program. The overall result of this and other projects indicates that man can survive and function while submerged for long periods of time in the sea.

After the feasibility of man's dwelling under water for extended periods of time was established, questions arose concerning man's specific capabilities and limitations under water. Some of these questions had already been partially answered in the SEALAB studies and others like it, but there were many other questions concerning underwater visual capabilities, motor skills, perceptual-motor coordinations, and so forth that remained unanswered. In the last few years, there have been a number of studies designed to obtain additional information relating to man's ability to function under water. These studies have identified various factors that will have an effect on performance. For example, there are "water" effects, such as neutral buoyancy, viscosity, reduced sensation, encumbrance of equipment, and the attention that must be paid to the diving procedures in order to insure safety. There are also other kinds of factors. For instance, in very cold water, the "cold" effect is superimposed on the "water" effect and may act directly on psychomotor performance and more indirectly on central processes by causing distraction from the task at hand (Bowen, 1968, p. 461).

Based on underwater research, it would appear that future underwater operations may have to rely less on the diver and more on better-designed equipment. As Bowen and his associates (1966, p. 198) point out, "There is a need to develop many features of diving equipment so that various man/equipment combinations can face the underwater environment and underwater tasks without the present reliance on diver courage and skill which, high though they may be, are often relatively inadequate resources for the tasks at hand."

ISOLATION AND SENSORY DEPRIVATION

The initial interest in the area of isolation and sensory deprivation was based on theoretical considerations. However, interest has been sustained by some practical questions that have arisen concerning space-flight operations, submarines, POW camps, and many other situations in which man may be isolated, confined, and exposed to stimulus impoverishment. In both the simulated lunar-exploration study and the SEALAB programs, confinement was considered an important variable.

Isolation, as we will consider it, refers to a situation in which a person is removed from his accustomed environment; confinement is a reduction of the freedom of movement that the individual typically enjoys; sensory deprivation refers to a reduction from some normal level of sensory input in one or more of the sensory modalities. Sometimes the sensory input is not reduced a great deal but is no longer "patterned"—that is, the input no longer varies as it typically does. Actually, in the typical laboratory situation or, for that matter, in the real-world situation, all three occur together. Isolation can be viewed as representing some degree of sensory deprivation and, in most instances, isolation and confinement occur simultaneously.

Various approaches have been utilized in laboratory studies of isolation and sensory deprivation. Generally, a subject is placed by himself in a small, soundproof room. Different procedures are then followed to reduce sensory input or to minimize its patterning. For example, consider one of the first investigations in this area.

Bexton, Heron, and Scott (1954) had subjects (individually) spend several days reclining on a bed in a small room. Subjects wore translucent goggles that permitted them to distinguish light but prevented form discrimination. During the time they were in the room, the subjects were exposed to a constant level of masking noise. Tactual and kinesthetic stimulation were reduced to a minimum by requiring the subject to recline and to wear gauntlets or "tubes" on the appendages. Thus there was reduced sensory input and its patterning was minimized. These investigators found that subjects displayed a great deal of restlessness, had poor motor control, fluctuated emotionally, and, after being released from the test room, showed a decrement in IQ performance. One of the most interesting findings, however, was the fact that subjects tended to have very vivid visual hallucinations during their confinement.

Many studies have followed the same general procedure (isolation in a small room and reduced or nonstructured stimulation), but other procedures have also been used. For example, Lilly (1956) drastically reduced the level of stimulation of his subjects by submerging them in a tank of water maintained at near-body temperature. He also found emotional fluctuations and hallucinations.

In these investigations, the researchers have been concerned with the effects of isolation and stimulus impoverishment on a number of aspects of behavior. There is considerable evidence that the subject's perception may be affected under these conditions with distortions of visual shapes, decreased efficiency in vigilance tasks, reduced color discrimination ability, changes in perception of movement, and of course a variety of hallucinations. There is little evidence that motor performance is affected by isolation although there may be poorer eye-hand coordination and a decrement in tracking performance. There is also some evidence in the literature that intellectual functioning may be temporarily impaired by isolation. Susceptibility to propaganda has been shown to increase with confinement.

One of the more apparent effects of sensory isolation is changed emotional behavior. Although the subjects are typically relaxed and find confinement pleasant for a short period of time, this feeling of relaxation and contentment soon gives way to confusion and general irritability. Of some interest to researchers has been whether, on the basis of various personality and other types of tests, the emotional reaction of a person to an isolation situation can be predicted. In general, although a few studies have shown relationships between some tests and ability to withstand confinement, data in this area are lacking.

EXCESSIVE STIMULATION

In contrast to the unusual environment that is characterized by stimulus deprivation or impoverishment, some environments are unusual because of the excessive stimulation that is present. We will consider two of this kind of environment—one involving vibration and the other involving noise.

Vibration

Vibration is encountered in many kinds of man-machine systems. It is common in most types of vehicles used for transportation and is also a common condition in heavy industrial machinery. Grether (1971) points out. "The possibly harmful effects of such vibrations are, quite naturally, a matter of real concern. Harmful effects might occur in terms of either physical injury and health hazards or impairment of human work efficiency and safety" (p. 203). Grether goes on to say that:

Only in the past ten years has research on human performance during vibration received significant attention. Among the reasons for attention to this area has been increasing military interest in high-speed flight at low altitude, where air turbulence causes a very rough or jolting ride. As manned space flight became a matter of serious interest about a decade ago, it was realized that rocket launches could produce vibration environments severe enough to raise questions about astronaut performance. However, some of the earliest and best studies of vibration and performance . . . arose not from any of these aerospace problem areas, but from concern about vibration in trucks, farm machinery, and earth-moving vehicles.*

*Reprinted by permission of the Human Factors Society.

FIGURE 4-3. Although there is a tendency to think of unusual environments in terms of space stations or underwater laboratories, men operating heavy equipment such as that shown here may encounter "unusual" environments including excessive vibration, noise, heat, or cold. (Photo courtesy of Publicity Division, South Dakota Dept. of Highways, Pierre, S. D.)

A common type of vibration experienced is of a repetitive or cyclic type. This kind of vibration is usually defined in terms of frequency in cycles per second (the term *Hertz* or Hz has been adopted in place of the cycles per second notation), the amplitude of the vibration, and the direction of the motion in relation to the body of the subject—chest to back, right-left, or vertical. However, another kind of vibration, which is more complicated and difficult to specify, is the noncyclic or random oscillatory movement such as is encountered in ground vehicles moving over irregular terrain or in aircraft flying through turbulent air. Although there are several methods of defining this type of random-motion environment, these methods are technical and beyond the scope of the present chapter. Most of the research that has been conducted has made use of sinusoidal vibration in the vertical axis with the subject seated. However, considerable research has also been conducted in low-flying, high-speed aircraft (random motion).

In conducting studies dealing with the effects of vibration on human performance, the investigators must exercise care that they do not expose subjects to a vibration level that will result in physical damage. Studies with animals have shown that vibration, if intense enough, will kill the animals. Some studies with human subjects have found that severe chest pains result from high levels of vibration; moderately severe gastrointestinal bleeding, which persists for several days, may also result. In addition, other forms of injury may take place. Consequently, the psychologist who wishes to study vibration must proceed with caution. Studies of human performance under vibration conditions have typically been performed at vibration levels well under the human tolerance limit.

Many of the studies on vibration have been in a frequency range between 1 and 30 Hz. Under 1 Hz, the amplitudes of motion are usually quite large, such as those found in ships at sea, and the whole body tends to follow the motion. Above about 30 Hz the vibratory energy is likely to be absorbed at the point of contact, such as the bottom of the feet or the buttocks, and will have little effect on the rest of the body.

A review of the data on the effects of vibration on performance does not yield a particularly consistent picture. The effects of vibration on performance can be caused by direct interference with the activity that is of interest or, because of physiological changes caused by vibration, the effects on the activity may be more indirect.

There is evidence that vibration, particularly of the sinusoidal type, will affect performance on certain kinds of visual tasks. This is not surprising since vibratory motion of the head and eyes might be expected to cause a blurring of the retinal image as well as some difficulty in fixating on a small object. Research has shown that there is a loss of visual acuity with increased frequency and amplitude of vibration. However, studies have also shown that this loss can be compensated for by increasing the size of the visual details (letters or numbers) that must be read under vibration conditions, or by using some form of head restraint.

Most studies dealing with reaction time and perceptual judgment tasks of various kinds have found little or no performance loss due to vibration. Tracking tasks of various kinds, however, have frequently been shown to be adversely affected by vibration with decrements that are proportional to the vibration. Other kinds of motor activities have also been shown to be affected by vibration.

After surveying the literature dealing with the effects of vibration on human performance, Grether (1971) made the following generalizations concerning these effects:

1. Vibration causes an impairment of visual acuity that is proportional to vibration amplitude and is greatest at frequencies in the range from 10 to 25 Hz.
2. Vibration causes impairment of human tracking ability proportional to vibration amplitude and is greatest at very low frequencies, i.e., below 5 Hz.
3. Other tasks that require steadiness or precision of muscular control are likely to show decrements from vibration.
4. Tasks that measure primarily central neural processes, such as reaction time, monitoring, and pattern recognition, appear to be highly resistant to human performance degradation during vibration [p. 213].*

Noise

Man is constantly being bombarded with sound; some he needs to hear, some he wants to hear, and much he doesn't want to hear because it is meaningless or too intense. When the sound is unwanted it is termed *noise*. This definition is extremely subjective because one man's music is another man's noise, but often as the sound intensity becomes too great the sound may become noise to both people.

There is a range of sound intensity that is desired by man. If sound is too quiet (as in some experimental soundproof rooms) the sounds of internal body functions, such as heartbeats and blood flow through the ears, are heard. If sound is too loud, damage may be done to the hearing apparatus, resulting in temporary or permanent hearing losses.

In the mid-1800s the widespread use of steam boilers resulted in a consequent widespread development of "boilermaker's" deafness in workers exposed to the intense sounds of the hammering and riveting of metal plates together. Modern industry continues to present many intense sounds to workers, from presses and weaving looms to drop forges and heavy machinery. The adoption of machinery in the office has seen constant increase in the sound levels of office equipment such as typewriters, duplicators, and adding machines. Even the once-quiet world of the mathematician has become filled with loud, continuous sounds of computer hardware necessary for completing computations and printing answers. In every case, as societies change from agricultural to industrial communities, there has been an increase in noise.

*Reprinted by permission of the Human Factors Society.

Noise Intensity. The basic unit of measurement of noise intensity, or loudness, is the *decibel*. When you see sound intensity expressed in decibels, there are two important factors to keep in mind. In the first place, the decibel is a ratio expression indicating the relative difference between two sounds. However, this information has meaning only if we have some reference value. An arbitrary reference value has been established. Because intensity of sound is actually a measure of sound pressure, a reference value of 0.0002 dynes per square centimeter is used. A dyne is a unit of pressure. The second point to keep in mind is that the decibel scale is a logarithmic scale. If a sound is 100 decibels more intense than another sound, then it is ten billion times more powerful. Figure 4-4 shows the decibel levels for a number of sounds, some of which will be familiar to you. On this scale, at about 120 decibels, the pain threshold is reached. In other words, a sound at this level will actually cause a person to experience a painful sensation.

Research Approaches. In studying the problem of noise, researchers have been concerned with a number of different variables. For example, many studies have been conducted dealing with the effects of long exposure to certain noisy conditions on hearing loss. Other investigations have dealt with the effects of various types of noise on human performance, emotions, moods, and so forth. Still other studies have been concerned with the attitudes of people toward certain noise sources, such as jet aircraft and highway transportation systems.

Hearing loss. Experiments concerned with noise-induced hearing loss present the researcher with some problems. Records of industry can be examined to determine the approximate exposure to sound of persons who have since discovered that they have a hearing loss. This serves as a rough guide of the effect of some particular sound level on hearing loss. However, such factors as the frequency or frequencies of the sound, distance from the source, age of the worker, and a number of other independent variables may have contributed to the observed hearing loss. The well-controlled laboratory experiment will reveal which variables are most suspect, but nothing can duplicate the exposure the worker might have received. The advantage of laboratory results is the certainty of the results; specific antecedent sound levels can be related to observed hearing losses. With this certainty comes the problem of induced hearing loss itself. No experimenter would approach the situation with the intention of damaging someone's hearing. Human subjects might be exposed to noise and the effects observed, but ethics require that the experiment be stopped if a decrement is observed. As a result, there is no certainty that

71

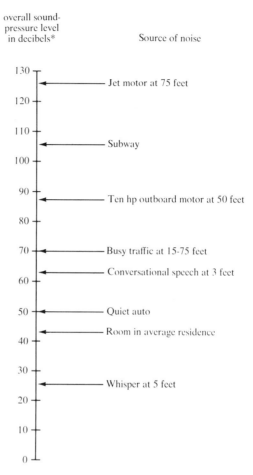

overall sound-
pressure level
in decibels*

Source of noise

130 — Jet motor at 75 feet
120
110
— Subway
100
90 — Ten hp outboard motor at 50 feet
80
70 — Busy traffic at 15-75 feet
60 — Conversational speech at 3 feet
50 — Quiet auto
40 — Room in average residence
30
20 — Whisper at 5 feet
10
0

FIGURE 4-4. Sound pressure levels for a number of different sounds. (0 decibel = 0.0002 dynes per square centimeter.)

higher noise levels would continue to damage hearing; perhaps the noise had already done the greatest amount of damage possible. To ascertain the limits of noninjurious exposure to intense sounds, animals are often used. There is no direct generalization from the animal studies to humans, but there are no serious discrepancies between induced hearing loss in animals with specific noise conditions and those observed in men exposed (without intent to induce a hearing loss) to the same sound.

Regardless of the difficulties encountered in research in the area of noise-induced hearing loss, there is little question that it does take place. At one time the concern was primarily with industrial noise and noise in certain other occupations, but more recently, with the hard-rock groups, it appears that there may be a whole generation with noise-induced hearing loss.

Noise and performance. Because noise is associated with so many different environments, there has long been an interest in the effects noise may have on various kinds of human performance. Research in this area has led to a number of conflicting finds; some studies show impaired performance, some show no effects on performance under noise conditions, and some show improved performance. It has been recognized for some time that noise and performance form a complex situation with variables associated with the task itself, with the noise, and with the subject all interacting to determine whether there is a performance change.

Warner (1969) conducted an investigation concerned with the performance of subjects attempting to determine quickly and accurately whether a 'target" was present among a number of "nontarget" figures presented by means of a slide projection system. A target was an odd letter among an array of similar letters (for example, an O among C's or an E among F's). Subjects performed this task under no noise, 80, 90, and 100 decibels, with the noise being of an intermittent nature (on-off, on-off). Warner found that, as the intensity of the noise increased, the number of errors made by the subjects decreased. There were significantly more errors made (an error being an indication by the subject that a critical target was present when there was none present or, conversely, indicating that there was no target when one was present) during the no-noise condition than under the 100-decibel condition. In this study, then, noise facilitated performance.

In later studies (Warner and Heimstra, 1971, 1972), subjects were tested on a similar task, but the difficulty level was varied by increasing or decreasing the number of letters shown on a given display. Under one condition only 8 letters were used; in another condition 32 letters were utilized. Noise was presented at 100 decibels, but the on-off ratio was varied. Therefore, under one condition the subject received noise that was on for 30% of the time and off for 70%; in another condition it was on for 70% and off for 30%; in still another condition it was on for 100% of the time. Subjects were tested under four noise conditions—zero noise, 30%, 70%, and 100%—as well as two levels of task difficulty (8 letters and 32 letters). Results showed that the 30% noise condition had a facilitating effect on performance, but the 70% and 100% conditions had a negative effect. Again, the complex interaction of noise and task variables becomes apparent when results of studies such as this are considered.

Attitudes toward noise. The acceptability of a particular sound depends a great deal on a person's particular attitude or configuration of attitudes related to the sound. Many sounds that might be tolerated on the job are not acceptable at home, where both the meaning and the attitude toward the sound are different. Levels of intensity of sound from contemporary music groups may far exceed legal limits of exposure in work situations, yet the sounds are sought rather than shunned. The only difference is the attitude of the majority of the listeners toward the sound.

Although there has been some research in this area, it has become apparent that attitudes toward noise are complex and may be caused by many factors that are difficult, if not impossible, to quantify.

chapter
5

Hazards of the
Environment: Accidents

According to statistics released by the National Safety Council (1971), there were 114,000 accidental deaths in the United States in 1970. There were 10,800,000 disabilities caused by accidents, of which about 400,000 were classified as permanent impairments. The economic impact on the country due to accidents was estimated to be at least 25 billion dollars.

The magnitude of this problem is staggering. In one year, for example, more Americans are killed on our highways than have been killed in all the years of the war in Vietnam. More Americans over the years have died from accidents than have died from combat wounds in all of our wars. If we disregard the human suffering and consider accidents from a purely economic point of view, the financial cost of accidents is also impressive in terms of medical expenses, lost wages, reduced production, and so forth. Also, our medical system, which is already overburdened, has a tremendous extra load imposed by accident victims. Of the approximately 50 million persons injured in 1969, the majority required medical treatment of some sort, whether in physicians' offices, emergency or outpatient departments of hospitals, or at the scene of the accident. Many of those injured required hospitalization, occupied beds for many millions of hospital days, and required the services of thousands of hospital personnel. Viewed from any perspective, accidents must be considered one of the major medical problems confronting our society today.

Because accidents are such a major problem, efforts are being made to reduce the frequency of occurrence of accidents and their severity when they do occur. Programs aimed at accident prevention are multidisciplinary, involving professionals from a number of different fields. The programs range from local safety campaigns to large-scale, government-financed action programs. Research projects at a number of different levels are concerned with accident prevention. These projects range from laboratory studies designed to better understand some of the human variables in accidents to large evaluation studies aimed at determining the effectiveness of various kinds of accident-countermeasure programs. Although the majority of the research is concerned with vehicle accidents (see Chapters 9, 10, and 11), investigations dealing with many other kinds of accidents are also being conducted.

Psychologists are active in this research at all levels. Some psychologists are studying aspects of human behavior in laboratory settings and are attempting to relate their findings to accidents. Others are trying to design and evaluate various accident-countermeasure programs in schools, industries, recreational areas, and other settings. Still other psychologists are employed by the government in key positions in various of the federal safety programs. We will not be able to discuss all of the different accident-prevention areas in which psychologists work. However, we will attempt in this chapter to give a broad overview of the field and include enough representative studies to give you some idea of what psychologists are doing to help solve the accident problem.

WHAT IS AN ACCIDENT?

One might assume that a definition of *accident* is not necessary because everyone knows what an accident is. The problem, however, is that there are too many different views of what constitutes an accident. Even researchers in the area will often argue about definitions. This has led to a great deal of confusion.

One point of view, often held by the general public and even by some research workers, is discussed by Haddon, Suchman, and Klein (1964). In their comprehensive book dealing with accident research, these authors point out that:

Accidents seem to be commonly regarded . . . as resulting from causal sequences that are somehow intrinsically different from those that lead to disease and to other everyday events. As a reflection of this, accidents remain the only major source of morbidity and mortality which many continue to view in essentially extra-rational terms. "Luck," "chance," and "acts of God" are all culturally acceptable explanations of accidents, although such concepts have gradually fallen into disuse in explaining the causation of disease [p. 2].

Obviously, the "chance" view of accidents is such that research and countermeasures based on this point of view would require theologians and philosophers rather than scientists. Most researchers prefer more substantial definitions, although not all agree about just what the definition should be. Many define an accident as the occurrence of unexpected physical or chemical damage to living or nonliving structures; the damage is caused by a rapid transfer of energy in such ways and such amounts that animate or inanimate structures are harmed.

Other researchers would argue that physical damage is not necessarily a consequence of an accident. Suchman (1961) suggests that, in describing an event, the term *accident* is more likely to be used if the event manifests the following three major characteristics:

(1) *Degree of expectedness:* The less the event could have been anticipated, the more likely it is to be labeled an accident.
(2) *Degree of avoidability:* The less the event could have been avoided, the more likely it is to be labeled an accident.
(3) *Degree of intention:* The less the event was the result of deliberate action, the more likely it is to be labeled an accident [p. 30].

An accident, then, can also be defined as that class of events involving a low level of intention, avoidability, and expectedness. As Suchman points out, this definition includes not only events that lead to bodily injury (medical accidents) but also those unexpected, unavoidable, and unintentional acts such as losing things or forgetting appointments (behavioral accidents).

In the broadest definition, then, any unexpected event might be considered an accident. However, in terms of prevention, statistical analysis, and statistical comparisons, an accident is usually considered an unexpected event in which either damage or injury is sustained.

ACCIDENT COUNTERMEASURES

When utilized in the injury-control or accident-prevention context, a countermeasure is a technique or program that is designed to reduce the frequency of accidents and/or the severity of injury if an accident does occur. Many of the people in the accident-prevention area are involved, in one way or another, with the development of various types of countermeasures.

Unfortunately, the development of countermeasures in the past has been based mostly on a "common sense" approach and not on the basis of research. If a particular countermeasure looked good to the developer, it was often implemented with no effort made to evaluate its effectiveness. An example of a "common sense" countermeasure is the "kerb drill," which has been used in England for a number of years to teach young children safe street-crossing practices.

In England, young children are required to memorize a "kerb drill." In the form of a short poem, it warns them to look to the left and right when crossing a street; if they do so, they will not get run over. The children can memorize this poem quite readily and, from a common-sense point of view, it would appear to be a simple but effective countermeasure. In 1967 Pease and Preston conducted a study designed to evaluate the effectiveness of the little poem. They concluded that many of the children simply stopped at the curb, repeated the drill, and then went ahead regardless of the traffic situation. The children assumed that the mere act of saying the poem would insure their safety. Also, many children who used the "kerb drill" did not comprehend the concept of directionality. Therefore, they responded to left and right as parts of a static environment rather than as a relational idea of a direction.

Although there are many specific types of countermeasures, they are either designed to modify the behavior of people so that they are less likely to have an accident, modify the physical environment so that an accident either cannot occur or is reduced in severity, or some combination of the two. For example, the spot advertisements that you see on television concerning various safety habits are attempts at modifying behavior. The air bags that will rapidly inflate if the car is in an accident are examples of physical-environment modification-type countermeasures. An example of a countermeasure that requires both approaches is seat belts in automobiles. The seat belts have been installed and represent a physical modification, but, in order for them to do any good, behavior-modification techniques must also be employed in order to convince the occupants of vehicles to buckle the seat belts.

Much of the effort in accident-prevention research is either directly or indirectly aimed at the development of countermeasures. Though the researcher in the laboratory who is interested in some aspect of human behavior that may relate to accidents will, perhaps, not be directly concerned with countermeasures, someone else may use his data in order to develop a new countermeasure technique. It will be apparent from this chapter that there are a multitude of variables involved in the event that we label an accident; in order for a countermeasure to be effective, these variables must be taken into account. A valuable contribution of research in accident prevention is the identification and definition of these variables. Once the variables are known, systematic development of countermeasures can be accomplished more readily. A basic problem, however, is that the variables associated with one class of accidents may be quite different from those associated with other types of accidents. Therefore, a countermeasure that may be effective for one class of accidents may not be effective in another situation. Most major accident-prevention programs will consequently require a variety of countermeasure techniques.

Countermeasure Research

We have suggested that too many countermeasures are based on "common sense" and not empirical data. Why is this the case? Possibly one of the primary reasons is that research on countermeasure development and effectiveness is time-consuming and difficult. Also, until relatively recently there has not been a great deal of interest in accident-prevention research in the United States. Consequently, there is a shortage of well-trained investigators to carry out the required type of research.

Although countermeasure research is often complicated, the basic experimental design is straightforward. Generally, the first stage involves the development of the particular technique or program, the second stage involves implementing it, and the final stage includes the evaluation of the countermeasure. There are a number of factors that must be taken into consideration in the development and implementation stage, including decisions about whether behavioral- or physical-modification methods should be used, which techniques should be employed, and what the ratio of cost to effectiveness should be (that is, the amount of accident prevention to be achieved per dollar spent). Psychologists are often involved in these decisions, but generally they are more interested in the evaluation aspects because of their unique training in experimental design and evaluation techniques. However, it is important that the individual or group who will be doing the evaluation be involved with all phases of the program. Too often researchers are asked to evaluate existing programs; this is very difficult, if not impossible, to accomplish in a scientific fashion.

As an example of the steps in evaluation of a countermeasure, let us consider an imaginary series of films that have been developed to train first graders in safe street-crossing habits. Before the films are used, the first step involves gathering base-line data concerning pedestrian accidents of first-grade children in a number of different areas where we plan to try out the films. This is a very important step since it permits an evaluation of the effectiveness of the films in reducing this type of accident. The next step involves showing the films to some of the children in the areas that are selected and not showing the films to others, who would be considered *controls*. We once again collect data over a period of time concerning the frequency of pedestrian accidents in these areas. Possibly, the children who are shown the films show a lower incidence of accidents than those who are not shown the film. The frequency of accidents of children in the control group probably will be about the same as the frequency obtained in the base-line data. If the children who view the film have significantly fewer accidents than the controls, we can assume that the films are an effective countermeasure.

Actually, the film example is a greatly simplified situation. In the first place, frequency of accidents as a criterion measure for evaluating counter-measure effectiveness leaves a great deal to be desired. Although an accident may not seem to be a rare event, it really is. Consider, for example, the millions of safe street crossings that children make for each crossing that results in an accident. Consequently, in order to use accidents as a criterion measure, it is necessary to utilize very large samples of subjects so that enough accidents occur to make statistical analysis possible. Because of this, some interest has been expressed by a few researchers in the use of certain categories of high-risk behavior instead of actual accidents as criteria in evaluation studies. In other words, some form of high-risk behavior would be observed and its frequency obtained before a countermeasure is implemented and, following exposure to the countermeasure, the frequency of this behavior would again be obtained. If it were reduced significantly from that of a control group, the countermeasure would be assumed to have had some effect. Before this can be done, however, research is needed to identify and define *high-risk behavior* to establish whether or not the behavior is actually related to accidents. A step in this direction is represented in a recent investigation. Heimstra, Nichols, and Martin (1969) systematically analyzed the street-crossing behavior of kindergarten children. As the children approached and crossed an intersection near their school, they were filmed by a concealed cameraman. Later these films were analyzed by means of single-frame analysis techniques and a number of categories of behavior were identified and defined. Included as high-risk behavior was not stopping at the intersection and not looking to the left or the right for traffic. A number of other behavior categories were also involved but were not defined as high risk. It was found that significant differences existed between boys and girls in terms of the frequency of high-risk behavior demonstrated (boys had a higher frequency) and that there were a number of other factors that contributed to this behavior (such as whether the children were in groups or alone, whether they were running or walking as they approached the intersection, and so forth). The next step in this series of research projects is to determine whether this behavior can be modified by various types of countermeasures.

The importance of countermeasure evaluation in accident-prevention research cannot be overemphasized. Programs that are implemented just because they "look good" may in fact do no good at all and in some instances may even do harm. They are also expensive; in an area that is chronically underfinanced, funds must be spent on programs that have demonstrated effectiveness.

APPROACHES TO ACCIDENT-PREVENTION RESEARCH

Because the area of accident-prevention research is so broad and encompasses so many different fields—industrial accidents, home accidents, recreational accidents, vehicular accidents, and so forth—we make no attempt to cover the many specific approaches utilized by researchers. However, some methods are more common than others; in this section we will be concerned with several of these approaches.

The Epidemiological Approach

One way of looking at an accident is to consider it the result of a combination of forces from at least three sources—the *host* (usually man himself), the *agent* (an automobile, a sharp object), and the *environment* in which the host and agent find themselves. Epidemiological research is aimed at identifying as many factors as possible associated with the host, agent, and environment and their relationship to accidents, as well as the complex way these factors may interact to produce an accident. This type of research may range from the gathering of statistics concerning certain types of accidents to rather detailed studies in which attempts are made to establish causal relationships of a complex nature. The former type of study—descriptive epidemiology—usually does not contribute a great deal to the understanding of what causes accidents. However, it is necessary in order to identify the general areas from which accident problems are originating and to determine their relative importance. For example, the present concern with hazardous toys is based on descriptive epidemiological data showing that there are a substantial number of injuries to children each year due to dangerous toys.

After a problem area has been identified, more detailed epidemiological research is needed on specific host factors (such as age and sex), agent characteristics (such as sharp points of a toy or one that shatters too easily), and environmental factors that may influence the host and agent. With properly conducted epidemiological research, a great deal of information is made available to those who are concerned with developing countermeasures for a particular class of accidents. This type of research involves much more than just going out in the field and asking questions about accidents. There are many sources of data ranging from hospital records to interviews, for investigators conducting epidemiological research. Actually, properly conducted epidemiological research is a highly sophisticated endeavor involving careful survey and sampling techniques and elaborate statistical analysis of the data that are obtained.

The Experimental Approach

Aside from the subject matter involved, the experimental approach applied to accident research is no different than when utilized in other areas. Although the independent and dependent variables may be somewhat different in accident research, the experimental approach is the same.

There has been considerable laboratory research on various aspects of driver behavior and vehicular accidents, but there has been relatively little experimental work in other accident areas. However, laboratory research in a number of areas of psychology does have direct applications to the accident-prevention field. Thus studies conducted in sensation and perception, decision making, fatigue and motor performance, and many other areas may provide valuable information to the researcher who is dealing with the human factors in accidents.

The advantages and disadvantages of laboratory studies that have been discussed in previous chapters also apply to accident-prevention research. There is always the question of the applicability of the laboratory findings to the real-world situation. However, the advantage of studying human accident variables in the laboratory is that the subjects do not have to be exposed to hazardous conditions.

An experiment, of course, does not have to be carried out in the laboratory but can be conducted in the field. Research carried out in the field under carefully arranged conditions could prove quite useful. A considerable amount of this kind of research has been conducted in the area of vehicular accidents. It would also be a useful approach in studying other kinds of accidents, but there has been little effort in this direction.

Other Approaches

There are, of course, several methods for studying behavior. Behavior can be studied by employing the naturalistic-observation method, by interviewing subjects in some depth (the case-study method), by testing groups of subjects, and by using the experimental method. We have already mentioned the use of the experimental method in accident research. The naturalistic-observation approach, while not commonly used, can be an effective method for certain kinds of accident-prevention research. For example, the study in which children were filmed as they crossed a street (Heimstra, Nichols, & Martin, 1969) involved naturalistic-observation techniques. Testing and case-history methods have also been utilized to research accidents, particularly in studies that have attempted to relate some personality or behavioral variable to accident frequency (such as the accident-proneness concept). The particular approach selected by the researcher depends, of course, on the nature of the problem that he is investigating.

SOME EPIDEMIOLOGICAL DATA

When we scan the accident statistics, some interesting facts quickly become apparent. There are, for example, certain types of accidents—specifically, motor vehicle accidents—that kill many more people than other kinds. Age is an important variable, and we find that particular kinds of accidents are associated with particular age groups. Sex is also a variable, with the death rate from accidents among males considerably higher than among females. As might be expected, certain occupations are much more hazardous than others in terms of the probability of being injured or killed by an accident.

Types of Accidents

Obviously, there are thousands of different kinds of accidents that may seriously injure or even kill a person. However, certain types are much more common than others and make up the greatest share of recorded accidents. When deaths from accidents for both sexes and all ages were calculated, statistics for 1968 showed that 114,864 people died from accidents. A further breakdown shows:

Motor vehicle	54,862 deaths	Firearms	2,394
Falls	18,651	Ingest food, object	3,100
Fires, Burns	7,335	Poison (solid, liquid)	2,583
Drowning	7,372	Poison (gas)	1,526

Age

An infant under 1 year of age is more likely to die from mechanical suffocation or from the ingestion of a food object than any other kind of accident. In contrast, a person over 75 years old is more likely to die from a fall than another type of accident. At all ages in between, however, the most common cause of accidental death is a motor vehicle accident. Fire or burns are the second most common type of fatal accident for children from 1 to 4 years. From 5 to 44 years, the second most common accidental death is by drowning. Over age 44, falls rate second as causes of accidental death.

For children from ages 1 to 14, accidents claim more lives than the six leading diseases combined; for youths from 15 to 24, accidents take more lives than all other causes combined. Diseases, however, begin to "catch up" after this age, and for the group between 45 and 64 years of age, heart disease, cancer, and strokes all claim more lives than accidents.

Sex

In the 1-to-14 age group, boys have about twice as many fatal accidents as girls. However, in the 15-to-24 age group, four out of five accident victims are males. Just why these differences exist is not clear, although some interesting speculations have been made concerning the reasons. Perhaps it is due to societal pressures, which tend to encourage risk-taking and aggressive behavior in boys while discouraging this same sort of behavior in girls.

Occupation

There are wide differences between various occupations in terms of the frequency rate of accidents and the severity of the accidents if they do occur. The National Safety Council, an organization that furnishes leadership in the safety movement, tabulates data of this sort. The 1970 injury rates reported to the National Safety Council for a number of industries are shown in Figure 5-1.

There are other variables that epidemiological research shows are important factors in accidents. For example, the 1967 statistics compiled by the National Center for Health Statistics show that the accident death rate per 100,000 population for nonwhite males was 102.4 whereas for white males it was only 77.6. Socioeconomic variables are important, particularly in childhood accidents, since exposure to hazard tends to be concentrated among children whose families are lowest on the socioeconomic scale.

There are other variables that could be listed. However, the ones we have discussed should be sufficient to point out that epidemiological research is important in defining the factors that contribute to accidents. Those responsible for establishing countermeasures must have other kinds of information as

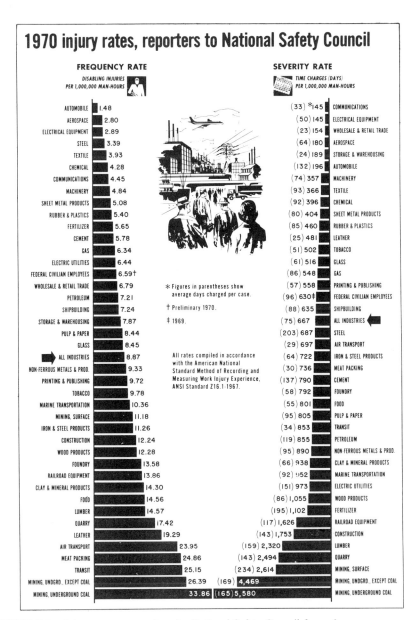

FIGURE 5-1. Injury rates reported to the National Safety Council for various occupations. (From *Accident Facts*, 1971 Edition. Reprinted by permission of the National Safety Council.)

well. Some of this information is obtained through the various research approaches we discussed previously.

ACCIDENT-PREVENTION RESEARCH
WITH CHILDREN

Although we could discuss accident-prevention research in a number of different fields such as industry, the home, recreational areas, and so forth, for several reasons we will restrict our discussion to research in accident prevention with children. In the first place, a discussion of research in all of the different areas is well beyond the scope of this chapter. Secondly, research on childhood accidents presents the investigator with some unique problems not encountered in the other areas; although accidents are a serious problem for all age groups, they are particularly serious for children.

The View of the Child as a Miniature Adult

Frequently, a countermeasure aimed at reducing children's accidents does not work, and the designers of the countermeasure are puzzled. To them it looked like a very logical approach that should have been effective. One reason that the countermeasures designed for children often are not effective is because the developers do not consider the fact that the child's sensing, perceptual, decision-making, and response capabilities are quite different from those of the adult. The "kerb drill" is an example showing this misunderstanding of children's capabilities. Thus an important area of research for psychologists interested in accident prevention for children is that of determining the capabilities of the behavioral systems of the child.

There is available, of course, a considerable amount of developmental-psychology research, which should be of use to the accident-prevention researcher. Unfortunately, all too frequently this basic research does not give the kinds of answers needed to design countermeasures. It does reveal something about the child's capabilities in a laboratory setting, but it does not tell us a great deal about why a child failed to see an approaching car or, if he did see it, why he failed to get out of the way.

A Behavioral Model of the Child

In Chapter 7 the various functions required of the human element in a man-machine system are discussed in some detail. These functions include detection, identification, interpretation, decision making, and response. A child performs similar functions in his everyday interaction with his environment. A schematic of a child's behavioral system, which consists of a series of subsystems, is shown in Figure 5-2. These subsystems work together and interact in such a fashion that an input, in the form of stimuli in the environment, is transformed to an output, in the form of a response. As we know, sometimes the response is such that the child is involved in an accident. Let us consider these various subsystems and how they might function or malfunction to cause an accident.

Sensing Subsystem. The sensing subsystem includes the various sensory receptors, nervous pathways to the brain, and certain sections of the brain. Not a great deal is known about the sensory capabilities of small children. On the basis of some types of accidents involving poisonings, one might assume that taste in a small child differs considerably from that of an adult. The difference in their tastes may explain why a child swallows turpentine or some other chemical agent that, to the adult, tastes "awful." Perhaps it does not to the child.

Identifying Subsystem. The identifying subsystem is responsible for organizing sensory input and giving it meaning. It is often referred to as the perceptual or perceiving subsystem. A child may be involved in some kinds of accidents because of limited perceptual capabilities. For example, there is evidence that a child cannot localize sound as efficiently as an adult. Similarly, in studies concerned with the ability of children to perceive movement out of the "corner" of their eye (peripheral vision), it has been found that a child's ability is significantly inferior to an adult's. Both of these perceptual abilities—sound localization and peripheral-movement detection—may be impor-

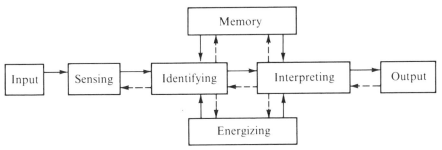

FIGURE 5-2. A model of the behavioral system of a child showing the various subsystems and their relationships. These various subsystems may be involved in behavior resulting in an accident.

89

tant in street-crossing behavior and may be one reason that children are frequently involved in pedestrian accidents.

The Memory Subsystem. This is the subsystem that is involved with learning and memory. Obviously, there are many rules about safe behavior that a child must learn and remember. Often the safety programs that are designed for children expect too much of this subsystem; children are simply not capable of learning and remembering all the rules and regulations.

The Energizing Subsystem. The energizing subsystem is concerned with motivation and emotion. Perhaps the child has seen a car approaching and knows the rules about running into the street, but his pet races into the street in front of the car. If the energizing subsystem overrides the other subsystems, the child will rush out to save his pet and be struck himself.

The Interpreting Subsystem. The interpreting subsystem is involved with the higher mental processes such as thinking and decision making. This is probably the critical subsystem as far as children's accidents are concerned. We have already given one example of "misinterpretation" in which children learned a short poem designed to teach good street-crossing habits. Recall that many children thought that just repeating the poem would protect them while crossing the street.

There are many other examples in which children interpret situations incorrectly and, because of this, may have an accident. For example, the skull and crossbones is a common symbol used to warn that the contents of a bottle or can are poison. However, some children interpret the symbol to mean "bone medicine" or that the container has something to do with pirates. Warning signs of various kinds are often misinterpreted by children and may actually entice the child into a dangerous situation.

We do not know a great deal about how children perceive and interpret hazardous or risky situations in their environment. What may seem to be an obviously dangerous situation to an adult may appear attractive and perfectly safe to a child. Recently, a large-scale study designed to investigate how children interpret hazardous situations was carried out by Martin and Heimstra (1970). In this study a "perception of hazard" test was developed. It required a subject to rate a large number of photographs, which depicted various hazardous situations and varying degrees of hazard. The subject rated the photograph on a five-point scale ranging from "no danger" to "very dangerous." The photographs included scenes involving firearms, street crossings, falls, electrical appliances, poisons, and so forth. The test, which was demonstrated to have a high reliability, was administered to about 1500 first-, third-, and fifth-grade children. It was also administered to a number of "judges" who were experts in the area of accident prevention; the scores of these experts were compared with the children's scores. It was found that a number of variables had an effect on the children's perception of the degree of hazard depicted in a given photograph. Sex differences were quite apparent. Socioeconomic background of the children was an important variable, as was rural-urban background. Similarly, the age of the subject was important: fifth graders perceived more or less hazard in certain scenes than the first and third graders did.

Further analysis of the data has shown that there are a number of children who can be considered "low perceivers" of hazard. They tend to see very little danger in any of the photographs, even those where the danger should be quite obvious. There were also a number of "high perceivers," who saw danger in nearly all of the photographs, even when no danger was meant to be depicted. In a follow-up study, the parents of the low and high perceivers were interviewed, and accident records of the children were obtained. It was found that the male low perceivers had had significantly more accidents in the past than the high perceivers had.

There is need for a great deal more research dealing with the interpreting subsystem of children before effective behavior-modification countermeasures can be designed. Obviously, if the child misinterprets the meaning of the countermeasure, its effectiveness will be limited.

The Output of the System.   Even if the child senses the stimuli, identifies the sensory input, and interprets it correctly, he may still have an accident if he is not capable of making the correct physical response. A child may simply not have enough strength to make an appropriate response. In some instances, countermeasures can be designed with the child's response limitations in mind. For example, it is possible to design the door on a refrigerator so that even a small child can push it open from the inside. This would prevent entrapment, which still occurs relatively frequently.

For each of the problems, a number of examples could be given in which lack of knowledge about children's capabilities makes the design of effective countermeasures difficult. However, a large-scale research program will be required in order to obtain this type of information, and unfortunately there is no indication at present that such research will be undertaken. Rather, the trend seems to be in the direction of attempting to modify the environment so that the child is better protected. Instead of training a child regarding the dangers of poisons, the major effort presently is in designing bottles with caps that cannot be removed by children, medicine cabinets that cannot be opened, and so forth. Whether these attempts will be successful remains to be seen.

THE THEORY OF ACCIDENT PRONENESS

Everyone has known an individual who seems to have a disproportionate number of accidents. Is this individual accident-prone? An idea that has been popular among a number of researchers in the area of accident prevention is that a high frequency of accidents are incurred by certain individuals because of some type of personality characteristic. Considerable interest has been expressed in attempting to identify the personality characteristic or characteristics that will make a person more likely to have an accident than individuals who lack the characteristic.

Interest in the theory of accident proneness has fluctuated. At one time there was a good deal of excitement generated by this theory, and considerable research was conducted in an attempt to support this view. However, some investigators began to take a closer look at the theory and raised some serious questions on statistical, methodological, and theoretical grounds.

In the first place, since chance plays a part in many accidents, it is not surprising that during any given period of time a certain proportion of the population would have a high number of accidents by chance alone. Actually, a statistical model (called the Poisson distribution) indicates that 9% of the population should have 39% of the accidents and that 39.5% of the people should have 100% of the accidents. If the accident-proneness hypothesis were used as an explanation of a given distribution of accidents, then the distribution would have to differ significantly from that predicted by the Poisson distribution.

Also, for the hypothesis to hold up, the membership of the accident "group" would have to remain essentially unchanged over time. Therefore the number of accidents that people have in two time periods (for example, one two-year period compared with another two-year period of their lives) should be highly correlated. The evidence suggests that membership in the accident group changes and that the small group who has a high frequency of accidents during one period will be replaced with another group that has more accidents during another period.

Frequently in accident-proneness research the investigators have failed to control for environmental exposure or risk. Because certain individuals are more likely to be exposed to hazard, they may have more accidents and be labeled accident-prone. Studies should attempt to equate the exposure factor, but often they do not. Similarly, certain age groups are sometimes called accident-prone. However, in these cases there are often social and cultural predisposing factors that may contribute to a higher accident rate and not accident proneness. Thus the young male driver is much more likely to have an accident than drivers in various other age groups but would not be considered to have a personality characteristic that makes him accident-prone.

For these reasons, and for many others, most researchers in accident-prevention areas have not been overly impressed with the theory of accident proneness. Although there have been recent well-designed and controlled studies suggesting that there may be more to this theory, data are still scarce. The theory of accident proneness does deserve a limited place in accident research, but it probably does not deserve the central place that was reserved for it for quite a period of time.

part

2

MAN AND HIS WORKING ENVIRONMENT

Psychologists have been concerned with man and his working environment for many years, and the impact of psychological research can be seen at all levels within this environment. Although the activities of psychologists in industries and other organizations are varied, one of their primary tasks is to attempt to "fit the man to the job" by means of various selection and training techniques. Some of the problems associated with effective selection and training and some of the techniques used by psychologists in fitting the man to the job are discussed in Chapter 6.

The effectiveness of an individual in a work environment can often be enhanced through appropriate selection and training procedures. Sometimes his effectiveness can be further increased by psychologists who utilize their knowledge of man's capabilities and limitations in an effort to "fit the job to the man." Frequently, this involves the application of psychological principles to the design of machines and equipment in order to make the man-machine relationship as compatible as possible. Some of the activities of these psychologists, called human-factors engineers, are discussed in Chapter 7.

A more recent area of interest to psychologists has to do with the manner in which the working environment will influence the behavior and general well-being of the workers. These researchers are concerned with factors in the working environment that will motivate the worker and lead to satisfaction with his job. How job motivation and satisfaction are studied and some of the variables that affect them are discussed in Chapter 8.

Fitting the Man
to the Job

Organizations differ a great deal in the requirements they impose on their employees. Even within a single organization or industry, requirements may range from those needed for successful operation of a simple piece of equipment to those needed for complex decision making. Because of these diverse requirements, most organizations make some attempt to *select* individuals who, because of certain attributes or abilities, appear to be more likely to succeed in a particular job than other individuals. Also, once an individual has been hired for a job, most organizations make some effort to *train* the person so that he is more effective.

As the title of this chapter implies, proper selection and good training are required to "fit the man to the job." Placing a man in a job he cannot perform effectively can be expensive for the organization in terms of replacing the individual, reduced production, accidents, expensive "incorrect" decisions, and so forth. These costs are often compounded since, due to various types of union-management agreements, it might be difficult to fire a person who is not suited to a particular job.

Although the need for good selection and training is generally recognized, changes in technology over the last few years have made the selection and training process a difficult one. At one time, many jobs were simple, and it was not particularly difficult to select and train men for them. Because jobs have become much more complex, the requirements for them are harder to

Photo courtesy of Travel Division, South Dakota Dept. of Highways, Pierre, S.D.

specify and measure. Consequently, it is much harder to select and train persons for these jobs.

Selection and training are two important activities that occupy the time of a number of psychologists. Most are located in industrial settings, but others are involved with these activities in military organizations and in many other types of settings. As you will see in this chapter, different techniques are employed, depending on the particular job that a person is to be selected and trained for. However, there are a number of basic considerations involved in establishing selection and training programs; it is these that we will be primarily concerned with in this chapter.

SELECTING THE MAN FOR THE JOB

It should be apparent that before a man is selected for a job a good deal must be known about the particular job. For example, what requirements will it impose on the individual? What are the job objectives? What duties are required? What characteristic patterns of behavior will be necessary in order for a person to get the job done? In order to obtain this information, the job is analyzed. The resultant *job analysis* can be used to determine the qualifications and behaviors needed to fill the job. The analysis can also be used to obtain information that is needed for establishing training programs, for improving job efficiency, and sometimes for establishing wage structures.

The Job Analysis

Essentially, a job analysis consists of a description of the various tasks required of a person doing a particular job. The characteristics of these tasks are described, and the behaviors and abilities required to perform the tasks are listed. A number of different methods of job analysis are used; they range from simple questionnaire techniques to rather elaborate procedures that gather information about a job from a number of different sources. Basically, however, each of the various techniques can be classified as falling into one of two general approaches. In one case, the current job holder is requested to describe what he does at his job (the interview approach). Techniques in this approach may range from relatively informal interviews to highly structured questionnaires, diaries, and checklists. In the second approach, an investigator analyzes a job by observing what a current job occupant is doing and then, in some systematic fashion, describing what has been observed (observation approach). With this second approach, the job analyst may actually work at the job for a period of time instead of just observing. In some instances, a combination of interview and observation may be used (observation-interview technique).

In the interview approach, a worker (or workers) will be called from his job and interviewed extensively about all of the activities involved in the performance of the job. Usually a worker is interviewed alone, but in some cases a group interview technique is employed. The questions in a group interview may be similar to those asked in an individual interview, but this approach is much less time-consuming. The technical-conference method, which is also an interview approach, brings together a number of "experts" in place of the actual job occupants. These experts, who are persons with a high degree of knowledge about a particular job, meet with the job analyst and attempt to provide him with information about all of the characteristics of the job. In a variation of the interview technique, workers may be required to complete questionnaires, fill out check-lists, or record all of their activities in a log book or diary. (This latter method is typically used with higher-level executive jobs.)

With the observation-interview technique, the analyst goes to the job and interviews the occupant as he actually works. The job analyst observes the worker and questions him about his various activities. After observing and interviewing a number of job incumbents, the analyst combines the data into a single job analysis.

A variety of specific techniques can be employed when using the *observation* approach. The observer may stand near a worker and, by means of a checklist, record various activities that take place. Sometimes motion pictures are made of a job occupant as he performs his job; these films are then subjected to analysis. An interesting variety of this approach involves the job analyst himself actually performing the job. This allows him to gain firsthand information about the behaviors required to perform the job. By systematically recording everything that he does on the job, the analyst is able to arrive at a comprehensive picture of what is required of the job occupant.

Regardless of the type of job analysis utilized, it gives the psychologist who is concerned with selection a good idea about the kinds of individuals who would be most likely to fit the requirements of the particular job.

The Selection Process

The techniques of personnel selection are aimed at identifying those individuals who have the interest, motivation, and capability to succeed at a given job. The individuals who are selected are assumed to be better risks for job success than those who were rejected by the selection technique involved. If the technique is effective, individuals who are better risks will be selected.

If it is not effective, then selection, for all practical purposes, is a random process, and there is very little difference in terms of probable success between those selected and rejected.

Underlying the selection process is the fact that individuals differ on virtually any measurable ability or attribute. Obviously, if people did not differ there would be no problem in selecting a person for a job because anyone hired would have the same potential for succeeding. Since individual differences do exist, however, personnel selection is aimed at identifying those persons who, because of certain abilities or potential abilities, are better risks for job success than persons who do not possess the particular abilities.

In attempting to accomplish this objective, the industrial psychologist may make use of a number of selection techniques and devices. These include a wide variety of tests, biographical inventories, personal references, interviews, and so forth. Basically, however, all of the methods are aimed at evaluating individual differences, which make certain persons more likely than others to succeed at some job.

The Selection Model

Ideally, the technique employed for selecting personnel for a job would identify all individuals who will succeed at the job and all those who will not succeed. If we had such a technique, whether it was a test, an interview, or whatever, we could say that we had available a perfect *predictor or selection device*. Unfortunately, this type of predictor is not easily come by.

An important task of the industrial psychologist is developing selection devices and then evaluating their effectiveness. If he were just to devise a predictor that "looked good" and then utilize it for selecting new employees, he would not know whether employees selected on the basis of the predictor were any more likely to succeed at the job than new employees who had been randomly selected. How, then, is the effectiveness of a predictor determined?

Along with the predictor (or selection device) that is administered to potential employees, the psychologist must also develop some sort of indicator of what constitutes success on the particular job involved. This is called the *criterion* and is sometimes difficult and expensive to determine. For example, considerable effort is made to select the right men to train as military aircraft pilots. However, what determines successful performance as a pilot? Similarly, what constitutes good driving performance in an automobile? The problems associated with this type of criterion are taken up in more detail in the chapters dealing with the highway transportation system. In less complex tasks, however, such as operating a lathe, a drill press, or a typewriter, it is not as difficult to arrive at some sort of criterion of good performance.

After developing *predictor* and *criterion* measures, the psychologist evaluates the effectiveness of the predictor by determining the relationship (correlation) between the scores obtained on the predictor measure and on the criterion measure. Suppose, for example, that a psychologist has developed a test that he thinks will measure the abilities required for successful operation of a machine in a factory. "Successful operation" has been established on the basis of the number of perfect units produced by the operator in a given period of time. The predictor, then, is the test, and the criterion is the number of units produced. The psychologist administers the test to a number of workers who are already on the job and then obtains data about the number of units each worker produces in a given period of time.

The next step is to correlate the predictor scores with the criterion scores in order to determine if a real and meaningful relationship exists between the two. Various correlational techniques are employed. A high positive correlation between the predictor and criterion measures is generally thought to indicate that the predictor will be useful in selecting individuals for the job.

The procedure of relating the predictor to the criterion is called *assessing the validity* of a predictor. More specifically, the procedure would assess *concurrent* validity, since the predictor and criterion measures were obtained concurrently from workers already on the job. Sometimes, however, the predictor test is given to all newly hired employees; then at a later date (often many months later) the performance of the workers is carefully evaluated. Next the relationship between their predictor test scores and their performance is established. If a relationship between the two does exist, we say that the predictor has *predictive* validity. Generally, predictive validity is more meaningful than concurrent validity in the development of predictor measures, but it is more expensive and difficult to obtain. Models of the two procedures used to determine the validity of a predictor are shown in Figures 6-1 and 6-2.

There are several steps involved, then, in the traditional selection model. In the first place, the job must be analyzed. Based on information from the job analysis, the predictor and the criterion must be selected. Next it is necessary to obtain measures on both from workers on the job. Then the criterion and predictor measures are statistically compared. Actually, the cautious investigator may take one more step, which is called *cross-validation*. If the result of the validation step looks promising, then the last step is to repeat the entire procedure. This cross-validation insures that the results of the first investigation did not occur on the basis of chance factors alone. After all of these steps

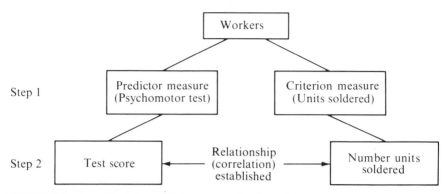

FIGURE 6-1. A model of the validation strategy for determining concurrent relationships between predictor and criterion measures. In the first step of this model, workers are administered the two tests either together or very close in time. The second step involves determining whether a relationship, usually in the form of a correlation, exists between the two scores obtained from the measures. In this example, a score on a psychomotor task was used as a predictor score while the number of units soldered in a given period of time was utilized as the criterion score. Obviously, the particular job or task would determine the type of measures that would be utilized. (From N. W. Heimstra and V. S. Ellingstad, *Human Behavior: A Systems Approach.* Copyright 1972 by Wadsworth Publishing Company, Inc. Reprinted by permission of the publisher, Brooks/Cole Publishing Company, Monterey, Calif.)

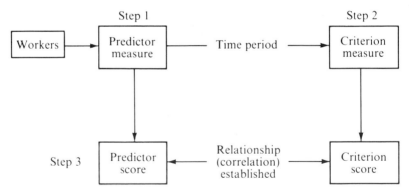

FIGURE 6-2. A validation strategy for determining predictive relationships between predictor and criteria measures. The first step involves testing a group of newly hired workers on the predictor measure that has been selected. After a period of time, possibly many months, the same workers are tested on the criterion measure (Step 2). The third step consists of determining the relationship between the predictor scores and the criterion scores. (From N. W. Heimstra and V. S. Ellingstad, *Human Behavior: A Systems Approach.* Copyright 1972 by Wadsworth Publishing Company, Inc. Reprinted by permission of the publisher, Brooks/Cole Publishing Company, Monterey, Calif.)

102

have been followed, the psychologist is then prepared to make recommendations for implementation of his selection techniques.

Obviously, the various steps outlined may be more or less difficult depending on the complexity of the tasks or jobs that are involved. As we have indicated, it is one thing to make use of a selection model of this sort to select lathe operators or secretaries and another thing when we are concerned with selecting airline pilots or astronauts.

The selection model discussed here can be considered a "traditional" or standard model. However, as Korman (1971) points out, "the process of personnel selection and the development of appropriate methodologies relating to it is be no means a closed, decided procedure" (p. 178). Because more and more situations develop where the traditional model is not appropriate, psychologists have become interested in developing alternative personnel-selection models for use in these situations. The traditional model, however, has much to recommend it; when it can be utilized, it probably constitutes the most desirable approach.

Some Predictor Devices

There are a number of predictor devices that are commonly used, including a wide range of psychological tests, selection interviews, biographical inventories, and personal references. In some cases only one of the devices will be utilized for selection. However, in most cases various combinations will be used in order to give the individual in charge of selection more information on which to base his decision.

The Interview. Regardless of the extent to which psychological tests and the other available selection techniques are employed, a personal interview is almost always conducted with the job applicant. Many personnel men have considerable faith in their ability to determine from an interview whether the applicant is a good risk for the job. However, on the basis of available data, it would appear that this faith in the interview is largely unfounded. Most data indicate that there is little relationship between predictions of job success based on personal interviews and actual job success. Thus, regarding the validity of interviews in predicting success, Blum and Naylor (1968) state:

In only a few of these research studies does one find the interview emerging as a meaningful predictor of either job or training success. While in a number of cases it has demonstrated moderate validity, in most of these it adds little to any multiple prediction over and above what can be obtained with more standardized test instruments. . . .[p. 154].

One reason, of course, that an interview may not be a valid predictor is that the applicant does not always tell the truth. A study by Weiss and Dawis (1960) showed that this may often be the case. These investigators checked the accuracy of interview information obtained from 91 physically handicapped persons by comparing interview information and various available records. Questions regarding age, sex, marital status, education, age at disability, and many more were asked during the interview. The investigators found that 100% of the individuals interviewed reported their sex correctly, but significant percentages gave inaccurate answers to all other questions. For example, 55% gave inaccurate reports on whether they had received prior financial aid, 33% about age at disablement, and so forth.

Biographical Inventories and Personal References. Along with the interview, biographical inventories (application blanks) and letters of references are required by nearly all companies. The biographical inventory can be criticized on several counts. In the first place, it is easy for an applicant to bias responses in his favor. Even when he is being honest, it may be difficult to recall accurately the items required on the inventory. Depending on the criterion used to measure job success, studies evaluating the validity of biographical inventories have resulted in mixed findings. In some instances, the inventory predicted reasonably well; in other instances it had no predictive validity at all.

Although there are many difficulties associated with using letters of reference in selecting applicants for a job, it is still a very common procedure. These letters can, of course, be highly inaccurate and misleading, since most applicants ask for references from individuals who will write a "good" letter.

Mosel and Goheen (1958, 1959) conducted several studies concerned with the validity of letters of recommendation. In these studies, which involved civil-service personnel, the investigators made use of the *Employment Recommendation Questionnaire* (ERQ), which is a civil-service recommendation blank covering a number of characteristics of a potential employee. The form is filled out by a previous employer or someone acquainted with the employee's abilities. In one study (1958), the investigators used ERQs from over a thousand employees in 12 skilled occupations and related the ERQ scores to supervisor performance ratings of the employees. In only four occupations did the ERQ scores relate significantly to the performance ratings, and these relationships were still too small to have any practical significance.

In another study, Mosel and Goheen (1959) attempted to determine whether there was a relationship between the content of the ERQ (what kind of statements were made about the employee) and the kind of person doing the recommending. They found that personal acquaintances were the most lenient in their recommendations, followed by previous subordinates, co-workers, and, finally, previous employers. However, further analysis regarding the *validity* of these recommendations showed that former acquaintances and supervisors had the most valid recommendations.

Tests as Predictors. Probably the most effective, commonly used predictors are tests that measure some aspect of behavior that has been demonstrated to be important for successful performance on a particular job. There are many types of tests used as predictors; we can make no serious attempt to discuss them here. However, there are a number of ways of categorizing these tests into various groupings, and we will briefly discuss some of these groupings to give you an idea about the kinds of tests that may be used as predictors.

Achievement and aptitude tests. An aptitude test is assumed to measure and predict a person's potential in some area; the achievement test is assumed to measure the person's level of skill or ability at the time the test is taken. Often, a test can be considered both an achievement and an aptitude test, since a measure of present skill level may predict future performance.

Paper-and-pencil tests and performance tests. On a paper-and-pencil test, the testee records his response to some item on paper. With a performance test, he does not make a written response but is graded on some performance measure.

Speed and power tests. In some cases, accuracy is not as important as speed, and a person is told to complete as many items as possible in a given period of time. This is a speed test. In other cases, the testee may be allowed all the time he needs, and accuracy of response is weighted very heavily (a power test).

Individual and group tests. Group tests, which can be administered simultaneously to large numbers of testees, are usually more economical in that nearly anyone can administer them. Individual tests, on the other hand, usually require someone who has been extensively trained; consequently, they are more expensive.

Sometimes tests are categorized on the basis of the particular behavior they are designed to measure. For example, there are intelligence tests, personality tests, vision tests, mechanical aptitude tests, driver behavior tests, and so forth. These types of tests obviously also fall within one or the other of the categories listed above.

As you might expect, the effectiveness of tests as selection devices will vary considerably, depending on the nature of the criterion for which they are used as predictors. Many tests have turned out to be quite useful as predictors; others are useless. The effectiveness of a test is generally the result of a long developmental procedure. Test construction is a field in itself and requires sophisticated procedures and well-trained researchers.

Ethical Problems in Personnel Selection

At present, there are factors other than predictor-test performance that must be taken into consideration in the hiring process in an organization. For example, if hiring (or firing) can be shown to be discriminative on the basis of ethnic background or sex, then the Civil Rights Act of 1964 has been violated. A critical problem facing the psychologist who is concerned with developing a selection procedure is whether or not the tests he devises are, indeed, discriminatory.

In some selection procedures, particularly those involving executives, personality tests of different types are frequently involved. These tests may require a person to describe a number of aspects of his personal life. The tests typically become part of the executive's personnel file and can possibly be used in an improper fashion if someone does not understand the implications of the test. This raises the problem of invasion of privacy.

There are other problems in addition to those of discrimination and invasion of privacy in the traditional approach to personnel selection. Although space does not permit going into these problems, some psychologists feel that they may be serious enough to affect the future of personnel selection. For instance, Korman (1971) says that "the future of personnel selection itself, as an organizational improvement process, may have a limited future. Such a statement, while somewhat strong, may nevertheless be justified on the basis of increasing societal pressures against organizational procedures which may serve to perpetuate already existing societal problems" (p. 221).

TRAINING THE MAN FOR THE JOB

The selection procedure is just the first step in fitting the man to the job. Through selection, a number of new employees join the organization. Because of performance on selection devices, these employees are considered to be good risks at being successful on the job. In most cases, however, the new employee is not ready to step directly into the system since he does not as yet possess all the knowledge and skills required by the job. These are developed by the process of *training*.

The Development of a Training Program

Earlier, we found that the development of an effective predictor required a number of steps. This is also the case with the development of a training program. At one time the establishment of training programs was a rather haphazard procedure, but a considerable amount of research has since been conducted dealing with the design of training programs. Much of this research was supported by the military (which is often confronted with training requirements that are somewhat unusual in terms of number of men trained and the time available for training).

The first step in the development of a training program involves a *job description* similar to that required in the selection model. On the basis of the job description, the psychologist is then in a position to *specify the training objectives*. In this phase, a systematic attempt is made to describe the knowledge and skills that a person must acquire in order to be successful at the particular job.

The third step in the development involves the *construction of criterion measures*, which are needed to evaluate changes in the trainees' behavior as a result of the training program. Several types of criterion measures are utilized in training programs. They may involve paper-and-pencil tests or performance tests in either a real or a simulated work environment. Sometimes a criterion test will be given before training (*input criterion*) in order to measure the level of performance at that stage and another test given after completion of the training (*output criterion*). The latter criterion test is used to determine whether the student has mastered the objectives of the course and whether he can perform the job effectively.

In the fourth phase, *instructional procedures are developed*. During this stage, decisions must be made concerning the selection of specific subject matter—how and when it will be presented, training devices and simulators to be used, testing procedures to be used during the program, and so forth. The final, or fifth, phase involves the *evaluation* of the program along with revisions that may be necessary. During this phase, the output criterion measure is administered, the effectiveness of the program is evaluated, and new training materials may be developed; then the training is administered to a new group of students to see if the new procedures are more effective.

Objective of a Training Program

As we have indicated, the primary objective of a training program is to impart the necessary knowledge, skills, and attitudes required for successful performance on a job. However, there are also other objectives that effective training programs can accomplish. In addition to increasing the proficiency of the trainees, a carefully developed program may result in reduced training time and costs. Often the objective of training-program research is the development of a new program that is shorter and less expensive than some existing program. In organizations such as the military, shorter training programs, regardless of cost, may become very important in times of national emergency. A considerable amount of the training-program research supported by the military has been aimed at reducing the length of existing training without subsequent reduction in performance capability. In addition, sometimes the research objective is to develop a program that can effectively train personnel who have certain characteristics preventing them from being trained in other types of programs.

Goffard, Heimstra, Beecroft, and Openshaw (1960) attempted to develop an electronics training program that could be used to train army personnel whose aptitude scores in electronics were too low for them to be admitted to the standard training program. After the investigators analyzed the job and determined what specific skills the job would require, an experimental training program was developed. A criterion measure was also developed. The basic design called for comparing graduates of the experimental course with graduates of the standard course. For purposes of the study, low-aptitude personnel were admitted to the standard course so that both the experimental training program and the standard program contained men with aptitude scores ranging from very low to very high. Graduates of both programs were administered the criterion test. It was found that in the experimental training program, low-aptitude personnel did as well as those with considerably higher aptitude scores in the standard course. With the experimental program implemented, the Army could include a number of men with low aptitudes in their pool of prospective electronic trainees.

Selecting the Training Program to Be Used

There are a variety of different training methods, or combinations of training methods, available to the psychologist who is setting up a training program. His selection of an appropriate method will be based on a number of factors, including *who* is to be trained, *what* is to be taught, costs, time allowed, and so forth.

Much training that goes on in industry and in other organizations falls under the general heading of *on-the-job training* (OJT). There are different approaches to OJT, and some are quite effective. Typically, the trainee works in the same situation that he will work in after his training period is over. Consequently, the problem of transferring what he has learned in training to the actual job is often reduced.

The advantage of OJT is that it does not cost much because the new employee is usually able to produce while he learns. There are also disadvantages. All too often the trainer who supervises the OJT is far from a qualified instructor. Also, too often the OJT programs are not established in a systematic and organized fashion and no evaluation of their effectiveness is made.

Frequently the training programs that are established in civilian and military organizations are not very different from those that you have probably been exposed to. Although generally of relatively short duration, they may involve classroom presentation complete with demonstrations, films, laboratories, and often simulators (the trainee can be exposed to situations quite similar to those he will encounter after training). Sometimes these training programs are designed to develop basic skills in a particular area, but many training programs are aimed at developing advanced skills and knowledge. Thus an employee or military man might receive initial training in a given area shortly after entering the industry or the service, work on the job for some period of time (perhaps years), and then enter an advanced training program of some sort.

Of particular interest to a number of psychologists has been the establishment of training programs that are designed to train supervisory personnel. These programs, often called *leadership-training programs,* began to be developed when it was recognized that supervisors needed special abilities and skills—skills that could be acquired through training in the same way that the assembly-line worker needed training to handle his job.

Typically, it is taken for granted in leadership training that the trainee has a considerable amount of technical knowledge. Consequently, little emphasis is placed on technical material. Instead, the aim of most leadership training is to develop skills in decision making and/or human relations. Decision making is considered the essence of any supervisory or managerial position; if a position does not involve decision making, it is not a leadership position. Training in decision making is therefore central to most leadership-training programs.

There are a number of approaches to this kind of training. The *case-study* approach is based on the assumption that behaviors required of leaders can best be attained through detailed study and discussion of particular "real" problems associated with actual organizations. *Role playing* involves setting up some type of problem situation and assigning trainees roles to play. For example, one trainee may be assigned the role of a foreman and another the role of a worker who is having problems with the foreman. In front of the other trainees, the "foreman" and "worker" play out solutions that they think might develop in the real situation. After a role-playing session, the other trainees can discuss and comment on the various solutions to the problem that were obtained.

Training by *simulation* has become quite popular as a method of developing decision-making capabilities in leaders. Various types of situations that may develop in a real organization are simulated and the trainees are placed in these situations. Although there are many versions of the simulation technique, we will consider just one—the *in-basket simulation* technique.

With this technique, a trainee is first given a good deal of background information about a particular organization or situation. He is then furnished with a number of memos, letters, and so on that might be expected to be found in the "in" basket of an executive in that organization. The trainee then responds to these letters and memos as though he were the executive. He may be called on to solve problems, make decisions, set up agendas for meetings, and so forth. Typically, a critique takes place after a session with the "in" basket.

We have in no way exhausted the many types of approaches that are involved in training programs but those we have discussed should give you some idea about how diverse training programs can be. However, the objectives of all programs are basically the same   to give the trainee knowledge, skills, and attitudes that he did not have when he entered the program.

New Training Approaches

In recent years, several new approaches have been developed for training and are becoming increasingly popular. One of these is *programmed instruction.* You probably have encountered various types of programmed instruction, since textbooks based on this concept are available in many fields. Similarly, *computer-assisted instruction* is growing rapidly. Another new approach is called *adaptive training.* All of these new approaches are discussed in detail in Chapter 20.

chapter

7

Fitting the Job
to the Man

In the previous chapter we saw how psychologists, by means of selection and training procedures, attempt to fit a man to a particular job. Other psychologists take a different approach to the man-job relationship and are concerned with adapting the job to the man. They attempt to do this by applying their knowledge of human behavior, its capabilities and limitations, to the design of work environments and machines.

Why is it necessary to design work environments? Although the engineering capabilities of modern technology are remarkable, all too often the engineer's dream has turned out to be a nightmare for the human operator. Machines are sometimes designed so unrealistically that operator errors increase and gross malfunctions occur, sometimes with devastating results. In other cases, the job environment is such that performance may be affected by such variables as improper lighting, noise, vibration, heat, cold, and so on. Again, errors and sometimes serious accidents are the result.

What can psychologists do about these kinds of problems? Along with the engineers and other professionals, psychologists called human-factors engineers are involved in attempts to design machines and work environments that complement human abilities and compensate for human limitations. Basically, human-factors engineers are interested in helping design machine and work environments that (1) permit optimal human functioning in the kinds

Photo by Sam Sprague.

of tasks required of the operator and (2) provide maximum system efficiency in attaining the goals for which the system was conceived.

In attempting to achieve these goals, human-factors engineers deal with such topics as the distribution of functions between men and machines, the design of controls and displays, the design of safety, survival, and training equipment, and the integration of entire work environments to meet the needs of the human operator. In this regard, the human-factors specialist may specify workspace layouts (normal environmental conditions involving illumination, noise, and so forth) and may determine the effects of unusual environmental situations (such as those encountered in space and under water) on performance.

Obviously, we cannot even begin to discuss the many factors that may be involved in attempting to adapt the machine or the job to man. Rather, we will restrict our discussion in this chapter to some of the approaches used and some of the problems encountered by human-factors psychologists who work with man-machine systems. Since our society is so machine oriented, improving the man-machine relationship is an important activity of many psychologists.

MAN-MACHINE SYSTEMS

Man-machine systems can be defined several ways. For our purposes, a man-machine system consists of several components, both human and machine, that are designed to work together to achieve a specified goal. These systems can vary from extremely elaborate arrangements of men and machines to very simple systems. The requirements imposed on the human in a man-machine system will vary considerably, but typically they can be listed under the general headings of sensing functions, data-processing functions, and controlling functions. A simplified schematic representation of a man-machine system is shown in Figure 7-1. Note in this figure that there is an input and an output to the system. Man's sensing function (input) is involved when he reads the various displays, the data-processing function is involved when he utilizes the information he has received from the displays, and the controlling function (output) is involved when, based on the data-processing step, the operator manipulates some controls of the machine.

Man's role in man-machine systems, then, is typically that of a data transmission and processing link inserted between the displays and controls of the machine. In this capacity, the human operator receives information from the displays in the form of signals, interprets such information, and transforms it into appropriate responses directed at the controls of the machine.

114

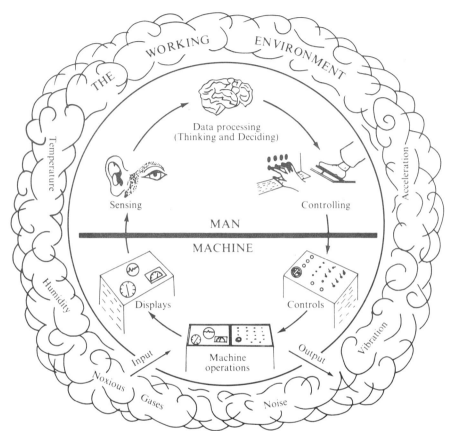

FIGURE 7-1. Simplified schematic representation of a man-machine system. (From A. Chapanis, *Man-Machine Engineering.* Copyright 1965 by Wadsworth Publishing Company, Inc. Reprinted by permission of the publisher, Brooks/Cole Publishing Company, Monterey, Calif.)

Much of the human-factors research in man-machine systems has been aimed at the modification of displays and controls to better suit the operator.

Considerable research has been conducted in an effort to more fully understand man's capabilities and limitations as a data-processing link in man-machine systems. Although the human operator performs a great variety of tasks in these systems, two types of tasks—*vigilance* and *tracking*—have been emphasized as subjects for research because of their importance in many different kinds of systems.

Vigilance Tasks

In most systems, the human operator must monitor various displays (dials, lights, meters, and so on) in order to be informed about system malfunctions, or he may have to be alert for the occurrence of some type of critical signal, such as the appearance of a signal on a radar scope. The ability of the operator to perform these monitoring, or vigilance, tasks has been investigated under a variety of different experimental conditions in an effort to determine what variables affect performance and how performance can be improved.

In some studies, a phenomenon known as *vigilance decrement* has been found. Thus if a given number of signals are presented to a subject over a lengthy period of time, the subject tends to miss increasingly more signals as the test session progresses. Research has shown that a number of variables contribute to the decrement. For example, the number of signals missed is related to the intensity of the signals, the duration of the signals, and the frequency of the signals. Similarly, personality variables and other characteristics of the observer have been found to be related to vigilance performance. Research has also shown that vigilance performance can be maintained at a high level by adding secondary tasks (which tend to keep the observer alert), by duplicating critical signals in other sensory modalities (presenting an auditory signal at the same time a visual signal is presented), by adding rest pauses, and by giving the observer stimulants (such as amphetamine).

An analysis of the vigilance task reveals that several important human functions are required if the task is to be performed effectively. These functions, which are also important in many other types of situations in which human operators perform, include (1) *detecting* the information signal, (2) *identifying* the signal, (3) *interpreting* the signal's meaning, (4) making a *decision* about which responses are appropriate, and (5) emitting the appropriate *response*. These functions of the human operator—detection, identification, interpretation, decision making, and response—have all been studied by psychologists in both basic and applied research; the human-factors engineer needs all such information available on the human operator for his work with man-machine systems.

Tracking Tasks

The type of signal that the operator monitors may be discrete (occurring only occasionally) or it may be constantly varying. With a discrete signal, the operator may make a discrete response, such as pushing a brake pedal at the onset of a red traffic light. With a continually varying signal, however, the operator's response may also have to be continuous. For example, as you drive a car, the roadway can be considered a constantly varying input signal and the manipulation of the steering wheel can be thought of as a constantly varying response, or output. *Tracking behavior* involves matching the operator outputs (steering) with the operator inputs (what the driver sees).

Because tracking is required in one form or another in so many different types of man-machine systems, it has been subjected to a considerable amount of study. Specific types of equipment have been developed to study tracking behavior, and there is a great deal of research literature dealing with it. However, regardless of the complexity of the equipment used, most tracking tasks fall into one of two classes—pursuit or compensatory.

In *pursuit tracking*, the operator has control of some sort of moving element that he attempts to keep on a moving target of some type. For example, if you were to attempt to keep a spotlight (controlled element) on a running person (target), you would be engaging in a form of pursuit tracking. Obviously, the pursuit-tracking tasks involved in most man-machine systems are somewhat more complex than this. However, the important characteristic of this type of tracking is that both the controlled element and the target move.

In the second major class of tracking, called *compensatory tracking*, there is only one moving element. It is controlled by the operator in such a way that it is held stationary over the fixed target from which it tends to move away if not controlled. Thus with some types of weapons systems, the operator sees two "blips" on a radar screen. One blip (the target) remains stationary in the center of the screen while the second blip (representing a missile that the operator can manipulate) is held on the target by means of some controls. If the operator does not "track" properly, the blips will begin to separate on the screen as the missile gets "off target." By adjusting various controls the operator again brings the two blips together, and the missile is back on target.

Measures of tracking performance have been dependent variables in a wide range of studies. Some researchers have been concerned with the effects of variables such as alcohol, drugs, fatigue, age, sex, and noise on tracking performance; others have been interested in manipulating "task" variables, such as target speed and the way the controlled element is guided. A considerable amount is now known about the human operator's ability to perform tracking tasks under a variety of conditions.

Obviously, in most man-machine systems the operator will be required to do many other things besides monitor and track. We have emphasized these two particular tasks because they are involved in many common man-machine systems.

Man-Machine Allocation

In assisting with the design of a man-machine system, the human-factors engineer may be asked for advice on which functions of the system should be assigned to the human operator and which to machine components. Basically, the question that must be answered in deciding on allocation of functions between man and machine is which one can best perform the function. Human-factors engineers have spent considerable time comparing the relative abilities of men and machines for various tasks, and numerous lists have been developed summarizing such comparisons. This type of list (see Table 7-1) is interesting to read, but there is some question about its usefulness. For example, a list of machine limitations may be out of date before it is even published. In utilizing a list of this sort for designing systems, the design engineers must keep several other things in mind. Comparisons of man and machine capabilities may reveal that machines are highly accurate and efficient in tasks such as arithmetic computation. However, when a machine fails as the result of overload or some other complication, it is likely to break down completely or make errors of a dramatic nature. Man, on the other hand, is characterized

TABLE 7-1. **Man versus machines. (From N. W. Heimstra and V. S. Ellingstad,** *Human Behavior: A Systems Approach.* **Copyright 1972 by Wadsworth Publishing Company, Inc. Reprinted by permission of the publisher, Brooks/Cole Publishing Company, Monterey, Calif.)**

Man is more capable	Machines are more capable
In situations requiring improvision or adaptation.	In the storage and retrieval of coded information.
At tasks involving unusual or unexpected events.	In the processing of large amounts of information in a short period of time.
At tasks involving the detection of targets in high noise backgrounds.	Of reliable performance of highly repetitive tasks.
In performing tasks involving inductive reasoning.	By being relatively insensitive to extraneous factors.
In the usage of entirely new solutions or those developed in related situations.	In the sensing of stimuli that are outside man's normal sensitivity range (sounds above 20,000 cps).
In the usage of uncoded information.	In the maintenance of a performance level over a long period of time.
In the perception of complex stimuli in highly varied situations.	In the exertion of great force in a precise and consistent manner.
In the use of subjective judgment based on previous experience.	In performing tasks involving deductive reasoning-recognition or categorization tasks involving previously experienced stimuli.
At anticipating stimulus input.	By being able to simultaneously handle numerous inputs.

by *graceful degradation*—that is, under conditions of adversity his output will more closely resemble the desired output. It must also be kept in mind that man is more flexible and can reach the same goal by a variety of different methods. Similarly, man's experience provides him with characteristics that cannot easily be compared with those of machines.

There are other factors involved in deciding which functions of a system should be allotted to man and which to the machine. Cost, for example, may be a factor, as well as maintenance considerations and social implications. This latter factor has become more and more important with the advent of automation because many functions that were previously performed by man are now performed by machines.

THE DESIGN OF DISPLAYS IN MAN-MACHINE SYSTEMS

As indicated previously, much of the effort of human-factors engineers has been involved with the design of displays and controls in man-machine systems. There is a sound reason for this interest. Man acts as a link or interface between the displays and the controls in a typical man-machine system. Before emitting a response directed at the controls, the man must first *detect* the information signal, *identify* it, *interpret* its meaning, and *decide* what the appropriate response should be. The type of display that is used to present such information to the operator may greatly facilitate these particular functions or may reduce the speed and precision with which these functions can be performed.

To determine typical errors made in the use of displays, Fitts (1951) conducted a survey of pilot errors that were made in responding to various displays. The greatest number of errors in this survey involved the interpretation of display signals. The most frequent error was misinterpreting instruments whose indicators made multi-revolutions. The next most common error was misinterpreting the direction of indicator movements. The third most frequent error was failing to respond to warning lights or sounds due to inadequate detection characteristics of the displays. Finally, the fourth most common error was misinterpreting as a result of poor legibility of numbers and letters.

Some Types of Displays

The human operator processes many kinds of information that he can receive *directly* from the environment by means of his sensory and perceptual processes, but there are other kinds of information that he cannot sense directly.

119

In these instances, *displays* are needed. A display presents information *indirectly* in either a reproduced or symbolic form. For example, the gas gauge, oil-pressure indicator, and speedometer are examples of displays. You cannot directly sense the oil pressure, you need a display to give you this information indirectly.

There are different ways of classifying displays, but most can be categorized as either *dynamic* or *static*. As their names suggest, dynamic displays such as the speedometer and the gas gauge will change through time, whereas other types of displays (such as signs, charts, and graphs) remain fixed over time. The kind of information that displays are used to present can also be called *quantitative* (involving actual numerical values), *qualitative* (such as hot, cold, warm), or *dichotomous* (which indicates "on" or "off," "yes" or "no," and so forth). Some examples of quantitative displays are shown in Figure 7-2.

We typically think of displays as presenting information by means of the visual channel, but this is not always the case. Some displays that are effective involve other sensory modalities—for example, auditory or cutaneous displays. Generally, *auditory* displays serve warning functions in systems. For instance, a loud buzzer may be used to alert the operator of a malfunction. Typically, auditory displays of one sort or another are appropriate when the visual sense is already overloaded, when critical or infrequent signals must be presented, or when the operator must move around a great deal.

Information can also be transmitted to the human by means of stimulation of the skin. Displays of this type are called *cutaneous* or *tactual* displays. Possibly the best-known type of cutaneous display is Braille, used by blind persons. Braille is also an example of a *static* tactual display. On the other hand, *dynamic* tactual displays make use of changes in vibration or electric shock in order to transmit information.

Research using electrocutaneous displays to present information in tracking tasks has been conducted by Hofmann and Heimstra (1972), Nichols (1970), and Schori (1970a). In these studies, error information concerning tracking performance was presented either by a visual, auditory, or electrocutaneous mode. The results of these investigations show that for certain types of tracking tasks, electrocutaneous displays can be used as effectively as visual or auditory displays for presenting error information to the operator. In some cases, it is even more effective. Similarly, in a study comparing auditory, visual, and electrocutaneous displays in a vigilance task, the electrocutaneous display was found to be quite effective (Damkot, 1969).

Increasing the Effectiveness of Displays

In designing displays, the human-factors engineer must keep in mind the human functions of detection, identification, interpretation, and decision

120

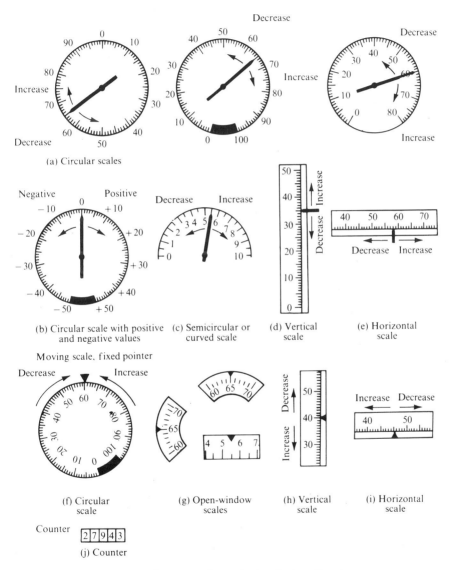

Fixed scale, moving pointer

(a) Circular scales

(b) Circular scale with positive and negative values

(c) Semicircular or curved scale

(d) Vertical scale

(e) Horizontal scale

Moving scale, fixed pointer

(f) Circular scale

(g) Open-window scales

(h) Vertical scale

(i) Horizontal scale

Counter

(j) Counter

FIGURE 7-2. Examples of various types of quantitative displays. Certain features of these displays are discussed in the text. (From *Human Factors Engineering* by E. J. McCormick. Copyright 1957, 1964, 1970 by McGraw-Hill, Inc. Used with permission of McGraw-Hill Book Company.)

making. The *detection* function is primarily dependent on the principle of display visibility; display visibility, in turn, is affected by such variables as the relationship between the size of the displayed information and the viewing distance, the brightness of the displayed information, the ambient illumination involved, the color of the display, and the manner in which the display contrasts with its surroundings. A considerable amount of research has been conducted dealing with detection of displays, so the design engineer has available a number of handbooks, which give various specifications required for displays under many different kinds of conditions.

The process of *identification* is largely dependent on the ability of the operator to discriminate characteristics of the displayed information. Primarily, this involves the properties of *legibility* and *readability* with number and letter displays. Again, the engineer has available data that have been obtained through research concerning such factors as stroke width of the number or letter, form of the characters, background, size, spacing, and so forth. By following the available guidelines, the engineer can greatly enhance the identification function.

Interpretation of the information displayed is influenced by the manner in which it is presented. One of the most important factors in presenting displayed information is that *stereotypes* should be adhered to whenever possible. Stereotypes are commonly accepted meanings given to directions of movement, figure-ground relationships, color, and so forth. For example, in most displays, movement to the right, up, or clockwise is usually interpreted as an *increase* in whatever the display represents. In contrast, a movement to the left, down, or counterclockwise usually represents a *decrease*. When indicator movement is in the opposite direction (for instance, movement to the left indicating an increase), interpretation is much more difficult and error may result. Similarly, a red light used to indicate safe operation would present a problem since the stereotype of red is danger.

These factors are taken into account in the design of a particular display. However, in developing displays for man-machine systems, there is much more involved. For instance, the amount and the nature of the information presented by the displays of a system will also contribute to the *decision-making* function. When too much information is displayed, the operator's decision-making function may be affected in that he is "overloaded" by all the information that he is bombarded with. Thus one of the first principles of display design for systems is to eliminate all unnecessary displays or unnecessary information presented by displays. Another design principle is to present information in the simplest and most usable form. This facilitates interpretation and, indirectly, the decision-making process. Therefore, it is easier to interpret a qualitative or dichotomous display (such as an oil-pressure warning light) in most cases than a quantitative display (an oil-pressure gauge).

There are, of course, many other considerations involved in the design of display layouts for complex systems. For example, the requirements imposed on an operator monitoring only one or two displays may be quite different from those imposed when a large number of displays must be monitored. In some cases, the displays are rescaled in such a fashion that when all measures are within prescribed limits, the indicators on all displays point in the same direction; therefore, an indicator reflects a malfunction when it points to "12 o'clock." On which of the two display panels shown in Figure 7-3 would the malfunction be most readily detected by the operator?

A great deal more can be said about display design, but we can summarize the more common considerations involved. These include:

(1) Eliminating all unnecessary displays.
(2) Selecting appropriate sensory channels.
(3) Substituting qualitative and dichotomous displays for quantitative displays whenever possible.
(4) Making displays as legible and readable as possible with regard to such variables as figure size, spacing, and type, as well as illumination, contrast, and color.
(5) Preserving stereotype relations, such as direction of movement and color.
(6) Being consistent.

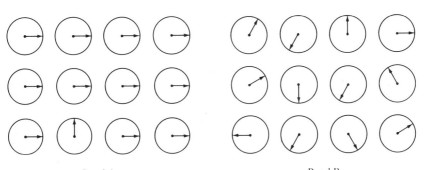

Panel A   Panel B

FIGURE 7-3. On some display panels, when there are a number of displays to be monitored, the task of the operator is made easier by having the indicators on all displays point in the same direction when everything is functioning properly. If the "12 o'clock" position represents a malfunction, on which of the panels shown would the display indicating a malfunction be most readily detected?

DESIGN OF CONTROLS IN
MAN-MACHINE SYSTEMS

There are, of course, many different kinds of controls that can be found in various types of systems. These may include push buttons, toggle switches, knobs, cranks, foot pedals, levers, steering wheels, keyboards, and so forth. Basically, however, controls are mechanisms by which the operator transmits "information" to the system. Displays, on the other hand, transmit information from the system to the operator. Proper design of controls is another important area in which human-factors psychologists are often involved. Even if the display design is excellent in a man-machine system, poor control design will introduce errors that may cause serious consequences.

In a study dealing with the types of errors that pilots make when using their controls, Fitts and Jones (1961) found that the most frequent errors were those in which different controls were confused with one another. The second most common error was moving a given control in the wrong direction. Next was forgetting to use a particular control, then accidentally moving the wrong control, and finally, inability to reach a control because of the design of the cockpit.

Obviously, any of the errors above could have resulted in an accident. As a matter of fact, one study during World War II showed that there were over 400 accidents in a 22-month period because pilots confused landing-gear and flap controls.

Designing Effective Control Systems

Many of the problems associated with the design of effective control systems are similar to those encountered in the design of displays. One of the first considerations in control design, as in display design, is the *principle of parsimony*, which is the elimination of all unnecessary controls. Related to this process is the *integration* of controls so those formerly requiring two hands for their operation (such as certain types of handwheels) are replaced with controls that require only one hand (levers or joy sticks). In the design of controls for a system, the human-factors engineer must be careful that he does not "overload" the operator's hands by designing too many hand-operated controls. Often some controls can be replaced with foot pedals. However, such changes must be made with system requirements in mind, such as the degree of accuracy and speed needed. There is a considerable body of research literature available concerning human performance with various types of hand- and foot-operated controls.

124

After relieving the hands of any overload, the designer attempts to replace controls requiring continuous operation or adjustment with those that require only positional or dichotomous movements. An example of a continuous control is the steering wheel of the car; the gearshift lever is a positional control; the ignition is an example of the dichotomous ("on-off") control. Obviously, continuous controls cannot always be replaced with other types, but, when possible, it is desirable from the operator's point of view.

After all unnecessary controls have been eliminated and manual and continuous controls have been minimized, the human-factors psychologist then takes a close look at ways in which the manipulation characteristics of the controls can be optimized. At this stage, proper *control coding* and *control arrangement* become important.

Control Coding. Being able to distinguish between controls is important, particularly when many controls must be manipulated, such as in an aircraft or in other types of complex man-machine systems. Controls are *coded* in various ways to make them more distinguishable.

The most common method of coding controls is simply to label them. However, in many systems this cannot be done because of the extra time required for reading the labels, extra space needed for the labels, dim illumination, and so forth. *Shape* and *texture* coding are two other techniques that are frequently used. Some examples of shape coding are shown in Figure 7-4. It is difficult for an operator to confuse controls like these, even if he cannot see them and must rely only on tactual information. Note that the shape suggests the purpose of the control. In texture coding, the surfaces of the controls or control knobs are varied to improve tactual discrimination. Thus certain control knobs may have a rough texture, others smooth, some "knobby," and so forth.

Control Arrangement

Controls can also be arranged in such a fashion that errors in their use are reduced. Probably the most important principles of location coding (arrangement of controls) are the *frequency-of-use* and the *sequence-of-use* principles. When the frequency-of-use principle is followed, the most frequently used controls are placed in preferred locations in relatively close proximity. Controls that are used less frequently may be placed farther away. In some systems, however, proper operation requires that certain controls are manipulated in a prescribed sequence. In this case, the sequence-of-use principle might be followed, and the controls would be arranged to correspond with the sequence

Design of Controls

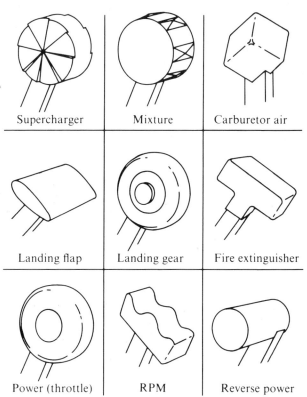

Supercharger	Mixture	Carburetor air
Landing flap	Landing gear	Fire extinguisher
Power (throttle)	RPM	Reverse power

FIGURE 7-4. Shape coding can improve visual and tactile identification of the controls. When possible, functional shapes are selected that suggest the purpose of the control. (From *Human Engineering Guide to Equipment Design* by C. T. Morgan, J. S. Cook, III, A. Chapanis, and M. W. Lund (Eds.). Copyright 1963 by the McGraw-Hill Book Company, Inc. Used with permission of the McGraw-Hill Book Company.)

in which they are to be used. Sometimes a *functional* arrangement is followed, in which controls with related functions are placed together. In other cases, arrangements according to *importance* will be followed, with the most important controls having the best locations.

There are a great many more factors that the engineering psychologist must consider when designing displays and controls for a particular system. It should be apparent from our brief discussion of displays and controls that in complex systems these cannot just be "tossed into the system." Instead, a good deal of thought must be given to the proper displays and controls to be used.

THE TOTAL JOB SITUATION

As pointed out previously, there is a great deal more involved in fitting the job to the man than just designing effective controls and displays. Human-factors engineers are also concerned with the design of the total job situation. Often, they must carefully analyze a system to ensure that the requirements imposed on the human operator correspond with his capabilities and limitations. They must be sure that the speed and accuracy requirements are within his limits and that he is not *overloaded*. On the other hand, they must also be concerned with *underload*, a situation in which the operator does not have enough to do. The human-factors engineers may also be concerned with eliminating environmental factors, such as noise, vibration, inadequate lighting, heat, and cold, that may have detrimental effects on the operator's performance.

Actually, when the total job situation is considered, it rapidly becomes a complex, many-faceted problem. It is one thing to improve the physical working conditions, achieve optimum man-machine compatibility, and, in general, achieve maximum comfort and safety for the human operator. It is another thing to attempt to consider all of the factors that may affect the human operator in a particular system. The big difficulties in fitting jobs to men are not all technological. Many of the problems require social considerations for their solution. For example, what do we do to system efficiency when we isolate employees who enjoy social contact, force employees into positions of competition when they would rather cooperate, and use men as replaceable links in a system when these men need a sense of dignity and individuality? Some of these types of problems will be discussed in the next chapter.

RESEARCH IN HUMAN-FACTORS ENGINEERING

On several occasions in the previous pages we have mentioned that the human-factors engineers have available to them handbooks and other types of literature concerning specifications for controls, displays, and work-environment conditions. Very often when design problems arise, the human-factors specialist will not have time to conduct his own investigation to determine which type of display or control would be most effective for the particular system involved. Rather, he must rely on the information he has available and make recommendations based on this information.

Most of the information that the human-factors engineer has available in his handbooks and other references is based on careful research. A number of psychologists working in university laboratories, applied-research institutes, industry laboratories, government laboratories, and many other settings are engaged in research that will be incorporated in these various handbooks and references and will be used by psychologists and engineers in the design of equipment. Frequently, however, the designers are confronted with problems in new systems for which no answers are to be found in the literature; then they conduct their own investigations. For example, a few years ago an engineer who was concerned with designing controls to be manipulated under weightless conditions would not have found much in his handbooks to help him.

Although the human-factors engineer will engage in a variety of different kinds of research projects in an effort to answer applied problems, most of these investigations will fall into one of three categories: the *laboratory* experiment, the *simulation* study, or the *field* study. You will recall that in the laboratory experiment, the variables are rigidly controlled by the experimenter, who carefully defines and measures his dependent variable, manipulates one or more independent variables, and attempts to control the nuisance variables. The field study is a researcher's attempt to study some aspect of behavior in the ongoing, real-world situation. If the research is properly conducted, the investigator will have more confidence in the applied value of his findings from field research than from most laboratory experiments. However, because of the fact that the investigator has less control over many variables in field studies, the results of this kind of investigation often are ambiguous at best. The simulation study is essentially a combination of the laboratory and field study, in that simulation attempts to duplicate a real-world environment on a small scale in a laboratory. The experimenter can exert considerable control over variables in a simulation study, but he still doesn't know how his results apply to the real world. Often all three approaches will be used by a human-factors engineer in his attempt to solve a particular problem.

In order to illustrate these approaches, let us consider a hypothetical problem. Suppose that a human-factors engineer has been asked to make recommendations about the most effective steering-gear ratios for a new automobile that is being designed. The steering-gear ratio will determine how much a steering wheel has to be turned in order to turn the vehicle a given amount. It is recognized that a higher gear ratio is desirable at high-speed driving in order to give precise control, whereas to provide easier low-speed maneuvering and minimize steering wheel turning, the ratio should be low. The human-factors psychologist must take these factors, along with many others, into consideration in his recommendation.

As a first step, the psychologist might set up a laboratory study to investigate the effects of various steering-gear ratios on performance in a tracking task of some type. He designs a piece of equipment in which, by means of a steering wheel with adjustable gear ratios, the operator attempts to keep a controlled element on a moving target whose speed can be adjusted. The independent variables that will be manipulated, then, are gear ratio and target speed. The dependent variable will be some measure of performance, such as the amount of time "off target" during a trial. The experimenter will assign subjects to various gear-ratio/target-speed conditions or, perhaps, will test the same subjects under all conditions with the sequence of conditions presented in a random fashion. After he has tested all the subjects as many times as he feels is necessary, he will analyze his data by statistical methods and determine whether differences in performance under the various conditions are significant.

This type of study will give the investigator some idea about the effectiveness of various steering-gear ratios. He may find, for example, that at certain ratios the subject simply cannot "track" at all, whereas at other ratios performance ranges from adequate to excellent. However, the researcher cannot state with any certainty which ratio would be the best in the real-world situation. He has, instead, a good idea about the range of ratios that might be acceptable.

Another approach that the investigator might then take is to select several of the steering-gear ratios and modify a driving simulator in such a fashion that subjects can be tested with the different ratios. As you will see in Part 3, there are a number of drawbacks (also advantages) to using simulators in research. One problem is measuring tracking behavior, and only a few simulators are designed so that this measure can be obtained. Assuming that he has such a simulator, the researcher can then determine the effects of the several steering-gear ratios on driver performance in the simulator. This study will give him a much better idea about what the most effective ratios are.

As a final field study, an actual automobile might be instrumented so that several gear ratios can be selected for use and various instruments installed to measure the driver's performance. Again, the problem of measurement is a serious one since tracking behavior is difficult to study in an actual car. There is a question about how meaningful, in terms of driver behavior, many measures that are typically obtained in instrumented vehicles actually are. However, at some point the investigations must come to a halt and the human-factors engineer must make a recommendation based on the data he has collected. Usually his recommendations are correct.

chapter
8

Man and the Organization

In the preceding chapters we have seen how psychologists working in various types of industrial and organization settings attempt to fit a man to a particular job by means of personnel selection and training procedures. We also noted that other psychologists are concerned with the machines and the work environment associated with the job and attempt to fit the job to the man. Both steps are important in enhancing the effectiveness of a particular system. However, before maximum system efficiency is achieved, there are a number of other aspects of man's role in an organization that must be understood and taken into account.

Psychologists in organizations are particularly interested in the factors that contribute to job motivation and job satisfaction. Psychologists are continually being asked why one worker, who has no more basic ability than another, is a much more effective and competent worker than the other. Why does one worker decide to loaf while another consistently works hard? Why are some workers satisfied with a particular job when others are not? What is it about certain jobs that makes nearly all workers dissatisfied? These and many similar questions are of interest to psychologists who are concerned with understanding the relationship of man to the organization.

Although some psychologists may view these questions as interesting from a theoretical point of view, others are seeking answers in order to help solve some very practical problems that confront organizations today. We hear a

Photo by Sam Sprague.

great deal about blue-collar workers' growing dissatisfaction with their production-line jobs. This dislike is being reflected in increased job turnover, absenteeism, shoddy workmanship, alcoholism, drug problems, and, in many instances, deliberate sabotage of the product. Job dissatisfaction is not restricted to the blue-collar worker; increasing numbers of white-collar workers are also unhappy with their jobs.

Organizations are aware that job dissatisfaction is a major problem and are instituting changes and procedures to reduce it. However, before this can be effectively accomplished, a great deal more must be known about the factors that are responsible for job satisfaction or dissatisfaction. Psychologists are attempting to determine what these factors are and how they can be modified to serve the needs of the individuals in organizations.

MAN'S NEEDS IN ORGANIZATIONS

Until relatively recently, it was thought that if you paid a worker enough and gave him some fringe benefits, he would be satisfied and motivated. However, it is now apparent that when an employee makes a decision to work effectively, it is a complex decision based on a great deal more than just the reward, or perhaps punishment, that is associated with a particular level of work performance.

Man, whether in his role as a worker or in the variety of other roles that he may fill, has certain *needs*. Super and Bohn (1970) define need as "a lack of something which, if it were present, would contribute to the well-being of the organism. It is a condition that is lacking, a force that organizes behavior, driving the individual to act (or not to act) in certain ways to change an unsatisfying condition" (p. 21). This concept of need has important implications in the study of why people behave differently in organizational settings.

Investigators interested in motivation have developed a number of classification schemes for listing and categorizing different kinds of needs. One categorization of needs has found particular favor with many psychologists in organizations. Maslow (1943) suggested that needs can be arranged in a hierarchical fashion; and when a need at a lower level of the hierarchy is satisfied, those at a higher level emerge and demand satisfaction. Maslow's "need hierarchy" places physiological needs, such as hunger and thirst, at the lowest, or basic, level. He then has safety needs, social needs, esteem needs, and self-realization needs, in that order, in his hierarchy.

How can needs of this kind affect the performance of an individual at his job? We cannot discuss the theorizing and research findings in this area to any great extent, but let us briefly consider how some of these needs relate to the organization.

Generally, a person's physiological and safety needs are met. The average worker makes enough money to adequately fulfill the basic physiological needs, such as food and drink for himself and his family. Similarly, the safety need is usually met in modern industry. Consequently, according to the need-hierarchy concept, the higher-level needs begin to emerge and assume importance.

The social needs, which are next in Maslow's hierarchy, are complex and can assume a number of different forms. However, social needs such as "togetherness' and "belonging" are becoming increasingly difficult to attain in our society, both in and out of the work situation. Studies have shown that much of the motivation of workers in industries can be attributed to this need, but that in many organizations it is a difficult need to satisfy.

Esteem needs, which are still higher in the hierarchy, are even more complex than social needs and may be more important. An individual in any job wants to feel that what he is doing is worthwhile and that he has achieved some status and prestige. Obviously, there are many production-line jobs, as well as others, in which these feelings of self-esteem would be difficult to develop. How much self-esteem is there associated with a job in which a worker does the same thing eight hours a day and a new worker, with a few hours of practice, can do the job equally well?

The self-realization need is the most difficult of all to fulfill. Essentially, it represents the need for an individual to employ his skills, or potential, to the fullest. A person who feels that he is putting forth to his full potential, according to the need-hierarchy concept, has achieved the highest level of motivation. Again, how much opportunity for self-realization is there on the typical production-line job?

Maslow's need-hierarchy concept is not popular with all organizational psychologists, but it has value in that it calls attention to the complicated nature of worker motivation. For example, few psychologists now believe that a high level of motivation can be achieved simply by manipulating monetary incentives. The old saying that "man does not live by bread alone" is particularly applicable to the problems of man's relationship to organizations.

MOTIVATION AND HUMAN PERFORMANCE

It is generally assumed that all behavior is motivated; because the concept of motivation is so important in psychology, there has been a great deal of research in this area. A number of books and countless articles in scientific journals have been published dealing with this topic. One might assume, then, that a psychologist who was interested in worker motivation in an organization would be able to find out all that he needed to know by spending some time poring over the available literature. This is far from the case. Relatively little of the research deals with human behavior, and much of what does has little implication for workers. There has been some research, however, dealing with motivational variables and human performance that, although not always dealing directly with work situations, does have implications for workers.

Performance Goals

In recent years, psychologists have begun to study the effects of *conscious goals* and *purposes* on task performance. Just what determines an individual's goals in relation to a particular task involves a complex interaction of variables, including characteristics of the task, instructions and feedback about performance, personality, level of arousal, and previous experience. These as well as other factors contribute to how a person "sets" his goal. One approach to the study of factors involved in the process of goal setting is based on the concept of *level of aspiration*.

Basically, level of aspiration is the standard by which an individual tends to judge his own performance at a task or job. Based on his past experience with the task, a person tends to aspire to a particular level of performance. Generally, if you ask a person what level he hopes to achieve on the task, he will cite a level somewhat higher than he usually achieves—that is, the level of aspiration is slightly higher than the person's typical performance. Thus a golfer who usually shoots 15 over par will probably aspire not to a par game, but to perhaps five above par. His degree of satisfaction with his game then is dependent on how close the score he achieves is to the score he aspires to make.

Recently, several studies were conducted that attempted to establish more clearly the relationship between the conscious goals, or level of aspiration, of individuals in regard to a particular task and their performance on the task. Studies reported by Locke (1968) and Locke and Bryan (1967, 1969) indicate that goals can both energize and direct behavior on a task. It has been shown that hard goals often produce a higher level of performance than easy goals and that specific hard goals produce a higher level of output from an individual than do goals of the "do your best" type. In general, it can be concluded that performance goals are related to, and can account for, the level of performance on a number of different types of tasks.

It may be difficult for the industrial psychologist to apply findings such as these directly to the worker in an organizational setting. What is required

134

is a better understanding of how to *manipulate* goals to achieve the maximum performance from an individual. Locke (1968) points out that goals can be manipulated in several ways, such as instructions, setting time limits on tasks, and other incentives. He goes on to say:

> In most real life work situations a combination of all of these incentives are employed. A worker is hired and instructed on what to do and how fast to do it; he is given or gets knowledge of performance either from others or from the task itself; he may compete with others for promotion; he is paid for working, he is evaluated by his supervisor, and sometimes he participates in decision making. All of these factors can be considered ways of (1) getting the subject to set or accept work goals, and (2) retaining his commitment to them and insuring persistence over time [p. 185].

One way of viewing the relationship of goal setting and performance is encompassed in the *concept of par* or *tolerance*, which has been proposed by Helson (1964). Basically, this concept suggests that a person consistently sets his level of aspiration *below* what he is actually capable of achieving on a particular task. There is evidence from several studies that a person's performance rarely reaches the potential level of which he is capable. One of the tasks of the psychologist in an organization is to attempt to determine what variables will bring the achieved level of performance closer to the potential level.

A question of interest concerning the concept of level of aspiration has to do with how a person may react if he consistently fails to reach his goals. Suppose that the goals a person sets for himself in an organization are too high for him to achieve. It may be that repeated failure to achieve goals will result in a reduced level of aspiration. Personality theorists have suggested that personal frustration (with resulting behavioral manifestations) may arise because of a discrepancy between the level of aspiration and the level of performance.

Group Influences on Performance

It is apparent that people frequently are influenced by others in terms of the level of aspiration they establish and the conscious goals they set for themselves. There has been a considerable amount of laboratory research dealing with an individual's performance under social conditions, but not much is known about group influences in a real-world work situation.

Research has shown that individual performance is affected by the presence of other persons—that is, an audience. In some studies the presence of an audience facilitated performance on certain types of tasks; in other studies subjects did worse when an audience was present. Careful analysis of the type of tasks involved showed that if a task is well-learned and the subject is proficient at the task, then an audience will probably improve the performance. However, if the task is not well-learned, then an audience will probably have an adverse effect. When the task requires complex intellectual functions, the presence of others seems to have a disruptive effect.

In some studies other individuals perform the same task that is undertaken by the subject who is being studied. Even though these "coactors" do not interact directly with the subject, they may have a marked effect on his performance at a task. Again, however, the situation is complex: some studies show that the presence of coactors leads to better performance, but other studies find poorer performance results.

Although studies demonstrating the influence of social factors on task performance in a psychology laboratory are numerous, just how this influence exerts itself is not completely understood. It is even less understood in the case of a worker on the job. That group influences are important, however, was shown many years ago in the now classic Hawthorne studies (1939).

In the late 1920s and early 1930s, a series of investigations was conducted at the Hawthorne Works of the Western Electric Company. These studies initially were designed to determine the effects of illumination and other physical factors on the productivity of workers. Before long, however, the researchers began to discover some things that were quite different from what they had expected. Consequently, their research took new directions. They found that physical factors did not have much effect on production. However, they also found that social influences such as group approval, democratic as opposed to authoritarian-type leadership, and the expectancies of other workers concerning performance did have a marked effect on production. Although the methodological procedures may have left something to be desired, the Hawthorne studies must be considered some of the most significant investigations conducted in the field of industrial psychology. They opened up a host of problems, generated theories and controversies, and established for the first time the importance of factors such as leadership style, group standards, and other social influences on worker performance.

Incentives and Worker Motivation

It should be clear by this point that incentives are not the only factors that contribute to worker motivation, although they are important. The concept of incentives forms the basis for most of the practices that are found in traditional organizations. Korman (1971) points out, "In its simplest framework, 'incentive' theory states that if (1) a man thinks that some kind of outcome is desirable, and (2) he can get the outcome by performing at a given level, then (3) he will be motivated to perform at that given level" (p. 49).

An incentive, then, is something that is introduced to motivate a person to achieve some goal. There are a variety of incentives, both financial and nonfinancial, that will tend to bolster an individual's activities in the direction of some goal. Incentives can be rewards such as pay, promotion, security, good working conditions, fringe benefits, and so forth. However, both competition and cooperation can also be thought of as incentives. Competition requires a person to strive to do better than another, and cooperation requires that several individuals contribute to a common goal. Competition is more common as an incentive, but cooperation incentives may turn out to be more useful.

There have been a number of studies concerned with incentives. Many of these studies have found that salary is not as important an incentive as factors such as security and opportunity for advancement. However, the rank assigned to a particular incentive depends on characteristics of the individuals doing the ranking. Age, sex, marital status, and education have been found to have an effect on rankings. For example, most research indicates that salary is not the most important incentive; however, in a study of college students by Dudycha and Naylor (1966), salary was given the highest value.

Although it may seem strange that salary is not rated highest in most studies, there are several possible explanations. It has been suggested that the reason pay, as an incentive, is not rated very high is that it is not actually related to merit in many work situations. This raises a question, of course, about whether pay can be used as an incentive for better job performance if the organization does not use job performance as a basis for determining pay. In other words, if one does not feel that his job performance will affect his pay, then pay cannot serve as a very effective incentive.

Some investigations have shown that incentives are important as motivational factors in work situations. However, it should be kept in mind that worker motivation is a complex subject about which we still have a great deal to learn. It should be apparent from our brief discussion that there are many factors that contribute to motivation. Eventually, research will tell us how to *integrate* these various factors to insure that at least the majority of workers are motivated to perform at a high level on their jobs.

JOB SATISFACTION

Closely related to the problems of worker motivation are those associated with *job satisfaction*. A simple straightforward definition of job satisfaction states that "job satisfaction is a favorable feeling of a person toward his job situation."

The primary questions of interest to psychologists have to do with what factors contribute to this "favorable feeling," how we can measure job satisfaction, and how job satisfaction relates to performance on the job.

Measuring Job Satisfaction

Over the years, a variety of techniques have been developed to measure job satisfaction. Just how effectively they perform this function, however, is uncertain. All too often it has been found that data obtained with one method correlated only slightly with data gathered by a different method. Data-collection techniques employed in job-satisfaction studies have included interviews, questionnaires, rank-order techniques, sentence-completion techniques, and critical-incident approaches.

Structured *interviews* are sometimes used to obtain information about job satisfaction from workers. Generally, however, the interview is not used as the only technique in a study but is combined with others. Sometimes it is used as a method for gathering information that can be used for the development of other techniques. The problems associated with interviews (specifically, reliability and validity) have already been discussed in Chapter 6. The same problems are encountered with interviews in job-satisfaction studies.

Questionnaires are probably the most common technique employed. There are a variety of types used, depending on the occupations involved and the kind of information the researcher is seeking. With *rank-order* techniques, the employee ranks a number of characteristics of a particular job in terms of their importance (to him) to job satisfaction. Sometimes the worker is presented with a list of characteristics and ranks these; in other studies he is asked to make up and rank his own list of characteristics. With *sentence-completion* techniques, the employee is presented with a series of incomplete sentences that, when completed, will describe his attitude toward a job characteristic. Thus he might be presented with an incomplete sentence such as "The supervisor on my job is . . . " and be asked to complete the sentence. This approach is relatively new in the study of job satisfaction.

The *critical-incidents* approach to assessing job satisfaction is also relatively new. With this technique, a worker is interviewed and asked to describe, in great detail, times when he felt exceptionally good about his job and times when he felt exceptionally bad about his job. From these data, the researchers can determine the factors that seem to be important to a worker's job satisfaction and dissatisfaction.

Herzberg and co-workers (1959), who developed the critical-incident technique, investigated the aspects of job environments that were satisfying or dissatisfying to accountants and engineers with this technique. Their study has led to a theory of job satisfaction that has received a great deal of attention. Herzberg found that "satisfying" jobs are characterized by opportunities to experience achievement and recognition, to advance in jobs that are of interest, and to have a sense of responsibility. Salary as a motivating factor was rated below these. Feelings of dissatisfaction were attributed to different aspects of the job, such as incompetent supervisors, poor company policy, and so forth.

Regarding the general area of measurement of job satisfaction, Blum and Naylor (1968) make an important point. They suggest that " . . . job satisfaction can be measured in one of two ways. One method is to investigate the specific factors on the job and the resulting attitudes. The other, which is much more comprehensive, includes the overall factors that contribute to satisfaction in life. Neither method is necessarily right or wrong. However, progress can be made in this important field only after there is an understanding of the many factors which are involved . . . " (pp. 384–385).

Factors Influencing Job Satisfaction

A wide variety of factors have been shown to be associated with job satisfaction. These can be divided into two broad types: characteristics of the individual that have an effect on job satisfaction and characteristics of the job itself. Sometimes these are referred to as *intrinsic* and *extrinsic* variables.

Characteristics of the individual. In a review of the literature on job satisfaction, Fournet, Distefano, and Pryer (1966) discuss a number of the more frequently studied individual characteristics that are associated with job satisfaction. These include *individual differences, age, education, intelligence, sex,* and *occupational level.*

Individual differences. If people did not differ, then once the factors influencing the satisfaction with a particular job were understood, everyone working at that job would react the same and be satisfied. However, because of the existence of individual differences, the study of job satisfaction becomes much more complicated. Studies have shown that, because of differences in attitude, expectations about a job, reactions to authority, and so on, the same job may be extremely satisfying to one person and equally dissatisfying to another.

Age. It has been suggested that there is a relationship between age and job satisfaction. Initially, the young employee tends to be satisfied with his job, perhaps because of the newness. After the first few years, satisfaction decreases and then begins to increase again as workers continue with their jobs.

139

However, any relationship between age and job satisfaction is far from established.

Education and intelligence. Some studies have found relationships between education and intelligence and job satisfaction; other investigations have not. The effect of these variables on satisfaction is unclear. It would seem, however, that if the extremes were considered, some relationships might be established. For example, a worker with a high IQ would probably not be satisfied with a routine, nonchallenging job, and a low-IQ individual might not be satisfied on a job that required a great deal of intellectual endeavor.

Sex. It is likely that for women, job satisfaction depends on variables that are somewhat different than those for men. Currently, of course, there is a great deal of dissatisfaction being expressed by women in virtually all types of jobs, but it is probable that it is not sex per se that is responsible. Rather, it is the fact that because a worker happens to be a woman, she may often be discriminated against in terms of pay, job level, and promotional opportunities. In the little research that has been conducted, women receiving the same pay as men and having the same social position in a job situation were as satisfied as or more satisfied than the men.

Occupational level. It appears that job satisfaction increases as the level of the job progresses. These seem to be the most consistent findings in all of the research on job satisfaction. In most cases, a person who holds a high-level job is more satisfied with the job than a person who holds a lower-level position.

Characteristics of the Job. Fournet and associates (1966) list a number of job characteristics that have been related to job satisfaction. The *organization* and *management* of the company to which the worker belongs can be an important variable, and administrative practices can be directly related to job satisfaction. Satisfaction may also be associated with the *immediate supervisor's* personal interest and support for the worker. *Social factors,* such as whether or not the worker is a member of a group, are important, with group members tending to be more satisfied than those who are not regular members. *Job security* has been found in some job-satisfaction studies to be a very important variable, although it seems to be more important in causing job dissatisfaction when it is absent than in causing satisfaction when it is present. A job that is *monotonous* may be less satisfying than an interesting and varied job. *Pay,* as we have seen, is an important variable but not as important as it was once thought to be.

One job characteristic that has received relatively little attention and that may be vital in the whole job-satisfaction process is *communication.* Although a considerable amount of research has been conducted in organizations dealing with enhancing the effectiveness of communication networks, both horizontal and vertical, these studies were generally aimed at increasing the efficiency of the organization. If the effects of new communication procedures were found to increase or decrease job satisfaction, these findings were typically secondary. There are findings from laboratory studies, however, that suggest the role of communication may be an important one. Studies have been conducted in which subjects are placed in different kinds of groups and allowed to communicate only in a specified manner—that is, to all other members of the group, to only certain members, to only a "key" member, and so on. The groups are typically assigned certain problems to solve or tasks to accomplish and the effect of the particular communication network on performance is evaluated. An interesting finding of these studies is that certain types of communication networks are much more satisfying than other types. Satisfaction is particularly high for the member of the group who is in the "key" position. Another interesting finding, however, is that satisfaction is not necessarily related to performance on the task. Subjects in the network in which satisfaction is the highest may do the poorest on the problem or task. The relationship between communication and job satisfaction is an area in which a great deal of research remains to be done.

Personal Versus Job Characteristics in Job Satisfaction

We have seen that a variety of personal and job characteristics may be important determinants of job satisfaction. According to Herzberg and co-workers (1959), whose study using the critical-incident technique has already been mentioned, job satisfaction and job dissatisfaction are caused by qualitatively different job factors. Workers attribute their satisfaction to certain aspects of the job, and they attribute their dissatisfied feelings to aspects that are usually different from those associated with job satisfaction. Herzberg found that when the workers interviewed were describing times when they felt exceptionally good about their jobs, these descriptions included such things as recognition, achievement, advancement, and responsibility. On the other hand, when exceptionally bad work periods were described, things dealing with company policy, supervision, working conditions, salary, and so forth, were typically included.

In a later study (Wernimont, 1966), *intrinsic* factors (recognition, achievement, responsibility, and so on) were compared with *extrinsic* factors (salary, company policy, working conditions, and so forth) in relation to the role they played in job satisfaction or dissatisfaction. Nearly twice as many extrinsic factors were reported for dissatisfying situations as for the satisfying situations. The findings of this study correspond closely with those of the Herzberg study in terms of the factors important in satisfying situations, but the job factors contributing to dissatisfaction were somewhat different.

In both the Herzberg and Wernimont studies, engineers and accountants were used as subjects. One might expect that extrinsic factors would be more important in providing satisfaction for blue-collar workers since they typically have less opportunity for the intrinsic motivators. However, in a study dealing with this kind of worker, it was found that intrinsic factors as well as extrinsic factors were important in job satisfaction (Malinovsky & Barry, 1965).

Obviously, the whole question of job satisfaction is highly complex, with satisfaction dependent on a host of both intrinsic and extrinsic factors. We are just beginning to achieve a basic understanding of the many factors involved in this complex process. Regardless of the factors contributing to job satisfaction, there is another key question that must be considered. What effect does job satisfaction, or dissatisfaction, have on a person's performance on the job?

Job Satisfaction and Work Performance

The problems we have discussed concerning job satisfaction may be of interest from a purely theoretical point of view to some researchers, but most investigators are concerned with the relationship between job satisfaction and job performance. The assumption underlying efforts to improve job satisfaction is that the satisfied worker is going to perform better on the job than the dissatisfied worker.

There are some serious problems in attempting to investigate the relationship between job satisfaction and job performance. You may recall from Chapter 6 when criterion problems were discussed that, in many situations, it is difficult to measure job performance adequately. The problem is complicated even further, of course, by the fact that it is difficult to measure job satisfaction. The available research suggests that there is very little relationship between job satisfaction and job performance. Performance, in this case, refers to how well the worker actually does his job or accomplishes his assigned task. On certain other types of measures, which are not directly related to job performance, there does seem to be a relationship. Thus there is some evidence that the higher a worker's satisfaction with his job, the less likely he is to resign. Similarly, there is also some indication that satisfied workers are absent from the job less often than dissatisfied workers. However, in general it must be concluded that the relationship between satisfaction and job performance is not clearly established.

142

part

3

MAN AND THE HIGHWAY
TRANSPORTATION
SYSTEM

In recent years, an increasing number of applied psychologists have become involved with various of the problems associated with the highway transportation system. This has been due in large part to the growing concern with the tremendous annual loss of lives, the economic impact of vehicular accidents, and the realization that the human operator is responsible for a large share of these accidents.

Psychologists are attacking these problems from a number of different directions. Many researchers are conducting investigations aimed at developing a better understanding of what happens when a person drives a car. Research approaches utilized by these investigators and some of their findings are discussed in Chapter 9.

Still other psychologists are concerned with the effectiveness of the current driver-training programs and are attempting to evaluate these programs. The problems encountered by investigators conducting these evaluative studies and the conclusions drawn from this research are considered in Chapter 10.

Some special problems associated with man's role in the highway transportation system are dealt with in Chapter 11. The effect of alcohol and other drugs on driving performance is discussed along with other variables that may lead to decreased efficiency in performing the driving task.

chapter 9

The Human Factor
in the Highway
Transportation System

For the last several years, over 50 thousand Americans have been killed annually in automobile accidents. In addition, several million are injured each year. It is estimated that the annual economic loss from highway crashes is over ten billion dollars. Obviously, because of the vast loss of life, the tremendous number of injuries, and the huge economic loss, motor vehicle accidents must be considered one of the most serious hazards confronting us today.

Because of the magnitude of this problem, substantial efforts have been made to reduce the number of accidents and to minimize the injury resulting when accidents do occur. Although a variety of countermeasures have been developed in the attempt to achieve these goals, most of the countermeasure approaches fall into two broad categories. One approach involves the modification of the vehicle and roadway so that accidents are less likely to occur and, if they do take place, injury is reduced or eliminated. These can be considered physical or environmental countermeasures. Seat belts, energy-absorbing steering columns, improved roads and operating environments, padded dashes, and inflatable air bags are a few examples of this type of countermeasure.

The other approach involves the modification of the behavior of the drivers so that they become more efficient and safer operators of motor vehicles. Driver-education programs, for example, can be considered a behavior-modification approach. Defensive-driving programs, which have become

Photo courtesy of Travel Division, South Dakota Dept. of Highways, Pierre, S. D.

popular in recent years, are also examples of this type of approach. Similarly, the rationale behind the traffic-court system is that, through legal sanctions, the behavior of certain kinds of drivers will be modified.

One problem that advocates of the behavior-modification programs encounter is that relatively little is known about the complex behavior required to operate a motor vehicle. Although the driving task may not seem particularly complex to you as a seasoned driver, you need only think back to your initial attempts at driving to realize that it is indeed a highly complicated task. An important role of the psychologists interested in traffic safety and injury control is to define more adequately the requirements of the driving task and to obtain information concerning the kinds of behavior that are involved in driving.

Many psychologists are actively engaged in research aimed at answering these and other questions related to driver behavior. In this chapter we will be concerned with the approaches these investigators utilize in attempting to answer these questions and some of the conclusions they have reached concerning this particular type of behavior.

THE MAN IN THE SYSTEM

The motor vehicle, the highway traffic environment within which the vehicle is driven, and the operator whose task it is to link or interface the vehicle with the environment can be thought of as subsystems that, in combination, make up the public transportation system. When all of these subsystems are functioning and interacting properly, the end result is the safe and efficient conveyance of persons and material from one physical location to another. When, for one reason or another, these subsystems fail to function properly, there is a reduction in efficiency at best and a fatal accident at worst.

Obviously, for the public transportation system to be safe and efficient, a great deal of attention must be paid to the design of the vehicles involved and the environment in which these vehicles are to be driven. Government agencies currently exist whose responsibilities include the establishment of standards and guidelines for the construction of safer vehicles and safer operating environments. Unfortunately, it is a more difficult task to attempt to establish standards and guidelines for the "construction" of safer drivers.

It is sometimes tempting to view the driver as a simple mechanical link between the highway and the vehicle, but this view is greatly oversimplified. There are a variety of factors that determine the effectiveness of the driver at any given time. It is these factors that have been of interest to psychologists concerned with the problems presented by the human subsystem in the public transportation system.

As a link, or interface, between the vehicle and the highway, the driver performs various operations that are basically the same as those performed in other man-machine systems. These can be categorized as input, central-processing, and output operations. The input operations involve the sensing of stimuli that impinge on the receptors of the body. "These stimuli constitute information which is operated upon or transformed by the human operator. The central processing operations consist of the identification and interpretation of the incoming information in order to determine what response, if any, is appropriate. The output operations are the motor responses produced by the driver" (Schori, 1970b, p. 155). The driving task is complex; it is the input, central-processing, and output operations performed by the driver.

Ellingstad (1970a, p. 177) points out that there are two broad classes of factors—pre-operational and operational—that may contribute to the way a driver behaves in a given situation. Every driver brings to the driving task certain physical and mental characteristics, which may influence his performance. These are *pre-operational* factors. The pre-operational status of the driver is determined by such things as his physical status (which includes his ability to sense and process information from both the vehicle and driving environment), attitudinal and motivational variables, and the level of driving skill that is brought into the driving task. These, in turn, help determine how he performs on the tasks that are actually involved in driving—that is, (1) the search-and-scan tasks, (2) the perceptual tasks, (3) the decision-making and cognitive-response tasks, and (4) the physical responses that are required for operating the vehicle.

In terms of operational factors, the first two tasks correspond to an information-input operation, the third task to the central-processing operation, and the last task to the output function. Both the pre-operational and operational factors involved in driver behavior have been and still are subjected to considerable research by psychologists in an effort to better understand the human requirements in the transportation system. Eventually, an understanding of these requirements will lead to the development of effective training programs for drivers as well as more efficiently designed vehicles and operating environments.

RESEARCH APPROACHES TO THE STUDY OF DRIVER BEHAVIOR

What methods and techniques does the psychologist employ in his efforts to understand driver behavior better? A variety of approaches is used. In some instances the researcher makes use of carefully controlled laboratory studies that are designed to answer a specific question about some aspect of driver behavior. In other situations he may attempt to study the behavior of a driver who is actually operating a vehicle on the highway. In other types of studies, driver behavior is investigated in elaborate driving simulators designed to realistically simulate many of the conditions encountered in actual "on-the-road" operation of a vehicle. In other kinds of investigations the psychologist may be interested in determining whether personality and attitudinal factors are important variables in driver performance, and he will measure these characteristics in an attempt to relate them to measures of driver behavior, like accident frequency or number of driving violations. Other approaches may also be used, depending on the question to be answered and the interests and training of the psychologist involved.

Although there are many specific techniques used by traffic-safety researchers, most methods can be classified as either *naturalistic* or *laboratory* methods (Warner, 1970). In the study of driver behavior, investigations conducted "on the road," with a driver operating a real vehicle, are considered "naturalistic." Actually, a naturalistic study would typically involve the presence of the researcher or some type of recording device in the car, so it would not be completely natural. Some investigations have involved taking motion pictures of drivers without their knowledge and then analyzing the behavior demonstrated in certain types of situations. This approach can also be considered a naturalistic technique.

The naturalistic method has some advantages in that behavior is studied in its natural habitat and the results may therefore be more generalizable; however, it also has disadvantages. For example, it is difficult to control or identify all of the numerous variables that may affect the driver's performance. A single variable cannot typically be isolated and observed so that its role in the functioning system may be assessed. As Warner (1970) points out, "This disadvantage of the naturalistic method becomes the foremost advantage of the laboratory investigations in traffic safety research. Laboratory research provides for controlled manipulation of a single variable or several preselected variables" (p. 213). In a laboratory study the investigator will typically select a limited number of variables and will carefully study their effect on some aspect of driver behavior. For example, the researcher might be interested in what variables are important in determining how fast a person can depress a brake pedal. This could be studied in the laboratory, and the effects of variables (such as age, sex, fatigue, alcohol, drugs, and so forth) on reaction time could be determined.

There are also disadvantages to the laboratory method. Warner (1970) suggests that the "most severe criticism of laboratory research is the 'sterility' or unnaturalness of laboratory methods. White laboratory jackets and standardized instructions reduce the reality of the situation" (p. 213). Another criticism of the laboratory method, at least in terms of driver-behavior research, is that various events that occur in the real driving situation are difficult to present in the laboratory. Thus it is difficult to simulate an "accident" in the laboratory setting. In addition, if an attempt were made, it would not have the same connotations for the person as a real accident would have.

There are other relative advantages and disadvantages to both methods, and one of the important decisions a researcher must make is which method is most appropriate for his purposes.

Some Research Tools in the Study of Driver Behavior

When studying driver behavior by either laboratory or naturalistic methods, the researcher has at his disposal a number of tools and techniques. In the laboratory, the psychologist may investigate the various human operations—input, central-processing, and output—in a variety of ways. These techniques have been used for many years by investigators who were not concerned with driver behavior, but rather with the study of basic human functions and processes. For example, in terms of input operations, most of the sensory input that the operator requires is visual. Thus all the techniques that have been developed for studying visual acuity, dark adaptation, night vision, color vision, glare, contrast, depth perception, and visual-channel capacity can be used to study these processes in terms of their importance in driver behavior. Similarly, techniques have been developed to study the central-processing operations of memory, pattern recognition, decision making and risk taking, and some of the findings are applicable to the driving situation. Psychologists interested in psychomotor performance have developed a number of procedures and techniques that have been useful in studying the output operations involved in the driving task.

Psychologists studying driver behavior have used many kinds of equipment originally designed for other types of research. For example, several sophisticated data-recording systems developed for use in laboratories have been installed in research vehicles and used in on-the-road studies to record a variety of different measures of driver performance. Similarly, physiological recording equipment designed to measure physiological responses to stress (the Galvanic Skin Response or GSR), heart rate, and other types of physiological responses have also been used in driver-behavior studies. A particularly useful piece of equipment that has been used in a number of studies is the *eye-movement camera,* which records on movie film the scene a person is viewing and the exact spot at which the person is looking. However, other kinds of equipment and apparatus have been designed specifically for use in driver-behavior studies. Examples of these kinds of equipment are *driving simulators* and *instrumented cars.*

Driving Simulators. As the name suggests, driving simulators are devices designed to simulate the driving task. These devices are often categorized as either *whole-task simulators* or *part-task simulators.* A whole-task simulator is designed to simulate the entire driving task, whereas the part-task simulators attempt only to simulate certain aspects or parts of the entire driving task. According to Schori (1970b):

The operator's task in a part task simulator is similar only in certain aspects to that of a real driving task. Such simulators are generally developed in order to investigate a specific problem or a specific class of problems. Thus, they can be made as simple or as complex as the problem necessitates. An investigator wishing to measure response time from the accelerator to the brake upon the occurrence of an emergency signal might construct a part task simulator which consists of nothing more than an accelerator pedal, a brake pedal, a mechanism to produce a visual warning signal, and a timer [p. 164].

The operator's task in a whole-task simulator is assumed to be similar to that involved in the operation of an actual vehicle. The operator "drives" as though he were actually in a vehicle on the road and is typically confronted with a changing visual scene. He responds to this scene by making the appropriate steering, accelerator, and brake adjustments. In some types of simulators the visual scene changes as the driver makes these adjustments. For instance, if the driver turns abruptly to the right, the visual scene reflects the turn and the driver is confronted with the same type of view he would have if he turned off the road in a real driving situation. Similarly, if he depresses the accelerator, the visual scene passes before him more rapidly. A simulator of this type, in which the visual scene reflects the control adjustments of the operator, is called a *closed-loop simulator.* In other types of simulators the visual scene is independent of the control adjustments of the operator; these are called *open-loop simulators.* Simulators that make use of motion-picture systems to provide the visual scene are examples of open-loop simulators. Sometimes closed-loop simulators are referred to as *unprogrammed* simulators; the open-loop types are called *programmed* simulators.

Whole-task simulators are also often classified on the basis of the manner in which the visual display is presented. Thus some versions make use of a system in which a television camera with a special lens system is moved over a large terrain board containing miniature roadway systems, model buildings, trees, and so forth. When the operator (seated in a "mockup" automobile) makes control adjustments, these adjustments are reflected in movements of the small television camera. The operator, who is looking at a television monitor or a screen on which an image is projected, is confronted with a moving visual scene very similar to one he would view from an automobile. As he manipulates the accelerator, brake, and steering wheel, the television camera moves and produces corresponding changes in the visual display. This is a closed-loop or unprogrammed-type simulator. Figure 9-1 is a schematic of this type of simulator.

In motion-picture simulators, the operator is also seated in either a standard automobile or a mockup and views a screen through the windshield of the car. A variety of films of driving environments can be presented. These films are typically taken with special cameras mounted on cars and can include scenes ranging from heavy freeway traffic to deserted country roads. With simulators of this type, the control manipulations of the operator will have little, if any, effect on the visual scene. However, when the driver accelerates, the projectors run faster in some motion-picture simulators, giving a limited

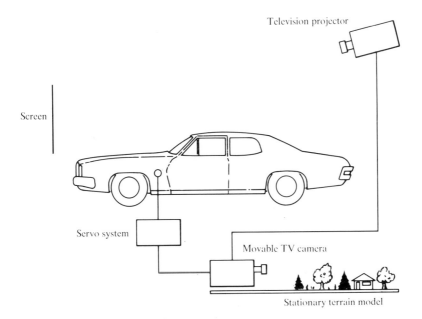

FIGURE 9-1. A schematic representation of a driving simulator utilizing a television system.

153

sensation of increased speed. Sometimes steering corrections will move the projector slightly and give the impression of a slight change in the car's direction. Motion-picture simulators, however, are classified as programmed or open-loop simulators. A schematic of a motion-picture simulator is presented in Figure 9-2. With this model, the driver also sees a scene projected on a screen behind the car when he looks in his rear-view mirror or over his shoulder. This adds more realism to the situation.

Another unprogrammed or closed-loop simulator is the *point-light-source simulator*. A simulator of this type, which is presently being utilized in Heimstra's laboratory, consists of an automobile mockup and a visual projection system. This particular type of simulator is shown in Figure 9-3. The mockup is situated in front of a translucent screen, and the operator responds to an image projected onto the rear of the screen. As the driver operates the controls in the mockup, he causes the model driving environment, or terrain model, to move past the stationary point of light. The terrain model consists of a transparent disk on which roadways have been painted and to which buildings, signs, vehicles, trees, and so forth are attached. These objects can be either solid or transparent. As the terrain model, under the control of the operator, moves under the light source, transparent objects in front of the light are projected in considerable detail onto the screen. Solid objects are projected as dark shadows.

The visual display on a point-light-source simulator is very sensitive to the control manipulations of the driver. When he accelerates, the terrain model

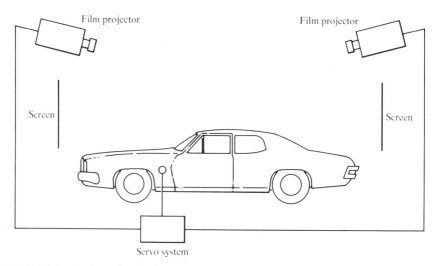

FIGURE 9-2. A schematic of a driving simulator that makes use of motion pictures to present the visual scene to the operator.

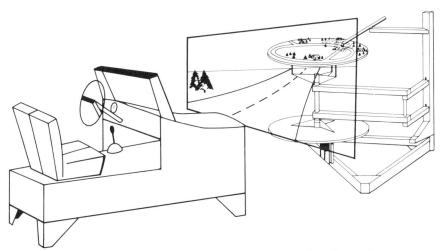

FIGURE 9-3. An illustration of a point-light-source simulator such as that used at the University of South Dakota. See text for an explanation of how the simulator operates.

moves more rapidly past the light source and results in the same kind of visual "feedback" he would receive if he were to accelerate in a real vehicle on the road. Steering changes result in changes in the direction of movement of the terrain model, and braking slows the movement of the model. In both cases, the driver sees changes in the visual scene that are quite realistic.

There are advantages and disadvantages associated with the use of simulators in driving research. One obvious advantage is the increase in safety. Situations that would be hazardous to investigate in actual vehicles on the road can be safely studied in simulators. For example, investigations concerned with the effects of various drugs on driver behavior are often conducted in simulators rather than in real cars. Another advantage is that the investigator can exert a higher degree of experimental control in simulator studies; the variables that he is interested in can be more adequately defined and controlled. There are other advantages. However, simulators also offer some disadvantages as research tools. In the first place, a simulator that is unprogrammed and realistically simulates the real-world driving task is a very expensive piece of equipment, and the cost of developing or acquiring such a simulator is prohibitive to many organizations. Also, a simulator, as the name implies, only simulates the real-world situation. It is still not clear whether many of the research findings from simulator studies can be generalized to situations involving the operation of a real vehicle in a real driving environment.

The simulators that have been discussed are sophisticated models that have been designed for research purposes. There are also a number of types

155

of simulators that have been designed for training student drivers. The role of simulators in driver-education programs will be considered in the next chapter.

Instrumented Research Vehicles. Another approach to the study of driver behavior is to equip actual vehicles with various types of recording devices and other kinds of equipment, and then study the performance of drivers as they operate the vehicle on the road. There are several versions of instrumented vehicles in use; one of the most sophisticated is the Highway Systems Research (HSR) car, which was developed by researchers at the Ford Motor Company and is now manufactured by the Chesapeake Systems Corporation. Performance measures are obtained by means of sensors attached to various parts of the automobile and to the driver. Thus the frequency of steering reversals, accelerator reversals, and brake applications as well as physiological measures from the driver can be obtained. These measures are stored on a magnetic tape recorder located in the trunk of the vehicle.

The HSR car is an example of a complex instrumented vehicle in which numerous behavioral responses of the driver can be obtained simultaneously. In some cases, however, the investigator may be interested in only one or two particular responses, requiring much less in the way of instrumentation. For example, in a study by Jones and Heimstra (1964), which was concerned with how accurately experienced drivers could estimate the time necessary to pass a lead car in the face of an oncoming vehicle, the only instrumentation required was a pair of stopwatches. In other investigations, eye-movement cameras have been used to study the eye-movement patterns in drivers. Actual vehicles can be instrumented in many ways, depending on the purpose of the investigations.

Measurement of Driver Performance

We have pointed out previously that the driver in his role as an interface between the vehicle and the highway performs input, central-processing, and output operations. The output operations are the motor responses produced by the driver, and in most of the research dealing with driver behavior these are the operations that are measured. However, it should be kept in mind that these responses are very much dependent on the input and central-processing operations. For example, we may measure the time it takes a driver to move his foot from the accelerator to the brake when a red light appears. Our measure, in this case, deals with an output operation. However, in order for this operation to take place, the driver must first have sensed the light (input operation) and then have made a decision to respond (central-processing operation). We are measuring an output operation, but the efficiency of the input and central-processing operations are often inferred from these measures.

Some Types of Measures. An important decision for researchers interested in driver performance, one that is often difficult to make, is what performance measures to use. In some cases the measures are dictated by the particular study the investigator has in mind. For example, an investigator concerned with some aspect of the visual task (such as visual search) required in driving might record the eye movements of drivers. Another researcher who is interested in the effects of certain kinds of drugs on steering performance might measure the number of times the driver makes small or large steering movements. In some cases the measure might be the number of accidents or traffic violations in a given period of time. Possibly one of the most common types of measurement involves an observer who sits beside the driver and rates his effectiveness on a number of different areas of driver performance. Everyone who has taken an examination for a driver's license has been exposed to this type of measurement. Obviously, there are many kinds of measurement that can be utilized. We will discuss specific studies dealing with driver behavior later in this chapter.

Often, however, the investigator is concerned with obtaining as broad a picture of driving performance as possible. In studies of this sort, a battery of performance measures may be used. For example, the Highway Systems Research (HSR) car provides for the measurement of a number of operator-performance measures, including:

(1) The number of small steering movements (micro reversals).
(2) The number of gross steering movements (macro reversals).
(3) The number of changes in accelerator pedal position.
(4) The amount of time the accelerator is not depressed.
(5) The number of brake applications.
(6) The amount of time the brake is held depressed.

In addition, measures such as total trip time, delay time, time that the car is in motion, the average speed, and the number of speed changes are obtained. The HSR car is also equipped to record various physiological indices that may be important for a particular study. The steering wheel is gold plated, and acts as a sensor for measuring either heart rate or GSR. This sensor system eliminates the restriction of movement that is associated with systems that attach electrodes to various parts of the body.

Some simulators have measures similar to those discussed. For example, the point-light-source simulator at the University of South Dakota (Ellingstad, 1970b) has heart-rate and GSR measures, but it is also equipped to obtain the "tracking" error of the subject. Tracking error is based on the lateral placement of the simulated vehicle to the left or right of the center of the lane in which it is being operated. This type of error occurs in the operation

157

of a real vehicle, in that you "weave" slightly (even when sober) as you drive, but it is difficult to measure in an actual car. In certain types of simulators it can be measured quite accurately.

Validity of Measures. In considering the measures of driver performance, whether in a simulator or in an instrumented car, an important question must be kept in mind: the measures tell us a good deal about how a driver is performing in a given situation, but do they tell us anything about whether the person is actually a "good" or a "bad" driver? It is critical that all measures obtained in driving studies be validated against actual criteria of good or bad driving performance. As you will see in the next chapter, it is difficult to define what a good or bad driver is. However, several of the measures obtained in the HSR car have been shown to differentiate between drivers with accident histories and those without, between experienced and inexperienced drivers, and between drivers with and drivers without histories of traffic violations (Greenshields & Platt, 1967; Ellingstad, Hagen, & Kimball, 1970). Studies like these suggest that results of driving studies are meaningful indices of driver behavior.

When measuring driver behavior in a simulator, other problems must be considered. For instance, the question of how closely the simulator measures parallel the measurements obtained in an actual car must be answered before much confidence can be placed in research findings from simulator-based studies. Unfortunately, very few studies have been conducted that have attempted to "validate" simulator measures against measures from actual vehicles. An excellent study of this type was conducted by Ellingstad (1970b), who tested the same subjects in both the HSR car and a point-light-source simulator. Both the vehicle and the simulator were instrumented to obtain similar types of behavioral measures. Ellingstad found that a high correlation existed between the subjects' scores in the simulator and the HSR car, indicating that, indeed, the measures obtained in the simulator were valid. Many more validation studies of this kind will be necessary, however, before investigators can be sure that the measures obtained in a simulator are meaningful for real-world driving.

SOME INVESTIGATIONS OF DRIVER BEHAVIOR

In the previous pages we have discussed some of the research approaches, techniques, and tools that psychologists utilize in their attempt to gain a better understanding of the complex form of behavior we call "driver behavior." In this section we will consider some of the studies that have been conducted by these researchers.

Pre-Operational Factors

Recall that there are two broad classes of factors that contribute to the way a driver performs—pre-operational and operational factors. The former refers to the mental and physical characteristics that the driver brings with him to the driving task, and the latter refers to the factors required to perform the driving task.

Physical Status. The physical status of the motor-vehicle operator is determined by the functioning of a number of physiological and psychological systems that make up the human organism. Ellingstad (1970a) suggests that in terms of their role in determining the performance of the driver, these psychophysiologic systems can be grouped into at least three major categories— sensory processes, sensory-effector coordination, and tolerance to transient effects. Drivers come to the driving task with different capabilities in these areas. For example, as Ellingstad (1970a) points out:

Vision, of course, is the primary input channel to the human operator. The status of this sensory channel is determined by the operator's static, peripheral, and dynamic visual acuity; the extent of his visual field; and the response of his eyes to varying levels of illumination. These functions will determine, basically, whether the driver will see objects in his driving environment. Additional visual capabilities are required in the areas of depth and motion perception and color vision [pp. 177–178].

Obviously, individuals will differ considerably in their ability to perform these various visual functions and their driving performance may reflect these differences. Actually, few studies have been attempted that were designed to relate a driver's visual capability to accidents or other measures of driver performance.

Burg (1964) tested several thousand volunteer driver-license applicants for both dynamic and static visual acuity. The former type of test involves an acuity measure based on a moving visual "target"; the latter utilizes a stationary target. Among other findings, Burg reported that there was a positive relationship between good dynamic visual acuity and good driving records (lack of citations). However, he found no relationship between either type of visual acuity and the number of accidents the drivers reported.

Even if the driver does possess adequately sensitive sensory-receptor systems, there is the additional pre-operational requirement that he be able to process and act on the information received. A common measure of sensorimotor coordination is simple reaction time. Similarly, a wide variety of psychophysical judgments involve sensorimotor coordination. "The capacity of the operator to make judgments of closure rate, the velocity of oncoming and intersecting vehicles, and the estimation of intervehicular distances can be thought of in terms of sensorimotor coordination and judgment" (Ellingstad, 1970a, p. 179). Although a number of attempts have been made to relate various measures of sensory-effector coordination with accidents and traffic-violation records, the attempts have generally been unsuccessful.

Another pre-operational factor of some importance is the tolerance that a driver may have for various transient effects such as fatigue, drugs, noise, or other factors in his internal or external environment. Studies have shown that these factors will have an effect on driving performance, but very little work has been done on how individuals differ with respect to the effects that these agents will have on their performance. The capacity of the driver to withstand the effects of alcohol, drugs, fatigue, and so on will help determine his level of functioning in the driving task.

A study by Rainey and co-workers (1959) involved two groups of subjects. One group was made up of Air Force drivers who had a history of accidents, and the other group was accident-free airmen. A large number of psychological tests was administered to these drivers, including several psychomotor tests, such as simple and complex reaction time, eye-hand-foot coordination, and depth perception. Analysis of the results of these tests showed that there were no differences between the accident-free and the accident-repeater groups.

Attitudinal-Motivational Factors.   The attitudes and motivation that a driver brings to the driving task may be important determinants of driving performance. Consequently, the concept of attitude as it relates to driver behavior has been the topic of investigation for a number of researchers. There are many who feel that the attitudes of drivers may be a very significant factor in how they drive. They also feel that modification of these attitudes may result in significant changes in driving behavior. Since an attitude can be defined as a predisposition to behave in a certain way, it is often suggested that changing a bad attitude toward driving may result in a change for the better in driving habits. Whether or not this is actually the case, however, remains to be demonstrated.

A study by Schuster and Guilford (1964) had as its major aim the development of attitude scales that would differentiate between two groups of problem drivers (traffic-violator and accident-repeater drivers) and better-than-average drivers. In other words, they were interested in developing a test that, when administered to drivers, would be reasonably accurate in predicting which of the three groups the driver would most likely be in. The results of their study, which involved nearly 2000 drivers, showed that their test was predictive—that is, they were able, on the basis of the test results, to predict which individuals were likely to become problem drivers.

In another study by Schuster (1969), a large number of negligent drivers attended a driver improvement class that was intended to improve their attitudes toward driving. Another group did not attend the class but was simply interviewed. Records were kept of accidents and traffic violations for several years after the drivers attended the class or were interviewed. There was an improvement, but it was the same for both groups. The conclusion drawn was that the class did not help the driving behavior any more than the improvement interview alone. Incidentally, both groups, even after improvement, were worse than the average drivers in California, where the study took place.

Although considerable research has been conducted in the area of driver attitudes and their relationship to driving behavior, we can draw few firm conclusions from the results of these investigations. Lucas (1970), in a review of the literature dealing with attitudes and driver behavior, states that " . . . based on these investigations, it would be difficult to state, with any degree of certainty, what attitudes and personal characteristics, if any, are related to accidents, violations, or to other aspects of driver behavior" (p. 151).

Driving-Skills Factors. Another pre-operational factor that is important in determining how the driver will perform in the driving task is the level of driving skill that is brought into the task. Ellingstad (1970a) points out that there are two broad areas encompassing the range of pre-operational driving skills. The first such area includes the psychomotor skills required in the operational tasks. The second area includes what might be considered driving knowledge and includes cognitive processes, driving rules, and so forth. The topic of driving skills, and how they are acquired, will be discussed in detail in the next chapter, when the problem of driver education is taken up.

Operational Factors

In considering the operations of the driver as either input, central-processing, or output, there are a number of tasks that can be classed under each of these operations. We will restrict our discussion to only a few of these tasks, which can be of particular importance in determining driving performance. These include (1) a search-and-scan task, (2) a perceptual task, (3) a decision-making and cognitive-response task, and (4) the physical responses or output task. As pointed out previously, the first two of these tasks can be considered input operations, the third a central-processing operation, and the fourth an output operation.

The Search-and-Scan Task.   The driving task represents a dynamic situation in which the driver must actively seek information about his operating environment. Some of this information will be obtained through the auditory channel and some through the kinesthetic channel, but the great majority of information that the operator needs for adequate driving performance is transmitted via the visual channel. Consequently, the major amount of search-and-scan research has involved this sensory modality.

When a driver attempts to guide a moving vehicle on a roadway, he must visually sample a continuously changing environment. The roadway's geometry, surface condition, traffic density, and rate of traffic flow are not constant; they are constantly changing. The driver must adopt techniques for conducting the "visual sampling," and the techniques he selects will determine the "particular characteristics of the environment to which visual attention is directed, the sampling time allowed for input from these characteristics of the environment, and the patterning of the search and scan activity" (Ellingstad, 1970a, p. 181).

A number of approaches have been used in attempting to isolate and analyze visual search-and-scan behavior. However, one of the best techniques involves the use of eye-movement recording equipment. A motion-picture camera is mounted on a helmet worn by the driver and films the scene ahead of the driver. By means of special equipment, a spot of light is aimed at the cornea of the eye and the reflection of this spot is also filmed. The end result is a movie that shows whatever scene the camera was aimed at and a small spot of light superimposed on the scene, which is the point at which the driver was actually looking.

In a study by Zell, Rockwell, and Mourant (1969), the changes in eye-movement patterns during the acquisition of driving skill by novice drivers was investigated. Results showed that, initially, the novice driver spends a great deal of his visual fixation time in the immediate proximity of his vehicle—that is, looking at the road very close to the front of the car. As experience is gained, he spends more of his time looking farther ahead of the vehicle. It was also found that drivers tend to fixate points farther from the vehicle as the speed of the vehicle is increased.

A considerable amount of experimental work has been done on the eye-movement recording system by Rockwell and his co-workers at Ohio State University and by other investigators. Studies using this system have shown that eye-movement patterns change when the driver has been drinking alcoholic beverages and that fatigue and other transient variables will also have an effect on eye-movement patterns. However, the question about whether drivers who have many accidents have different patterns of eye movement from drivers with no accidents remains unanswered.

The Perceptual Task. Although the search-and-scan task will determine to a large degree the amount and kind of input that the operator receives, the perceptual task involves the operator's reaction to these sensory inputs. The perceptual task has at least two basic functions. One is the identification and recognition of cues that are important to the driving task. Obviously, a driver at any given time receives a large sensory input, and only part of this input is relevant to the driving task. Thus a driver might see a horse in a pasture beside the road, but it will not be identified as task-relevant. An approaching car, however, would be. The second function is to relate these cues to information that the driver has already stored in his memory system. For example, the approaching car might be weaving back and forth; because of stored information about this kind of behavior, this cue might suggest to the driver that the oncoming vehicle is driven by a drunk.

A number of studies have been conducted concerning the design of vehicles that would facilitate the identification and recognition function. For example, the detection and recognition of turn-signal indicators of one vehicle by the driver of another is a critical factor in safe driving. Mortimer and Olsen (1966) investigated the variables that influence the attention-getting quality of automobile front-turn signals. They found that amber-colored turn indicators were the most effective in terms of detection. Amber lights are also most readily detected under adverse weather conditions. They also found that the location of the lights may be a variable in detectability. For example, under daylight conditions, when a turn-signal lamp was placed in the chrome surface of the bumper, it was detected less readily than if placed away from the chrome bumper surface. Under night conditions, turn-signal lamps placed near the headlights required a greater length of time to be detected than those located further away from the headlights.

In relating the cues available from the sensory input to stored information, the driver must typically make a number of judgments. For example, consider the processes that are involved when you follow another car on a roadway. In this car-following situation, you receive a number of cues from the car ahead. The principal cue produced by the lead vehicle is the change in retinal image as the distance between your car and the lead car changes. As you come closer, the retinal image gets larger. Based on these retinal cues, as well as several others, you judge the relative velocity and closure rate, and, based on these judgments, you modify your driving behavior. Similar judgments are required when you attempt to pass a lead car. Judgments of vehicular velocity (of both your own vehicle and the lead vehicle), rate of change in speed, and various distance judgments are required. In a passing situation, it is also very important that accurate judgments be made concerning the velocity of oncoming vehicles. Research has shown that most drivers cannot make this type of judgment with great accuracy.

Jones and Heimstra (1964) studied the passing-judgment process in an on-the-road investigation. In this study, the driver was asked to report to the experimenter (who rode with him) the last possible moment that he thought he could pass a lead car when another car was approaching from the opposite direction. However, the driver did not actually attempt the pass. It was possible for the experimenter to determine, from records of speeds, distances, and so on, whether the driver could have actually made a safe pass or whether he would not have had time to make a pass if he had actually attempted to do so when he indicated that it was the last safe moment. Of 190 such judgments (10 per subject), 93 were *underestimates*—that is, judgments that would, in an actual passing situation, either result in an accident or require evasive action on the part of the drivers involved.

The velocity-distance judgment situations are probably the most critical functions required by the perceptual task. Most of the remaining perceptual functions are somewhat "static" judgments, in contrast to the dynamic characteristic of the velocity-distance judgments. Some of the cues for the static-type judgments arise from physical context of the highway environment, such as driver reactions to road signs. Perceptual-task inputs also arise from other vehicles and from the vehicle the driver is operating. Typically, the latter type of input is visual and involves the driver's monitoring visual displays in the vehicle, such as dials and lights. However, as Ellingstad (1970a) points out, "A set of perceptual demands representing information transmitted from vehicle to operator which has not received adequate research evaluation and attention concerns cues impinging upon kinesthetic and proprioceptive receptors. ... A common situation of this type is encountered in relation to the detection and correction of vehicular skid" (p. 189). Thus it appears that in most cases of skidding, a corrective response is made by the driver before he detects the skid visually. Rather, it is the movement of the vehicle, which he detects through kinesthetic and proprioceptive receptors, that usually gives the driver his first cue that a skid is beginning.

The Decision-Making Task. The ability of a driver to make rapid and correct decisions may be the most important aspect of the driving task. It is also the least understood. When you drive a car, you are constantly required to make decisions. In some cases you may decide not to pass another vehicle on a curve, but at some other time you might attempt that maneuver. People run red lights and stop signs because they decide to do so. They drive when they are drunk even though they know the risk involved. However, virtually no investigations exist that are concerned with decision making and risk taking on the part of drivers. Obviously, this is a critical area and should be thoroughly researched. Perhaps it has not been studied because it is a much more difficult area to investigate than many other aspects of driver behavior.

The Output Task. Basically, a driver exerts control of his vehicle in two dimensions: he controls the position of the vehicle on the roadway, and he controls the speed of the vehicle. The position of the car on the highway (lateral placement) is maintained through manipulation of the steering wheel, and control of the vehicle's speed is maintained by means of the accelerator and the brake. These control activities have been subjected to considerable research, both in the laboratory and in instrumented research vehicles. Studies have dealt with the effects of alcohol and other drugs on vehicle control, with variables such as age, physical disabilities, fatigue, and mood and their relationship to steering and speed control, and with many other variables.

In a recent study, the relationship between driving experience and these control activities was studied. Ellingstad, Hagen, and Kimball (1970) exposed two novice driver groups (one group with less than 10 hours of driving experience and a second novice group with between 10 and 20 hours) and an experienced group of drivers to a simulated driving task. A point-light-source simulator, described earlier in the chapter, was used. Among the measures obtained from the subjects were fine and gross steering movements, speed control, and lateral placement (the position of the simulated car on the roadway). Comparison of the performance of the three groups showed that each group revealed a characteristic pattern of response. The experienced drivers tended to make relatively few steering inputs (both gross and fine), maintained a high rate of speed, and showed a small amount of lateral position error. The more experienced novice drivers made fewer steering adjustments than the experienced drivers. The two novice groups showed similar lateral position scores but made more lateral placement errors than the experienced group.

In terms of the speed-control task, both novice groups exhibited about the same average speed, but the more experienced novice drivers were much more variable in their control of vehicular speed than the inexperienced novices. The authors suggest that the initial acquisition of response skills in the driving task creates a situation in which the most attention is paid to the maintenance of the lateral position of the vehicle at the expense of vehicular speed. The least experienced drivers made many steering inputs and maintained the speed at a constant, low rate. The more experienced novice drivers maintained about the same position control, but with fewer steering inputs. However, this group showed extreme variability in speed maintenance, accelerating to a high rate of speed, slowing abruptly, and so forth. The authors suggest that the integration of the two control activities is an important aspect of the acquisition of driving skill.

It should be apparent that driver behavior, which most of us take for granted, is actually a very complex form of behavior. A considerable amount of research effort has been directed at understanding the driving task requirements better, but a great deal more research is needed. With an ever-increasing number of drivers and automobiles involved in the public transportation system, it becomes increasingly urgent that more investigators turn their attention to the problems associated with man as the driver of an automobile.

chapter

10

Training Man for His Role in the Highway Transportation System

The highway transportation system becomes more complex each year. Millions of new vehicles, millions of new drivers, and thousands of miles of new roadway are added to the system annually. With a complicated system of this type, it is important that all of the subsystems—the vehicle, the operating environment, and the man—function properly. The new drivers added to the transportation system are often inadequate and even dangerous. One of the purposes of driver-education programs is to insure that a new driver entering the system has been brought to at least a minimally acceptable standard of ability.

The idea of educating the driver was initially conceived as part of the "balanced approach" against accidents, which was developed in the 1920s. Driver education became part of the "three E's" of accident prevention—education, engineering, and enforcement. The quality of engineering and enforcement has progressed a great deal over the years, but the quality of driver-education procedures remains extremely variable. As a matter of fact, the value of the entire driver-education program has been questioned by a number of individuals.

We have already discussed the complexity of the driving task (Chapter 9). As might be expected, it is no simple undertaking to train individuals to properly execute this task. Those who have attempted to teach someone how to drive are painfully aware of the difficulties associated with this type of

Photo courtesy of *The Minneapolis Tribune.*

training. When we consider that driver education on a national basis involves millions of students with all types of backgrounds, thousands of teachers of varying quality, and many different kinds of training programs, it is not surprising that there are problems associated with driver-education programs. For example, what are the most effective methods of teaching a person how to drive? How does one measure the effectiveness of these methods? The objective of driver-education programs is to train good drivers, but how do we define a "good" driver? What criterion can we use? Are graduates of driver-education programs any better drivers than those who learn to drive from parents or friends? These are a few of the problems with which individuals in the field of driver education must deal.

A number of psychologists are actively working in this area in an attempt to solve these problems. As you will see, many of the problems remain unsolved, despite the efforts of these researchers. One of the aims of this chapter is to illustrate how formidable a challenge programs of such a magnitude as driver education present to research.

THE STATUS OF DRIVER EDUCATION

Since its beginning about 40 years ago, high school driver education (HSDE) has grown to a stage where several million students graduate from the program each year. If the present trend continues, virtually all eligible students in high schools all over the nation will be taking HSDE in the near future. You might conclude from this that there is no question that HSDE is valuable since many millions of dollars and man-hours are being invested in this program. Actually, it will become apparent as you read this chapter that there are many serious questions being raised concerning the effectiveness of driver education. There are a number of respected researchers who feel that this program does very little to reduce highway accidents.

A number of psychologists have been actively engaged in research on problems dealing with driver education. For example, there are researchers who are attempting, by means of various approaches, to determine whether driver education is effective and does actually result in reduction of accidents and traffic violations. Other psychologists are concerned with the development of methods for adequately evaluating driver performance so that the effects of driver-education programs can be determined. Still others are interested in the methods and procedures used in HSDE programs. These and other research questions will be discussed in some detail later in this chapter. As we indicated earlier, there seems to be a genuine question in the minds of many experts in the area of traffic safety about whether or not HSDE is of any real value. Many other experts are equally certain that it is of value, but all would agree that the HSDE programs as they exist today leave much to be desired. The programs have some obvious "flaws," which reduce the potential effectiveness of driver education. These include inadequately trained teachers, lack of standardization of courses and their content, and lack of accident-avoidance training, to name only a few.

Teacher Preparation

If driver education is indeed ineffective, then much of the blame rests on the training the teachers in the program receive. When the first HSDE courses were introduced, there were no qualified instructors to conduct these courses. Teachers from various disciplines (particularly physical education) taught driver education on a part-time basis for extra remuneration. At best, these instructors received a short summer course to prepare them for their HSDE teaching; most of them received no instruction at all. Nichols (1970) points out that "As a result of this method of obtaining instructors, not only were poorly trained personnel incorporated into the program, but there was also a tendency for driver education to become a teaching endeavor of secondary importance to instructors and administrators alike. Teachers from other disciplines often 'picked up' driver education as a sideline activity to supplement their primary salaries . . ." (p. 58).

Although there has been some improvement in recent years in teacher preparation, deficiencies in this area remain a major problem. Most articles by advocates of driver education agree that deficiencies in teacher preparation are still the major weakness in the HSDE system.

Course Standardization and Content

In addition to the variable and often inadequate training of the teachers who are involved in HSDE, the contents of driver-education programs vary considerably. According to Nichols (1970), these programs " . . . vary erratically from state to state, city to city, and even from school to school within a particular city. Although a few major texts are used consistently across the nation, some courses consist of classroom training only; others include behind-the-wheel training in addition to the classroom phase. Also, some schools have excellent facilities such as driving simulators, multiple-car driving ranges, dual-control cars, and other teaching aids; other schools have varying amounts or none of such facilities" (p. 61).

Because of the wide variety of approaches, facilities, and techniques associated with HSDE programs, an assessment of the usefulness of these programs is difficult. The lack of course standardization is a problem still far from being satisfactorily solved.

Accident-Avoidance Training

One of the primary purposes of driver education is to reduce the frequency of accidents. However, in programs that offer behind-the-wheel training, most of the time is devoted to procedures such as parking and backing up. Obviously, these basic procedures must be learned, if for no other reason than that they are necessary in order to pass the driver's license examination. Little if any time is spent in the training of accident-avoidance procedures, which might save the driver's life. Although advances have been made in accident-avoidance training in some HSDE programs, such training is the exception rather than the rule. Most investigators who have looked carefully at the HSDE programs feel that they do not prepare a student for even the simplest of emergencies. There are a number of other reasons why HSDE is not as effective as it should be. However, poorly trained teachers, lack of standardization of programs, and lack of accident-avoidance training are probably the most important factors. Efforts are being made to overcome these difficulties. The federal government is beginning to play a more active role in the area of driver education and is furnishing financial support as well as guidelines for the administration of these programs. Hopefully, in the near future, these criticisms will no longer be applicable to HSDE programs. However, they do exist at present, and you should keep them in mind when the controversy over the effectiveness of HSDE programs is discussed.

THE CRITERION PROBLEM IN DRIVER-EDUCATION RESEARCH

Whenever a researcher wishes to evaluate the effectiveness of any kind of training program, whether it is a program to train drivers, pilots, lathe operators, or electronic technicians, he must have some sort of indicator of what "success," or proficient performance, involves for the driver, pilot, operator, or technician. The measure that he develops for this purpose is called a *criterion measure*. An adequate criterion measure is essential before the effectiveness of any kind of training program can be accurately evaluated. Driver-education programs are no exception to this rule.

One might assume that, with the number of students involved in HSDE programs and the amount of money spent each year on these programs, adequate criteria exist to evaluate the effectiveness of HSDE. Unfortunately, this is not the case. Although several types of criteria have been used in studies designed to evaluate driver education, there are no *adequate* criteria available.

A number of unique problems are associated with the development of criterion measures for use in driver-training programs. In the first place, the development of a criterion measure depends on an understanding of what constitutes successful performance on a job or task. For example, suppose we were concerned with developing a criterion measure to determine whether a program for training lathe operators was effective. We could ask supervisors and foremen what they expected from a qualified lathe operator in the way of acceptable units produced in a given period of time. Our criterion measure then might be ten acceptable units per hour, and we could check the effectiveness of our training program against this measure. Consider, however, this question: what constitutes successful driving?

In the previous chapter, the problem of defining the driving task was discussed in some detail. You may recall that a variety of measures of driver performance exist, which are used by researchers interested in driver behavior. However, there are very few data that would allow us to state that a driver who scores high (or low) on performance measure X can be classified as a "good" or "successful" driver. Consequently, because we are not sure of the relationship between most of these measures and good or bad driving, there has been a tendency on the part of researchers to make use of two criteria that, at first, appear to be natural indices of "good driving." These are *accident rates* and *violation rates*.

Number of Accidents as a Criterion of "Good" Driving

Several studies have shown that graduates of HSDE programs have fewer accidents than drivers who learned to drive on their own or were taught by parents. Based on the demonstrated difference in accident rates, advocates of driver education were quick to claim that the value of driver education had been proven. They felt that the accident rate was a valid criterion of "successful" driving, and if the HSDE graduates had fewer accidents than non-HSDE graduates, the program must be serving its purpose.

When we look carefully at the use of accident rate as a criterion, however, it quickly becomes apparent that there are some problems with this particular measure. For example, in most studies that have shown differences in accident rates between graduates of HSDE programs and nongraduates, the accident records of trainees and non-trainees were obtained from police files. These records show the number and nature of accidents that the individual has been involved in, but they *do not* show the number of miles the person drives (quantity of exposure) or the conditions under which he drives (quality of exposure). Suppose, for some reason, that the students who enroll in HSDE programs tend to drive fewer miles under conditions less likely to produce accidents than students who do not take HSDE. Obviously, we might expect the HSDE graduates to have fewer accidents because they drive less and under safer conditions. There are research findings indicating that students who enroll in HSDE programs *do* drive significantly fewer miles than students who do not enroll in such courses. Further, there are indications that students who enroll tend to drive under safer conditions than students who do not enroll. Obviously, these factors tend to cast some doubt on the use of accident rates as a criterion of "good" driving. When these factors are taken into consideration in the analysis of accident rates, the differences between HSDE-trained drivers and nontrainees often disappear.

Traffic Violation Frequency as a Criterion of "Good" Driving

Studies have shown that persons who have completed driver-training programs have fewer traffic violations than those who have not enrolled in such programs. The same criticisms that are raised regarding the use of accident rates as a criterion of driving success can also be raised against the use of traffic violations as a criterion. Once again, the problems of quality and quantity of exposure are encountered. Typically, in studies equating these variables, differences in the number of traffic violations between HSDE graduates and the nongraduates tended to disappear.

Besides the variables of quality and quantity of exposure, there is another factor that adds to the difficulty of using accident and traffic-violation rates as criteria for evaluating the effectiveness of driver-training programs. Some investigations have shown that the students who enroll in HSDE programs are different in terms of personality, IQ, socioeconomic background, and so forth from persons who do not enroll in these programs. Perhaps these factors, and not the training received in the HSDE programs, cause the reduced accident and violation rates that some investigators claim are due to the HSDE training.

Conger, Miller, and Rainey (1966) analyzed the accident and violation records of three groups of young male drivers. These records were based on the first four years of driving experience. Group 1 consisted of drivers who had completed a driver-training program; group 2 consisted of drivers who wished to take driver education courses but, for various reasons, were unable to; group 3 consisted of drivers who did not wish to take driver education and did not. The initial analysis of accident and violation records showed that drivers in group 1 had fewer violations than drivers in the other two groups, but they did not differ from the drivers in the other groups in responsible accidents. However, the analysis also showed that the drivers in group 1 had by far the lowest driving exposure in terms of miles driven per year. Drivers in this group also had the highest average IQ. When the records were reanalyzed with drivers in the various groups matched for exposure, IQ, and socioeconomic background, it was found that differences in violations no longer existed. However, the second analysis showed there were differences in accident rates between the groups, with drivers in group 1 having fewer accidents. The authors concluded by calling attention to the fact that the results of studies purporting to show differences in driver behavior between students who have and have not had driver education may be influenced by factors other than the driver-training experience itself.

Some Other Criteria

Possibly the most obvious criterion for determining whether a driver-education program is effective is to take the graduate out in a car and see if he can drive. If you drive, you were exposed to this type of performance evaluation when you were examined for your license, and you are probably well aware of its limitations. However, there are a number of standardized rating scales available that can be used by observers for rating the performance of a driver. Although these scales differ in terms of their construction and what might be required of the observer, basically all involve a list of items or phrases that describe various aspects of driver performance. The observer rates the driver on each of the items. In some cases, the reliability (the relationship between the scores of two observers rating the same driver) of these rating scales is quite high.

With the development of instrumented cars and sophisticated simulators, these devices may eventually be effectively utilized in the evaluation of driver-education programs. Perhaps in the future all graduates of HSDE programs may be tested on instrumented vehicles or simulators. However, because of the expense of these devices, it is probable that this will be some time in the future.

The lack of adequate criteria for the evaluation of HSDE effectiveness is a genuine problem—one of which researchers in the field are aware. Most studies that are now being conducted in this area are designed to take the limitations of the testing criteria into consideration. However, the fact that it is difficult to define the driving task, to determine who is or is not a "good" driver, and to evaluate the effectiveness of existing training programs raises a number of additional problems in other areas of driver-training research. For example, researchers are concerned about what should be presented to the students in HSDE programs. We have already mentioned the problem of course standardization and course content. Questions exist regarding the number of classroom hours compared to behind-the-wheel hours that should be included in a HSDE program. Similarly, there is an interest in substituting a certain number of hours in a driving simulator for some of the behind-the-wheel hours. Different programs have utilized different combinations of classroom work, behind-the-wheel hours, and simulator hours, but very little can be done to evaluate the effectiveness of these various programs until we have better measures of what constitutes "good" driving. A number of psychologists are attempting to solve these problems in spite of the obstacles encountered in this kind of research. It should be kept in mind, however, that the fact we have no adequate criteria against which the effectiveness of programs can be compared imposes a serious limitation on research in this area.

EVALUATION STUDIES OF DRIVER-EDUCATION PROGRAMS

We have already pointed out that one of the major controversies in the area of driver education is whether the program justifies its cost in terms of reducing injury and death on the highway. A considerable number of studies have been conducted at both state and local levels to determine whether HSDE reduces the number of accidents and violations. One of these studies (Conger, et al., 1966) has already been cited. In considering evaluation studies, some of which will be described below, several factors must be kept in mind. First, the problems associated with the use of accident and violation rates as criteria are inherent in most of the studies. Second, many of the studies have been conducted by agencies and institutions that have openly advocated and promoted driver education. Also, many of the effectiveness studies have involved a rather limited sample of drivers. However, there have been several relatively large studies involving many thousands of drivers and extended periods of time.

The Connecticut Study

In this study, the effects of various forms of driver education on the driving records of nearly 50 thousand young drivers were analyzed. The results of this study indicated that students who had completed HSDE programs had 40% fewer violations than parent-trained drivers, and 45% fewer violations than drivers who had been trained in commercial driving schools (Connecticut Department of Motor Vehicles, 1964).

The Illinois Study

The records of over one-half million young drivers were observed for a year. Results showed that untrained drivers had more than twice as many violations as HSDE-trained drivers at age 16, and nearly seven times as many violations by age 20. Overall, it appeared that driver-education students had one-half as many accidents and one-third as many violations as did nondriver-education students (American Automobile Association, 1964).

The New York Study

A total of 960 driver-education trained high school students were matched with an equal number of untrained students. They were matched on such variables as academic status, sex, and school attended. The driving records of these drivers were observed for over a year, and the results showed that the untrained students had 22% more accidents than the trained students. An important feature of this study is that it did recognize the need to control for some variables other than whether or not a driver had received HSDE training (New York Department of Motor Vehicles, 1964).

Several other studies support the viewpoint that driver education is "paying its way" by reducing accidents. There are, however, studies that support the other point of view—that is, that driver education does not reduce traffic accidents or violations.

Two studies conducted in New Jersey found that untrained drivers had records superior to those of trained drivers. In one of the studies (American Automobile Association, 1964), an attempt was made to compare the effects of a complete driver-education course that included behind-the-wheel training, a course that involved classroom instruction only, and no driver education at all. Results indicated that untrained drivers had better subsequent driving records than either group of trained drivers.

Probably one of the most damaging studies dealing with the effectiveness of driver education was conducted by McGuire and Kersh (1969). The study by these investigators won the 1968 Metropolitan Life Award for research in accident prevention. Space does not permit a detailed discussion of their procedures and findings, but one of the principal conclusions of this study was that "All research properly conducted to date indicates that driver education, no matter of what quality, bears no causal relationship to highway accident frequency, accident severity or violation frequency" (National Safety Council, 1968, p. 122). Needless to say, this study has resulted in heated controversy between those who advocate driver education and those who do not—specifically, those who research the driver-education program.

Although it would be desirable to conclude this section with some definitive statement about the worth (or worthlessness) of driver education, it should be apparent from the few studies discussed that this is not possible. It should also be apparent that the problems associated with driver education are a formidable challenge to researchers. They are not the sort of problems that can be solved by a few psychologists working independently on small parts of the problems. Rather, solution of the problems will require a sustained effort by teams of investigators before substantial headway is made in the improvement of HSDE programs and in the ability to assess the quality and effectiveness of these programs.

SOME QUESTIONS ABOUT TRAINING
PROGRAMS

Up to this point we have been primarily concerned with the graduate of the HSDE program and the difficulties associated with the evaluation of his effectiveness as a driver. Although it was pointed out that the quality of HSDE programs may suffer from poorly trained teachers, lack of course standardization, and too little accident-avoidance training, there are also other factors that affect the quality of these kinds of training programs.

Over the years, a number of psychologists and other researchers have systematically investigated various methods and approaches in an effort to determine which are most effective for training men for a variety of different skills. For example, hundreds of psychologists are employed by military organizations to study training problems. Similarly, other government organizations as well as private industries utilize the services of psychologists to help solve problems associated with training employees. Because of these interests, a considerable amount is known about effective training procedures.

In Chapter 6 we pointed out that the development of any training program involves much more than just tossing together a few books, lectures, and demonstrations and then exposing a trainee to these materials and assuming that he is trained. Rather, if a training program is to be effective, there are a number of steps that must be followed during the development of the program. Let us consider the driver-education programs in terms of the steps, or stages, of development required for the establishment of any training program.

One of the first steps is a *task analysis* that, if properly conducted, will describe the behavior that is required of the person in performing the task—in this case, driving a car. Until recently, no detailed and systematic task analysis of the driving task had been conducted. However, the Department of Transportation, which is very interested in improving driver-education programs, has recently had a task analysis of this type conducted (Human Resources Research Organization, 1969). This analysis is extremely detailed and should prove useful in the development of training programs in driver education. In order to illustrate how detailed an analysis such as this can be, consider the analysis of the task of starting an automobile. As can be seen from Table 10-1, a relatively simple procedure such as this can involve a rather comprehensive task analysis. An analysis of this type was conducted for all of the tasks involved in driving, including steering, backing up, stopping, skidding, and so forth.

TABLE 10-1.   An analysis of the task of starting an automobile.

Task Description: Operator Starts Car
Task Analysis:
  1. Operator sets gearshift lever. If there is an automatic shift, he places it in park or neutral.
  2. Operator depresses accelerator to set choke. If there is no automatic choke, he pulls out manual choke slightly.
  3. Operator releases accelerator and then depresses slightly.
  4. Operator inserts key into ignition and turns it to *on* position.
  5. Operator checks that oil and generator warning lights are on.
  6. Operator turns ignition key until starter is heard.
  7. Operator holds key in starter position until engine starts.
  8. Operator releases key and listens for sound of engine.

Based on the task analysis, the researcher is able with some degree of accuracy *to specify the knowledge and skills* that an individual must have for performing the task and *to determine the objectives* of the training program. These steps in the development of a training program are still not completely specified in the driver-education programs, but progress is being made. Although most administrators of driver-education courses have assumed that they knew what was needed in the way of knowledge and skills and what the objectives of

179

their programs were, these assumptions were not necessarily true. However, with the availability of a driving-task analysis as thorough as that of the Department of Transportation's, the necessary information is now available for the specification of these skills.

After a task analysis, specification of skills required, and the determination of training objectives, the next step is the actual construction of the training program. This involves the selection of specific subject matter, deciding how and when it will be presented, selection of training devices and simulators, and so forth. This is still a major problem in driver-education programs.

Typically, those involved in driver education have paid great homage to a training program based largely on the element of time. The formula of 30 classroom hours and 6 hours of behind-the-wheel training has become virtually sacred, even though there is no evidence that the 30 + 6 formula has any particular virtue. As Boyer and McAvoy (1968) point out, "By simply requiring the 30 and 6 formula, driver education is almost the only discipline within a school that bases its requirements upon clock hours rather than on performance" (p. 23). Even when the 30 + 6 formula has been followed, there has still been a great deal of variation in what is covered in the classroom phase and the procedures followed in the behind-the-wheel phase.

A considerable amount of interest has been shown in recent years concerning new techniques for use in the driver-education courses. We cannot deal with all of the new approaches, but we will consider one promising new technique—the use of driving simulators as training devices in driver-education programs.

Simulators were discussed in some detail in the previous chapter. They were research models, but the versions used in driver education are very similar. Typically, these are programmed open-loop simulators that rely on motion pictures for their visual displays. Although the use of this kind of simulator has become quite common, a number of questions about its utilization in the training programs remain to be answered. For example, can simulators be used to replace some hours of behind-the-wheel training? Should students be trained in simulators in addition to the normal amount of behind-the-wheel training? How effective is training in a simulator in terms of transfer to the real driving task? In other words, will training in a simulator facilitate, in terms of reduced time or better performance, the learning of the actual driving task? What sort of design factors are important in the simulator to insure maximum transfer from the simulator to the real vehicle? These are only a few of the questions that confront the people who are interested in using simulators in the driver-education program. Attempts are being made, however, to answer these questions.

180

Bishop (1967) attempted to determine whether sufficient transfer of learning occurred from simulator instruction to actual driving to permit the substitution of simulator instruction for part of the behind-the-wheel experience in the traditional driver-education program. He worked with several groups of trainees: one group received the typical six hours behind the wheel, another group received a number of hours of simulator training and only three hours of actual driving, and a third group received no simulator time and only three hours behind the wheel. A fourth group received no instruction. All four groups were tested before and after training on knowledge and attitudes about driving, and the first three groups were also tested for driver competency.

With the exception of the fourth group, which received no instruction, there was an improvement in driving knowledge and attitudes in each of the groups. However, more importantly, Bishop was able to conclude from his findings that a driver-education program combining 12 hours of simulator experience with three hours of actual driving compares very favorably with the conventional six hours behind the wheel.

The implications of Bishop's study (and other studies that suggest simulator experience can be substituted for actual driving) have some importance for administrators of driver-education programs. Advantages of a program that combines simulator and behind-the-wheel experience are that more students (quantity) learn more about driving (quality) with less expense (cost).

Although most investigators concerned with developing training programs in driver education agree that simulators may serve a useful purpose in these programs, there is still some question concerning the kind of simulator that will be most effective as a training device. Consequently, research is now being conducted by the Department of Transportation that is aimed at specifying the requirements of a training simulator. Obviously, research model simulators such as those described previously are far too expensive for use as training simulators. However, if the purpose of the training simulator is to reduce the time required for learning to drive or to improve the level of performance in the real vehicle, then the training received in the simulator must "transfer" to the actual car. Some interesting questions have been raised and are currently being investigated regarding the characteristics of a simulator that are most important to insure that maximum transfer takes place.

For example, how important is movement of the simulator? Should the system simulate the movement of an actual car so that you "feel" the acceleration (or deceleration)? How important is the degree of clarity, or resolution, of the visual scene? Perhaps the most important question has to do with whether or not the simulator should be programmed or nonprogrammed. Questions are also being raised about whether, for many of the skills involved in driving, part-task simulators may be more effective than whole-task simulators.

181

There are many other problems associated with the construction of driver-education training programs. However, these problems are being studied by a number of psychologists and other researchers, and it is likely that some major advancements will be seen in the next few years.

One other step in the development of a training program should be mentioned. Typically, the last step is an *evaluation of the program.* The problems associated with the evaluation of driver-education programs have already been discussed in detail. However, this is a very critical step in the development, and, until we do have methods of evaluating these programs, we will not have the "feedback" to know whether or not the programs are effective.

OTHER KINDS OF TRAINING PROGRAMS

We have been primarily concerned with the driver-education program that takes place in the high school setting and is typically part of the school curriculum. There are several other types of driver-education programs that are not associated with school systems. There are, for example, a large number of *commercial driver-education* schools, which, for a fee, train prospective drivers. The primary function of these schools has been to train adults to drive, but they also train a considerable number of teenagers.

Most of the same comments that have been made concerning the HSDE programs can also be made about the commercial programs. Once again there is the problem of evaluating these programs. There is some argument about the relative effectiveness of commercial and HSDE programs, but few studies comparing the two programs have been attempted.

If we think of driver-education programs as being designed to prepare the human element of the highway transportation system for at least minimal functioning within the system, we can think of *driver-improvement programs* as being designed to raise the level of performance of certain drivers already within the system. There are several types of driver-improvement programs currently in operation.

Driver Improvement for the Professional Driver

Two of the most commonly used systems for improving the performance of professional drivers are the Smith system and the Smith-Cummings-Sherman (SCS) system. Both of these systems place particular emphasis on the development of visual techniques for evaluating traffic situations and recognizing conditions that are hazardous. Emphasizing the visual aspects of driving, these systems stress such principles as (a) aim high in steering (look far enough ahead), (b) keep your eyes moving, (c) get the big picture, (d) leave yourself an out, and (e) make sure they see you. Students attend a forty-hour (five-day) program, which consists of both classroom and behind-the-wheel training. A study by Payne and Barmack (1963) compared the performance of 60 drivers trained by the SCS system and 60 drivers not trained by the system. Analysis of accident records controlled for age, driving experience, and road exposure showed no significant differences between the groups in number of accidents, although the trend was for the trained drivers to have somewhat fewer accidents. An interesting finding of this study, however, was that the students of one particular instructor had significantly fewer accidents than the students of another instructor. This finding tends to emphasize the importance of instructor capabilities in any type of driver-education program.

Driver Improvement for the Public

A majority of the driving public has never had a formal course in driver education. There is also little doubt that the average American driver does not drive to the best of his ability. Consequently, interest has been shown in the development of programs for improving the driving performance of the general public. One example of this type of program is the well-known Defensive Driving Course (DDC). The primary attributes of this course are that it is highly standardized, aimed at accident avoidance, and interesting to the student. The course consists of eight hours of classroom lecture, visual aids, and discussion, and is conducted by highly-trained instructors who are licensed to teach the course. Well over a million drivers have now taken the DDC.

The critical question, of course, is: does this type of training do any good? Advocates of the system are convinced that it does. However, the effectiveness of DDC must still be considered questionable since there is very little in the way of data from well-controlled investigations that show that DDC is, indeed, effective.

Driver Improvement for Problem Drivers

Some drivers continue to accrue violations and accidents regardless of the warnings issued by legal authorities. These people are called problem drivers, although other types of drivers such as medically impaired drivers or the driving alcoholics may also be placed in this category. Several types of driving improvement programs have been established that are aimed at rehabilitating the problem driver. These programs may consist of warning or advisory letters, personal interviews, driver-improvement clinics, probation, or suspension of the violator's driver's license. Although the research findings regarding the effectiveness of these various techniques have been conflicting, there have been some positive indications for some of these techniques.

Kaestner, Warmoth, and Syring (1967) investigated the effects that three different types of letters had on the driving records of the recipients of the letters. The letters were (1) a photocopied standard form letter, somewhat threatening in its contents; (2) the same letter but personally typed, addressed, and signed; and (3) a personalized "soft-sell" letter, which was less threatening than the form letters. The results of the study showed that the photocopied form letter was no more effective than no letter at all in terms of reduction in violations over a six-month period. Personalizing the standard letter, however, resulted in a reduced number of violations. The recipients of the "soft-sell" personalized letter had the fewest accidents of all. The greatest improvement for both types of personalized letters was for drivers under 25 years of age.

Campbell (1959) evaluated the effects of advisory letters, suspension of driving licenses, and probation on the subsequent records of problem drivers. He concluded that all three procedures were effective in reducing subsequent violations. Campbell found that probation was more effective in improving driving records than suspension, and that when suspension was involved, less severe suspensions had more beneficial consequences than did more severe suspensions.

Interviews and clinics have involved both group and individual approaches. Group approaches may be desirable in that a number of problem drivers can be worked with simultaneously, but there is considerable question about the effectiveness of the group approach. Although there is some evidence that interviews and clinics can have some positive effects, the effectiveness of these procedures remains questionable. Certain available data indicate that they have no profound beneficial effect on subsequent driving records of problem drivers.

chapter

11

Some Human Problems in the Highway Transportation System

We have seen that man's role in the highway transportation system is that of a link, or interface, between the vehicle and the roadway. We have also seen that significant problems exist in regard to defining the task of the human element in the transportation system and determining how to train him for the task and how to evaluate the effectiveness of his training. Although these problems are substantial enough, man also presents some other unique problems for the system.

If the system is functioning properly, the various subsystems—the vehicle, roadway, and driver—must all function efficiently and safely. A "breakdown" in any of these elements can result in an accident. The vehicle and roadway may sometimes break down and cause an accident, but the human element is most frequently responsible for the sequence of events that results in the highway accident. The reasons for the behavior that results in an accident are not always clear.

One thing that is clear, however, is the fact that the human element of the highway transportation system is extremely variable and diversified. Some drivers operate vehicles safely, do not have an accident for many years, and may never even have a violation of any kind. Others have accidents occasionally and now and then pick up a traffic citation. For a third group,

Photo courtesy of Safety Section, South Dakota Highway Patrol, Pierre, S. D.

accidents and violations are not at all uncommon; and, for still others, safe and efficient driving appears to be the exception rather than the rule.

Psychologists have long been interested in the causal factors that result in a performance decrement or breakdown of the driving task. They have wondered whether there are certain types of personalities more likely to be high-risk drivers than others and whether a driver's attitude toward driving may be related to accidents and violations. A number of other causal factors have also interested researchers. Particular concern has been shown regarding the effects of alcohol on driving behavior; recently, a great deal of interest has been shown in the effects that other kinds of drugs have. Similarly, researchers have attempted to determine the effects of fatigue and other forms of stress on driver behavior. In this chapter we will consider some of the variables that may be responsible for the breakdown of the human subsystem in the highway transportation system.

THE DRINKING DRIVER

Alcohol and the Body

As is true with any other type of drug, the effect of alcohol is largely determined by the concentration at which it arrives at its site of action, the brain. There are several factors that will determine this concentration, such as the rate of *absorption* of the alcohol into the system, the rate of its *distribution* through the system, and the rate of its *elimination* from the system. Alcohol is absorbed primarily from the stomach and the small intestine into the bloodstream. Dilution of alcohol, such as in beer and wine, will retard the absorption process, as will the presence of food in the stomach. Distribution through the bloodstream is rapid, although the distribution is dependent on the size of the individual. Elimination occurs primarily by oxidation, but some elimination takes place in the breath and urine. Contrary to popular belief, the elimination process is not significantly affected by cold showers, black coffee, exercise, or sleep.

For research purposes, the investigator cannot just "guess" how much alcohol the subject has absorbed into his bloodstream. Rather, he must measure the blood-alcohol concentration (BAC) and utilize these measurements in his research. One method of determining BAC is to actually draw blood from a subject and analyze the specimen. However, since some studies require a number of BAC measures on one subject, the blood-sample technique can become rather traumatic. Another technique requires only that a subject exhale into a tube; his breath is then analyzed. After a person has had a drink of an alcoholic beverage, a small amount of alcohol remains "on his breath" and can be analyzed. Studies have shown that measures obtained with this technique correlate very highly with measures obtained from actual blood analysis. Consequently, because of the ease of utilization, the breath-analysis technique has become quite common in alcohol research.

The results of breath analysis (or blood analysis, if that method is used) are often used to construct blood-alcohol curves. The curves are, in a sense, a graphic representation of what happens to alcohol after it enters the body. They are obtained by plotting BAC on the vertical axis and time on the horizontal axis. A typical curve is shown in Figure 11-1. It can be seen that the shape of the curve, indicating the rate of absorption and elimination of alcohol, varies with the amount of alcohol taken. A larger alcohol intake gives a faster rise and a slower fall in BAC.

A number of important aspects of the blood-alcohol curve are not apparent from the graph itself but are worth mentioning. It is important to remember that the graph shown is only a "typical" one. The curves can vary in shape as a result of many factors, such as body weight, rate of drinking, amount of food in the stomach during the drinking period, type of alcohol, and prior drinking habits of the subject. Figure 11-2 shows the approximate average amount of 80-proof liquor a 150-pound person would have to consume in a one-hour period to reach various BACs. Despite the many factors affecting the blood-alcohol curve, it is a useful predictor of behavior once it has been obtained, because behavior after the consumption of alcohol depends to a great extent on the concentration of alcohol in the blood and brain.

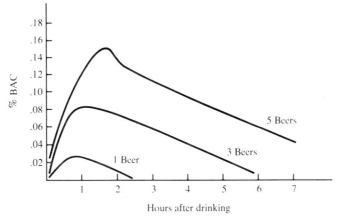

FIGURE 11-1. Typical BAC curves that might be expected for a 150-pound man after drinking one, three, or five "hi-point" beers.

189

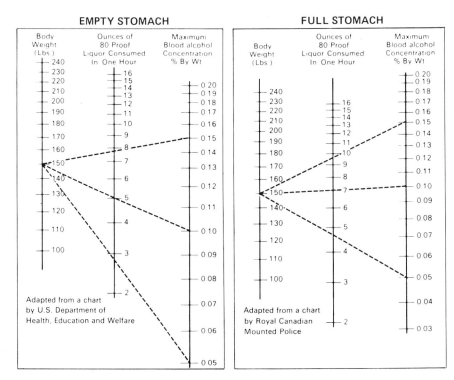

FIGURE 11-2. Chart showing the average amount of 80-proof liquor a 150-pound person would have to consume in a one-hour period to reach a BAC of .10%. To determine the approximate average number of ounces of liquor needed for a person of a particular weight to reach the .10 level, draw a line from "body weight" to .10%. The line will intersect the average number of ounces needed to produce a BAC of .10%. (Courtesy Allstate Insurance Company.)

The BAC is utilized by authorities to establish the legal level of intoxication for drivers. In some states, the legal level is 0.15% BAC. In other words, with a BAC of 0.14%, one is considered sober enough to drive; if it is 0.15% or above, one is legally drunk. This is still true, despite evidence indicating that at 0.15% a driver is 25 times as likely to cause an accident as at zero level. However, at present many states are following federal guidelines and lowering the legal limit to 0.10%.

There are some problems, however, in utilizing a particular BAC level as evidence of drunken driving. Thus research has shown that the same BAC can correspond to different degrees of "drunkenness," depending on whether it is measured on the rising or falling side of the BAC curve (see Figure 11-1).

For example, a subject may appear sober at a 0.12% BAC when measured on the falling side of the blood-alcohol curve; however, he appears quite drunk at the same BAC when measured on the rising side of the curve. In other words, it is important to know at what point on the curve a blood or breath sample was obtained.

Alcohol and Behavior

Although a considerable amount of research has been conducted dealing with alcohol and behavior, a great deal is still not known about how and in what way alcohol affects behavior. This is particularly true in the case of driver behavior. It is recognized that drinking increases the probability of an accident, but it is not clear what behavioral processes are affected.

In attempting to better understand the effects of alcohol on the driving task, researchers are often required to make use of data from laboratory studies not designed to study driver behavior. Although the tasks that were utilized in these studies may seem to be similar to certain aspects of the driving task, generalizations of the results of these laboratory investigations to the actual driving task must be made with caution. However, these kinds of studies do give us valuable information about alcohol and behavior.

Typically, these laboratory studies have been concerned with reaction-time tasks, various kinds of psychomotor tasks, sensory processes, and intellectual functions. No attempt will be made to summarize the many investigations conducted in these areas, but some general statements about the findings can be made.

Generally, the results of reaction-time studies show that reaction time is lengthened at relatively low blood-alcohol levels. Similarly, most studies show that motor performance is impaired at low and moderate blood-alcohol concentrations. There is some evidence that sensory functions show a decrement under relatively low BACs and that intellectual functions are quite resistant. At one time it was assumed that alcohol first affected judgment, inhibition, and memory; then loss of coordination, with speech, hearing, and visual difficulties; then stumbling, falling, and eventually coma (Martin, 1970, p. 111). However, more recent research suggests that, with increasing blood-alcohol concentrations, the sensory functions are the first to show a decrement, then the motor functions, and finally the intellectual functions.

Although there are a number of exceptions, most studies dealing with alcohol and driving fall into one of three general categories. These include simulator studies, in which the effects of alcohol on performance in a driving simulator are investigated; studies with drivers at various BAC levels operating an actual vehicle on driving ranges and courses; and studies that attempt to gather statistics concerning the involvement of drinking drivers in accidents (*epidemiological* studies).

Simulator Studies. The advantages and disadvantages of studying driver behavior by means of simulators were discussed in Chapter 9. A key question with any simulator-based investigation is: do the measures taken in the simulator predict the behavior in the real automobile? In many of the early alcohol investigations involving simulators, the simulators were rather simple devices. For example, several studies have used simulators that required a subject to operate standard-size driving controls, which regulated the lateral movement of a miniature car on a moving belt or "roadway." Although valuable information can be obtained from devices of this type regarding the effects of alcohol on various motor skills (such as tracking behavior), in terms of driving behavior the task was something like controlling the movement of the car in front of you by moving the steering wheel of your own car. Obviously, there is a real question about the validity of findings from simulator studies of this type.

Recently, however, alcohol studies have been conducted with the sophisticated research simulators discussed in Chapter 9. Several studies have been conducted using the point-light-source simulator at the University of South Dakota. You may recall that the measures obtained from subjects driving this simulator have been validated against measures obtained in the Highway Systems Research car operated under actual highway conditions. Consequently, there is reason to believe that the findings regarding the effects of alcohol on performance in the point-light-source simulator would also hold true in actual driving.

Martin (1971) utilized a point-light-source simulator and measured driving performance of subjects under three conditions—zero BAC, 0.05% BAC, and 0.10% BAC. Performance measures taken included the micro steering wheel reversals (steering movements of $2\frac{1}{2}$ degrees in any direction), macro steering reversals (8 degrees or over), and the maintenance of the simulated vehicle within the confines of the driving lane (tracking error) as well as several other measures. Martin found that there were no significant differences in tracking error between the three conditions. In other words, subjects at 0.05% and 0.10% BAC could maintain the position within a driving lane of the simulated vehicle as accurately as the zero BAC subjects. Analysis of the steering-wheel movement measures, however, revealed some interesting differences between the three conditions. On the micro reversal measure, a smaller number of reversals is usually associated with "better" driving. It was found that at the 0.05% BAC level the subjects made *fewer* micro steering reversals than did the subjects at the zero BAC level. In other words, at the 0.05% level their performance was actually facilitated. At the 0.10% level, however, performance was significantly worse than at the zero or 0.05% levels. Macro reversals did not differ between the zero and 0.05% levels, but at the 0.10% level there were significantly more macro reversals.

Since virtually all studies with simulators have shown either no change in performance or impaired performance due to alcohol, the fact that Martin found an improvement in performance at a low BAC level is of particular interest. The popular view has been that driving ability is impaired at any BAC level, and that this impairment increases linearly as a function of increasing BAC. However, a number of investigators are now beginning to question this *linear-deterioration hypothesis*. Although it is too early to say that at some low BAC levels "facilitation" of performance will usually be found, this possibility must be considered.

Behind-the-Wheel Studies. Studies in which subjects with various BAC levels actually drive cars are typically restricted to short driving courses and involve such tasks as backing up, driving in a straight line, parking, and stopping. In most cases, these courses are closed to traffic and all driving is done at low speeds. A variety of measures has been used in these studies, including the number of markers (stanchions) hit, the amount of time required to complete the course, measures of close-quarters maneuvering, and a number of other types of "errors" that can be recorded by an observer (rough stops and starts, stalls, racing the motor, and so on). Almost without exception, studies of this type have shown that alcohol impairs performance on most or all of the test measures.

One might assume that the behind-the-wheel studies have more validity than simulator studies, but this assumption is not necessarily correct. For instance, Carpenter (1962) states:

Although a driving course experiment very closely resembles actual driving, even to the extent of using real cars, it cannot be taken for granted that it is the same thing. This is emphasized by the kind of behavior required in these experiments, e.g., backing the car into a narrow space. It may be that the behavior in response to this requirement is an excellent diagnostic element for the true driving situation, but this is not known. In both the driving course and the driving simulator, the measurements show very clear changes, most often deterioration, with alcohol, but these measures may be completely beside the point in actual driving as it normally occurs [p. 303].

Epidemiological Studies. In epidemiological investigations, statistics are carefully gathered concerning the percentage of all accidents in a given locale

193

that involve a drinking driver. A number of different techniques are available to researchers who follow this approach. Often blood samples are taken at the scene of accidents, and road blocks may be set up and breath samples taken to get an estimate of the percentage of drivers who are not drinking (or who may be drinking but do not have accidents). The results of these kinds of investigations are often quite startling.

For instance, the Grand Rapids study (Borkenstein et al., 1964) is one of the most complete and best controlled epidemiological studies conducted. It took place over a one-year period, and data were obtained from accidents of all types—not just fatal accidents, as is often the case in these studies. In this study, 9,353 accident drivers and 8,008 control (nonaccident, similarly exposed) drivers were examined. The investigators found that alcohol was a major contributing factor in accidents. A driver with a BAC of 0.10% had about seven times the probability of causing an accident as a driver with zero BAC; at 0.15% BAC the drinking driver had more than 25 times the probability of causing an accident. Interestingly enough, an analysis of the data obtained indicated that at 0.04% BAC a driver was no more likely—and perhaps somewhat less likely—to cause an accident than at zero BAC.

Data also show that drinking drivers are involved in an inordinate number of automobile accidents. There are indications that about half of all fatally injured drivers have been drinking; about two-thirds of all drivers responsible for their fatal accidents have been drinking; and 70% of the drivers in single-car fatal accidents have been drinking. It can be safely concluded that alcohol is the largest single factor leading to fatal crashes.

Although the problem of the drinking driver is recognized and a variety of efforts are being made to "get the drunk off the road," there are some rather basic questions about alcohol and behavior that are still not completely answered. For example, at what blood alcohol concentration (BAC) is a person actually too drunk to operate a vehicle? Statistics show that a driver with a BAC of 0.10% has six or seven times the probability of causing an accident as a driver with a zero BAC. Yet there are many individuals whose behavior is hardly affected at the 0.10% level. Also, relatively little is known about the specific components of the driving task that are most affected by alcohol. Is it the input operation, the central-processing operations, the output operations, or all of these that deteriorate as alcohol is taken into the system? These and other questions are of interest to researchers.

Can We Solve the Problem?

With the realization that drinking drivers are involved in an inordinate number of automobile accidents, countermeasures ranging from slogans to

194

prohibition have been attempted. Most of the countermeasure attempts have been uninspired and unscientific in their development, application, and evaluation; they have had very little, if any, effect, in terms of reducing the number of accidents involving alcohol.

Very recently, however, a large-scale attack against the drinking driver has been undertaken by the Department of Transportation. Although it is far too early to evaluate the Alcohol Safety Action Programs (ASAP), which are being developed by the Department of Transportation in many states, these programs appear to hold a great deal of promise. The ASAP programs will include a variety of countermeasures, such as increased law enforcement, treatment of alcoholics, clinics, legal sanction, and many more.

One of the strong points of the ASAP programs is the rigorous evaluation that is being made regarding the effectiveness of the countermeasures. Typically, these evaluation processes involve the gathering of a considerable amount of pre-countermeasure data concerning the percentage of accidents involving drinking drivers, the percentage of drivers who drive while drinking, and so on. Similar measures are obtained during the countermeasure program, and additional post-countermeasure studies are made. With evaluation programs of this kind, the effect of the countermeasure procedures can be evaluated. Many psychologists are involved in the ASAP programs, particularly in the evaluation phase.

DRUGS AND DRIVING

In Chapter 15 the problems associated with the use of various drugs are discussed in some detail. In this section we will be concerned with a more specific problem—the effects of drugs on driving behavior.

When we think of drugs and driving, we generally tend to think of the various illegal drugs (hallucinogens, narcotics, and so forth) and not the legal drugs (over-the-counter or prescription drugs) as the primary problem. However, this is probably a false assumption, since evidence suggests that the users of legal drugs may present a greater threat in traffic situations because they most frequently use drugs while they drive. In considering the problem of drugs and driving, it must be kept in mind that any drug, when used in excess, can be harmful to the body and can be potentially hazardous in a traffic situation.

Actually, we know relatively little about the relationship between drug use and traffic accidents. There has been considerable speculation in recent years that drug users may contribute more than their "share" of highway accidents, but as yet little empirical data support this speculation. There are reasons for this lack of data. Although it is relatively simple to determine whether a person involved in an accident has consumed alcohol, it is very difficult to detect the presence of many of the commonly used drugs. Thus no satisfactory tests are available for the detection of hallucinogenic drugs, such as marihuana, LSD, STP, and mescaline. The presence of amphetamine is also difficult to detect. Because of these detection problems, epidemiological data are scarce concerning the frequency of accidents in which drugs were involved.

How Bad Is the Problem?

Several approaches have been utilized in an attempt to determine the incidence of drug use in the driving population and the relationship between drug use and highway accidents. One approach is to analyze blood samples taken from crash victims. In most cases, these studies have screened for only a limited number of drugs, since, as previously mentioned, tests are not available for many drugs.

In a study conducted for the State of California Highway Patrol (1967), investigators obtained blood samples from a large number of single-vehicle crash victims. Drugs that could be detected by the screening method included barbiturates, several types of tranquilizers, a stimulant, an antidiabetic, an anticonvulsant, and an anti-infectant. Results of the analyses showed that 13% of the crash victims had at least a detectable concentration of drugs in their blood. Traces of barbiturates and tranquilizers were found in 9% of the cases examined. Other investigations similar to the California study have also reported a percentage of the drivers involved in fatal accidents with detectable concentrations of drugs in their blood.

Another approach involves studying the driving records of known drug users. Investigations of driving records of these individuals show that they tend to have much higher violation records and, in some studies, higher accident rates. Smart, Schmidt, and Bateman (1969) examined the accident rates of 30 psychoactive drug abusers. Included in this group were persons addicted to or dependent on barbiturates, tranquilizers, or stimulants. Half were also dependent on alcohol. Analysis of the driving records of these drug abusers showed that they had accident rates about twice as high as expected for their age, sex, and driving exposure. Most of the excess in accident rates was contributed by those in the group who were addicted to amphetamines.

In a more recent article, Kibrick and Smart (1970) reviewed the studies dealing with the incidence of psychotropic drugs in the general population, in samples of drivers, and in samples of accident drivers. They concluded that:

Investigations have varied in terms of drugs studied, reliability of data collection procedures and criteria for choosing sample populations. This variable plus lack of replicative investigations makes the generation of conclusions tentative at this time. The studies cited did show that as high as 35 to 50% of the general population risk driving after drug use at least once per year and suggest that 11 to 15% of accident drivers have taken a psychotropic drug prior to their accident. Psychotropic drug use is most likely to be found among certain drinking driver groups, especially the fatally injured. The authors indicate that the veracity of drivers' statements about drug use is very low and drug use estimates derived from questioning are probably very conservative. Further research is recommended in associating the use of psychotropic drugs with driving errors or with responsibility for accidents [p. 73].

Although it would appear that a number of drivers risk driving after having taken drugs, the effect that this drug use has on increasing the probability of being involved in highway crashes is not clear. Considerably more research will be needed before it can be stated with any certainty that drug use is a major factor in accidents. At present, it appears that such use is not making a large contribution to automobile accidents. As yet, it is certainly not creating nearly the problem that alcohol usage creates (Nichols, 1971).

Effects of Drugs on the Driving Task

Although the contributions of drug users to the highway-accident figures is not clear, a number of researchers have attempted to determine the effects of various drugs on the driving task. Most of these investigations have utilized driving simulators of one kind or another. Many different kinds of drugs have been used in these investigations, although at present no studies have been reported that examined the effects of the more potent hallucinogens (such as LSD) or the narcotic drugs on driving-related skills.

Generally, these studies have shown that over-the-counter (nonprescription) drugs do not appear to have any adverse effects on the driving task. Typically, sedatives, tranquilizers, and stimulants have been found to impair performance. In the case of the sedatives and tranquilizers, impairment can usually be attributed to drowsiness, inability to concentrate, and extreme relaxation. With stimulants, the impairment is attributed to such factors as irritability, overactivity, a tendency to overestimate one's ability, and a lack of concentration.

In recent years, because of the widespread use of marihuana, there has been considerable concern about whether its use might impair driving performance. This drug has been subjected to only limited study in relation to the driving task, but research has failed to indicate any significant deterioration in driving performance as a result of marihuana usage.

In a 1969 study (Crancer et al.), the effects of marihuana and alcohol on a simulated driving task were investigated. The subjects were 36 marihuana users who were tested on a driving simulator under three different conditions. In one condition they were tested with no drug (neither marihuana nor alcohol), in another condition they were tested while "high" on marihuana, and in a third condition they were tested while legally drunk (0.10% BAC). The results of the study showed that the performance of these subjects was no worse when "high" on marihuana than when tested under the no-drug condition. However, at the 0.10% BAC level, their performance was nearly 50% worse than when under the no-drug condition. The researchers, however, are careful to point out that generalizations from a simulator-based study of this type to on-the-road performance must be made with caution, and that additional research is needed to substantiate the findings of their study.

One factor that tends to make studies dealing with drugs and driving difficult to interpret is that a large number of excessive drug users are also excessive alcohol users. In some instances, when drugs and alcohol are used together, there is an interaction that produces a whole new dimension of possible effects. Thus the measurement of the effects of a single drug on driving is only a first step. Its effects must also be measured in combination with alcohol (and other drugs, since combinations of drugs are used). Obviously, a great deal of research remains to be done before we can understand the problems that we confront with the "drugged" driver.

THE FATIGUED DRIVER

It is generally assumed that, after a period of time operating a motor vehicle, the driver is subjected to certain mental and physiological changes; together, these changes constitute "driver fatigue." It is also generally assumed that this type of fatigue will impair driving ability. However, there is actually little evidence that a decrement in driving performance does take place when the driver is fatigued. Most investigations have shown no relationships or, at best, very slight relationships between fatigue and driving performance.

There are several factors that make research in this area difficult. First, an investigator is confronted with the problem that we have discussed in some detail in previous chapters—that is, the problem of defining driving performance and finding adequate techniques for measuring it. Second, the nature of the fatigue process is not understood. We all use the term *fatigue* and think we know what it means, but it is actually a complex process, resulting from a variety of causes and manifesting itself in a variety of ways. It is difficult to measure fatigue, and in most studies it is defined in terms of the amount of time a person has been engaged in a task. Thus it is assumed that someone who has been driving for six hours is more fatigued than someone who has been driving for only one hour. Attempting to determine the effects of a process so difficult to define (fatigue) on a task equally difficult to define (driving) presents investigators with some unusual problems.

The fatigue that develops after a period of time in a driving task is quite different from the muscular fatigue caused by sustained physical work or exercise. One can view fatigue in the driving task as consisting of two components—the fatigue produced by the driving itself (called *operational fatigue*), and fatigue from other sources (which may not be specifically related to the driving task). Thus a person may be fatigued before beginning the driving task because of physical exertion, and this may then have an effect on his driving performance. From a practical point of view, it is difficult to separate the effects of the two components, although studies have been conducted that tend to emphasize one or the other.

Despite the problems associated with the study of fatigue and driving, a number of researchers have attempted to investigate the effects of fatigue on driving performance. These studies have made use of simulators, both part and whole-task, and actual vehicles. Although most of the research suggests that fatigue does not impair driving performance to any great extent, there have been some exceptions.

In discussing the fatigue process in driving, Crawford (1961) suggests that there are a number of stress factors inherent in the driving situation. Heavy traffic, unfavorable weather conditions, and so forth, may serve as stresses and result in a condition described as "stress" fatigue, which might lead to more impairment of performance than normal driving fatigue. This may be very common in driving situations, but it is difficult to investigate in on-the-road studies.

In a study by Heimstra (1970), the effects of stress fatigue on performance in a simulated-driving situation were investigated. Fifty-four male subjects were assigned to three equal groups and tested for a six-hour period in a driving simulator. A number of performance measures, including tracking, speed control, reaction time, and vigilance, were obtained from each subject. In one group, subjects received an electric shock whenever errors were committed on one of the tasks. Thus if tracking error exceeded certain limits, a shock was administered; if the speed exceeded or fell below a specified limit, shock was also given. In other words, shock administration was *contingent* on performance. A second group of subjects received electric shock at random during the six hours (*noncontingent group*), whereas a third group (the *control group*) operated

FIGURE 11-3. Often weather factors may contribute to the problems encountered by the human elements in the highway transportation system. (Photo courtesy of Travel Division, South Dakota Dept. of Highways, Pierre, S. D.)

the device for six hours without shock. Previous research had shown that subjects who received an electric shock because of poor performance were "stressed"; subjects who received shock at random were not.

Results showed that subjects in the contingent (stressed) group performed at a lower level than did subjects in the other two groups. There was a significant decrement in tracking performance as well as on the reaction-time task for subjects in the noncontingent and control groups. On the speed-control task and the vigilance task, subjects in the stressed group performed significantly poorer than subjects in the other groups. There were no significant performance decrements on any of the tasks in the case of the control and noncontingent groups. Since much of the fatigue encountered in driving situations may also involve various degrees of stress, it would appear that the effects of this type of fatigue on driving performance should be subjected to more research.

It has been suggested that one reason for the lack of findings showing fatigue-induced driving impairment is that most of the studies have not exposed subjects to long enough periods of time at the task. Silver (1964) points out that one might expect performance to remain constant over extended periods of time but that, at some point, performance will show an abrupt decline. Essentially, he suggests that the effects of fatigue are cumulative, and, at some point, the "accumulation" will be such that an abrupt decline in performance will occur.

Ellingstad and Heimstra (1970) designed a study in an attempt to determine whether the "abrupt decline" did take place during sustained performance in a driving simulator. Fifteen male subjects performed on a simulated-driving task for a total of 15 hours—that is, three five-hour periods separated by two 15-minute breaks. A number of performance measures were obtained during this period. These measures included a tracking measure, a vigilance task, two reaction-time tasks, mental multiplication tasks (which required the solution of simple multiplication problems without paper or pencil), and a digit-span task (which required the subject to repeat as rapidly as possible a set of digits presented to him orally by the experimenter).

A significant decrement in tracking performance was found over the 15-hour period. However, the decrement was gradual and showed no abrupt decline. There was no apparent decrement in performance on the other tasks. As a matter of fact, there was actually an improvement in performance on the vigilance task and on one of the reaction-time tasks.

The Ellingstad and Heimstra study did not find an abrupt decline in performance, but the "abrupt-decline" hypothesis cannot be rejected, since the time allowed for the cumulative fatigue effects may not have been sufficient in this study. However, if it takes much longer than 15 hours of driving to reach a point where the abrupt decline in performance does occur, then the practical aspects of such a finding would be of less interest. That is, if the abrupt decline did not take place until the operator had been driving for 25 to 30 hours, we would be dealing with a relatively rare event, since few individuals drive for that period of time.

Psychologists have conducted a number of other simulator-fatigue studies, which involved varying periods of time. They have also investigated fatigue effects when subjects were required to operate actual vehicles, sometimes for long periods of time. For example, Safford and Rockwell (1966) studied the effects of fatigue on driver performance in an actual vehicle. Measures obtained included a record of vehicle velocity, accelerator position, steering-wheel reversals, and brake-pedal depressions. Subjects were told that they would receive different amounts of money, depending on how long they drove, up to 24 hours. The route over which the subjects drove involved an 80-mile section of a major highway. The speed limit was 70 mph. Subjects were instructed to make eight round trips and were given a 15-minute rest period at the end of each round trip (160 miles). Drivers were instructed not to speak to the experimenter who rode with them. Only three of the seven subjects completed the test.

In general, the results of the study did not reveal any significant decrement in driving performance after long periods of driving. However, an important finding of this study was that the subjects showed great variability in performance, with some much more affected by fatigue than others. Typically, studies of driver performance do not show decrements due to fatigue. This does not mean, however, that some type of impairment in driving does not take place as a result of fatigue. What it may mean is that we do not yet have the capability to measure this impairment.

SOME OTHER DRIVER VARIABLES

Along with the driver variables already discussed (the drinking driver, the drugged driver, and the fatigued driver), there are other driver variables that may be important determinants of driving performance. For example, it is thought that various physical diseases may play a role in contributing to the incidence of traffic accidents. There is also the possibility that individuals with psychiatric diseases may have a higher probability of being involved in a traffic accident than "normal" individuals. Similarly, transient states, such as anger, depression, and anxiety, may affect driving performance. Some research has been conducted in these areas.

Physical Diseases and Driving Performance

Almost every disease known to medical science could at some stage interfere with the safe operation of a motor vehicle. With most physical disorders, when the conditions become extreme enough to affect driving performance, those affected are not likely to be driving and consequently pose no traffic safety hazard. However, with some diseases, extreme conditions can occur quite suddenly, with potentially serious results. This is particularly true of disorders that might suddenly interfere with motor control, consciousness, or perception. Although there are a variety of diseases that might result in these conditions, particular interest has been directed at the possible relationships between accidents and diabetes, heart disease, and epilepsy.

There are several approaches typically utilized by researchers interested in determining if a relationship exists between various physical disorders and traffic accidents. In some cases it is possible to determine from license applications and so forth the drivers who have certain disorders. The researcher then keeps a record of the number of accidents that these individuals have over a given period of time and compares these records with a control group of drivers who do not have the disorders. However, since the disorders were reported by the people who had them, it is possible that someone in the control group was disabled but did not report it. Therefore the validity of this kind of study is questionable.

Another approach is to attempt to determine whether a particular disease was a contributing factor in a traffic accident. This is often difficult to accomplish, but some data are available. For instance, for all accidents in which individuals suffering from diabetes are involved, it appears that only about 10% of these accidents are due to the diabetes itself. Similarly, for all accidents involving individuals suffering from cardiovascular disease, only about 5% of the accidents are thought to be caused by the disorder. The results of the investigations of this type, as well as others, suggest that cardiovascular diseases contribute relatively little to deaths or serious accidents on the highway. Also, enough data are not available to state with any degree of certainty that epilepsy and diabetes contribute significantly to the accident rate. However, this is another area in the field of traffic safety that must be thoroughly researched before we understand the relationship that does, or does not, exist between various physical disorders and highway accidents.

Psychiatric Diseases and Driving Performance

Mental illness exists on a continuum, with varying degrees of severity. At some point the degree of severity becomes such that hospitalization is required. These individuals do not drive and consequently pose no problem for those concerned with psychiatric diseases and driving. However, there are a number of psychoneurotic individuals whose driving is in no way restricted. Although neurotic symptoms may manifest themselves in many ways, perhaps one of the most serious is the suicidal tendency. Some investigators believe that suicide and homicide by automobile are attempted much more frequently than is generally recognized.

The data available strongly suggest that individuals with psychological or psychiatric problems have a significantly higher automobile accident rate than individuals in the general driving population. Studies of driving records of former mental patients show that they have nearly twice as many accidents as control drivers with the same type of driving exposure. Other studies have revealed that former mental patients may have an accident rate as much as

30 times as great as the normal population. However, these investigations must be considered preliminary; more detailed studies will have to be undertaken before any definite quantitative relationships between mental illness and highway accidents can be established.

The Angry Driver

A variable frequently assumed to be of importance in determining driver performance that has received very little verification is driver mood. Thus, although it is often suggested that a driver may be a greater accident risk when he is angry, there is little evidence to support such a conclusion. There are obvious reasons for this. For example, we might interview drivers involved in an accident and ask them if they were angry (or depressed or anxious) when they had the accident, but we would not be able to put much confidence in their responses. Since mood is a very transitory state, it would also not make much sense to administer "mood tests" to a number of drivers and then follow their driving records over a period of time.

One possible approach is to determine the mood of a person and then immediately test him in a driving simulator. This technique has been utilized by Heimstra, Ellingstad, and DeKock (1967) in a study that attempted to determine the effects of operator mood on performance in a simulated-driving task. A large number of subjects, both male and female, were given a test designed to describe their moods. Scores on a number of "mood factors," such as aggression, anxiety, concentration, and fatigue, were obtained. Immediately following the mood evaluation, subjects were tested in a driving simulator. It was found that subjects who had high scores on the mood factors of aggression, anxiety, and fatigue performed poorly on the driving task, in comparison to the subjects who scored low on these factors.

Although this study suggests a relationship might exist between driving and operator mood, it is probable that the measures used (tracking, vigilance, reaction time, and so on) may not be the aspects of the driving task most affected by mood states. Thus the driver's risk-taking and decision-making processes, which may be more critical in terms of what is normally considered good or bad driver performance, may also be the processes that are most impaired by mood. The angry driver may still be able to perform on the various tasks measured but may tend to take excessive risks while driving. If you think back on your own driving experience, you can probably recall at least one incident when you took an unnecessary risk because you were angry.

part
4

SOME INTERPERSONAL PROBLEMS

Increasingly, psychologists are turning their attention to the problems generated by what might be called interpersonal relationships of the individuals in our society. These interpersonal problems are numerous and complex, but several stand out because of their potential threat to man's well-being and even to the structure of society as we know it. For example, a great deal of concern is being expressed regarding the population explosion and the possible effects that the resulting overcrowding may have on the individual's health and behavior. The research in this area is sparse, for psychologists are just beginning to study overcrowding. Some of their research and conclusions are presented in Chapter 12.

Although aggression and violence have been of interest to behavioral scientists for a number of years, only recently has there been a concentrated effort to understand the underlying causes of this kind of behavior and to develop approaches for its modification. We are far from solving the problem of aggression and violence in our society, but advances are being made; they are discussed in Chapter 13. Similarly, because of the tremendous increase in crime in recent years, more and more psychologists are beginning to study criminal behavior in the hopes of preventing crime and rehabilitating the criminal. Research in this area is considered in Chapter 14.

chapter
12

The Problem
of Overcrowding

We hear a great deal about the approaching worldwide population disaster, with predictions of starving millions, revolutions, war brought about by population pressures, and many other dire threats. Frequently we are told that in the not-too-distant future there will be "standing room only" for man. There are many who consider the threat of overpopulation as serious as, or perhaps even more serious than, the threat of nuclear warfare. The latter may be easier to control. No one appears to have any good idea about what should be done about the population explosion. The agriculture experts seem to agree that the solution is not to be found in increased food production and that we must look to the population experts for the solutions. These experts, however, admit that at present they cannot solve the problem and toss it back to the agriculture specialists.

It would seem that there are many aspects of the population crisis that should be of interest to psychologists; after all, they are interested in behavior. Obviously, overpopulation exists because of a very fundamental form of behavior. Sexual behavior itself has been studied extensively by psychologists and many other researchers, but little of this work is related to birth control. Recently, however, some psychologists have been more interested in areas such as attitudes toward fertility control and abortion, as well as the ethical implications of population policies (Smith, 1972). Nevertheless, an article by Bartz (1970) accusing psychologists of dozing through the population crisis is an

Photo by Sam Sprague.

accurate reflection of the current situation. More recently, Buckhout (1972) pointed out that the "population problem has provoked more talk than research or action . . ." (p. 16).

One of the natural effects of overpopulation is overcrowding. In many instances, people are forced to live in closer and closer proximity to one another. Again, a natural question that psychologists are asked that they do not have a very good answer to is: what happens to human behavior when overcrowding occurs? There is a great deal of anecdotal data concerning the effects of over-crowding (the "tense" city dweller as contrasted with the "relaxed" small towner), but there is only a small amount of empirical data concerning the effects of overcrowding at the human level. However, a considerable body of data dealing with overcrowding in various species of lower animals is avail-able, and some of these studies shed some light on the problem of human overcrowding.

It should be pointed out, however, that psychologists are increasingly interested in overpopulation and that a growing number of research projects are getting underway. Perhaps, when someone attempts to review the literature in this area in a few years, he will have a formidable task on his hands.

POPULATION DENSITY AND ANIMAL RESEARCH

If we have a fixed amount of space and keep increasing the number of animals in it, the population density increases. At some point on the popula-tion-density continuum, crowding occurs. Just when and under what circum-stances a human begins to feel "overcrowded" depends on many factors, most of which are not at all understood. Consequently, in attempting to discuss the effects of overcrowding on behavior, we are forced to rely to a large extent on research that has been conducted with lower animals under controlled conditions. Since we already discussed several animal studies dealing with popu-lation density and behavior in Chapter 2, our consideration of this topic in this chapter will be brief.

Numerous studies with animals have shown that the population size of many mammalian species in self-limiting. That is, after the population reaches a certain density, it tends to stabilize, regardless of the amount of available food. It is thought that this is due to a stress response on the part of the animals and that this stress is developed through social pressures. The physical reactions to the stress result in physiological changes, such as increased adrenal size, reduced gonadal activity, and a consequent reduction in reproduction.

There are also a variety of behavior changes associated with increased population density and overcrowding. Although these findings are of considerable interest, any generalizations from rodents to man must be made with a great deal of caution. Thus, in discussing the speculation about man based on these kinds of studies, Clough (1965) says:

In my view, there are too many basic differences to justify much of this speculation. For one thing, historically, human populations have shown only a steadily increasing growth over thousands of years—or no significant change in the case of some isolated peoples. There has never been the regular, short-term rise and fall seen in the rodent populations. For another difference, although it is probably true that humans crowded into urban centers are plagued by certain mental and physical diseases of civilization, their birth rates are not greatly inhibited (if at all) nor their mortality rates increased. In fact, the birth rates are comparatively high among the people who live with the poorest conditions of nutrition, housing and, perhaps, even emotional and mental hardships [pp. 204–205].

Studies have shown that overcrowding will result in stress in animal populations and that the population will stabilize or be reduced because of this; in addition, other animal studies have implications for those concerned with the effects of overcrowding at the human level. Consider the sometimes striking results when crowding is combined with chemical stress. For example, a number of studies have shown that the toxicity of amphetamine is ten times (or more) greater when mice are placed in small groups following injection than when they are placed in isolation. This amphetamine-toxicity effect, showing that amphetamine is more lethal to mice in aggregate than in isolated conditions, has been found to be modified by several variables, including the prior social experience of the mice used in the study (Mast & Heimstra, 1962).

In a series of studies conducted by the authors, the effects of various social conditions on the response of rats to different kinds of drugs were determined (Heimstra & McDonald, 1962a; Heimstra & McDonald, 1962b; McDonald & Heimstra, 1965). It was found that, in many instances, the behavioral response to a particular drug was modified by the presence of other rats. Somewhat similar findings have been reported at the human level; certain types of drugs will tend to have little or no effect on a subject's mood when the subject is in isolation but will have a considerable effect when the subject is placed in a group.

Along these same lines, Dubos (1965) reports that the effects of crowding produce susceptibility to what he refers to as "crowd diseases." His suggested hypothesis is that crowding affects tissue response in that there is a decrease in the resistance to infection. In one investigation, mice were infected with a standard dose of Trichinella and then were either isolated in individual jars or caged in groups immediately after infection. Fifteen days later, when these mice were sacrificed and examined, it was found that all of the grouped animals had large numbers of worms in their intestines, whereas only three out of 12 of the isolated mice displayed any sign of infection. Although exposure to the infection had been identical, apparently the crowding had increased the ability of the parasite to invade the intestinal wall.

Studies such as these only emphasize the complex nature of the problem that confronts the researcher who is concerned with the effects of crowding on behavior. Not only may the crowding produce direct-behavior effects; it may also produce a number of effects indirectly, in that it may stress the animal (or man), reduce his resistance to diseases, cause him to respond in a different and unpredictable fashion to drugs, and affect him in a variety of other ways.

OVERCROWDING AND HUMAN BEHAVIOR

Not a great deal can be said about the effects of overcrowding on human behavior, simply because there is not a great deal known. With the general lack of systematic data on crowding and human behavior, investigators have been forced to speculate concerning the influences of overcrowding. These speculations may be interesting, but whether or not they hold up remains open to question.

An investigator attempting to study overcrowding is confronted with a number of obstacles. For example, the parameters of overcrowding in humans are only vaguely defined, if at all. Most of us would agree that the ghettos are overcrowded and unpleasant, but what are the optimum population-density conditions for humans? Crowding means different things to different people. For some, living in a densely packed dwelling is the preferred way of living; for others, it is virtually unbearable. For example, the authors, who are accustomed to the prairies of South Dakota and the mountains of Montana, both find that even a few days in a large city is a stressful and unpleasant experience. On the other hand, we frequently have visitors from large urban areas who find the lack of population density in South Dakota and Montana unpleasant. The question, then, about the point on the density dimension at which humans feel crowded is a difficult one to answer. Undoubtedly, a number of factors, such as past experience, personality variables, situational variables, and even nationality, contribute. Thus Hall (1966) describes the customs of various national groups to illustrate the sense of "proper space" between persons and points out that there are wide differences among nationalities in this regard.

Obviously, since there is a paucity of empirical data on overcrowding, there is relatively little theoretical material available. However, Milgram (1970), in an article called "The Experience of Living in Cities," presents an interesting point of view. As Milgram points out, any individual in a large city will see large numbers of different kinds of people in close proximity. He argues that these are not psychological facts; rather, they are external to the individual. What is needed is an idea that links the individual's *experience* to these demographic facts. He suggests that this can be accomplished through the concept of *overload.*

Overcrowding as a System Overload

A system, as we have indicated in previous chapters, involves an *input,* a *transformation* process of some sort, and an *output.* The term *overload* refers to the system's inability to process inputs because there are either too many inputs for the system to handle or because successive inputs arrive so fast that one cannot be processed before the next one arrives. When overload occurs, the system must make some type of adaptation. It must establish priorities or make choices between inputs, sometimes "holding back" on one input while another is processed or perhaps sacrificing an input entirely. Milgram points out that "City life, as we experience it, constitutes a continuous set of encounters with overload, and of resulting adaptations. Overload characteristically deforms daily life on several levels, impinging on role performance, the evolution of social norms, cognitive functioning, and the use of facilities" (p. 1462).

There are a number of specific adaptive responses that city dwellers make in order to reduce the overload brought about by the many inputs to the system. Milgram suggests that one adaptive response to overload is to allow less time for each input. This is reflected in the typically superficial, transitory social relationships that tend to be established in urban environments. Milgram also lists a number of other adaptive responses.

A second adaptive mechanism is disregard of low-priority inputs. Principles of selectivity are formulated such that investment of time and energy are reserved for carefully defined inputs (the urbanite disregards the drunk sick on the street as he purposefully navigates through the crowd). Third, boundaries are redrawn in certain social transactions so that the overloaded system can shift the burden to the other party in the exchange; thus, harried New York bus drivers once made change for customers, but now this responsibility has been shifted to the client, who must have the exact fare ready. Fourth, reception is blocked off prior to entrance into a system; city dwellers increasingly use unlisted telephone numbers to prevent individuals from calling them, and a small but growing number resort to keeping the telephone off the hook to prevent incoming calls. More subtly, a city dweller blocks inputs by assuming an unfriendly countenance, which discourages others from initiating contact [p. 1462].

Milgram goes on to point out that a fifth adaptive response made by city dwellers is to "filter" the intensity of social inputs, which results in only weak or relatively superficial forms of involvement with other individuals. Finally, cities develop specialized institutions, which tend to shield the individuals from inputs that would otherwise overload the system. For example, various agencies are formed (such as welfare agencies) that help handle financial needs of people who would otherwise be out on the street as "an army of mendicants continuously importuning the pedestrian."

Milgram's overload concept, then, at least presents us with a framework in which to consider the effects of population density and human behavior. Certainly, it suggests some lines for future research. For example, a necessary first step will be to study behavior in small towns, where overload is assumed not to be present. Actually, there is some research comparing behavior in large cities and small towns, and this will be mentioned later. In most instances, however, there are no data available on which to base comparisons of behavior in cities and towns. Consider, for example, the question of bystander intervention in crises.

Bystander Intervention. If the adaptation to an overloaded social environment were to be carried to its ultimate, it would result in complete disregard for the needs of anyone who is not perceived as being relevant to one's own personal needs. At this extreme, a person would refuse to become involved in the needs of someone else, even if the other person urgently needed help of some kind. An example of this sort of response was apparent in the Genovese murder in Queens in 1964. Miss Genovese was attacked and stabbed repeatedly over an extended period of time. It was later determined that 38 of her neighbors had heard her screams for help, but none came to her assistance or even called the police until after she was dead. Some argue that this could only happen in a city, with its social overload, and would not take place in a small town. However, this is of course speculation, since there is no evidence of its truth.

Regardless of whether this sort of thing could happen only in a city, it has led to some research in the area of bystander intervention. A series of laboratory studies dealing with variables that influence bystander intervention have been reported by Latané and Darley (1969). These studies involved a number of different experimental conditions. However, in all of the studies a situation was contrived in such a fashion that the experimenters could observe the reactions of "bystanders" (who were actually subjects in the studies) to various kinds of "emergency" situations. Thus, in one study, subjects were placed in a supermarket, where they thought they were going to assist in a survey. They were placed in a room, either alone or in a number of other conditions involving either one or two other people (friends, strangers, and so on, some of whom were "in on" the experiment and others who were not). Shortly after entering the room, the subject heard a loud crash from a room next to his and then moans and cries as though someone had been hurt. The main dependent variable was whether the subject took any action to help the victim and how long it took him to do so. When subjects were alone, 70% of them intervened or went to the assistance of the "injured" person. However, under all the conditions when more than one person was present, the percentage who intervened dropped remarkably. This was also the case in several similar types of studies conducted, which involved fake emergencies and bystander intervention. In general, it appears that the larger the number of bystanders, the less likelihood there is that any one of them will intervene in an emergency.

Lack of involvement, then, as an adaptation procedure to cope with overload, is represented at one extreme by failure of bystanders to intervene in an emergency situation when someone needs help. However, there are other less extreme examples of this type of response. For instance, refusal to do favors is also a lack of involvement, as is the withdrawal of simple courtesies.

"Lending a Hand" to a Stranger.   Milgram (1970) points out that another difference thought to exist between city and town dwellers is their willingness to assist a stranger in some noncrisis situation. He discusses an unpublished study by Altman, Levine, Nedien, and Villena of the City University of New York comparing the behavior of city and town dwellers in offering a type of aid that increased their personal vulnerability and required some trust of strangers.

These investigators individually rang doorbells in the city and in small towns, explained that they had lost the address of a nearby friend, and asked to enter the home and use the telephone. The criterion used in this study was the willingness of householders to allow the investigators, who were strangers to them, to enter their homes to use the phone. The investigators (two males and two females) made 100 requests for entry into homes in the city and

60 in small towns. In all cases, there was a sharp increase in the proportion of entries achieved by the experimenters in the small towns. In fact, although there was some difference between experimenters in their success in entering the homes, they all did at least twice as well in the small towns. In all cases, the females were more successful than the males.

Perhaps one other study will serve to illustrate the kind of research that may differentiate between behavior in big cities and, in this case, a smaller city. Zimbardo (1969) made arrangements for an automobile to be left for 64 hours near the Bronx campus of New York University and another car to be left near the Stanford University campus in Palo Alto, California for the same number of hours. In both cases, the investigators removed the license plates from the vehicles and left the hoods open. The cars were observed continuously for the 64 hours and photographs were taken at various times.

Zimbardo states: "What happened in New York was unbelievable! Within ten minutes the 1959 Oldsmobile received its first auto strippers—a father, mother, and eight-year-old son. The mother appeared to be a lookout, while the son aided the father's search of the trunk, glove compartment, and motor. He handed his father the tools necessary to remove the battery and radiator. Total time of destructive contact: seven mintes" (p. 287). By the end of the first 26 hours the car had been stripped of everything worthwhile and then random destruction began. In less than three days, what remained was a battered, useless hunk of metal. Many of the people involved in the "contacts" were well-dressed, white adults. As Zimbardo further points out: "In startling contrast, the Palo Alto car not only emerged untouched, but when it began to rain, one passerby lowered the hood so that the motor would not get wet" (p. 290).

Obviously, we are dealing with a complex situation, and whether city dwellers differ greatly from town dwellers in many types of behavior remains to be determined. Of course, if this is found to be the case, it is also probable that no single explanatory concept will be adequate to deal with all of the findings. However, overload is an interesting concept that does give a needed framework to an area almost devoid of any theoretical interpretations. In his article, Milgram (1970) gives a number of other examples to support his position and also discusses other aspects of urban experience that are interesting. However, space does not permit a more detailed analysis of Milgram's views, and we will now turn to several other investigations related to overcrowding.

Some Other Studies of Overcrowding

With the growth of large cities, there has been an increased demand for all kinds of services. This has frequently resulted in long, frustrating waiting lines, or queues, at airports, banks, and so forth. You probably spend at least some of each day in a line of one kind or another. Mathematicians and operations researchers have recognized for some time that queues are inefficient and time-consuming and have become concerned with shortening and speeding up lines, but only recently have psychologists become interested in the "psychology" of waiting lines and how this form of aggregation influences behavior.

In a study concerned with the social psychology of waiting lines, Mann and his co-workers (1970) discuss the unique set of social rules and behavioral regularities associated with waiting lines. The investigators studied a number of waiting lines in field experiments in which people were queued for tickets for football games, plays, and so on. However, in some cases, they formed their own queues experimentally in libraries and in other settings. They considered a number of aspects of waiting lines, such as the social structure, queue-jumping, and other kinds of behavior observed in queues. It was found that the queue's social structure is focused on preservation of members' rights to periods of absence without loss of position in line. This is accomplished in several ways, although there is a clearly defined "protocol"; and if the protocol is not followed, an individual might lose his place in line. Although queue-jumpers violate the basic norm of the queue, physical violence is rarely used to eject them. Interestingly enough, the favorite hunting ground of the queue-jumper is not at the front of the queue but somewhere near the tail.

Another interesting form of behavior was noted in some lines. When it was known that there was a limited number of items available (a hundred tickets to a football game, for example), many more people than this will typically line up. In one study, Mann asked every tenth person in a line to estimate how many persons were ahead of him. Up to the point where the tickets were likely to run out, there was a tendency to overestimate the number ahead. In other words, if there were 100 tickets available, people up to about 100 in the line would estimate that there were more people ahead of them than there really were. After the "critical point" (100), the mood of the queuers began to change, and people constantly underestimated the number of persons ahead of them. The investigators called this the wish-fulfillment hypothesis. The researchers also found that the longer the line, the stronger was its drawing power and that a rapidly growing line tended to draw bystanders into the line.

Studies such as this represent only one of many different kinds of unique approaches that will have to be undertaken if we are to understand the psychology of crowding and the many influences crowding has on behavior. Obviously, this is a complex area, and numerous variables interact in determining how a person behaves in a given situation. For example, analysis of the ghetto riots indicated that violence typically erupted on hot days. Thus the question

217

of the behavioral effects of combinations of environmental factors, such as overcrowding and heat, is also of interest. Again, virtually no research has been conducted in this area. However, a study by Griffith and Veitch (1971), which was conducted in a laboratory setting, casts some light on the relationship between "hot and crowded" conditions and behavior. In this study, subjects were tested in an environmental chamber under a normal temperature condition and under a hot condition. They were also tested under different "population densities" (small or large groups of subjects together in the test room). Several behavioral measures were utilized. Under the high temperature and high population density, subjects who were asked to evaluate a "stranger," based on various responses the stranger made on a questionnaire, indicated more dislike for the stranger than subjects in the other conditions. Similarly, the mood of the subjects was found to be negatively affected by the high-temperature/high-population conditions. Generalizations to the "real world" from studies of this type must be made with caution, but the results are certainly in agreement with what common sense has indicated to be the situation in the real world.

Some Additional Comments on Overcrowding

We have suggested previously that a basic consideration for the environmental psychologist who wishes to study overcrowding is the entire question of what constitutes crowding for human populations. For example, the 1970 Census Bureau indicates that there are 694,409 people in the state of Montana. The land area in square miles for Montana is 145,587. This means that, on the average, there are 4.8 persons per square mile for the entire state. Of this total, 370,676 dwell in what the Census Bureau calls urban areas. With less than 700,000 people in the entire state, it would appear somewhat ridiculous to be concerned with overcrowding in the state of Montana. However, the results of rather extensive surveys by environmental scientists show that a large number of people residing in Montana feel the towns and picturesque valleys are becoming overpopulated or crowded. This particular set of values or attitudes of the residents became most apparent to industries attempting to set up their businesses in the state of Montana.

One excellent example is the Big Sky Corporation, headed by television personality Chet Huntley. Among other things, the Big Sky project is developing a recreational center at Lone Mountain, Montana, which will be a year-round resort with skiing in the winter and everything from golf to fishing in the summer. Approximately 50 families live in this area at the present time.

However, by 1980, there may be as many as 10,000 people living in that same area. The original residents are very much concerned about the possible effects of the influx of large numbers of people on the environmental quality of the area. At the same time, the Big Sky Corporation is also very interested in any possible detrimental effects on the natural environment, for their success in this operation will depend on maintaining environmental quality if they are to continue to attract large numbers of people. As a result of the many complex problems facing the Big Sky Corporation and similar developments, the National Science Foundation has funded an extensive research project to deal with the problems involved with environmental control under the pressure of large numbers of people. Extensive interviews have been conducted with the existing residents in an attempt to determine what potential factors are involved in the perceived overpopulation of the area. It is hoped that these environmental psychologists will be able to come up with some kind of definition of values and attitudes people hold toward the concepts of crowding.

Peters and Bentzen (1971), in discussing the problems of human crowding, have come up with a suggestion that certainly warrants serious consideration. Assuming that we are going to have a "crowded future" (and all indications support this assumption), planned adaptation will be necessary. These writers suggest that it is time psychologists and educators begin applying their knowledge to the design of ways to achieve crowded living without pathological consequences. They feel that programs should be started with young children to prepare them for the future. This would involve developing personality characteristics of nonaggression, flexibility, warmth, and friendliness, which would better prepare them for living under high-density conditions. It may very well be that, in the final analysis, approaches such as this will offer the most satisfactory solutions.

POPULATION CONTROL

When we consider the psychological aspects of overcrowding, we are, of course, dealing with one of the effects of overpopulation and not the cause. Although some psychologists have been turning their attention to the overcrowding factors, others have begun to consider the basis for overcrowding—that is, too many births. Obviously, the issue of birth control is a controversial, emotion-laden area that psychologists and other researchers must deal with cautiously because of potential "emotional backlash."

What can psychologists do regarding this issue? In the first place, we require a better understanding of the existing attitudes toward parenthood, motherhood, marriage, sex, contraception, abortion, and so forth. Psychologists can be useful in measuring these attitudes; indeed, some research is currently being undertaken in this area. The reason for acquiring a better understanding of these attitudes is that it will probably be necessary to modify them in order to develop effective birth-control programs. In order to accomplish this, concentrated educational efforts will be required. Not only will the attitudes, beliefs, and behavior have to be modified, but some system must be established to encourage remaining single or childless. Obviously, this will be difficult to do, since remaining single or (if married) childless is contrary to existing attitudes.

Discussing some of the things psychologists should be doing concerning the problem, Bartz (1970) states:

Perhaps they can suggest effective means of providing contingent material reinforcement to promote remaining single or childless, perhaps they can help develop effective national methods of behavioral control or, let us use the word, manipulation. If human behavior has to be "manipulated" in order to halt humanity's rush to oblivion, then we should not shy from the notion. Psychologists have some knowledge of the effects of overcrowding on living organisms and are aware of the importance of environmental variables on behavior. If for some people religious beliefs interfere with effective birth control, then psychologists could provide direct help to them in discarding obsolete human-damaging notions, instead of waiting for foot-dragging theologians to finally get around to it themselves. If the concept of sexual behavior being "for" reproduction is an outmoded holdover from primitive times when more men meant greater tribal strength and were needed for species survival, perhaps psychologists could help bury such "purpose" explanations [pp. 501–502].

There appear to be a number of aspects of the overcrowding problem that psychologists could deal with, but the best interdisciplinary behavioral science skills will be required to attack the problem effectively. Many ethical and social complexities must be taken into consideration, and the task will not be a simple one. However, it is becoming increasingly urgent that a full-scale research program in this area be undertaken and that the results of the program be incorporated into population control programs immediately. Indeed, there may be "standing room only" sooner than we think.

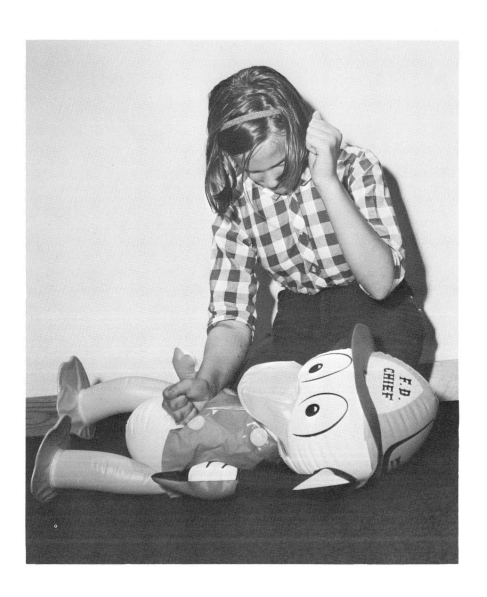

chapter
13

Aggression
and Violence

Many of the issues that are of most concern to people at the present time have, as a common element, violence in one form or another. War, urban riots, crime in the street, student unrest—all are issues that deeply disturb many persons. All involve violence. If a survey was to be conducted among laymen about what they considered the most significant contribution psychologists could make to the problems confronting society, a large proportion would probably answer that psychologists should do something about violence.

Actually, psychologists are attempting to do something about violence. There has been a great deal of research in the area of aggression. Attempts have been made to determine the causes of aggressive behavior and how it can be modified. Much of this research has been conducted in laboratory settings, and, unfortunately, the findings from this research have been difficult to translate into action that will result in an actual reduction in violence. However, more and more research of an applied nature, which is directed at specific questions concerning aggression and violence, is being undertaken. For example, what role does violence depicted on television play in the development of real-world violence? Does urban decay lead to violence? Do masculine ideals, associated with American culture, encourage physical violence? These and many other questions are being considered by psychologists in the hope that the answers may provide some solutions to the problems that aggression and violence present to our society and the world.

SOME VIEWS ON AGGRESSION

Although there are a number of different views about the cause of aggressive behavior in humans, no one particular view satisfies all of the researchers in this field. Basically, the various theories fall into two major categories—the "instinct" theories of aggression and the theories that consider aggression a learned form of behavior. We will not elaborate on either point of view, but we will consider some of the basic concepts associated with both.

The Instinct Theories of Aggression

One theory of aggression that received some interest for a period of time was advanced by Sigmund Freud. The notion was that aggression was brought about by a constantly driving internal force, whose energy must be released in one way or another. Freud felt that the energy was derived from the "death instinct," which everyone supposedly has. Attacks on other individuals, as well as other forms of aggressive behavior, were thought to be outlets for the energy of the death instinct. There is little research support for this particular view of aggression; currently, very few people take it seriously.

A much more popular instinct theory of aggression, one which is taken seriously by many investigators, is that advocated by Lorenz (1966) and other ethologists. These researchers differ somewhat on specifics, but, basically, they all feel that much of human behavior, including aggression, can be traced to man's "animal nature." Aggression is a spontaneously engendered, or instinctive, drive. In other words, aggression is an intractable part of human nature; it is biologically determined. To these individuals, the environment and learning play little, if any, role in the development of aggressive behavior.

Because the instinct theories tend to provide easy formulas for explaining aggression, they have become quite popular. The authors of articles and books dealing with the instinct approach to aggression tend to make use of a great many analogies between these behaviors and those of lower animals. For example, Lorenz feels that man is remarkably similar to the greylag goose in behavior. Most of us would agree that man, on occasion, does behave like a goose, but we would not carry the analogy quite as far as Lorenz and some of the other ethologists do.

There is a belief among many investigators who have been concerned with the study of aggressive behavior for a number of years that the instinct approach is an oversimplification of a complex topic. We suggest that the student who might be interested in a more detailed criticism of the instinct approach read a short and well-written article by Berkowitz (1969) in which he discusses some of the "simple views on aggression."

Learning Theory Approaches to Aggressive Behavior

In 1939, Dollard and co-workers published a monograph entitled *Frustration and Aggression,* which provides what is still a popular theoretical framework for the analysis of social aggression. Later Berkowitz (1962) utilized the concepts employed by Dollard in a much more detailed analysis of aggression. Berkowitz's book, called *Aggression: A Social Psychological Analysis,* is representative of the approach to explaining aggressive behavior that employs learning theory rather than instinct.

Most of the investigators who do not follow the instinct theory of aggression regard aggression as developing in response to some form of *frustration.* Generally speaking, frustration is thought to arise when some ongoing goal-directed activity is interfered with. Thus you want something, you attempt to get it, something interferes with your achieving your goal, and frustration is the result. According to Berkowitz (1962), such interference will usually "produce an emotional reaction, *anger,* the intensity of this emotional state being a function of certain aspects of the frustration" (p. xi). He further points out that anger, in turn, is a condition likely to make aggressive response occur. That is, anger heightens the likelihood of hostile behavior. Aggressive or hostile behavior is defined as behavior aimed at the injury of some object. However, the strength of the aggressive response, the nature of the response, or whether or not a response even occurs when goal-directed behavior is obstructed depends on a number of things. Berkowitz (1962) points out:

> This is not to say that learning experiences do not influence the nature of the reactions to obstructions. Prior experiences can (1) affect the individual's definition of his immediate situation and, thus, determine (a) whether he perceives frustrations, and if so, (b) which of his drives are thwarted; (2) determine whether any other response tendencies are aroused that are stronger than the elicited aggressive responses; and (3) govern the exact nature and intensity of the aggressive and nonaggressive responses [p. 49].

Frustration, then, does not automatically lead to aggressive acts. Learning plays an important role in determining what kind of behavior will be demonstrated in response to some type of frustration. Again, we can think in terms of reinforcement and nonreinforcement. If some form of aggressive behavior has been reinforced when used as a response to frustration, then exposure to the same frustrating situation again will probably result in the same aggressive response. For example, if a child throws a temper tantrum because the achievement of some goal is frustrated (such as obtaining an extra cookie or an ice cream cone) and then is given what he is after (the cookie or cone) in order to stop the tantrum, then that particular aggressive response has been reinforced and may very well occur again. On the other hand, if he is turned upside down and whacked solidly on the rear, the overt aggression may very well not occur the next time the same frustration takes place. (Some theorists would argue, however, that this would serve as an aggressive model for the child to imitate and might lead to aggressive behavior.) The point, of course, is that, with a learning theory view of aggression (unlike the instinct view), something can be done to train children (and adults) to reduce aggressive behavior. In other words, aggressive behavior can be inhibited. Let us consider in more detail the inhibition of aggressive acts.

Inhibition of Aggression.   Dollard and co-workers (1939) state that "the strength of inhibition of any act of aggression varies positively with the amount of punishment anticipated to be a consequence of that act" (p. 33). Stated somewhat differently, the likelihood that an individual will openly attack someone varies inversely with the intensity of his fear of punishment relative to the strength of his aggressive inclination (Berkowitz, 1962, p. 74). All this is, of course, is an idea that most readers are familiar with. In other words, you may have had a very strong inclination to punch someone in the nose, but if that someone was big enough to survive the initial punch and damage you significantly in return, you probably stifled the impulse—unless, of course, your "aggressive inclination" was so strong that you were willing to risk the consequences.

There have been a wide variety of investigations showing that aggression can be inhibited. These studies have made use of a number of animal species as well as human subjects, and some of the variables that are of importance in inhibiting aggression have been isolated. As you might expect, an important variable is *anticipation of punishment* for an aggressive response.

Chasdi and Lawrence (1955) investigated the effects of punishment on aggressive behavior in nursery-school children. These children were divided into an experimental and control group, and both groups played with dolls during several observation sessions. In the second session, children in the experimental group that directed any type of aggressive behavior at the dolls were "punished" by means of a verbal reproof. During the third session the children in this group showed significantly less hostility toward the dolls than the children in the control group who did not receive the verbal punishment.

This inhibition of aggressive behavior by means of punishment holds true with a number of species of animals. For example, the authors were able to demonstrate this in a study in which they used fish as subjects (McDonald, Heimstra, & Damkot, 1968). In this study, a large number of green sunfish were paired, and dominance hierarchies were allowed to be established. The dominant fish repeatedly attacked the submissive fish. After the dominance relationship was firmly established, the dominant fish were removed from the tanks, and each one was paired with a fish that was slightly larger. The larger fish typically attacked the smaller fish and would do so repeatedly. After a period of this exposure, the dominant fish were then returned and re-paired with the previously submissive fish they had once attacked. However, this no longer took place. The aggressive behavior of the previously dominant fish had been inhibited by the "punishment" they received during their exposure to a larger fish.

Another important variable is the social status of the person toward whom the aggression is directed. Thus an employee might feel anger at something that an employer does but, typically, will not direct an overt aggressive response at the employer. Similarly, a private may feel aggressive toward a captain but will probably not show it. However, in situations such as this, it is still the anticipation of punishment that inhibits the aggression. In other words, an individual recognizes that other individuals with certain kinds of status are in a position to administer punishment of some type and, because of this, does not display an aggressive response toward them.

A person may inhibit aggression for reasons other than fear of punishment. He may also inhibit his hostile reactions and tendencies because of his own attitudes or reactions toward such kinds of behavior. If a person feels very strongly, for example, that responding aggressively is wrong, then he will feel guilty if he demonstrates such behavior. Consequently, he inhibits it instead. Certain types of religious groups, such as the Quakers, provide the most obvious examples of this type of inhibition.

There are a number of other situations in which aggression may be inhibited, and various studies could be cited. As we have indicated, a considerable amount of research has been undertaken in this area. However, the important point to remember is that aggressive behavior can, in fact, be inhibited.

Displaced Aggression.   In many cases the aggression that is developed because of frustration is directed at the source of the frustration. Sometimes, however, for various reasons (such as fear of punishment or the social status of the frustrator), the individual cannot direct his aggression at the source of the frustration and may, instead, *displace* it. The aggression may then be directed at an innocent person who is in no way responsible for the frustration. Thus the employee may not direct his aggression at the employer who is the source of his frustration but, rather, at his wife when he gets home after work.

A number of laboratory studies have demonstrated the displacement of aggression, and there is little question that this type response does take place. Displaced aggression may also be the cause of much of the hostility and conflict demonstrated in the real world, but it is more difficult to study in this case. Displaced aggression may operate within certain minority groups, for example, and, by means of riots and other violent acts, may be directed at stores, buildings, individuals, and so on that had little or nothing to do with the frustration. The targets selected by student demonstrators often appear to be victims of displaced aggression. There is some thought that displaced aggression may operate throughout an entire nation at times when there is cause for extreme frustration. Thus it has often been theorized that, as a consequence of their defeat in World War I, the German people were exposed to a variety of frustrations. The resulting aggression was displaced onto Jews and people of other nations that had once conquered Germany. The result, according to this theory, was World War II.

It is probable that our particular society imposes a variety of frustrations on members of many different groups and organizations within it. Quite possibly, the violence that has become associated with our society in recent years may be due to aggression directed either at the source of frustration (or the perceived source of frustration, which may not be the same thing) or due to displaced aggression. An important goal for research is to determine the nature of these frustrations, the probable causes, and methods that can be used to reduce them.

Laboratory Studies of Aggression.   As we have indicated, there is a great deal of laboratory data available on aggression. Although much of this research has been conducted with subhuman animals, there is also a sizable body of literature dealing with aggression in humans. How does a psychologist study human aggression in the laboratory under experimental conditions?

A number of different techniques have been utilized to elicit and measure aggression in the laboratory. On the assumption that frustration leads to aggression, many of the studies have deliberately set up laboratory situations that will lead to frustration on the part of the subjects involved. This can be done in several ways. Sometimes subjects are told that they have failed to perform adequately on a task (even though their performance might have been excellent), sometimes their efforts to accomplish some type of task are deliberately blocked by the experimenter, or sometimes they may be promised a reward that they do not receive. Obviously, there are a variety of ways a subject could be frustrated by various deception techniques practiced by the experimenter.

Aggression can also be elicited from a subject by means of direct attack. This does not imply that the subject is actually physically abused but, rather, is verbally attacked by the experimenter or an accomplice in the experiment. This procedure is often combined with the frustration procedure mentioned above. Thus a subject may be "failed" on a test of some type but may also be derided by the experimenter concerning his lack of intelligence and ability. For example, in one study subjects were given a box to carry across a room. The box was "accidentally" knocked out of their hands by the experimenter, who then berated them for their clumsy behavior and demanded that they pick up the contents of the box, which contained many tiny objects.

Obviously, the laboratory approaches are artificial, and this is a major obstacle in inducing anger and aggression. Typically, a subject comes to a psychology laboratory expecting his behavior to be studied and, in many cases, expecting to be deceived. The behavior he demonstrates may not be very similar to that he would demonstrate in the real-world situation. There are a number of methodological issues involved that are difficult to resolve in designing experiments for studying aggression with these techniques.

Several other approaches are common. For example, the so-called "role-playing approach" accepts the artificiality of the situation, and the subjects know it is unreal. The subjects are asked to act out certain situations that are inherently frustrating and may give rise to aggressive, hostile behavior. Buss (1961) reports a study in which college men and women acted out the following situation:

We are two acquaintances. I have been gossiping about you, talking behind your back. I called you a hothead and a cheat and said that you were completely dishonest and utterly unreliable. You heard about this, and since of course it is not true, you are very angry. Now you are confronting me [p. 43].

Despite the obvious unrealism that may be generated in the role-playing situation, some studies using this technique find surprising amounts of violence and aggression developing. For instance, in a very recent study conducted by

Zimbardo at Stanford,* a simulated jail was established, and students acted the parts of either guards or prisoners. In a very short period of time, the students playing the role of guards began to become extremely aggressive and to subject the prisoners to various forms of harsh discipline. Surprisingly, the students who played the role of the prisoners tended to take the abuse. Although the study had been planned to last for a number of days, it was called off before its completion because of the aggressive behavior demonstrated by some of the "guards." Similar changes in behavior have been observed in another study in which students were asked to play the roles of police and demonstrators. Again, astonishing amounts of aggression developed.

These techniques, then, represent some of the ways in which aggression has been elicited in laboratory settings. One difficulty, however, with laboratory research in aggression is what to use as the dependent variable. In other words, how can we measure aggression?

Measuring aggression. Measuring the frequency and intensity of aggression is one of the serious problems in this area of research. Because the investigator cannot usually allow actual physical aggression to occur in the laboratory, some psychologists have turned to indirect measures of aggression by means of tests, projective techniques, and learning tasks. Others, however, have continued to attempt to measure aggression directly. Let us briefly consider both of these approaches.

One method of indirectly measuring aggression is to ask the subject about his aggressive feelings in a particular situation. This can be done by means of an interview or, more commonly, by means of structured questionnaires of one kind or another. Other types of tests can also be used. Some studies have made use of projective tests, which make use of ambiguous material that, supposedly, permits a person to express freely the basic structure of his personality. It has been found that these types of tests have rather limited use as measures of aggression in the laboratory.

Most researchers would prefer to observe and measure aggression in a direct fashion. One common method is to observe the demonstrated aggression and then rate it on some scale. Sometimes checklists are used, and an observer merely checks the occurrence of a particular aggressive response that he observes on the part of the subject. Several of these techniques have been developed, and reasonably high correlations have been found between independent observers rating the same subjects. A number of studies have been conducted in which the frequency of aggressive responses against some object (such as a doll) was recorded after children had been exposed to movies, television,

*At the time of this writing, the report has not been published.

and frustrating situations that were assumed to have developed an aggressive reaction.

An interesting method of quantifying an aggressive response is by means of the "aggression machine," which was developed by Buss (1961). With this device, the mode of aggression is the delivery of an electric shock. The subject, who is being studied, is instructed to play the role of an experimenter in a learning experiment. The subject is instructed to deliver an electric shock, by means of the "aggression machine," when the person in the learning experiment makes an incorrect response. Actually, this second "subject"—that is, the one who is supposed to learn some task—is an accomplice in the experiment.

The subject, acting as an experimenter, is allowed to "punish" the accomplice for incorrect responses on whatever task has been designed for the study. The subject is allowed to select the level of shock intensity and duration. However, the accomplice actually *does not* receive the shock, although the subject is not aware of this. The dependent variable is the intensity and duration of the shock that the subject selects to "punish" the accomplice.

With this technique it is possible to use a variety of independent variables in order to frustrate the subject and modify the level of aggression demonstrated. Consider, for example, a recent study by Baron (1971), which made use of the "aggression-machine" technique. The researcher was interested in the effects that "innocent bystanders" would have on the subjects' use, or misuse, of the electric shock that they could administer to an accomplice. Manipulation of anger arousal was accomplished by means of asking subjects to give a written solution to a pressing social problem. Under one condition (nonangry) the evaluation of their responses was quite favorable, whereas in another condition (angry) the evaluation was insulting and unfavorable.

Following the induction of low or high levels of anger among subjects, they were introduced to the "aggression machine" and given instructions about the "learning" experiment they were taking part in and how they were to administer electric shock to the learner (actually an accomplice, of course). Subjects were tested under several conditions. In one case, they took part without exposure to any audience; under other conditions, subjects were viewed by two observers who, supposedly, were doing similar research. In one condition, the observers came early in the experiment, whereas in another condition, they came late. Thus there were three conditions under which angry and nonangry subjects were tested—with no audience, with an early audience, and with a late audience.

Results showed that the subjects in the angry group administered longer shocks to the accomplice than did the subjects in the nonangry group. However, it was also found that the aggression was influenced by the presence of an audience. The early audience seemed to have the most effect in that the angry subjects under this condition administered shorter shocks than angry subjects in the other conditions.

We could cite many more investigations that support the frustration-aggression hypothesis. However, in concluding our discussion on frustration and aggression, it should be pointed out that there are other responses to frustration besides aggression. For instance, a person sometimes responds to frustration with *apathy*—that is, extreme indifference to his surroundings and a general listlessness. Sometimes frustration is coped with by means of *rationalization*. Thus you might fail an examination, be frustrated, and then become aggressive toward the instructor or toward your roommate (displaced aggression). However, you might also rationalize and convince yourself that the examination was grossly unfair and that failure was no fault of your own. There are a number of other possible responses that can be made to frustration. However, our interest in this chapter is the response that we have discussed—aggression and hostility.

Another Learning Theory Approach to Aggression. Some investigators believe that physically aggressive behavior can be learned just like any other response. They feel that aggressive responses are learned largely through imitation or through direct rewarding of aggressive behavior. According to these theorists, preceding frustration is not required.

There is considerable evidence that this theory has merit. For example, experimental studies have demonstrated repeatedly that children who are exposed to adult "models" on television or in movies will later imitate aggressive behavior demonstrated by these models. Other investigations in the field have shown that most people, from school age through adulthood, learn from their peers and will share the group's expected standards of behavior and beliefs. If these expected standards of behavior include aggression and violence, this behavior will be demonstrated. Wolfgang and Ferracuti (1967) argue that violence is an expected and accepted mode of problem solving in many groups and that, in these groups, aggression and violence are highly valued forms of behavior.

There is also evidence that child-rearing practices may be very important in determining whether a child develops aggressive tendencies. For example, it appears that physically aggressive-punitive parents tend to have physically aggressive children. The reason for this is argued, but the evidence suggests that the child learns aggressive behavior from the parents.

Although the frustration-aggression hypothesis still seems to be most popular among aggression researchers, it should be kept in mind that aggression and violence represent complex forms of behavior; no single explanation is sufficient to account for all of the phenomena of violence.

VIOLENCE

Whether one wishes to accept the frustration-aggression hypothesis or not, the fact remains that some motivation instigates a tendency toward aggression. Whether this tendency results in actual aggressive behavior and, if it does, the nature and type of aggression demonstrated will depend on a number of factors. All too often, however, the aggressive response results in some form of violence.

What is violence? There have been various definitions, but all imply characteristics such as physical force, intense emotional excitement, or unjust coercion. Garver (1968) suggests that violence can be examined along four dimensions: personal or institutional, overt or covert. *Overt personal violence* would include physical assault, rape, mugging, and so forth, whereas *overt institutional violence* includes riots and wars. *Covert personal violence* involves threat rather than physical violence; *covert institutionalized violence* includes such phenomena as ghettos and institutionalized racism.

In discussing overt personal and institutionalized violence, Ilfeld (1969) adds the dimensions of intention and intensity. Thus, besides being an overt harmful act, violence must be intentional. The individual must recognize and accept his behavior. Intensity of the response is also important. For example, shoving someone may be a violent act, but it is certainly not as violent as choking or stabbing the person. Ilfeld, then, considers violence "intense, willful physical harm committed by an individual or a group against himself or another individual or group" (p. 676). He further distinguishes, however, between "good" and "bad" violence: the former is the kind approved by society or justified on moral grounds (such as self-defense with a weapon); "bad" violence is that which is outlawed by society.

More and more psychologists are becoming concerned with the phenomenon of violence. Regardless of their theoretical inclinations, these investigators recognize that violence is one of the major problems confronting our society, and they hope to be able, in some fashion, to help reduce violence. However, it quickly becomes apparent that it is one thing to specify the variables in a laboratory study dealing with aggression and quite another thing to attempt to identify the complex set of interacting factors that may instigate aggression and violence in the real world. Unfortunately, there is a paucity of empirical data in this area, and much of the writing on this topic has been speculative in nature.

Causes of Violence

Although we have stressed the learned aspects of aggression and violence in the preceding pages, we do not mean to imply that biological factors are of no importance. Thus some investigators see factors associated with central nervous system damage, chromosomal aberrations, and male sex hormones as predisposing an individual toward violence. However, although these biological factors may increase the person's tendency toward violence, his past experience and the particular situation he encounters are further determinants of whether his response is or is not violent.

Violence as a Learned Response.   We have stressed that the past experience of an individual is an important factor in determining whether or not he engages in violent behavior and the circumstances under which this kind of behavior will occur. The key question, then, is what kinds of past experience are of particular importance in the development of learned aggressive responses? Particular attention has been paid to child-rearing practices and to an individual's membership in certain groups or subcultures that advocate or highly value violence.

Wolfgang (1970), in discussing psychology and the reduction of violence, points out that the use of physical force to restrain and punish children is permitted and even encouraged in most cultures. He goes on to say:

> The application of force is a form of violence and may be used consciously to discipline the child to the limits of permitted behavior, to reduce the domestic noise level, to express parental disapproval, and even unconsciously as a displacement for aggression actually meant for other targets. This model of parent-child interaction is a universal feature of all human societies. The model is one that the child himself comes to ingest; that is, that superior force is power permitting manipulation of others and can be a functional tool for securing a superordinate position over others, for obtaining desires and ends [p. 311].

Thus the child imitates or models the aggressive behavior of the adult and, in this fashion, learns to be aggressive and violent. This type of behavior has been demonstrated repeatedly in laboratory studies. For example, consider the experiments by Bandura and Walters (1963). In these studies, the general experimental design called for dividing nursery-school children into three groups. One group was exposed to adult models who exhibited physical and

234

verbal aggression toward a large inflated plastic doll. The second group of children was exposed to adults who displayed inhibited and nonaggressive behavior, totally ignoring the doll. The third group of children was not exposed to adult models. Immediately after the exposure to the adults, the children were placed in the same play setting. Children who had observed the aggressive group of adult models were very aggressive themselves toward the plastic doll and imitated quite precisely the adult behavior. This kind of behavior rarely occurred in either the control group or the group of children that had observed the nonaggressive adults.

Experiments such as this, as well as other types of studies dealing with modeling behavior and imitation, raise the question about the role that violence portrayed on television and in movies may play. This is still a controversial issue. Early in 1972, a comprehensive report by the U.S. Surgeon General's Office (*Television and Growing Up: The Impact of Televised Violence*) was published, which suggested a possible link between TV violence and aggression. The primary conclusion of the report was that "the data, while not wholly consistent or conclusive, do indicate that a modest relationship exists between the viewing of violence and aggressive behavior." This conclusion was based on a comprehensive survey of the research that has been conducted in this field.

It was pointed out earlier in this chapter that a person's attitudes and feelings about violence can inhibit aggression and violence. If engaging in such behavior arouses feelings of guilt, the person is not likely to become aggressive. However, in many groups and subcultures in our society, the use of violence is viewed as an acceptable form of conduct, and the users do not have to deal with feelings of guilt. Rather, through membership in these particular groups and subcultures, the individual learns to respond to certain situations with aggressive and violent behavior, since this kind of behavior is the expected behavior of the group. As Wolfgang and Ferracuti (1967) point out, violence as a means of coping with one's problems and as a demonstration of masculinity and toughness is not only an acceptable but a highly valued form of behavior in various groups. Through learning, violence is incorporated as a standard response for many situations.

Situational Causes of Violence.   What situational factors contribute to violence? The tendency to respond violently may be learned through childhood experiences in the family and, later, through membership in groups that support violence. However, situational variables are still critical in determining whether violence takes place and the form in which it occurs. Ilfeld (1969) points out:

Of all the proposed causes of violence, situational factors are the most hotly debated, not because they play a questionable role in violence, but because they are more apparent and modifiable. In contrast to man's inherent nature or his social learning, situational factors are most visible as contributors to violence and are more easily changed [p. 680].

The situational causes of violence are complex and numerous, but most situations that elicit violence are associated with frustration of one kind or another. Earlier, we discussed this aspect in some detail. Needless to say, everyone encounters numerous everyday situations that are frustrating. However, of particular concern at present are the overwhelming frustrations encountered by large numbers of our society in the form of institutionalized racism, the frustrations encountered by students, and the frustrations generated by other social stresses. Spiegel (1968) suggests that a major source of frustration may be the basic incompatibility between our democratic ideals and the authoritarian practices that prevent large numbers from participating in our democracy. Obviously, we could go on and list a number of other factors. It is not our intent, however, to compile a list of the possible ills of society. Rather, the point is that there are many sources of frustration, which, in combination with other factors, may result in violence.

As Ilfeld points out, there are a number of other important situational contributors besides frustration. A precipitating event, such as a personal threat or news coverage of violent events, can result in violence. A situation with a low expectancy of punishment may also contribute to violence, as will situations with ready availability of weapons, alcohol, and drugs, group contagion, boredom, and strong obedience to one's leaders. There are other "instigating" stimuli, which will increase the probability that violence will occur in a particular situation. What makes the typical violent behavior difficult to analyze, however, is that very often frustration, as well as one or more of the situational variables listed, is present and will contribute to the violent act. The important point to keep in mind when thinking about the causal factors associated with violence is that we are dealing with an extremely complex form of behavior with multiple causes and that some of the simple explanations (and "cures") that have been presented in the past are not adequate.

Can Violence Be Reduced?

If the psychologists interested in the areas of aggression and violence were polled about whether or not psychological principles could be used to reduce violence, most would probably agree that this would be possible. There would be considerable disagreement, however, regarding the most suitable approaches to be used, and the disagreement would stem largely from the particular psychologist's view of the cause of aggression and violence.

For example, suppose the psychologist follows the views of Freud or Lorenz (discussed early in this chapter) and feels that aggression is a drive whose expression is spontaneous and inevitable? Psychologists with this theoretical learning argue that aggression will be expressed, and the only safe way of averting violence is to divert the aggressive drive into safe channels. Numerous suggestions have been made about how this can be accomplished. For example, sport activities of one kind or another may serve as diversions for the aggressive drive. Nonviolent participation in politics or a wide range of activities, such as clubs, unions, and community projects, have been suggested. Thus "militant enthusiasm" toward almost any endeavor may serve as a means of harnessing the aggressive drive. Possibly, then, one way of reducing violence would be to make more of these "substitute" activities available to the particular groups or subcultures in which violence is the normal expression of the aggressive drive.

The psychologist who feels that aggressive behavior is largely a socially learned form of behavior would be likely to suggest somewhat different approaches to the reduction of violence. Theoretically, at least, since violence is considered to be a learned response, learning principles should be applicable for reducing or extinguishing this response. For example, a learned response can be inhibited through aversive stimulation or through the strengthening of an incompatible response. Thus, by punishing the violent response with some form of aversive stimulation, the behavior should be reduced. The incompatible-response concept is quite simple in theory but more difficult in actual life. It involves finding a response that is incompatible with the violent response and then strengthening the occurrence of the incompatible response through systematic reinforcement. The slogan "Make Love—Not War" represents an example of incompatible responses.

Since much of the social learning that develops the aggressive and violent forms of behavior takes place through child-rearing practices or as a result of membership in various groups and organizations, these appear to be optimal targets for modification. Obviously, however, one does not easily modify the child-rearing practices of a society, and whether this can be accomplished remains to be seen. The modification of subcultures and groups in which violence is highly valued will also be difficult. Thus Wolfgang and Ferracuti (1967) suggest that the violent subcultures and groups will have to be disrupted and dispersed. They feel that members of groups who share a commitment to violence will have to be dispersed within the larger culture, which does not share these values. It is also apparent that this would not be simple and might create more problems than it solved.

Finally, the psychologist who believes that frustration and other situational variables are most critical in contributing to violence would suggest other methods of reducing violence. First, those frustrations that are most important and significant to various individuals and groups who tend to be violent can be identified and attempts made at their reduction. This method, of course, has wide implications and would include college students, minority groups, many other groups, and all of the numerous situations that lead to frustration. Identifying these situations is one thing; doing something effective about reducing the frustrations is something else. For example, we already know many of the causes of frustration for minority groups, but we have not been very successful in reducing these frustrations.

Modifying any other situational variable that is conducive to violence might reduce violence. For example, the availability of weapons adds to the magnitude of violence and, possibly, to whether or not it will occur. Making weapons more difficult to obtain might be effective in reducing violence. Similarly, increasing expectancy of punishment might, in some cases, have an effect. Personal threats, arrests, shootings, and news-media coverage of violent events are precipitating factors; modified or eliminated, they may divert impending violence. Obedience to some leader figure is also a situational variable that is important, as well as the presence of others with the same aggressive tendency. We like to think that other solutions should be available and used, but a method that is often effective in avoiding violence is dispersing the group and arresting the leaders.

CONCLUSION

In our brief examination of the causes of violence and the possibility of reduction, it should be apparent that there is no quick or easy solution to the problem of violence. In some instances, counterviolence may be effective and the only answer, but this does not get at the roots of the problem. Thus it will be necessary to change some basic attitudes toward child rearing and to modify various subcultures that advocate violence. It will also be necessary to change many situations that are now frustrating or contribute to violence in other ways. However, as Ilfeld (1969) points out:

> While the problem at times seems overwhelming, at least we know that violence need not be inevitable and that prevention is possible. Hope is provided by knowing that not all peoples are equally violent, violent behaviors which are learned can be unlearned, frustrations can be alleviated, weapons can be limited, and men can find peaceful alternatives for resolving conflicts [p. 688].

Crime

Many crimes involve acts of aggression and violence and, as such, could have been discussed in the previous chapter. Muggings, murder, assault, rape, and various forms of juvenile delinquency are obvious forms of violence. However, when we look at crime statistics, we see that violent crimes are much less frequent than theft and other crimes against property. Although crimes involving physical violence make up an impressive total, most major crimes do not involve violence. Many would argue that these crimes are also a form of aggression and that the criminal does injure the property owner or an insurance company, but it is a different, indirect form of aggression.

However, much of the thinking concerning the causes and possible methods of reducing crime parallels that discussed in the previous chapter concerning the causes and reduction of violence. For instance, many researchers feel that a variety of factors, including social learning and the response to frustration or other situational variables, contribute to the development of criminal tendencies. It has also been shown that, for most imprisoned men, the criminal behavior is only part of a larger pattern of maladjustment. For example, a significant number of prison inmates are borderline schizophrenics, psychoneurotics, alcoholics, and so forth. Thus the treatment and prevention of much criminal behavior may have to involve the same procedures that apply to abnormal behavior in general—procedures such as hospitalization, therapy, and correction of undesirable social conditions.

Photo by Sam Sprague.

There are many facets to the crime problem, and psychologists have been involved in a variety of different ways with this problem. They can make possibly the most important contribution by determining the underlying causes of criminal behavior and how this behavior can be modified. A number of applied psychologists are active in this kind of research. Some of these researchers study the personality characteristics of criminals, others are concerned with the environmental variables that may be important in determining criminal behavior, and still others are attempting to treat offenders and prevent further criminal behavior. Some idea about the diverse interests of psychologists working in this field can be obtained from the types of research reports published. For instance, in the *Psychological Abstracts*, several hundred studies are annually listed under the major headings of Crime and Criminals, Juvenile Delinquency, Law, and Prisons. A random sampling of the investigations reported will show studies dealing with the self-concept of criminals, chromosomal abnormalities in criminals, crime causation, criminal behavior, etiology of delinquency, determinants of homicidal acts, employee theft prediction, interrogation tactics, penal institutions, prison riots, probation and success in later life, and shoplifting. These represent only a few of the topics listed. Obviously, psychologists study a wide range of criminal behavior. In this chapter we will be concerned with some of the research in this area and some of the current thinking about the problem of crime and criminals.

THE MAGNITUDE OF THE PROBLEM

According to the Federal Bureau of Investigation statistics (Hoover, 1971), there were 5,568,200 reported crimes committed in the United States in 1970. Of these crimes, 731,400 were classified as violent and 4,836,800 as property crimes. The former refer to murder, forcible rape, robbery, and aggravated assault, whereas the latter are limited to burglary, larceny ($50 and over), and auto theft. A more detailed breakdown of crime rates by region for 1970 is shown in Table 14-1.

Although these statistics are in themselves impressive, what is particularly disturbing is the fact that crime has shown a steady increase over recent years. This is readily apparent from Figure 14-1, which shows the percentage of change in crime from 1960 to 1970. It can be seen from this figure that crime is up 176%; the crime rate is up 144%. On this figure, the crime rate refers to the number of offenses per 100,000 population, whereas "crime" indicates the actual number of criminal offenses committed.

It should be pointed out that statistics of this type tell only part of the story. Actually, there is no way of determining the total number of crimes committed. Many criminal acts occur that are not reported to official sources. Sometimes they are not reported because they are not discovered. Often they are not reported because the parties involved wish to avoid publicity. It is estimated, for example, that a significant number of forcible rapes go unreported to the authorities each year. Thus the FBI statistics are based on offenses that are known to the police, and these offenses represent only part of the total number that take place.

The FBI gathers considerable data regarding each type of crime. For example, consider murder in the United States in 1970. The data collected by the FBI reveals that males outnumbered females as victims of murder by more than three to one. Forty-four of every 100 victims were white and 55 were Negro, with the remaining 1% distributed among all other races. It was determined that six of every ten victims were between 20 and 45 years of age, with the largest number (30%) falling in the 20-to-29 age group.

The types of weapons used in committing the murders are shown in Figure 14-2. Firearms are the predominant weapon, with handguns accounting for by far the largest percentage; rifles and shotguns are a relatively small percentage. It is interesting to note how the type of weapon used will vary according to the region of the country. For example, Table 14-2 shows that, in the case of firearms, there is considerable difference in their use in Northeastern states and Southern states. Similarly, a knife or other cutting object is about twice

TABLE 14-1. Crime rates by regions of the country in 1970 (rate per 100,000 inhabitants). From J. E. Hoover, *Crime in the United States* (Washington, D. C., Federal Bureau of Investigation, United States Department of Justice, 1971).

Crime index offenses	North-eastern states	North central states	Southern states	Western states
Total	2,845.9	2,398.7	2,400.2	3,761.4
Violent	385.3	323.2	362.2	380.0
Property	2,460.6	2,075.5	2,038.0	3,381.3
Murder	5.8	6.5	11.2	6.4
Forcible rape	12.7	17.0	18.0	28.9
Robbery	232.8	172.7	130.2	157.5
Aggravated assault	134.0	127.0	202.7	187.3
Burglary	1,065.5	896.6	960.7	1,541.8
Larceny $50 and over	823.2	759.7	750.2	1,269.3
Auto theft	571.9	419.3	327.1	570.2

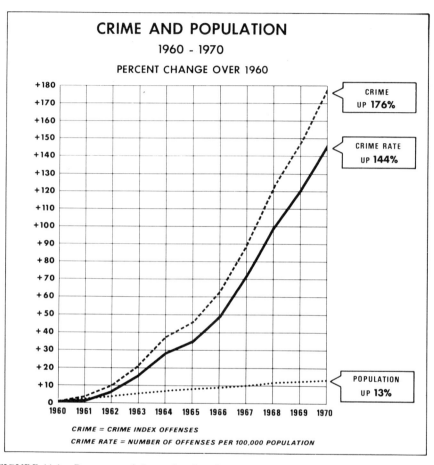

FIGURE 14-1. Percentage of change in crime from 1960 to 1970. During this period, the population was up only 13%, whereas crime was up 176%. From J. E. Hoover, *Crime in the United States* (Washington, D. C., Federal Bureau of Investigation, United States Department of Justice, 1971).

as likely to be used in a Northeastern state as in a Southern or North Central state.

Along with the statistics dealing with the incidence and nature of the crimes committed, the FBI also collects data concerning the characteristics of the persons who are arrested for these crimes. Thus, in 1970, persons under 15 years of age made up 9% of the total police arrests; under 18, 25%; under 21, 39%; and under 25, 52%. When only the serious crimes are considered,

TABLE 14-2. The types of weapons used for murders in different regions of the United States (percent distribution). From J. E. Hoover, *Crime in the United States* (Washington, D. C., Federal Bureau of Investigation, United States Department of Justice, 1971).

Region	Total all weapons used	Firearms	Knife or other cutting instrument	Other weapon; club, poison, etc.	Personal weapons
Northeastern States	100.0	49.9	28.3	9.9	11.9
North Central States	100.0	70.6	15.6	5.9	7.9
Southern States	100.0	73.1	16.3	5.6	5.0
Western States	100.0	56.6	18.4	13.4	11.6
Total	100.0	65.4	18.9	7.6	8.1

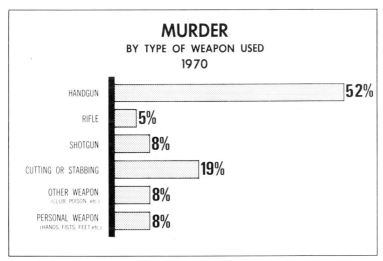

FIGURE 14-2. The types of weapons used to commit murder. It is apparent that the handgun is by far the most popular type of weapon. From J. E. Hoover, *Crime in the United States* (Washington, D. C., Federal Bureau of Investigation, United States Department of Justice, 1971).

20% of all arrests in 1970 were for persons under the age of 15 and almost one-half were under 18 years of age (Hoover, 1971).

In 1970, male arrests outnumbered female arrests by six to one. Thus only 10% of the arrests for violent crimes in 1970 involved females. However, female arrests were higher for larceny, and 19% of all property-crime arrests were females. Of some interest is the fact that, when all serious crimes are considered as a group during the period 1960–1970, arrests of males were up 73%, and the female arrests increased 202%.

CAUSES OF CRIMINALITY

Obviously, statistics such as those gathered by the FBI concerning crime and criminals are of value in defining the problem and revealing something about the characteristics of the offenders. However, there is much that statistics such as these do not tell us. They do not reveal, for example, the various personal and environmental factors that cause an individual to break a law and become a "statistic." It is this sort of factor that has been of particular interest to psychologists. Although it is still not possible to draw "psychological profiles" of various types of criminals, we do have a considerable amount of information available dealing with personal characteristics of criminals as well as environmental factors, which are important in developing this kind of behavior.

At the outset, a question must be raised about the definition of criminal behavior. As we have indicated, the FBI statistics are based on offenses that are known to the police—that is, a recorded incident in which a rule of regulation (a law) has been broken. Actually, if we define criminal behavior as breaking a law, we are all criminals. For example, a number of years ago (Wilson, 1951) it was pointed out that the average citizen would unwittingly break enough laws in a year to spend over a thousand years in prison and to accumulate fines of several millions of dollars. The point is that too much research has equated an arrest or conviction with criminal behavior. Perhaps, by definition, this is correct, but are we really studying a criminal when we are dealing with someone who breaks a law unintentionally? Some might question whether we are actually dealing with criminal behavior when we have an offender who may break a law repeatedly because he is unable to change an old established mode of response that is no longer legally permissible.

Lindner (1955) has suggested that criminals are those persons who, due to internal stress and pathological distortion, engage in unlawful behavior so they can satisfy their own needs or motivations. Ellingston (1948) views crime as whatever the dominant elements of a society view as being dangerous to the security and solidarity of the society at a particular time. Everyone learns what is and what is not "crime" for his society. There are other definitions of criminal behavior. Psychologists recognize the problem of definition, but most investigators still equate criminal behavior with conviction or arrest.

246

There are other problems encountered by investigators concerned with the personal and environmental origins of criminal behavior. There are many different kinds of lawbreakers, and different causal factors may be associated with each type. Thus one might expect that the personal and situational variables associated with murder would be quite different from those in cases of car theft, which, in turn, would differ from those involved in embezzlement. Consequently, one would not expect to find a cluster of personality variables or environmental variables associated with all criminals. In other words, there is no such thing as a "criminal type," although this was once a popular view. However, certain kinds of personal and environmental factors have been found to be related to criminal behavior, and it is these that we will be concerned with next.

Physical Characteristics

Not too many years ago, it was a commonly held belief that criminals had particular physiological or anthropometrical characteristics. At one time, considerable effort was expended in an attempt to list the physical characteristics of criminals (long lower jaw, flattened nose, symmetrical cranium, and so on). There is little in the way of scientific evidence, however, to support the view that criminals are physically any different than noncriminals, at least in terms of gross observable characteristics.

Recently, though, there has been considerable interest regarding a segment of the population whose genetic makeup includes a special form of one chromosome, known in genetic "shorthand" as the XYY chromosome. Some investigators believe that the possession of this special genetic feature may be connected with the tendencies toward violent crime. This hypothesis is based on the fact that there appears to be a disproportionate presence of this chromosomal feature in certain selected criminal and deviant populations as compared with its presence in nondeviant populations. However, it has been pointed out (Mulvihill, Tumin, & Curtis, 1969) that there is an absence of the required kind of information about this chromosome abnormality and violent behavior. Thus we do not know the true incidence of the abnormality in the population at large, the true incidence of the abnormality in so-called deviant populations, or whether these deviant populations are uniformly violent or assaultive. At present, the status of the research in this area is such that one cannot say with certainty that this genetic feature is connected with violence. However, the evidence does appear to implicate the XYY condition as being associated at least with a heightened tendency toward aggressive, antisocial behavior.

Currently, there is still a great deal of interest in this area, and ongoing research may provide a definitive answer in the near future.

Psychological Factors

In attempting to explain the cause of criminal behavior, the explanation can involve either, or both, of two factors: (1) factors inside the person, such as biological or psychological mechanisms, processes, or drives; (2) something outside of the person, such as social forces, values, or environmental factors that shape the individual's life. We have seen that there is little evidence for biological factors as an explanation for criminal behavior. What about psychological factors?

Although psychological factors are undoubtedly important in determining whether a person engages in criminal behavior, we must again emphasize that it is an interaction of these factors and environmental factors that result in the criminal act. We cannot say what weight is to be given to each of these factors in every case, but both are important.

Much of the work conducted in the area of psychological factors in crime has been aimed at determining whether those who have been convicted of crimes differ in personality characteristics from those who have not been convicted. In other words, are there personality factors that differentiate criminals or juvenile delinquents from others of comparable age, background, and so on who do not commit a crime?

A number of studies have found that adult and juvenile offenders differ from control groups on several personality characteristics. For example, research using the MMPI (Minnesota Multiphasic Personality Inventory) has shown that inmates (male prisoners) of a penal institution, compared to nonprisoners, scored in the direction of inadequacy on MMPI personality scales designed to measure prejudice, responsibility, dominance, dependency, and ego strength (Panton, 1959). In another study with the MMPI, a large number of ninth grade students were tested; two and four years later, their records were checked to see if they had been in trouble. It was found that certain items on the MMPI differentiated between the youngsters who did get into trouble and those who did not. The investigators (Hathaway & Monachesi, 1957) concluded that the members of the delinquent group were characterized by a basic resentment of restrictions, a love of danger, and a "youthful exuberance." There are many other similar studies comparing offenders and nonoffenders, and, often, differences in some personality characteristics are found. Sometimes, however, differences are not found. For example, Hurley and Monahan (1969) attempted a psychiatric, sociological, and psychological assessment of 50 male

248

arsonists and found no differences from controls on personality types. The arsonists tended to be typical in intelligence, measured personality, and anxiety. Thus it is probable that whether or not differences are found between offenders and nonoffenders on personality variables will depend a great deal on the particular criminal act involved, as well as the personality measures that are utilized.

Frequently, investigations of psychological factors in crime have made use of two or more groups of offenders, usually grouped on the basis of the type of offense committed or on some other variables, and attempted to determine if psychological differences existed between individuals in these groups. For instance, Davis and Brehm (1971) studied 91 male inmates (16 to 22 years old) of a juvenile unit of a prison. These prisoners were divided into three groups: one group had never had any experience with drugs, a second group had experience with hard drugs but was under sentence for crimes ranging from murder to breaking and entering, and a third group of inmates was under sentence for violation of state narcotic or drug laws. It was found that these groups of prisoners differed on a number of social, attitudinal, motivational, and MMPI factors. Results indicated that the factors of insecurity and dissatisfaction with the self, combined with little fear, characterize the drug user in contrast to the nonuser.

A number of other investigations dealing with personality characteristics of lawbreakers could be cited, but research suggests there are some characteristics that delinquents and criminals are more likely to possess than nonoffenders. Berkowitz (1962) has summarized these characteristics. It would appear that many delinquents and criminals:

1. Are unable to postpone their pleasures for too long.
2. Are easily frustrated and show strong emotional reactions.
3. Feel apart from others and may view other people with hostility and resentment.
4. Are aggressive.
5. Have inadequate moral standards, so that criminal behavior does not develop guilt feelings.
6. Hold attitudes that justify antisocial behavior.

Similarly, Coleman (1964) points out that "The great majority of persistent delinquents appear to share the traits which are typical of the antisocial personality. They are impulsive, defiant, resentful, guiltfree, incapable of establishing and maintaining close interpersonal ties, and unable to profit from their experiences in a constructive way" (p. 371).

In the previous chapter it was pointed out that one factor inhibiting aggression and violence is the feeling of guilt about such action. Typically, the studies dealing with criminals have shown that they do not feel guilty about their acts and, in fact, may view themselves as "good guys." For example, a study by Cudrin (1970) concerned the self-concepts of prison inmates. A number of inmates were asked to respond to interview questions that were designed to reveal how they viewed themselves as a criminal, as a bad person, bad company, and as an influence on children. The results showed that these men, who had continuously and severely violated laws, had no lasting sense of badness or evil about themselves. They admitted having violated the law, but they rejected the idea that they belonged to that class of people generally thought of as bad. They tenaciously held on to a favorable self-concept.

Under the heading of psychological factors that contribute to criminal behavior, one must also consider mental disorders that may be associated with illegal acts. Coleman (1964) estimates that in a small percentage of cases (about 3%), delinquent behavior is associated with a psychotic reaction and that in a large number of cases (10 to 15%), delinquent behavior appears to be directly associated with neurotic disorders. In a systematic investigation of 175 murderers, Guttmacher (1960) found that 53 were psychotic and 17 were seriously abnormal. On the other hand, in a staff report to the Commission on the Causes and Prevention of Violence (Mulvihill et al., 1969), it is pointed out that most studies indicate the mentally ill are no more likely than the general population to be involved in such violent crimes as assault, rape, or murder.

In summary, the research to date suggests that, although there are some personality characteristics that appear to be more common among criminals and juvenile delinquents than among the general population, the personality of the offender is not really a great deal different from that of the nonoffender. Certainly it does not differ enough so that, on the basis of personality tests, we can predict with a high degree of certainty that one person will probably engage in criminal behavior and another will not. However, if we also knew a great deal about the environment in which a person was raised and how he responded to situational variables, this information would increase our accuracy of prediction. We will now consider some of the environmental variables that are of importance in determining criminal and delinquent behavior.

Environmental Factors

In the previous chapter we discussed the various environmental factors that may be important in determining whether aggression and violence will occur. These same factors are important in considering criminal behavior. Thus we can think in terms of frustrations that lead to an emotional arousal predisposing the person to aggressive behavior. If the situational variables conducive to violence are present and the inhibitory factors are not present, then a violent act may occur. This may very likely be a criminal act for which the individual is arrested, prosecuted, and possibly convicted. We will not review the frustration-aggression hypothesis and its implications for criminal behavior, but the reader should keep in mind that this particular theory provides a framework within which a great deal of criminal behavior can be explained.

Similarly, much of what has previously been said about social learning of violence, the instigation of violence through membership in groups and subcultures that advocate this kind of behavior, and situational variables that contribute to violence also applies to many forms of criminal behavior.

For example, a great deal of social learning takes place in the home, and there is ample evidence to support the argument that delinquent behavior is reinforced and maintained within the family. Thus many delinquents come from homes in which parents and siblings are criminals or delinquents. Glueck and Glueck (1950) reported that 84% of the delinquents in the reformatories of a state came from homes in which there were criminals. Even if there are not any criminals in the home, there appear to be a number of other variables associated with the home environment that are important in determining whether a youngster becomes a delinquent. There is evidence that such factors as inconsistent discipline, parental rejection, and broken homes will increase the likelihood of delinquency. Also, a number of studies have shown that the fathers of delinquent boys frequently show sociopathic traits, such as alcoholism, brutality, antisocial attitudes, and so forth. There seems to be little question, then, that the home environment is important in forming this type of individual.

Other delinquents, however, appear to be more strongly influenced by their peer groups. Since their friends and associates consider violence and other criminal behavior proper and correct, they will kill, rob, steal, and commit other crimes in order to retain their membership in the group. A considerable amount of research has been conducted by psychologists and sociologists concerning the formation and characteristics of juvenile gangs. Vedder (1963) describes three different kinds of gang activities—*criminal, conflict,* and *retreatist.* Criminal activities are directed toward illegally obtaining money, conflict activities are associated with violence, and retreatist activities involve drugs and promiscuous sex.

Actually, in summarizing recent research in this area, Mulvihill and his associates (1969) point out that violence as a gang activity has probably been overemphasized and that the violence level in various gangs notorious for their toughness has been found to be quite low. In many gangs, the few members who persist in extreme aggression are considered to be "crazy" by other members. However, these gangs are characterized by criminal activities, such as robbery and burglary, and by their retreatist activities.

The importance of situational variables in determining whether a violent act takes place has been emphasized; these variables are also of importance in criminal behavior. For example, frequently auto theft involves a group of teenagers who spot a car with a key in the ignition and take the car for a "ride," sometimes for only a few blocks. If the key were not in the ignition, it is highly unlikely that the theft would take place. Similarly, such situational variables as the availability of a weapon, drugs, and alcohol or a door left unlocked in a store or house may all be stimuli whose presence in a particular situation will result in a crime.

The role of alcohol and drugs as situational variables in crime, particularly crime of a violent nature, has been receiving increasing attention (Burkett, 1972). No drug, narcotic, or alcoholic substance that is presently known will in and of itself *cause* the taker to commit a violent crime, but they may modify behavior capabilities that are already present and thus, indirectly, be a factor in the commission of such acts. In this way alcohol is found to be a factor in a high percentage of homicide cases. In some studies, as high as two-thirds of the criminal homicide events involved alcohol. It is also found to be a factor in a significant number of aggravated assault cases and in sexual offenses. It seems to have a minimal involvement in robbery cases.

Although there is convincing evidence that drug addicts contribute significantly to property crimes (since they frequently steal to support their habit), there is little evidence that there is a *causal* relationship between the use of drugs and the commission of crimes and violent acts. In other words, it is the person—not the drug—who performs the act. There is some concern, however, with certain types of drugs that greatly affect or change character and personality traits. For instance, it is quite possible that amphetamines, which can produce severe psychoses, may drive a person to violence. Similar dangers have been suggested for hallucinogens. However, just what the relationship is between such drugs and crime remains to be determined.

An adequate summary of the data that have been obtained on the physical, psychological, and environmental factors contributing to criminal behavior is beyond the scope of this chapter. There is a considerable body of existing literature, and research activity in this area is increasing. Our brief overview should, however, make it clear that criminal behavior is a complex form of behavior in which a number of factors, both personal and environmental, interact to produce the behavior. Perhaps in the future it will be possible to present a comprehensive theory that will explain all types of criminal actions, but this is not feasible at present. There are many complex and difficult problems confronting researchers in this field that must be overcome before a definitive explanation of the origins of criminal behavior can be offered.

PREVENTION OF CRIME

As some investigators attempt to understand the origins of criminal behavior, other researchers are attempting to determine the most effective methods for preventing crime. Obviously, we must understand what causes crime before we can prevent it; this may very well be the reason that efforts aimed at reducing and preventing criminal behavior have not been very successful.

In the staff report to the National Commission on the Cause and Prevention of Violence (Mulvihill et al., 1969), two approaches to the prevention of crime and violence are suggested. One approach is to eliminate the basic causes of crime and violence. The other approach suggested is to rehabilitate and integrate offenders.

Eliminating the Basic Causes

This approach, of course, implies that we know the basic causes of crime and violence, and, as we have indicated, this may not be the case. However, the recommendations of the staff report, if followed, would lead to a major social reconstruction program that would be certain to have an impact on virtually all behavior, including criminal. Unfortunately, although a solution that would eliminate the basic causes of crime would be the ideal solution, it would be difficult if not virtually impossible to implement. Consider, for example, the recommendations of the staff report, which are given below. Only the basic recommendations are presented here, but in the staff report each recommendation is presented in considerable detail with some concrete suggestions for how they might be implemented. The recommendations for the prevention of crime and violence through eliminating basic causes focus on:

1. The reduction of economic deprivation and degradation through programs concerned with jobs, income-supplementation, and homes.
2. The reduction of political alienation through programs designed to provide for greater community participation and through creation of new channels of communication between government and the poor, the underprivileged, and the unorganized.
3. The reduction of pathologies in child development through educational programs and family services.

4. The elimination of educational inadequacies through programs that provide equal quality education, enabling every child to secure the emotional and cognitive requirements for effective adult participation.
5. The creation of new roles for youth, so that young people can lend their energies, visions, and skills to the decision-making processes of this country and learn through such participation that peaceful change can be effected within the framework of democratic institutions.
6. The reduction or elimination of prejudice and discrimination that contributes so pervasively to the alienation felt by underprivileged groups.
7. An improved response to violence among intimates.
8. The reduction of violence by official representatives of the law.
9. A more effective and sensitive program against narcotic and drug use.
10. An improved response to the role of alcohol in violence.
11. A more comprehensive program of suicide prevention.
12. A more coordinated and exhaustive research effort.

Obviously, if all of the recommendations could be followed, we would have a much improved society. At present, however, it would appear that the second approach to the prevention of crime and violence—that is, prevention by rehabilitating and reintegrating offenders—might be a more realistic and feasible approach.

Rehabilitation and Reintegration of Offenders

As it presently exists, the system for rehabilitation of offenders is far from successful. That is does not restore significant numbers of people to normal, meaningful, law-abiding ways of life is apparent from Figure 14-3. Based on FBI data, Figure 14-3 shows the percentage of individuals who are released from custody and rearrested within four years. The staff report to the National Commission on the Causes and Prevention of Violence acknowledges these past failures in making their recommendations to the commission. Their recommendations, which are numerous and far-reaching, include suggestions for "particular treatment for particular offenders" and recommendations on restraint policies, rehabilitation, and reintegration.

For example, under the recommendation of particular treatment for particular offenders, it is suggested that every person found guilty of criminal activity should be treated as an individual. Thus we should focus on each particular personality and social situation, deciding which course of action is most likely to reduce future acts. The report points out that the soundest argument for restraint (prison) is probably its justification as punishment. However, it also points out that little is known about the deterrent aspects of

254

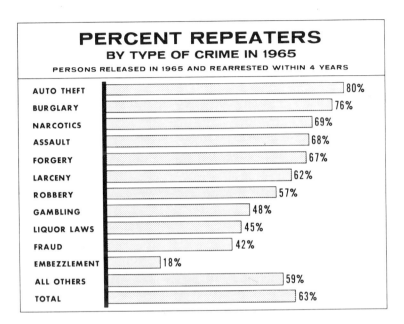

PERCENT REPEATERS
BY TYPE OF CRIME IN 1965

PERSONS RELEASED IN 1965 AND REARRESTED WITHIN 4 YEARS

AUTO THEFT	80%
BURGLARY	76%
NARCOTICS	69%
ASSAULT	68%
FORGERY	67%
LARCENY	62%
ROBBERY	57%
GAMBLING	48%
LIQUOR LAWS	45%
FRAUD	42%
EMBEZZLEMENT	18%
ALL OTHERS	59%
TOTAL	63%

FIGURE 14-3. The percent of repeaters by various types of crime. From J. E. Hoover, *Crime in the United States* (Washington, D. C., Federal Bureau of Investigation, United States Department of Justice, 1971).

incarceration and that scientific experiments should be carried out in this area. Perhaps restraint of some offenders does indeed serve to deter them from further crime, but in other cases imprisonment may produce negative effects and render offenders less capable of rehabilitation.

Although many would argue that an offender should be incarcerated as punishment regardless of whether it deters him from committing crimes later, many others are more concerned with programs for rehabilitation of the offender. Rehabilitation includes those institutional correction programs that are designed to modify the offender's behavior and attitudes so that he no longer commits crime. If locking a prisoner up in a cell serves this purpose, then it is a rehabilitation program.

Since evidence indicates that earning ability is an important asset if ex convicts are to lead crime-free lives, a strong recommendation of the report is that correctional institutions should upgrade educational and vocational-training programs and extend them to all inmates who can benefit from them. Along with training, rehabilitation should also involve personal guidance for the inmates in helping them gain self-understanding, developing interpersonal relationships, and acquiring positive social values. The report suggests psychological therapy of various types for this purpose.

Recommendations are also made concerning the extension of rehabilitation from the institutional to the community setting—that is, reintegration. The future of effective corrections policy lies in the direction of community-based treatment, usually as part of parole or probations operations but also as a basis for providing services for offenders who have left the corrections system completely.

The report suggests a variety of approaches for the reintegration process. Thus correctional institutions should adopt rigorous prerelease programs to prepare the offender for community reintegration. These programs should teach topics such as how to get a job and how to adapt to normal community life by means of conjugal and other sex-partner visits, short furloughs with families, temporary release periods, and so forth. It is also suggested that the prerelease program may be community-centered rather than institutionally based. Community "halfway" houses for released offenders have been suggested; psychological treatment, continuation of academic and vocational training, training citizens to accept and support ex-convicts, cooperation by employers, financial assistance to released offenders in the form of loans and unemployment insurance, as well as a variety of other "aids" have been suggested as part of the reintegration program.

Much of the thinking in relation to rehabilitation and reintegration has been in terms of young offenders, and a considerable amount of the research on rehabilitation has been concerned with these types of offenders. Different frames of reference have been applied to juvenile corrections with varying degrees of success. We will briefly consider several of these approaches to juvenile corrections.

Probation Approaches. The trend in the case of juvenile offenders has been away from imprisonment and toward the use of other alternatives. Probation has been a common approach. In fact, it turns out that very little time can usually be spent with any single offender by a probation officer; still, it is a widely used technique. Although the actual mechanics of probation may vary considerably in terms of requirements placed on the offender, rehabilitation procedures, and so forth, a number of studies have indicated that probation appears to be relatively effective. However, this raises an interesting question: what proportion of those placed on probation could do just as well on a suspended sentence without any supervision?

In a study of over 2200 delinquents assigned by several courts to probation, McEachern and Taylor (1967) found that dispositions of the cases fell into four general categories. One group (A) was dismissed by probation departments at intake and received no treatment. Another group (B) was placed on informal probation and received some treatment. Those in the third group (C) were made wards of the court but received no treatment, whereas those in the fourth group (D) were made wards of the court and received treatment. The researchers followed up the recidivism rates of those assigned to the various groups and found that delinquents who were made formal wards of the court (groups C and D) improved significantly more than those in groups A and B. However, more important, they found that delinquents who were never given any treatment improved more than those who were. In the group that committed the fewest offenses during the follow-up period were those who were made wards of the court but were given no treatment.

There are other studies on the effects of probation, but the results are confusing, and more systematic investigation is needed to answer a number of questions about this approach. As Empey (1969) points out, "On one hand, the evidence indicates that probation, as a helping and supervisory device, is highly limited. Its main function, instead, has been that of carrying out the formal rituals of legal and professional processing. On the other hand, the majority of offenders assigned to probation are successful. They do not recidivate. Why? In what way and from whom should probation operate?"

Incarceration. The second major approach to juvenile corrections has been imprisonment. Although it has become popular to condemn this procedure as a method of juvenile correction and many criticisms have been levied against it, "there is little in the way of hard evidence to support the view that a sheer avoidance of institutionalization will result in more successful adjustment. It is a lamentable fact that national statistics on recidivism after incarceration are not available" (Empey, 1969, p. 1404). Thus again there is a situation in which a great deal more research is needed before firm conclusions can be drawn.

Differential Treatment. The concept of differential treatment implies that offenders are not alike and that attempts should be made to match offenders with treatment programs—in other words, particular treatment for particular offenders. Any program following this theory is by necessity complex, since it calls for the differential diagnosis of offenders into subtypes, the selection and training of personnel to work with these subtypes, the establishment of a treatment program for each subtype, and so forth. Treatment programs might involve vocational training, therapy, or whatever else may seem appropriate. It is still too early to evaluate the few programs of this sort that are in existence, but preliminary data suggest that they may be effective.

Group-Oriented Programs.   Typically in programs of this kind, the offenders live together informally in small groups without the usual institutional guards and detailed routine. The groups work together on various projects, have group meetings, and in general follow principles such as those developed by Alcoholics Anonymous and Synanon (see Chapters 15 and 16), in which social reinforcement by group members for positive behavior is important. However, research on the outcome of these group programs has been inconclusive.

Learning Theory and Education Therapy.   Much of the theory behind juvenile correction has been based on what might be termed the "medical model" of delinquency. This model is like the medical model of abnormality, which is popular in behavior pathology. It views delinquent behavior as pathology, and corrective procedures are designed to return the delinquent to a state of "health." Some recent ideas, however, would replace the medical model with an "educational model" and emphasize the remedy of learning deficiencies, which are assumed to be responsible for the delinquent behavior. This approach is very similar to the behavior-therapy approaches used to treat mental disorders. Central to this approach is the immediate reinforcement of desired behavior by means of meaningful rewards, such as social recognition, peer approval, money, and so forth. This technique has shown that improvement will take place in learning academic materials and social skills within an institution. However, the effectiveness of this kind of approach remains to be seen after the juvenile has returned to the community, and there is little data on the impact of this type of therapy on the recidivism rate.

THE ROLE OF THE PSYCHOLOGIST

In the previous pages we have seen that efforts are being made to understand the causes of criminal behavior and how best to handle the criminal and delinquent after he has committed a crime. It is apparent that the information available is far from adequate; it is in the gathering of this information that psychologists will play a major role. There is an urgent need for an integrated, multidisciplinary approach, which will include studies of biological, psychological, social, and cultural factors that contribute to criminal behavior.

Thus psychologists are involved in research dealing with crime causation and criminal behavior in general. However, besides understanding the causes of this kind of behavior, we must also develop effective rehabilitation procedures. This will involve not only the development and implementation of new techniques and a systematic evaluation of their effectiveness but a more systematic approach to the evaluation of existing programs.

In attempting to solve the problems associated with criminal behavior, then, psychologists are involved at many levels. Basic research is needed to better understand the causes and nature of criminal behavior, and applied research is needed to develop and evaluate methods for reducing or eliminating this kind of behavior. Although the difficulties confronting researchers in this area are major ones, the magnitude of the problem itself is such that a concentrated attack is necessary.

part 5

SOME INTRAPERSONAL
PROBLEMS

The misuse of various drugs has become a major problem in our society today, and currently much concern is being expressed by government officials at all levels about the magnitude of this problem. Psychologists have been interested for some time not only in the misuse of drugs but also in the beneficial effects that various drugs may have in helping alleviate mental-health problems. Consequently, many psychologists are studying the causes of drug misuse and the effectiveness of various types of treatments, and many others are actively engaged in research dealing with the effects of drugs on both normal and abnormal behavior. Some of the approaches and problems confronting drug researchers are discussed in Chapter 15.

Along with drug misuse, the problem of alcohol misuse has been of interest to psychologists. Many investigations have been conducted dealing with the effects of alcohol on various aspects of behavior, but researchers are also interested in determining the underlying causes of alcoholism and how this problem can be most effectively treated. Theories of alcoholism as well as several of the treatment techniques are covered in Chapter 16.

Although a somewhat different type of intrapersonal problem than drug or alcohol misuse, aging also presents a number of unique problems for an individual. Because of improved health care, a larger proportion of our population now survives to encounter the problems associated with the aging process. Some of the effects of aging on behavior and the manner in which psychologists study the aging process are discussed in Chapter 17.

Mental health is a major problem area about which we hear a great deal. Thus we frequently hear statistics cited concerning the population of our mental hospitals, the search for effective treatment of the mentally disturbed, the approaches utilized by communities and regional groups to establish preventive programs, and so on. However, some areas of mental health are less well-publicized, such as problems associated with certain handicapped groups, with rural populations, with various minority groups, and with college students. These will be discussed in Chapter 18.

Although there are many other types of intrapersonal problems that psychologists deal with that could be included in this section, the final chapter deals with two problems that are not of the same magnitude as those previously discussed but that may be more important to you personally. Psychologists have been interested in why people smoke and overeat and why it is so difficult to modify or halt this type of behavior. Recent research dealing with smoking and overeating as well as explanations about about why this behavior occurs is considered in Chapter 19.

chapter
15

The Drug Problem

Although our society is confronted with a number of problems of staggering magnitude, the drug problem must certainly be considered one of the most serious. Although the estimates of just how serious this problem is will vary considerably depending on who makes the estimate, even the most optimistic reports paint a grim picture. Regardless of the criteria (loss of lives, economic loss, increase in crime, and so forth) used to measure the impact of drug abuse, there is little question that a point has been reached where massive action programs must be designed and implemented to counteract the problem. The beginnings of programs of this sort are now being funded by the federal government.

Attacks on the drug problem involve a number of different stages, including research, treatment, and education. Psychologists have long been interested in drugs, since many kinds of drugs will drastically modify behavior; consequently, they have been conducting research in this area for years. Typically, however, the research has been concerned with the effects of drugs on specific aspects of behavior and the evaluation of the effectiveness of drugs in the treatment of various mental disorders. Relatively little research has been done on the treatment of drug addiction and on education programs designed to counteract drug abuse. However, more and more psychologists are becoming involved in these areas.

Photo by Sam Sprague.

Because the drug problem has been receiving so much publicity, virtually all of you probably already know a considerable amount about drugs—their use and abuse. Consequently, we will not be concerned with a discussion of various types of drugs and their reported effects on behavior. Rather, we will concentrate on some of the methodological considerations involved in research with drugs and in attempts to treat drug users. By understanding how drug research is conducted and by becoming aware of some of the methodological pitfalls encountered in drug research, it is hoped that you will be in a better position to evaluate the often-conflicting reports that are published about the effects of drugs on behavior.

THE FIELD OF
PSYCHOPHARMACOLOGY

An important and relatively new applied area of psychology deals with the relationship between drugs and behavior. *Psychopharmacology,* or *behavioral pharmacology* as it is often called, is a combination of the techniques and concepts of experimental psychology and pharmacology to explore the behavioral effects of various drugs. Although the approaches utilized by researchers in this field are quite diverse, a study in this area will generally have one of four major objectives:

1. To identify and screen new drugs of potential value in the treatment of mental diseases.
2. To provide an understanding of the action of drugs—how a drug achieves its behavioral effect.
3. To make use of a drug as a tool or a means for the analysis of complex behavior.
4. To study drug toxicity, tolerance, addiction, absorption, distribution, and metabolism.

The objective of the investigation will determine to a large extent the particular approach that an investigator will use; however, there are a number of research design considerations that are important in nearly all drug studies. As has been true in the design of the experiments discussed in other chapters in this book, the investigator in drug research must be concerned with the independent and dependent variables he selects.

Independent and Dependent Variables in
Drug Research

Studies dealing with the behavioral effects of drugs take place in a variety of settings, ranging from laboratories to wards in mental hospitals. Subjects

264

may include a wide range of animals as well as humans. In fact, psychopharmacology is one applied area in which a great deal of the research must be
conducted with animals, because it is necessary, in many cases, to determine
whether it is safe to use a particular drug with humans. Thus very often the
behavioral effects of a new drug will be carefully studied on one or more
species of animals before any attempt is made to use the drug on human
subjects.

Regardless of whether the study takes place in a laboratory or a hospital
ward or whether it involves human or animal subjects, the investigator designing a study must take several factors into account. Among the many independent variables that are of concern in drug studies, a number, called *pharmacological variables*, are associated with the use of the drug itself. For example, one
of the basic variables is the quantity of the drug utilized. It is generally assumed
that, when other conditions are held constant, behavior may vary as a function
of the *dose* of drug used; this is one of the more important independent variables
in drug research. Another aspect of importance is the duration of action of
the drug, known as the *time response*. Drugs differ in the speed with which
they produce their effects after administration and in the duration of these
effects. Consequently, it is important to measure behavior several different times
after the administration of a drug.

There are several other pharmacological variables of importance. For
example, the *number of administrations* may be important, in that behavioral effects
that are not produced by a single dose sometimes appear during a series of
administrations. Similarly, the *frequency of administration* can be a variable. When

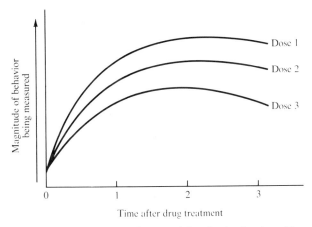

FIGURE 15-1. Dose-time response curves for several dose levels of a drug. Note
that the behavior being measured shows a change as a function of both the dose
used and the time at which the behavior is measured following drug treatment.

intervals between doses are long, more uniform effects (similar to single doses) may be achieved, whereas shorter intervals will sometimes produce a cumulation of effects. The *route* or *method of administration* of a drug may determine its speed of action, its metabolic rate, and its pharmacological effects. Sometimes oral dosage is best, sometimes various types of injections are used. These, as well as other pharmacological variables, must be considered by the researcher in designing his investigation.

There are, of course, other independent variables that must also be considered by the researcher. Many characteristics of the experimental situations (such as presence of other persons) and physical conditions (such as heat and light) may be variables, as will be various characteristics of the subjects themselves (such as sex, weight, and age). As is apparent, there are a great many variables that can be manipulated or must be held constant in drug studies.

Typically, in behavioral pharmacology, some aspect of the subject's behavior will constitute the dependent variable. The researcher must give a great deal of thought to the selection of an appropriate behavior pattern to be studied and to the techniques he will use for measuring the behavioral variable once it has been selected. Many behavior patterns—from simple psychomotor reactions to very complex forms of social behavior—serve as dependent variables in drug research; we will not attempt to list them.

Sometimes the techniques required for measuring the behavior are simple and straightforward, and sometimes they are very elaborate and complex. As an example of a study involving a simple form of behavior and a simple measuring technique, consider a study by Hurst and associates (1968). These investigators hypothesized that, under the influence of amphetamine, subjects' strength would increase and be more resistant to fatigue. To test this hypothesis, grip strength was measured by a hand dynamometer for both drug-treated and control subjects. It was found in this study that the grip strength of subjects receiving the drug was enhanced.

In contrast to a study of this type, consider the problems that might confront the investigator in selecting his dependent variable if he wished to test the hypothesis that amphetamine increased or decreased the amount of social interaction of subjects under various kinds of social conditions. The methods available for measuring social interaction are not nearly as simple as those available for measuring grip strength, but, of course, social interaction may be a much more relevant dependent variable.

The question of the relevancy of the dependent variable is a critical one, particularly when animals are used as subjects in drug investigations. Since one of the primary objectives of research in psychopharmacology is the selection of chemical agents that have potential therapeutic effects on aberrant human behavior, the old question of whether one can generalize results from studies of infrahuman animal behavior to the behavior of man assumes particular importance. How does one select the behavior patterns of animals to be studied? Essentially, the approach that is applied consists of the following steps:

1. An analysis of the human aberrant behavior pattern for its basic characteristics.
2. The selection of aspects of animal behavior that are as similar as possible to these characteristics.
3. Searching for chemical agents that affect these characteristics in animals.
4. Testing the effects of these agents on the human aberrant behavior pattern originally analyzed.

This approach begins with an analysis of the human aberrant behavior pattern for which chemical means of therapy are being sought and concludes with a determination of whether the behavior is indeed altered by the drug selected.

Some Other Design Considerations

The selection of the independent and dependent variables to be used in the investigation is a critical consideration in the design of studies in psychopharmacology. However, the investigator must also decide other design questions, such as whether he should have a *placebo* group and whether a *blind* or *double-blind* technique will be used.

Sometimes the behavior of a subject in a drug study will change, even though he has been given a substance that is known to have absolutely no behavioral effects. This is similar to the situation in which a patient "feels better" after the doctor has given him a coated sugar pill. This is the so-called *placebo effect*, and it is something that researchers must take into consideration in the design of their studies. Frequently, when human subjects are utilized in drug studies, one group of subjects will receive a pill that looks identical to those being given subjects in the experimental groups but that, in reality, contains no drug at all. The behavior of the subjects in this group will also be observed by the experimenters to see if behavior changes do in fact take place. If they do, they are the result of suggestion rather than drug action.

In most investigations, the subjects will not be informed about whether they have received a drug or a placebo. A study of this type involves what is called a *blind* (or sometimes single-blind) *technique.* Often, the person who is responsible for measuring the behavior of the subjects also does not know whether a particular subject has received a drug or a placebo. In this case, the technique is referred to as *double-blind*. Whenever possible, this procedure is desirable, since it prevents experimenter bias (even though it may not be intentional on the part of the experimenter) from influencing the results of the investigation.

The above considerations are of importance in laboratory and clinical studies concerned with the effects of drugs on behavior. Frequently, however, research is conducted in settings where the investigator has little or no control over design considerations. For example, we see many reports dealing with the effects of drugs (such as marihuana) on behavior. Sometimes these studies are carefully controlled and involve good experimental design. Too often, however, they will report, for example, that marihuana users tend to indulge in certain types of behavior (good or bad) and will assume that the behavior is due to the use of the drug. Rarely do these studies involve a control group of nonusers who are matched with the users in all of the important variables that may determine how they behave. Thus if a study attempted to match a group of users with nonusers in terms of age, sex, socioeconomic background, personality characteristics, intelligence, and so on and then found that the user group engaged in behavior quite different from that of the nonusers, we might be more confident that the different behavior was caused by the drug. Similarly, in such studies it is difficult to obtain reliable information about the amount of the drug used, the duration of use, whether or not other drugs have also been used, as well as numerous other variables that are usually considered to be of importance in drug investigations.

The Research Setting

As we have indicated, research in behavioral pharmacology takes place in a variety of settings. Much of the laboratory research has involved infrahuman subjects for several reasons. In the first place, a great deal of animal work is necessary in screening drugs before they can be used with human subjects. Secondly, unless a physician is available to assist him, the psychopharmacologist is not permitted to administer drugs to human subjects. Thus some research with human subjects has taken place in university laboratories, but the bulk of this research has been conducted in mental hospitals and in other clinical settings.

Because of the availability of attending physicians and a captive pool of subjects, the clinical setting has been, and will probably continue to be, utilized heavily as a facility for drug research. Unfortunately, most of these investigations suffer from shortcomings that render their findings questionable based on accepted standards of experimental research. Hollister (1968, p. 124) discusses these shortcomings in detail. First, most studies either have not specified their sample population adequately according to the behavioral abnormalities they possess or they have used different groups of subjects together. Second, most of the reported studies do not specify a treatment goal. Often a subjective evaluation of improvement is made and considered to be adequate by the investigator. Obviously, experimental bias can easily enter into the evaluation of a particular treatment. Also, much of the clinical work has been done without the benefit of control groups. Because of this, no objective evaluation of change in behavior can be made. According to Hollister, it follows that, due to lack of scientific rigor in this research, experiments typically make excessive claims about the therapeutic effects of these drugs.

These criticisms apply to clinical studies in which the aim of an investigation is typically to determine what, if any, therapeutic effects a particular drug might have. The same criticisms, however, can be made regarding many of the studies conducted that have been aimed at determining the harmful effects of drugs. The detrimental effects of some drugs are obvious even to the untrained observer, but there are other drugs whose effects cannot be so easily determined. With drugs of this type, such as marihuana, the results of various investigations are often conflicting, and no clear-cut statement about possible detrimental effects can be made. Consider, for example, the study of Kolansky and Moore (1971). These investigators reviewed the cases of 38 individuals from 13 to 24 years of age who smoked marihuana two or more times weekly between 1965 and 1970. The researchers reported that all of these individuals demonstrated adverse psychological effects. Of the 20 males and 18 females observed, there were eight with psychoses, four of which had attempted suicide. Of the 18 female patients reviewed, 13 unmarried ones became sexually promiscuous while using marihuana and seven became pregnant. These researchers indicated that no evidence of a predisposition to mental illness of any kind was found in these patients prior to the development of psychopathic symptoms when cannabis consumption was begun. It was their considered opinion based on these data that moderate-to-heavy use of marihuana in adolescents and young people without predisposition to mental illness could lead to problems ranging from mild ego disturbances to psychoses.

This study received a great deal of publicity when first published and stirred up considerable controversy. We will not review the comments, both favorable and critical, directed at this study, but it is likely that a large segment of our society who use marihuana on a fairly regular basis greeted this report with some skepticism.

DRUG ABUSE

Abuse of drugs is common to virtually all of the drugs that affect behavior—narcotics, stimulants, hypnotics, tranquilizers, and hallucinogens. In the past several years, the most publicized group of misusers of drugs has been the habitual users of narcotics. This is a very serious problem in the United States, and legal and medical authorities are constantly trying to exert control over the distribution and use of these types of drugs. However, the term "drug abuse" has come to refer to the use of any drug when the effect is not considered to serve a therapeutic function by medical or legal professionals. Defining the problem in this way, it is evident that both the so-called prescription and nonprescription drugs have been misused for many years by the adult population. For example, according to the U. S. Public Health Service, there were 178,000,000 prescriptions for mood-changing drugs filled by U. S. pharmacies in 1967. This was only a record of the drugs given for medicinal purposes. What is not known, of course, is the quantity of prescription drugs that was consumed illegally. The quantity must be large, however, for the U. S. Public Health Service estimates that of all manufactured barbiturates, more than half find their way into illegal channels (Public Health Service Publication No. 2098). The concern of the government is reflected by the FDA decision in early 1972 to reduce the production of amphetamines in the United States by nearly half.

Who Uses the Drugs?

What types of persons use these large quantities of illegal drugs? Recently, the Bureau of Narcotics and Dangerous Drugs devised a classification scheme categorizing the types of drug users. Some of these types may not be illegally consuming drugs, since the drugs may have been prescribed for them. However, these individuals misuse drugs. The *situational user* uses drugs for a definite reason, usually for a short time. In this group, one would find athletes who take stimulants before events to maintain peak efficiency and stave off muscle fatigue. Also in the group are truck drivers who find it necessary to stay alert on long drives and use stimulants. A housewife who takes pills for extra energy or to sleep after a difficult day also fits into this category. Second, there are the *spree users*. This category consists mainly of young people, particularly students, who try drugs first for curiosity and then for the "high" they produce. This group may or may not continue drug use, depending on the social contacts they maintain.

The third category suggested by this classification scheme is the *hard-core addict*. Although in the past years this group was primarily from the lower socioeconomic classes of our society, it is now represented at almost all social levels. The main distinguishing characteristic of the addict is that virtually all of his daily activities center around the task of supporting his habit. Narcotics are not the only drugs of choice found in this category: stimulant and depressant addiction is also common. The final category comprises what can be termed the *hippie* culture. Drugs are an important part of this group's social life. Unlike the hard-core addict, the drugs of choice for this group are usually hallucinogens, such as marihuana or LSD, and occasionally amphetamines. This group is largely composed of persons who are well-educated and come from middle-income families. They are like the hard-core addicts in that much of their time is centered on the experiences gained from drug taking and obtaining adequate drug supplies.

In an effort to better understand the motivations for the use of drugs of various kinds, some research has been conducted dealing with the differences in personality and other characteristics between users and nonusers. For example, some data suggest that personality differences exist between users and nonusers of marihuana. Hogan and associates (1970) found that users, compared to nonusers, were more socially poised, open to experience, adventuresome, impulsive, pleasure-seeking, and rebellious; on the other hand, nonusers tended to be more rule-abiding, inflexible, responsible, conventional, and narrow in interest. Grossman and co-workers (1971) reported that, in a study involving college students, those using marihuana were more creative and adventuresome than nonusers. Marihuana use in their study was associated with personality characteristics that many would tend to consider desirable. They also found, however, that the more a person uses marihuana, the more likely he is to try one or more other drugs. The fact that the personality characteristics of users tend to define a more "creative" person does not imply, of course, support for the use of the drug. Instead, it suggests that these types of individuals are more willing to try something new. Whether or not the use of marihuana is harmful remains to be seen.

Drug Dependence

Aside from the legal implications connected with drug abuse, chronic use of most chemical agents brings with it the problem of drug dependence. Two types of dependence are recognized—*physical* and *psychological*. When a user is physically dependent on a drug, he experiences withdrawal reactions

271

when he does not take the drug. For example, in the case of narcotic dependence, symptoms such as cold sweat, nausea, tremors, muscular aches and pains, mental depression, and vomiting begin to appear from 12 to 16 hours after the drug is last taken. Psychological dependence is reflected in the form of a feeling or craving for the drug. Either or both types of dependence may be evidenced, depending on the particular user's choice of drug. Continued use of drugs also brings with it the phenomenon of drug tolerance. This refers to the user's need for more and more of the drug in order to maintain its pleasurable effect on the body and to avoid the unpleasant symptoms associated with withdrawal.

The fulfillment of the need for drugs and the legal sanctions against possession and consumption of certain drugs combine to form a large part of the overall drug problem. In order to supply a habit that is expensive because of the risk to sellers and the demand of buyers, the chronic user is generally forced to resort to illegal means to obtain the funds for the drugs he needs.

What Can Be Done?

The drug problem is being attacked by psychologists from three fronts: research, treatment, and education. In the area of research, psychopharmacologists have studied the effects of drugs on the behavior of users. Research is also important as a source of information for legislators and law officials, who, in the last analysis, must make the judgment about what constitutes a potentially harmful and thus illegal agent. For example, marihuana has been considered by segments of the population to be less harmful and less addictive than alcohol, and they feel it should be legalized for those who wish to use it. This group is not small, and its demands for legalization have been increasingly heard. The exact extent of marihuana use in the United States is not known, but health authorities believe that as many as 8 to 12 million Americans have used the drug at least once in their lives. Other estimates have ranged as high as 20 million or more (Public Health Service Publication No. 1829).

It is obvious that the two sides of the marihuana dispute deserve consideration. Consideration should be given to relevant research findings by officials charged with the decision on this issue. Thus the report released in early 1972 by the President's Commission on Marihuana and Drug Abuse recommended some rather drastic revisions regarding the legal aspects of possession and smoking of marihuana. Whether or not these recommendations are implemented remains to be seen. In general, it appears that the negative cliches concerning the use of marihuana (such as genetic damage, physical and physiological addiction, predisposition to crime, suicide, pregnancy, and so forth) have not been supported. Again, however, the point must be made that more systematic research is required in many areas before we can really be sure about the effects of this drug on behavior.

In treating the class of drug user who constitutes a hazard to himself and to society, the psychologist and the medical practitioner carry the major part of the burden. If the user is apprehended and legally processed, treatment and rehabilitation sometimes follow. Treatment varies according to the particular drug on which the individual is dependent, but, as an example, consider narcotic dependence.

Successful treatment of a person addicted to narcotics presents a difficult problem. Not only does the addict need to be relieved of physical addiction and withdrawal, but his habit generally either has been a result of personality difficulties or has been accentuated by them. Physically, he can be withdrawn from narcotics with medical treatment. A major difficulty emerges, however, when he leaves the treatment center and attempts to take up his former life in society. When he returns to his past environment, it is difficult for him not to pick up his former habit, since most of his associates are usually addicts. It is also difficult for him to find suitable work. These problems add to the already large emotional strain of staying off drugs. Consequently, in order to successfully refrain from further drug use, the addict must be rehabilitated not only physically but emotionally and socially. Programs are being developed that, hopefully, will treat the psychological problems as well as the physical ones.

One approach to treatment of narcotic addiction is the use of the drug methadone. A methadone-maintenance program consists of supplying the addict with regular doses of methadone, which eliminates his desire for the harder drug. During the time of this treatment, the addict is closely supervised by medical personnel. Often he is also given supportive therapy and counseling by psychologists specifically trained to attack problems pertinent to the former user's social rehabilitation. Most reports on this type of program have been reasonably favorable. In a four-year study of methadone maintenance, Dole, Nyswander, and Warner (1968) reported 94% success in ending the criminal activities of former heroin users. They noted that most of these patients were now responsible and productive citizens. However, conflicting reports can be found in the literature, and much more research is needed before we can be certain that methadone is an effective tool in treatment of the addict. It is worthy of note that this type of program does seem to have a higher success ratio than other previously attempted approaches.

Other questions have also been raised concerning the use of methadone. It appears that methadone is addictive; consequently, treatment with this drug may simply be a matter of replacing heroin addiction with methadone addiction. This change may be highly beneficial, but little is known about the effects of methadone on behavior. If methadone therapy is to be widely utilized, this information will be necessary. For example, some interest is being expressed about whether or not methadone may have an effect on driving performance. This does not present a major problem at present, but if the use of methadone becomes widespread and then is proved to have a detrimental effect on a person's ability to operate an automobile, this may become a serious problem.

An approach to helping the addict that has generated some optimism among workers in this area is the social movement called *Synanon*. This approach, which has similarities to the Alcoholics Anonymous method discussed in the next chapter, attempts to provide a more or less autocratic family structure that makes demands on the patients as "members of the family." Actually, the key element for addicts is the form of group psychotherapy that is involved in the process. The group is led by a recovered addict, who makes use of a variety of techniques, ranging from empathy to ridicule and hostile attacks, in an attempt to stimulate the group members. The group attempts to extinguish the offending behavior (drug usage) through negative reinforcement while it attempts to reinforce new and more desirable behavior by means of social approval and other methods. In many respects, this approach is similar to the behavior-modification techniques employed in therapy—that is, the focus is on changing the behavior, and the underlying "mechanisms" are more or less ignored.

Psychologists are also involved in attempts to educate the public to both the harm of drugs to our society through their abuse and the benefits that can be obtained if they are properly utilized. There remains a tremendous need for the distribution of information based on objective studies of these agents to educators, law-enforcement officials, legislators, and the general public. Efforts in this direction are being attempted. Much information is already available, but a coordinated effort will be required to compile it into a practical and useful form. If this task can be accomplished, more efficient and safe use of drugs may result.

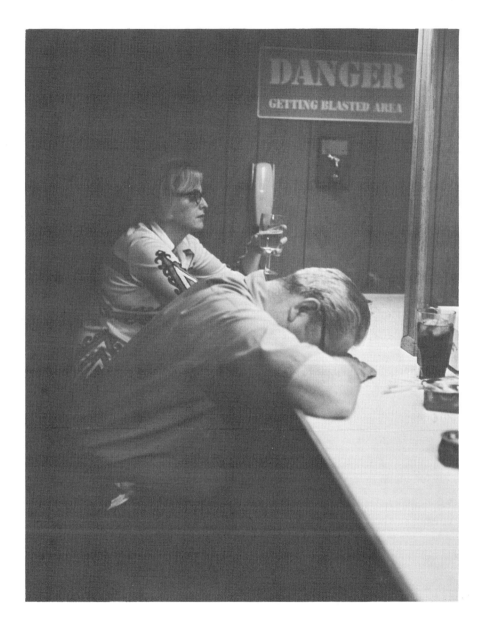

chapter
16

The Alcohol Problem

Alcohol, which is thought to have made its first recorded appearance in Meso-potamia some 5000 years ago, is known in some form or another to practically every society. As Leake and Silverman (1966) point out, "To millions of people it represents a source of food energy, an appetite stimulant, a digestive aid, a help in cardiovascular disease, a useful sedative, a lift in fatigue and a boon in convalescence and aging. It relieves the tensions of anxiety and actually is the most commonly used of all tranquilizers" (p. 5). At one time it was even thought to cure baldness, toothaches, and bad breath.

The destructive properties of alcohol, however, are becoming increasingly apparent. Currently, at least 85 million Americans drink alcohol on what can be called a "regular" basis. Four million of them can be considered "addicted" to alcohol, and an additional five million have a serious drinking problem, which results in marital strife, arrests, job losses, and so forth. It has been estimated that alcohol is involved in about half of the highway fatalities (which regularly run over 50,000 annually), in a significant number of pedestrian fatalities, and in other kinds of fatal accidents, including private aircraft. These kinds of statistics have led to the conclusion that alcoholism should be considered the third or fourth major health disease in the United States.

Many careful and thorough studies have been conducted on alcoholism and its physiological effects—that is, its absorption, metabolism, and removal from the body, as well as its action on various organs of the body. These

Photo by Sam Sprague.

data are imposing, but they are often puzzling, since they fail to explain many of the behavioral effects noted by those who drink alcoholic beverages. One reason for this is suggested by Leake and Silverman (1966) who state that "people very rarely drink alcohol itself. They take beer, wine, whiskey, brandy, gin, vodka, a highball, a cocktail or a mixture of sometimes quite astonishing ingredients. The effects of these real beverages, as used by real people under the conditions of real life, are often quite different from what may be observed in the most carefully controlled experiments with alcohol itself" (p. 5).

There are many psychologists and other researchers who are concerned with the effects of alcohol on behavior, and there is a great deal of research being conducted in this area. Much of this research is conducted in laboratories with lower animals, although the effects of alcohol on various aspects of human behavior are also frequently a subject of study. Thus the 1970 volume of the *Quarterly Journal of Studies on Alcohol* contained some 1300 original articles, abstracts, or titles, many of them dealing with alcohol and behavior.

In this chapter we will not be concerned with laboratory research. Rather, our attention will be directed at the problem of alcoholism, some of the theories concerning the etiology of this problem, and the attempts that are being made to correct the problem. Psychologists are actively engaged in all areas of alcoholism, and their contributions in this field have been of considerable value.

PHYSIOLOGICAL EFFECTS OF ALCOHOL

The literature on alcoholism is complex, immense, and perplexing. Probably no other single pathological state has attracted investigators from so many different fields. Perhaps part of this attraction for researchers lies in the fact that, in its morbid state, alcoholism is a well-defined clinical entity that, at the present time, has no reliable premorbid indicants. In other words, although alcoholism's behavioral and pathological symptoms are reasonably obvious once it has manifested itself, no one has yet been able to identify or predict the occurrence of alcoholism by psychological, physiological, genetic, or cultural indices. Consequently, this is a challenge for researchers (Lester, 1966).

The physiological effects of alcohol are now well-known. Contrary to popular belief, alcohol does not act as a stimulant but rather as a general anesthetic. As such, it acts as a primary and continuous depressant of the central nervous system. However, in a roundabout fashion, this depressant function of alcohol can result in apparent stimulation of a person. This is because of the unrestrained activity of various parts of the brain that have

278

been released or freed from inhibition due to the depression of inhibitory-control mechanisms by alcohol.

Also contrary to popular belief, it is not the cortex of the brain that is most sensitive to the effects of alcohol. Rather, it is an area of the brain called the *reticular system* that appears to be the most sensitive to the effects of alcohol. The reticular system is an important integrating center of the brain; the effect of alcohol depressing the reticular system is to release the cortex from this integrative control. The result is jumbled, disorganized thought processes as well as disrupted motor processes. The finest grades of discrimination, memory, concentration, and insight are lost. Confidence abounds, the personality becomes expansive and vivacious. Mood swings are accompanied by sensory as well as motor disturbances. Alcohol does not increase either mental or physical abilities, although the individual who has had a few drinks may firmly believe that this is the case.

Thus the physiological effects of alcohol fall neatly into the general class of central nervous system depressants, and the metabolic and cellular effects are well-identified.

Alcoholism

Despite the knowledge of the physiological effects of alcohol, virtually no agreement exists on the development of alcoholism in an individual. Although there is some difference in opinion, alcohol (unlike heroin and other opiates) is not usually considered a pharmacologically addicting agent. The World Health Organization (1955) states that:

Alcohol must be considered a drug whose pharmacological action is intermediate in kind and degree between addiction-producing and habit-forming drugs, so that compulsive craving and dependence can develop in those individuals whose make-up leads them to seek and find an escape in alcohol. With this substance the personal make-up is the determining factor but the pharmacological action plays a significant role. Damage to the individual may develop, but does so only in a minority of users. The social damage that arises extends, however, beyond these individuals themselves [p. 8].

Actually, it is not clear why alcohol is not considered an addicting drug, since withdrawal from alcohol can produce symptoms as severe as those encountered during withdrawal from heroin. As Jellinek (1960) points out, in some cases the criteria established for addiction with other kinds of drugs (increased tolerance, compulsive craving, dependence, and withdrawal symptoms) do occur during withdrawal from alcohol.

279

Perhaps the most cogent reason for excluding alcohol from the list of addicting drugs is the fact that addiction, in the pharmacological sense, occurs in a relatively small percentage of users of alcohol—somewhere in the neighborhood of 10%. It has also been pointed out that alcoholism may take from three to 30 years to develop, whereas heroin addiction can develop in only three or four weeks.

TYPES OF ALCOHOLISM

There is always an urge on someone's part to categorize and classify illness of any kind; alcoholism has not escaped. Actually, considering the large number of people involved and the damage that is done by the use of alcohol, categorization of alcoholics is largely an academic exercise.

The recognition by the American Medical Association of alcoholism as a disease has added considerable impetus to attempts to formulate conceptions of the etiology and treatment of alcoholism. E. M. Jellinek (1960), in his excellent book *The Disease Concept of Alcoholism*, has contributed greatly to the understanding of alcoholism by identifying and categorizing various types of alcoholism. These include:

1. *Alpha alcoholism.* A *purely* psychological dependence or reliance on the effect of alcohol for relief of bodily or emotional pain. There are no signs of a progressive process.
2. *Beta alcoholism.* That species of alcoholism in which such alcoholic complications as polyneuropathy, gastritis, and cirrhosis of the liver occur without either physical or psychological dependence.
3. *Gamma alcoholism.* That species of alcoholism in which (a) acquired increased tissue tolerance to alcohol, (b) adaptive cell metabolism, (c) withdrawal symptoms and "craving," and (d) loss of control are involved. In gamma alcoholism, there is a definite progression from psychological to physical dependence and marked behavior changes.
4. *Delta alcoholism.* Shows the first three characteristics of gamma alcoholism. In addition, instead of a "loss of control," there is an inability to abstain.
5. *Epsilon alcoholism.* That species of alcoholism that occurs with infrequent periodic bouts of alcohol ingestion.

Of these five alcohol drinking patterns, Jellinek does not consider either the Alpha or Beta patterns as conforming to the criterion of alcohol addiction. That is, the Alpha pattern is disqualified because the disturbance is viewed as a symptom of an underlying disturbance (relief of pain). Beta alcoholism is ruled out because, although there are pathological consequences (such as cirrhosis), there is no physical or psychological dependence.

The predominant forms of alcoholism in America (and therefore the types of greatest interest) are the Gamma, Delta, and Epsilon varieties. Most theories of etiology therapeutic treatments have focused on the inability to abstain and loss of control, because these phenomena are common to all three forms.

Phases of Alcoholism

A person does not just become an alcoholic overnight. Rather, there appear to be some rather distinct phases, or stages, through which a person progresses. Jellinek (1952) has outlined the series of stages commonly found in the development of alcoholism.

The Symptomatic Phase. During this stage, an individual who has been engaging in social drinking begins to experience a reduction in tolerance for tension, which is relieved by drinking. There is a transition during this stage from what might be termed occasional tension-relief drinking to nearly constant tension-relief drinking. This transition can take from several months to several years.

The Prodromal Phase. This phase is characterized by amnesic episodes, which involve periods of "blackouts." During these periods, the drinker may appear to be perfectly normal to observers but does not recall any trace of the activity the next day. During this phase, certain types of behavior often associated with the alcoholic begin to appear. There is an inclination to "sneak" drinks; to be nearly always preoccupied with alcohol in one way or another (for example, worrying about whether there will be enough to drink at a party he is going to and, just in case there isn't, preparing himself with a few shots before he goes); to gulp drinks instead of drinking them in a leisurely fashion; to begin to develop guilt feelings about drinking; and to avoid any references to drinking in his conversation.

Actually, the person may be drinking very heavily during this stage; however, often the drinking is not yet conspicuous to others. The individual may still have some insight into his own behavior and may not have developed the strong rationalizations about drinking that will follow later. At this particular stage, if the drinking problem is recognized, it is easier to stop than at later stages.

The Crucial Phase. When the person reaches this stage, he has reached a point at which, once he has started to drink, he loses control over his drinking. He cannot stop. However, he still has control over whether he will or will not drink on any particular occasion, so the crucial phase is characterized by frequent "going-on-the-wagon" episodes.

Along with the loss of control over drinking once he has started, during this phase the drinker begins to produce the typical alcoholic alibis and to rationalize away his drinking behavior. However, even though there is a great deal of rationalization, there is also a tendency for the drinker to begin to lose his self-respect during this period. He often attempts to compensate for this by extravagant gestures of one type or another; he also blames his problems on others and becomes hostile toward them, has persistent feelings of remorse, and so forth.

Much of the behavior commonly associated with the alcoholic takes place during this phase. He begins to drink early in the day, is drunk before evening, loses friends, may quit his job, becomes more isolated, and loses outside interests. Frequently there are also dramatic changes in family patterns leading to divorce or separation. He begins to hide his alcohol supply in unlikely places "just in case" someone wants to take it away from him. Also, at about this time, the neglect of proper nutrition may begin to lead to problems.

The Chronic Phase.   This phase is characterized by drawn-out drinking bouts, which may extend for days. In a small percentage of alcoholics, true alcoholic psychosis may develop (such as delirium tremens), and loss of morale is severe. At this point alcoholic tolerance may begin to disappear, and only about half of the alcohol that once was required may now get the person "stoned." When the alcoholic does begin to sober up, he is beset by so many fears, feelings of insecurity, guilt, tremors, and so on that he drinks to control these symptoms.

During this phase, the alcoholic begins to develop feelings of defeat, as his elaborate rationalization system starts to collapse. He may become religious and recognize that he needs help. If help is available and apparent to the alcoholic, at this point he may seek it.

THEORIES OF ALCOHOLISM

It has already been pointed out that alcoholism can be reliably identified in its morbid state but cannot be predicted on the basis of psychological or physiological indices in its premorbid state—that is, before obvious symptoms appear. This has led to the development of a variety of etiological theories and accompanying therapeutic techniques based on the assumed existence of some X factor, which is thought to be activated by the continued exposure to alcohol. Included in these theories are those that are based on nutritional, endocrinological, central nervous system, genetic, and pharmacological factors.

Nutritional Theories

For a number of reasons, many investigators have been led to consider nutritional or diet factors as a primary cause in the etiology of alcoholism. One reason is that the metabolism of alcohol as a caloric substance requires a unique enzyme action, which is produced through the liver. It is assumed that, if the body's metabolism of alcohol is disturbed in some manner, this altered response to alcohol may be reflected in a "craving" for alcohol on the part of the individual. Carrying this notion a step further, therapy that would alter or correct the metabolic disturbance should, at least theoretically, reduce the craving for alcohol. A variety of different techniques have been attempted, manipulating various dietary factors of alcoholics in the hopes of correcting the nutritional deficiency.

Although the notion of a nutritional basis for the etiology of alcoholism is appealing because of its simplicity, there is little experimental evidence that the metabolic processes of alcoholics differ from those of nonalcoholics. Neville and co-workers (1968) conducted a study that compared the nutritional status of a number of alcoholics with normal controls. They utilized 34 alcoholics between the ages of 25 and 59 years and 12 nonalcoholic controls. In this study, a detailed and exhaustive analysis of a number of nutritional factors was made, and comparisons between the alcoholics and controls were conducted. These investigators report that, in terms of vitamin utilization, caloric metabolism, and protein utilization, they were unable to differentiate between the alcoholics and the control subjects.

Obviously, in studies of this type, care must be taken to differentiate between cause and effect. The nutritional theory of alcoholism suggests that, because of some nutritional deficiency, a person has a craving for alcohol and consequently drinks. If proper care is not taken in studies in the nutritional-theory area, it is possible to find differences between alcoholics and nonalcoholics that are a *result* of the drinking, not the cause. For example, a researcher might find that alcoholics have a particular vitamin deficiency not often found in nonalcoholics. However, the vitamin deficiency may be the result of excessive drinking and may have nothing to do with the reasons for drinking—that is, why he started drinking in the first place.

Endocrinological Theories

Along with the nutritional theory, another popular theory of the etiological basis for alcoholism is the endocrinological theory. Basically, this theory suggests that the need to drink and the consequent alcoholism is caused by a hormonal imbalance in the system. The adrenal-pituitary complex has received the most attention in this regard. For one thing, it is involved in the stress response, and there is some feeling that drinking may be a response to stress. Also, the adrenal-pituitary complex is important in performing a central-regulatory function, and disturbance of this particular complex has a number of effects. Recent research, however, has led Verdy and Brouillet (1970) to conclude that the existence of a disturbance in the adrenocortical function in alcoholics has yet to be demonstrated.

Actually, some earlier research in the area of hormonal imbalance in alcoholics looked promising. Favorable results were reported following the administration of various hormones, and there was some excitement generated by this procedure. However, recent research has not demonstrated any simple therapeutic technique, despite the manipulation of virtually every hormone that has been identified.

Brain Pathologies

Some specific brain pathologies have been found to be associated with chronic alcoholics. This has led some researchers to hypothesize that some sort of central nervous system defect may be an etiological factor.

Some of the more frequent pathological conditions associated with chronic alcoholism are enlarged cerebral ventricles and cortical atrophy. Lemere (1956) has suggested that the frontal lobes of the brain, which are very important in many of the higher thought processes, are the most sensitive to alcohol and that continual exposure to alcohol produces irreversible damage in the frontal lobes. The destruction of the frontal area, according to Lemere, leads to the "loss-of-control" phenomenon, the need to drink.

If the loss of control is due to damage in the frontal lobes, then it would seem that surgery severing the frontal lobes from the rest of the brain should have some effect on the drinking behavior. The technique of psychosurgery was at one time a fairly common therapeutic procedure for treatment of psychosis. Recently this approach has been attempted with alcoholics in Poland. Markiewicz and Brennenstuhl (1969) performed sterotactic surgery on several chronic alcoholics. (This procedure involves severing the frontal lobe connections of the brain.) Although the results of the study were complicated by several pre-existing conditions and the death of one of the subjects, at least one of the patients was reported to have been abstinent for 21 months.

As a therapeutic technique, however, this type of surgery is unlikely to gain wide use, even if it is reasonably successful. The "cure" in these cases may be worse than the disease, with severe cognitive disturbances and a variety of emotional side effects.

284

Genetic Theories

The basic premise of the genetic theories is that a metabolic characteristic of alcoholics is genetically determined. This theory has appeal because the existence of individual genetic, and therefore metabolic, patterns is recognized. However, it lacks experimental verification, although it has been demonstrated that it is possible to breed "drinking" and "nondrinking" rats (Eriksson, 1969). The amounts of alcohol selected by the "drinking" rats, however, is still far below the intoxication level.

Pharmacological Theories

The fact that alcoholism requires from three to 30 years to develop has led to the speculation that alcoholism is basically a process of physiological change and adaptation, which, due to prolonged usage, leads to a permanent change. This, of course, is a theory of addiction similar to that postulated for heroin. We have already discussed the question of addiction to alcohol. Although prolonged usage of alcohol does produce true addictive behaviors in some individuals, it does so only in a minority (about 10%), compared to about 80 to 90% with heroin. In this regard, the World Health Organization (1955) has stated that:

It is now clear that, following discontinuation of alcohol after a prolonged period of very heavy drinking, severe withdrawal symptoms, which in a limited proportion of cases include convulsions or delirium, or both, may occur. These latter symptoms are more dangerous than are any of the manifestations of withdrawal of morphine.

However, they go on to say that:

These observations all lead to the conclusion that although there exist many clinical and biochemical analogies between alcoholism and opiate addiction, one must make a clear distinction between them, both in medical practice and in the medico-social or legislative measures concerning them [p. 3].

SOME OTHER THEORIES AND THERAPIES

Because alcohol is generally considered only partially addicting, a second major class of theories has been postulated. These are nonorganic and, basically, suggest that alcohol is used by the individual as a method or means for coping with the environment. In other words, rather than suggesting that the craving for alcohol is due to a biochemical or endocrinological factor, the nonorganic theories postulate that alcohol is consumed in order to satisfy an individual's psychological need or "craving."

Psychoanalytic Conceptions of Alcoholism

This theory views the use of alcohol as a symptom of an underlying personality defect. There has been a good deal of theorizing in this area. Most psychoanalytically oriented psychologists view the alcoholic as a person with a neurosis based on difficult family situations encountered as a child. The alcoholic is thought to have strong homosexual tendencies and "oral cravings," and the use of alcohol represents a running away from problems he cannot face or does not want to face—that is, a regression toward infantile experiences.

Generally, theorists with this point of view feel that the only satisfactory treatment for chronic alcoholism is intense and long psychotherapy. Some feel that not only the alcoholic but his whole family should be treated in order to improve the psychosocial environment of the alcoholic.

A variety of psychotherapeutic techniques have been utilized in attempting to cure alcoholics. Various types of individual therapy, as well as a number of kinds of group treatments, have been attempted by psychiatrists and psychologists. There is no satisfactory proof that any one of these approaches is more useful or more successful than any other. As Leake and Silverman (1966) state:

Under what are believed to be usual conditions, apparently no technique can help more than 20 to 25% of patients to abstain from alcohol for an appreciable period. Under optimal conditions, with highly competent therapists, highly motivated patients, strong support from family members and employers, and necessary treatment facilites, it has been claimed that 60% of the patients may achieve not necessarily complete abstinence but at least adequate control of their drinking [p. 124].

The frustrations involved in treating alcoholics with conventional therapy techniques are illustrated in a recent study by Newton and Stein (1971). These investigators studied the effects of several types of therapy on chronic alcoholics. The patients were assigned to one of three different programs: (1) a program that included small-group therapy, group therapy, and family psychotherapy, (2) an implosive-therapy group, which involved a form of behavior therapy, and (3) a detoxification treatment program, or "drying out." Evaluation of the effectiveness of the various treatment programs was determined by readmission rates of the treated patients. Patients in the detoxification and full-therapy programs showed readmission rates of 32 and 25% respectively, whereas those in the implosive-therapy program had a readmittance rate of 53%. This was surprising, since the implosive-therapy technique is considered a very "intensive" therapy procedure. Newton and Stein concluded that the intensity of therapy is of no practical significance in alcoholism treatment. Although these results are somewhat discouraging, they are typical of evaluation studies involving therapy techniques in alcoholism.

Learning Theory Formulations of Alcoholism

There have been a number of attempts to explain alcoholism within the framework of learning theory. One rather straightforward approach has been to explain the excessive ingestion of alcohol in terms of anxiety reduction. The basic notion is that anxiety is based on learned fear of some type and that alcohol will tend to reduce the anxiety of an individual. Since anxiety is an undesirable and an unpleasant emotion, when alcohol reduces the feeling of anxiety, it acquires a reinforcing value. Remember that a reinforced response tends to be repeated. Within this framework, then, the drinking response is thought to be a learned response, which is learned because it is reinforcing. If this is the case, since alcoholism takes from three to 30 years to develop, it stands to reason that it is a well-learned response, which will be difficult to extinguish.

With the idea that drinking is a learned response, several techniques designed to eliminate or extinguish the response have been developed. One method is aversive conditioning. In other words, by associating drinking with something unpleasant, the individual is "conditioned" not to drink. Instead of being reinforcing in a positive sense, drinking is made to be negatively reinforcing.

One of the earliest forms of aversive conditioning as a treatment for alcoholism was introduced by the Romans. They placed a particularly unpleasant looking eel in the wine cup of a drinker when he was not looking. Supposedly, the unexpected discovery of the presence of the eel was "aversive" enough so the person didn't want to drink anymore. We have little data available about the success of this particular technique.

A widely used technique of aversive conditioning that is somewhat more modern was developed by Lemere and co-workers (1942). In this procedure, nausea and vomiting are produced by intramuscular injection of a drug (emetine hydrochloride). Immediately prior to the nausea and vomiting, the patient is given an alcoholic drink. The idea is that, eventually, the smell and taste of the alcoholic drink will become associated with the less pleasant smells and tastes of the vomiting and the patient will no longer wish to drink. In other words, he will have been "aversively conditioned" to drinking.

Another aversive-conditioning technique involves the use of Antabuse (disulfiram). This drug causes a person to become violently ill if he drinks alcohol. When a person is on an Antabuse regime, the knowledge that he will become ill if he drinks has a strong deterrent value. If he does take a drink, even a number of hours after taking the drug, he may experience headache, palpitations, dizziness, nausea, vomiting, hypertension, apprehension, and difficulty in breathing. Unlike the technique described previously, with Antabuse the person does not have to get sick; he simply does not drink. With the emetine-hydrochloride technique, the drinking and nausea are "paired" together in order to condition the person.

Although the typical aversive-conditioning technique has involved a drug of some type that will actually cause physical illness, Cautela (1967) has made use of a nondrug form of aversive therapy. In this approach, a drinking history is first obtained from a patient (how often he drinks, where he drinks, what he drinks, and why he drinks). Cautela instructs the patient to visualize a drink and a drinking situation and then attempts, through suggestion, to build up in the patient sickening, nauseous feelings. The patient imagines himself taking a drink, vomiting over himself, other people, the bar, and so on, creating a bad scene in general. The therapist attempts to condition the patient so that the *desire* to drink is the aversive stimulus, instead of the drink itself. The patient is supposed to imagine the scene whenever he feels the desire for a drink. Not a great deal of data is available about the effectiveness of this procedure.

ALCOHOLICS ANONYMOUS

The "treatment" that an alcoholic receives through Alcoholics Anonymous (A.A.) represents a combination of group therapy, religious elements, positive social reinforcement for desirable behavior, and negative social reinforcement for undesirable behavior. The meetings of Alcoholics Anonymous groups represent a social movement that consists of personal testimony, concern for one another, group discussion, and a general social fellowship. There is a considerable degree of emphasis on testimony of members regarding how their behavior has changed for the better since they stopped drinking. Many of the characteristics of the Alcoholics Anonymous program apply to the Synanon movement, discussed briefly in the previous chapter, that is now current in drug-addiction treatment.

When an alcoholic joins A.A., new role behavior is expected of him. Within his group, there is strong and rapid positive reinforcement for behavior such as sobriety, working in a family context, and being a responsible individual. The members of the group do not pretend to deal with the underlying psychological problems but, rather, focus on behavior—that is, drinking. One might note the similarity between this approach and the behavior-modification techniques of therapy that we discussed earlier.

Although it is difficult to arrive at accurate figures about how successful a program such as A.A. is, they claim a 75% abstinence record. However, there is considerable selectivity in terms of the type of alcoholic that will approach an A.A. group, so it is dangerous to extend these figures to the general population of alcoholics.

CONCLUSION

Alcoholism is almost uniformly viewed as a chronic disorder, both in terms of the period of time involved in its development and in the difficulty of achieving a "cure." A "cure," however, does not mean the ability to return to "normal" drinking, although some psychiatrists view this as the desired goal. The commonly used term *recovered alcoholic* refers to a person who has recovered social functioning and has attained a substantial ability to refrain from drinking. Many therapists stress abstinence in their work with alcoholics, but few seem to feel the success of treatment should be judged solely on constant sobriety. Reductions in the frequency and lengths of episodes of destructive drinking, of hospitalization, and of days lost from work are all reasonable criteria for the effectiveness of treatment.

Because of the lack of evaluation of treatment of alcoholics as well as standard criteria, little is known about the relative effectiveness of different kinds of psychotherapy or other types of treatment. Information on "recovered" alcoholics is largely limited to statistics on readmission to the original treatment center. As almost nothing is known about patients who have been treated but are not seen again at the original treatment center, it is difficult to estimate what the eventual success-failure ratio is.

A commonly quoted statistic is from 25 to 50% success, with the "success" criterion of 10 to 15 days loss of working time or hospitalization per year. Unfortunately, this figure appears to apply to all treatment conditions indiscriminately (occupational therapy, individual or group therapy, aversive techniques, or LSD treatment), and there is little current enthusiasm expressed by therapists for any one treatment condition. It should be noted, however, that serious attempts to analyze the problems of alcoholism are relatively recent, and it is premature to express too much pessimism.

That there may be grounds for some optimism is evidenced by the increased concern of the federal government about the problems of alcoholism and alcohol abuse. In 1971, a Uniform Alcoholism and Intoxication Treatment Act was approved and recommended for enactment in all of the states. This act is designed to provide the states with the legal framework within which to approach public intoxication and alcoholism from a health standpoint as recommended by various professional organizations, the courts, and various commissions. The interest of the government has been further demonstrated by the creation of the National Institute on Alcohol Abuse and Alcoholism (NIAAA) as part of the National Institute of Mental Health. Other government agencies also have an active interest in this area. Thus, in February of 1972, a joint conference on the problems of alcoholism was sponsored by NIAAA, the National Highway Traffic Safety Administration, and the Law Enforcement Assistance Administration. Whether or not the concentrated attack on alcoholism by the various agencies will be successful remains to be seen, but certainly an effort is now being made.

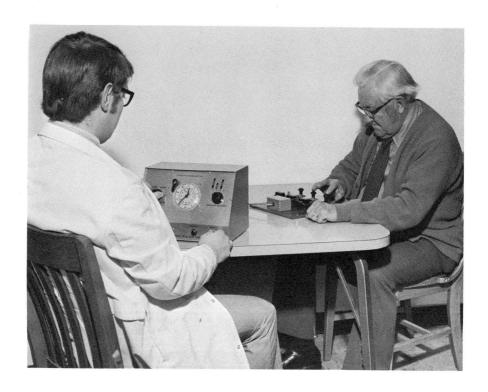

chapter

17

Aging

In recent years, there has been a marked shift in the age makeup of our population. Through the prolongation of life by new advances in medical science, the over-65 segment of the population is increasing disproportionately. By 1980, it is estimated that this age group will make up over 10% of the population, or somewhere in the neighborhood of 25 or 30 million people.

Although the problems of the aged are not new problems, these problems are becoming more apparent because of the increase in numbers of elderly people. As we grow older, there are certain biological, physiological, and sociological problems associated with the process. Thus, as the individual grows older, biological aging brings about a number of changes, such as a decline in muscular strength and increased susceptibility to disease and stress. Sociological aging involves a complex readjustment to retirement, changes of position in society, drastic changes in self-concept and attitudes, reduced income, more leisure time, and so on. Although some aspects of sociological aging may be positive and require only a minor amount of adjustment on the part of the individual, other aspects may be negative and present the elderly with severe adjustment problems.

Obviously, when we talk about biological and sociological aging problems, we are also talking about psychological problems. As the person grows old, the biological and sociological problems give rise to psychological problems as well. A number of psychologists are interested in these kinds of problems.

Photo by Sam Sprague.

There are also other kinds of psychological problems associated with aging. For example, reaction time and speed slows on various psychomotor tasks, deficiencies develop in memory and learning, and flexibility and creativity in problem solving decrease. Much of the psychological research in the area of aging has been concerned with the behavioral changes of the human organism that take place with the passage of time. Over the past decade there has been a substantial growth in this type of research, which has been notable even more for an increase in sophistication and scientific rigor than in volume. In this chapter we will discuss some of this research and the conclusions that have been drawn concerning the aging process and its effects on human behavior.

SOME THEORETICAL AND METHODOLOGICAL CONSIDERATIONS

Many of the theoretical questions concerning aging have to do with the characteristics of the process itself. For example, is the physiological aging of the body as natural and inherent a process as growth? Or is aging due to the gradual degenerative results of infections, toxins, traumas, and so forth? In other words, do aging and death result from the body's failure to eliminate waste products and repair damage caused by many factors that, with proper health practices, could be eliminated? Although questions such as this are of interest to researchers dealing with psychological aspects of aging, there are several theoretical questions concerning more specific relationships between aging and performance that are of more direct concern to the psychologist.

One of the characteristics of aging is that there is a reduction in the speed of functioning in various processes. Is slowing up a general factor that affects all processes? Is slowing up specific to each process? What is the relationship between speed and difficulty or complexity of the task when aged individuals are involved? Another critical question, often asked, is: does use preserve function? For example, one might ask if exercise promotes health and increases longevity, and whether active participation in intellectual activity preserves intelligence. Similarly, does active involvement in learning increase the capacity of a person to learn at an older age? Answers to questions such as these have practical implications, for, if use does indeed preserve function, it might be possible to modify downward changes in older individuals by providing appropriate environments with adequate stimulation and opportunities for participation.

Some Research Approaches to Aging

In studying the effects of aging on some aspect of behavior, the typical approach is to utilize subjects in several different age groups, test them on the behavior of interest, and, if differences exist, conclude that these differences are due to the age variable. In studies of this type, the dependent variable may be almost anything, such as reaction time, scores on various tests, learning, problem solving, or decision making. The independent variable is the subject's age. Thus an investigator may test four groups of subjects—one group between 20 and 25 years of age, another between 40 and 45, another between 60 and 65, and a fourth group between 80 and 85 years. He may test all four groups on a task involving problem-solving ability and be able to conclude that this particular ability is or is not affected by the age of the subject.

In other studies on aging, the independent variables can be external to the subjects being tested. In an approach such as that described above, all conditions may be held constant except the age of the subjects. However, in some studies the experimenter might be interested in the effects of some external independent variable (such as noise) on the performance of aged subjects. In this case he might still have several age groups, but part of each group would be tested under a noise condition and part would be tested under quiet conditions. With the proper experimental design and data analysis, the investigator would be able to determine if the noise had a greater effect on older subjects than on younger subjects.

In many studies of aging, the researchers tend to make use of available "captive" populations, such as those found in various institutions, old-people's homes, and hospitals. This may tend to bias the results of the studies somewhat, since there are many older independently living individuals whose capabilities may differ from those in institutions. However, it should be pointed out that most other areas of psychology also use captive populations. For example, a great deal of the psychological literature is based on data obtained from college sophomores, who, in many respects, are as atypical as the institutionalized elderly.

Birren (1970), who is one of the leading researchers in the field of psychological aspects of aging, suggests a somewhat different approach to an "experimental psychology of aging." He states:

An experimental psychology of aging would attempt to reproduce the changes in individuals associated with chronological age by manipulation of the independent variables. If, for example, one entertains the major hypothesis that a particular intellectual ability changes with age in adults because of disuse, then one can attempt to raise the level of the ability by increasing its use in selected adults [p. 124].

Birren's suggestion has several implications. Suppose that we were interested in studying the effects of disuse on a particular intellectual function or ability. If we were to take a group of elderly individuals who already showed a deficit in the ability, randomly assign half the group to an experimental condition in which they practiced on the particular ability while the other half of the group did not, and then tested them again at a later date, the results would tell us several things. First, perhaps there was no change as a function of the practice; that would suggest to us that the diminished function was not reversible. Second, improvement would suggest that the diminished function was, in fact, reversible. Improvement would also suggest that, indeed, the diminished function was a result of disuse and not due to physical changes in the system that could not be reversed.

Another implication of this approach for aging research has to do with longitudinal studies. For example, we might design a study in which a number of individuals were selected before they had reached a certain age, assigned to various groups, and exposed to different experimental conditions for a number of years. Thus one group might receive extensive practice on the particular intellectual function that is assumed to diminish with disuse and another group might not. If the diminished function were due to disuse, then one would predict that those in the group that did not practice would show an impairment in that function when they were old, whereas members of the practice group would not.

Obviously, this approach would present a great many difficulties, since we are just not prepared to do longitudinal studies of this type with human beings. Actually, it is even expensive and difficult to maintain and study animals for their entire life span, and very few studies of this kind have taken place. When they have been conducted, they have typically involved mice or other rodents. However, some studies of this kind are underway with higher animals. For example, as part of a program to study the effects of radiation on behavior and aging, Dr. Roger Davis maintained a colony of rhesus monkeys at the University of South Dakota Primate Laboratory for a number of years. Survivors of the initial colony are still being studied by Dr. Davis at Washington State University. Similarly, a new animal resource has been created in the life-span colony of beagles maintained at Colorado State University; the project is also concerned with radiation effects. Since many of the effects of radiation do not appear early, it is necessary that animals in these types of experiments be studied over long periods of time.

Although studies involving animals can give us a great deal of information about the aging process and its effects on behavior, it will still be necessary to conduct research with humans in order to develop a comprehensive psychology of aging. As Birren (1970) points out, "while practical reasons slow dramatic progress, the science seems to be moving toward an experimental psychology of aging . . . " (p. 125). As we indicated earlier, because of the very large number of aged in our society and the problems confronting these people, it is essential that our progress in this area become more dramatic.

HUMAN PERFORMANCE IN OLD AGE

The variety of topics that could be included under the heading of "human performance" are, of course, numerous; we will make no attempt to deal with all of the many areas of performance that have been investigated in relation to age variables. Rather, we will restrict our discussion to several of the areas that have been subjected to rather extensive research and about which a considerable amount is known or that are of particular importance in everyday life. These areas include speed and timing performance, as well as several of the higher mental processes.

Speed and Timing Behavior

One of the commonly observed changes in performance that occurs as an individual grows older is a tendency to slow down. Researchers have been interested in two aspects of this slowness—the reasons it occurs and the effects it has on the performance of various tasks.

There are probably several reasons for the overall reduction in speed of response of older individuals. In the first place, older persons frequently have a slower perception speed and are slower to recognize stimuli. Secondly, in many cases physiological changes due to aging have resulted in reduced sensory acuity. These factors may result in a reduction in sensory input, which, in turn, leads to a slowed response. However, as Birren (1964) points out:

Were this the only factor, then older adults would show quickness in self-initiated responses. Actually, the evidence indicates that all behavior mediated by the central nervous system tends to be slow in the aging organism. Hence, while reduced sensory input may contribute to slowing, it is not the only or necessarily the largest factor in the generalized slowing of old age. The reduced sensory input may itself be a manifestation of primary neural aging, in which transmission in the nervous system tends to be reduced because of the loss of cells and age changes in the physiological properties of nerve cells and fibers. In the view favored here, slowness of behavior is the principle manifestation of a primary process of aging in the nervous system [pp. 111–112].

Much of the data available concerning the reduced response speed of older persons have been obtained from various types of reaction-time studies. In a typical reaction-time study, the subject places a finger on a telegraph key and, at the onset of a light or buzzer, removes his finger as rapidly as possible. The time between the onset of the signal and the point at which the finger is removed from the key is the reaction time. A number of studies of age changes in simple auditory or visual reaction time shows that there is a considerable slowing between 20-year-olds and 60-year-olds, with the latter between 10 to 20% slower.

Sometimes the reaction-time tasks are made more complex. For example, the subject may have to respond to a particular type of signal rather than just a light, or he may have to make other "choices" between stimuli. For this reason, reaction-time tasks are often labeled "simple" or "choice," with the latter being more complex. Research has shown that older persons are also slower on choice-reaction-time tasks than younger individuals.

It is necessary to distinguish between speed in doing a task and timing. Speed, such as in a reaction-time task or in other kinds of tasks, refers to the fastest time in which a task can be performed. Timing, on the other hand, involves some kind of sequential relationship between the components of a task. Most tasks require that some sort of integration, or timing, of subtasks take place, and more is involved than just speed. The adverse effects of age on timing of more complex behavior than the reaction-time tasks has been demonstrated in a number of experiments involving a variety of tasks. Numerous studies show that old people require more time to complete the tasks or will finish fewer items in a prescribed period of time than young people.

A number of investigations could be cited to support the conclusion that there is a generalized slowness of behavior in older persons. However, there are still some questions about the reasons for this process and even more questions about the modifying conditions that might maintain an older person's potential for a precise and rapid response. It has been suggested that continuous high-level stimulation in later life might serve this function, but this is only a hypothesis.

Laboratory research, then, has demonstrated that there is a slowing of behavior as a result of age. What practical implications does this have? It may not be possible to reverse this process or to maintain a rapid response through practice (although we do not know if this is the case), but information of this kind may have some value in the design of environments for the elderly.

Unfortunately, most of the man-machine systems that we encounter are not designed with the elderly in mind. For example, consider the transportation system: driving on a freeway may require a series of rapid and timed patterns of behavior. We know very little—other than fatality statistics—about the aged driver's capability to drive in these situations. However, with the growing number of older people in our population, there will be a corresponding increase in older drivers; we may have to obtain a better understanding about their driving and, possibly, consider modifying the system to account for their capabilities. This is just one example of many that could be listed in which the reduced response speed of the elderly might have implications.

Learning and Memory in the Aged

It was once believed that learning ability declined from youth to old age. Support for this view was given by a number of descriptive studies. A number of investigations show that, on a variety of learning tasks, older subjects do not do as well as younger subjects. Some researchers argue that this is due to an overall decline in learning *ability* or *capacity* and can support their arguments with a considerable amount of data. However, others hold a more optimistic view. For instance, as Birren (1964) points out, more and more evidence suggests that changes with age in the primary *ability* to learn are small; when differences are noted, the changes often can be attributed to age deficits in perception, set, attention, motivation, and the physiological state of the person, rather than to any change in the primary *capacity* to learn. Thus, although differences between old and young subjects show on such measures as speed and accuracy of learning, the differences may be due to situational variables rather than ability. More research is needed, however, in order to determine which situational factors may limit the older individual's learning performance and which factors may facilitate it.

The opposite side of learning is memory, and this process in the aged has been subjected to considerable research. Old people, of course, are notorious for remembering, in minute detail, events that took place many years before and forgetting events that happened only a short time earlier. There can be little doubt that the ability to retain new information in a form which can be readily "retrieved" declines with age. As Talland (1968) points out:

This decline can be attributed to an impairment of the mechanisms active in either the acquisition or the retention of new information, and there is experimental evidence to support both explanations. Indeed, it seems quite probable that efficiency declines with age in all the processes that are involved in memory function, in recall and recognition as well as in the initial acquisition of information and whatever mechanisms subserve the storage of information [p. 94].

In considering the relationship between memory and age, it should be kept in mind that memory is a complex process of at least two types. One type of memory stores material for long periods of time—perhaps a lifetime; this is called *long-term memory*. Another kind of memory, however, involves temporary storage of a very short duration; it is called *short-term memory*. The question that has concerned researchers in the area of memory is whether similar processes are involved in the two kinds of memory. In other words, when you look up a telephone number and attempt to dial it immediately, is the same kind of process involved as when you attempt to recall something you learned years ago? A definitive answer to this question is not available, although some investigators have pointed out important differences between the two kinds of memory. Other researchers have argued that some of the processes involved in forgetting long-term memories are similar to those for short-term memory.

Most current thinking in the area of learning and memory has new incoming information stored in short-term memory before it is "transferred" to long-term memory. All of the information received in short-term storage, of course, is not transferred to long-term, and some is lost immediately. Whether or not the transfer to long-term storage takes place is dependent on several factors, including the individual's conscious decision to learn and "store" the material. Why and how the transfer takes place is a technical topic beyond the scope of this chapter. For our purposes, the important point to remember is that short-term memory is considered by many to be an essential step in the complex learning and memory process. Thus any deficit in short-term memory would result in many learning and performance-task deficits.

Because of the importance attributed to short-term memory, considerable research has been directed at this process. A number of investigators have attempted to prove that some of the age deficits found in learning and performance are due to an age decrement in short-term memory. An age decrement in short-term memory would account for the observed decline in overall learning ability as well as age deficits in problem solving and skilled performance. Craik (1968), in reviewing short-term memory and the aging process, points out that there is no lack of experimental evidence to show that this function does, in fact, become less efficient with increasing age. He concludes that the importance of age deficit in short-term memory has been established, and he cites a number of investigations revealing large age decrements in short-term memory to support his conclusions. All of the data on age-related deficits in learning and performance does not fit in with the concept of short-term memory impairment, but much of it does, and, judging from the current interest among researchers in studying short-term memory in the aged, this point of view is becoming increasingly popular.

Intellectual Functions

The research dealing with decline in mental abilities as a result of aging has often produced contradictory results. Thus, in some studies, definite and pronounced declines are found, whereas in other investigations, declines (if any) are slight. When the results of many studies are combined, they show a gradual decline in ability. However, what this "average" decline represents is really a mixture of two populations—the elderly who are relatively stable in their abilities and those who decline abruptly and seriously in their abilities (Birren, 1964, p. 194).

Although considerable research has been done on intelligence, a number of methodological problems are encountered by investigators concerned with the relationship of mental ability and age. What should be used as the criterion of mental ability? Typically, some form of intelligence test is used, and the performance of groups of old individuals is compared with groups of younger persons. This procedure has several disadvantages. Intelligence tests were not designed to be used with elderly individuals; in most cases, they were designed and validated with young subjects. There are other measurement problems. Jones (1956) discusses some of the other considerations involved in evaluating mental measurements of older persons:

The psychologist must always take account of the possible discrepancy between abilities and capacities. A person's ability, or his actual performance in a test situation, will approach his capacity if the test is appropriate for his educational level, and if he is working under strong incentive without handicap from internal or external distractions. Under these conditions the ability score will hug the capacity ceiling, and variations in capacities will be reasonably well reflected by variations in obtained test scores. At later ages it may be increasingly difficult to meet all of these conditions, and in addition there may be sensory or other physical handicaps which divorce ability from capacity, and which register an age decline due to extraneous factors rather than to essential changes in intellective process [pp. 137–138].

Typically, tests used to measure intellectual abilities will contain subtests that emphasize different abilities. Thus, in some cases, verbal ability may be critical, whereas on other subtests, speed of performance may be important. Often, the result of the test is reported as one score, which combines the various subtests. We have already pointed out that a decline in speed of performance

301

is characteristic of older persons, and there is considerable evidence to indicate that there is a consistent decline in performance in these types of subtests as a function of age. However, evidence for decline on verbal tests is much less clear; some studies even show a rise in performance with age.

Along with the measurement problem in studying intellectual functions of the aged are the questions concerning the use of longitudinal or cross-sectional techniques. In the former case, subjects would be studied for many years, and data obtained concerning the evolution of abilities over a long period of time. With cross-sectional studies, far more common, tests are administered to a number of subjects in different age groups, and comparisons are made of the performance of the various groups. Basically, what information from studies of this type tells us is the relative ability of various age groups composing a given population at a particular time. Cross-sectional studies are important for setting normative characteristics and showing trends, but they give us little information about what happens to single individuals as they grow older. Longitudinal studies, on the other hand, can give us these kinds of data. Consider, for example, a study by Birren (1968). In this investigation, Birren and his colleagues studied a small number of community residents (men over 65 years) in an effort to obtain information about the capacities of older, independently living, individuals. Initially, there were 47 subjects with an average age of 72 years. They were tested on several standardized tests, and the survivors were measured again five years and six years later. The results showed that some aged individuals had slight or no decrements, and others showed dramatic declines in scores.

These findings support Birren's (1970) hypothesis that "change in intelligence in late life, as measured by conventional techniques, is not normally distributed. It may show little or no change in some healthy men in the seventh, eighth, and ninth decades of life, while concurrently individuals, possibly comprising a subpopulation suffering erosion of health, may show dramatic decline . . . " (p. 125).

It should be apparent from the above material that the exact relationship between aging and intellectual functioning is not completely understood. There has been interesting research in this area and interesting speculation about the results of the research, but it is a difficult area to study. Much more research, probably of the longitudinal type, will be required before the relationship is understood.

Problem Solving and Decision Making

Among the higher mental processes that have interested psychologists for many years are those of problem solving and decision making. There are various definitions of problem solving. However, most psychologists would agree that problem solving involves the *discovery* of a correct response to a situation that is new and unique to the individual. Decision making, on the other hand, can be thought of as the process that leads to the *selection* of a response from among a number of already "discovered" or known alternative responses.

In recent years a good deal of theorizing has taken place concerning the nature of the problem-solving and decision-making processes. Although there is agreement on some basic concepts in these areas, there is a good deal of disagreement about how these processes take place. Our concern, however, is not with the theoretical formulations but rather with the changes that do, or do not, take place in these processes due to aging.

Although not many studies have dealt with the relationship between age and problem-solving ability, those that have been done indicate there is a reduction in this ability in older persons. However, explaining this deficit is difficult. It was pointed out earlier that situational variables, not ability per se, may account for some of the deficit. The same is true when problem-solving ability is measured. Thus what should be used as the criterion—speed, accuracy, or some other measure? That this may be important is shown in a study by Welford (1958) that involved a problem-solving task comparing young and old subjects. It was found that older subjects were as accurate as young subjects but required 85% more time.

In considering the findings that problem-solving ability appears to diminish with age, several other facts are important. Problem solving, as we have indicated, is a complex process involving many component abilities, each of which may change with age. In some instances, solving the problem may depend on the amount of information possessed by the individual. Since this tends to increase over the life span, problems that have familiar elements and rely on possessed information may be solved more efficiently by the old rather than the young adult. However, if the problem emphasizes memory-held instructions or perceptual capacity, the younger person may perform more efficiently than the older individual. Older individuals may not have as much "practice" in their daily activities in problem solving as do younger people. Thus Birren (1964) states that "age brings with it not only differential changes in component mental abilities, but it involves the adaptations of the individual to problem-solving situations. Because of adaptation, the problem-solving orientation probably declines as a function of years since school" (p. 194). In general, because of the complex nature of the process, there are no simple answers to the question of whether problem-solving capacity rises or falls over the adult years.

Much the same statement can be made about our knowledge of changes in decision-making capability as a result of age. We really do not know whether man's effectiveness for decision making changes over the life span. There is some evidence to indicate that there is a slowing of the decision-making process. However, much of the research in this area has been based on choice-reaction-time studies or other simple tasks in which the longer latency shown by older subjects was inferred to be caused by a longer decision time. Research dealing with the older individual's capacity to make decisions in a complex and changing society is scarce.

One aspect of the decision-making process that some researchers have been interested in is *risk-taking behavior.* In other words, some decisions may involve some element of risk: the person "weighs" odds and stakes and arrives at a decision based on the probability of some desirable or undesirable outcome of his decision. Thus, in a sense, when a person crosses a street in the face of oncoming traffic, he makes a decision that involves some element of risk. Many of the decisions that we routinely make can be considered "risky decisions." This is a relatively new area in psychology, and virtually no research has been conducted dealing with risk taking in elderly individuals; when it has been done, the results have not been clear cut.

It would appear, then, that the areas of problem-solving, decision-making, and risk-taking behavior, all closely related, should be subjected to more research. These are critical functions, and an understanding of how age affects them is necessary if we are to have a "psychology of aging."

chapter
18

Some Special Problem
Areas in Mental Health

Over the years it has become apparent that various groups, for a variety of reasons, have what can be considered "special" mental health problems. These problems may arise because of particular experience, or lack of experience, associated with certain groups or because of attitudes toward mental health that are held by large segments of our population. For example, certain problems arise because of sensory deprivation, in the case of deaf children, and cultural deprivation, in the case of certain minority groups. Similarly, we find that psychologists who attempt to work with rural groups encounter quite different types of problems than do the psychologists who work in urban areas.

Of course, a number of groups could be considered "special" in terms of mental health problems, and we cannot deal with all of these. Rather, we will restrict our discussion in this chapter to the mental health problems of the deaf, people in rural areas, the American Indian, and, finally, some special problems of college students. In our discussion, we will consider the etiology of the mental health problems with these groups as well as some of the special approaches being developed in an attempt to cope with these problems.

EARLY EXPERIENCE AND MENTAL
HEALTH

It has become axiomatic in psychology that what happens to an individual at an early age may have very profound influences later, in terms of mental

Photo courtesy of Travel Division, South Dakota Dept. of Highways, Pierre, S. D.

health. One of the basic assumptions of Freudian psychology is that particular events occurring during the developing stages of an organism will, in fact, have long-lasting effects, evident in later behavior. For example, traumatic events occurring in the very young, even though consciously forgotten by the individual, are thought to be the motivating force of abnormal behavior when the person grows older.

Verification of the hypothesis of the effects of early experience on adult behavior with humans involves a number of methodological problems. The typical approach has been to utilize adult subjects who are considered abnormal and, in some fashion, attempt to find out what might have happened to them as children to cause the behavior. Obviously, it is difficult to obtain accurate information about the childhood experiences of a 30-year-old patient. However, some interesting research with animal subjects has tended to support the notion that early experience is, indeed, critical in the development of later behavior. We will briefly consider a few of these studies in order to illustrate this point.

Critical Periods

For some years, researchers have been studying a phenomenon called *imprinting* in a variety of birds. Basically, imprinting is a process whereby a young bird develops a set of responses toward the most common moving object it perceives shortly after hatching. Numerous drastic examples have been used to demonstrate this phenomenon. For example, young birds such as ducks or geese can be imprinted on humans shortly after they are hatched and will continue to follow humans in seeming preference over actual mother ducks or geese. When these young birds become sexually mature, many will have little to do with members of their own species but will make sexual advances toward humans. This is an example, then, of the effects early experience in the first 24 hours of an organism's life can have on later adult behavior. This period of time is referred to as a critical period.

After the concepts of critical periods, early experience, and imprinting with birds had been firmly established, many psychologists turned to using other animals as experimental subjects and investigating more complex behaviors. Investigators have demonstrated that there are critical periods affecting rather complex social behavior in animals such as dogs (Scott & Langston, 1950). In brief, this research has indicated that, if young puppies are not allowed to interact with other members of the species, their later adult social behavior does not develop normally. Similarly, Harlow (1958, 1962) has conducted extensive research on the development of affective responses in rhesus monkeys. He has demonstrated quite dramatically that the development of affective responses has a critical period during the early life of the infant monkeys.

Sensory Deprivation

An interesting variation of the early-experience hypothesis has to do with the effects of early sensory deprivation. Traditionally, the sensory and perceptual responses of organisms have been thought of as essentially innate or primary. In other words, investigators considered sensory responses, such as touch and pain, very basic to the organism. It was thought that these responses would appear appropriately in the presence of a given physical stimulus, regardless of the background of the organism. However, it has been demonstrated in both dogs and chimpanzees that even the response to pain, such as the pain of being stuck with a pin, is not a naturally occurring response if the animal has undergone sensory deprivation during the critical period.

Using chimpanzees as experimental subjects, psychologists encased legs, feet, arms, and hands in cylinders, thus eliminating the opportunity for the subject to touch, feel, or manipulate external stimuli. Chimpanzees were maintained in this manner for almost the entire period of growth and development. After the period of development and the supposed critical period had passed, the cylinders were removed from the extremities. At this time batteries of tests were administered to the subjects in an effort to determine if any loss of function had occurred. It was no surprise that the animals were essentially incapable of manipulating objects with the fingers. It was a surprise, however, to discover that the inability of the subject to respond to sensory stimuli had generalized to the point of not recognizing pain, even when the stimulus was rather severe. The same general finding was reported for dogs when they were raised through the critical period in sensory-restricted isolation. As adults, these dogs would not respond to pain in the same way their litter-mates, which had been raised in an enriched environment, responded.

Studies of these kinds are important to a better understanding of some of the special mental health problems we will be discussing. For example, to understand the mental health problems of patients who have been deaf, blind, or sensory deprived in some other fashion since birth, we must realize that we are dealing with a human who has gone through the critical-period stages without acquiring the same kind of sensory input that individuals with normal hearing or vision have accumulated. As we have seen, the more complex social behaviors are also dependent on exposure during critical periods of development, or else they, too, become disrupted with the result being manifest in abnormal behavior. Finally, the same kinds of dynamics are evident in behaviors exhibited by small culturally deprived groups, such as those on isolated Indian reservations in the United States. Obviously, in most cases when there is some deprivation of a particular type, this deprivation will have generalization effects on a wide variety of behaviors. This generalization factor should be kept in mind as we talk about some of the special areas of mental health facing psychologists.

SPECIAL PROBLEMS OF THE DEAF

Although the point has been made that sensory deprivation in any modality induces a very broad variety of problems, this discussion will be concerned with mental health problems of the deaf. Obviously, much of what we have to say about the problems of the deaf would also apply to the blind. However, it is beyond the scope of this chapter to deal with all of the special groups. Consequently, although you should be aware that the blind also have unique problems of this type, we will restrict our discussion to the deaf.

There are many causes for deafness developing at various stages of life, but our primary concern in this chapter will be with those people whose hearing losses occurred prior to the development of language skills. Typically, this includes congenital deafness as well as injury- or disease-producing deafness prior to approximately 2 years of age. These individuals have not had the opportunity to develop personalities, including coping responses, with the aid of the auditory sensory modality. In other words, they have undergone sensory deprivation through a critical period for the development of their intellectual and emotional processes.

Personality Development in the Deaf

Although a great deal of effort has been directed toward determining the effects of deafness on school performance, language development, and reading ability, little effort has been directed toward understanding the problems of emotional and personality adjustment. One of the primary tasks for psychologists interested in problems related to the deaf is to ascertain ways in which that type of sensory deprivation does, in fact, modify the development and manifestation of personality adjustment.

A deaf child, of course, does not have the richness of meaning of words that goes beyond the simple spelling of that particular word. An example might be the word *mother*. Although the words would appear on paper as having meaning in a given context, the use of the word in the spoken language by people with normal hearing can be given a variety of meanings and suggestions, depending on the tonal quality expressed. The resultant loss of this richness in quality and the association of words and meanings restricts emotional involvement with these concepts for the deaf. These differences in emotional

310

qualities set deaf people off from those with normal hearing, and the result is that these people are very often labeled "different." Being perceived as different may, of course, have an effect on the personality development of the deaf child.

In his developmental process, a normal child goes through a period of approximately two years as a nonverbal being. Yet it is during this period that the child must learn to identify with his existing environment. He must learn to conform to the stimuli in that environment as well as dress and feed himself and establish emotional bonds with the physical and social components of his environment. As he progresses in his development, he has the channel of audition to constantly provide him with information, both as a sensing device to facilitate new learning and a means of reaffirming relationships already learned. This facility then enhances the progress and process of emotional development as the child continues to grow. When the deaf child reaches the stage at which audition should be making a major contribution to his process of development, the development of his emotional maturity is considerably disrupted.

Myklebust (1964) has proposed that the process of identification is a basic aspect of personality development and emotional maturity that the deaf child has a great deal of difficulty in developing. The concept of identification takes into account a wide variety of factors, such as general attitudes toward the total environment (family, community, state, other people, society) and an individual's role or relationship to all of these. In addition, the concept refers to the process of the individual adopting some kind of role model against which he may constantly test his behavior and self-concept. Obviously lack of auditory ability during this critical stage of development creates a situation in which the deaf individual may identify with grossly inappropriate concepts for the particular culture and society in which the child lives. A more specific example might be a female in our society who identifies with primarily male concepts and personalities and therefore has serious adjustment problems.

If we consider audition as a modality serving as a monitoring system for the stimuli coming from outside of the body, then not having this monitoring system creates some special kinds of difficulties. One of these problems is the psychological factor referred to as isolation. It becomes extremely difficult for a family to keep a deaf child informed of happenings not only within the family but within the entire social structure. The child thus becomes more isolated, giving the appearance of becoming autistic and withdrawn. There is, then, a deficiency of total experience of the feelings, emotions, and intellectual functioning when this monitoring system is not operative. In addition, the development of language is crucial in the process of internally integrating experience. When experience is not integrated internally, the deaf child's behavior appears less structured, more immature, and more immediately hedonistic than behavior in children of the same age who have normal hearing. This is a sample of the problems psychologists must face and deal with when working with mental health of the deaf. We will briefly look at some of the research that has been conducted.

Personality Studies of the Deaf

The study of personality in people with normal hearing is a difficult enough task. Numerous techniques have been developed, including projective tests, standardized personality assessments, and the clinical-interview technique. None of these standardized techniques are very useful when given to individuals that are nonverbal, because almost all of the tests utilized for the evaluation of emotional factors are dependent on and related to verbal facilities.

Some years ago, Brunschwig (1936) devised personality tests exclusively for use with deaf children. The language used in these tests was extremely simple, in an attempt to take into account the limited verbal abilities of the subjects. Although he was looking at a wide variety of factors, one interesting finding was related to the presence or absence of other deaf persons in the home. Rather consistently, deaf children coming from homes in which there were other deaf persons, either parents or siblings, were found to be much better adjusted than deaf children coming from homes in which there were no other deaf.

The typical finding in most studies has been that deaf children are emotionally immature. However, this finding is certainly questionable, since the "immaturity" comes from the comparison of the deaf children's scores with standardized norms in which the standardization had been done with children with no impairment. In a very extensive investigation, Myklebust (1964) administered the Minnesota Multiphasic Personality Inventory (MMPI) to large numbers of deaf and hard-of-hearing adults. A great deal of effort was made to control for differences between reading facility of the deaf and the level of expertise needed for comparison of the data with the standardized norm. He reports that if the results of the test are taken literally, the deaf males would definitely be more emotionally disturbed and immature than the average hearing male. This is true for almost all of the psychological categories measured by the MMPI. When comparisons were made between deaf males and deaf females, the females were consistently closer to the universal norms on almost all categories. Since the subjects were comparable in education, age, hearing loss, and socioeconomic status, this would suggest that deafness influences personality factors unequally in men and women.

Myklebust proposes a tentative hypothesis that hearing loss may have a major effect on psychosexual adjustment. For example, the interest scale on the MMPI measures feelings of masculinity and femininity. If males score high on the interest scale, this indicates femininity. High scores for females indicate masculinity. With the deaf, males' and females' scores on the interest scale were both high. The immediate suggestion from these high scores is that deafness feminizes the male and masculinizes the female. It is possible that these findings indicate that the inability to hear reduces the social sexuality prevalent in our society for people with normal hearing.

In summary, the research on emotional adjustment and personality for the deaf would indicate that these people definitely have characteristic behavioral attributes, which lead to different kinds of behavior problems than we typically see in the normal population. One of the obvious distortions involves the psychological reception of the individual by others as well as the entire environment. From the practical point of view, when providing therapeutic mental health, it becomes critical that therapists take into account many diverse consequences of early sensory deprivation during critical periods of development. Therapists must constantly seek meaningful methods of communication, both for understanding the problem and suggesting new learning methods for the patient. It remains, then, a challenge to the therapists to devise and implement appropriate techniques to provide help in these kinds of special cases.

RURAL VERSUS URBAN MENTAL HEALTH

Mental health workers providing services to rural areas find that there are many aspects of the rural environment that have produced qualitative as well as quantitative differences in behavioral manifestations associated with mental illness. Programs that have been successful in urban mental health clinics have not been as successful in rural areas for a variety of reasons. One factor is that the community response to mental health clinics is very different. This difference becomes quite clear when the mental health worker gets to know the attitudes of the people living in the area the center is designed to serve.

Psychologists attempting to set up rural mental health centers have found that, although there are some similarities between urban and rural populations, there are very important differences. To understand better what the rural mental health worker must face, we will look at a few of the attitudinal and personality factors that must be taken into account when working in rural areas.

The very nature of the geographic environment is important. The people living in small towns situated away from metropolitan areas do not have the same social and mental health services available to them as do people in urban areas. This is understandable, since the small population typically cannot afford the services of trained professional mental health workers such as psychiatrists and clinical psychologists. Support for these kinds of professional services is usually on the basis of population. This means that, in rural communities, these services are not available on any permanent basis and are seldom available even on a monthly basis. This sets up a situation in which the people do not develop any reliance on services and often are not even aware of their availability.

Rural Attitudes Toward Mental Health

Along with the problem of availability and utilization of mental health facilities in rural areas, the attitude toward mental illness is very different from the one we find in the highly populated areas. For example, if we consider the concept of mental health problems in the rural area from the standpoint of what it means to be "sick," we encounter some interesting problems. Thus Tranel (1970) states:

In order to be legitimately "sick" in the rural situation, one must be sick in a very identifiable way. It is scarcely enough to say that one is sick because of interpersonal stresses, since being sick implies that one is unable to function in his job. Interpersonal difficulties may prevent a person's adequate functioning in a service economy but not in the extractive economy of the rural work situation . . . it is difficult to imagine any of the usual forms of functional mental illness as a serious handicap to holding a job such as a sheepherder, a cowboy or a ranch hand . . . part of this aspect of the sick role in the rural condition is that in order to play the role because of mental illness one must show gross signs of disturbance. It is not enough to manifest mild neurotic symptoms to obtain the secondary rewards of the sick role. This is true not only because there are fewer professional people in the mental health and allied fields to hear and understand these complaints but also because mild symptoms are not vocationally handicapping in a primary level economy . . . [pp. 421–422].

Tranel then goes on to point out that very often the individuals who reach the professional mental health worker in rural settings show symptoms of mental illness that are much more gross than those that would be called to the attention of the psychologist in a more sophisticated social unit. In other words, people living in rural areas must be very "crazy" before they receive help.

The rural community, then, maintains a much higher tolerance for mental illness than we find in urban areas. Again, as suggested by Tranel, behavior disorders that would be disrupting or at least annoying to co-workers in an interpersonal relationship do not exist in the rural community, since the work performed is typically not of an interpersonal nature.

Some Other Factors

There are a variety of other unique factors that contribute to the mental health problem in rural areas. For example, members of rural communities dependent on agriculture are very unsure of the future. Programs developed by the government have not been universally acceptable or successful. Subsidy programs have tended to benefit the larger agricultural units more than they have benefited the small farmer or rancher. The tendency, then, has been for ranches either to grow or be absorbed. The attitude of the people becomes one of confusion and general skepticism that anyone anywhere really has any control over the situation. When we consider the dependence of agricultural interests on factors defying control (such as the environment), it is much easier to understand this skepticism.

One of the reported differences in rural-versus-urban lives most referred to by urban people is their amazement at the many references rural people make to the weather. However, the entire rural community in an agricultural economy is dependent on the weather. If there is not enough rain, crops don't grow; if there is too much rain at the time of harvest, crops are lost; if it freezes or if it's too hot, income is lost. This affects not only the farmer but the machinery suppliers, warehouses, agricultural production, grocery stores, bankers, realtors, car salesmen, and so forth. Again this contributes to a great deal of mistrust and skepticism toward control or authority of any kind. These, plus many other factors, add up to a very imposing task indeed for psychologists interested in providing previously nonexistent mental health services in rural areas.

SPECIAL MENTAL HEALTH
PROBLEMS OF MINORITY GROUPS

In our society, normal or abnormal behavior is defined by the dominant culture in that particular social unit, regardless of whether we consider the nation, state, county, or city as our target social unit. Typically, within any given social unit there will be identifiable smaller cultural units. When these smaller cultural units are ethnic minority groups having meaningful traditional behavioral patterns serving to identify and preserve the cultural integrity of the group, these behaviors are looked on as different from the dominant cultural group. Since the predominant social values of the United States evolve around what has been referred to as the "WASP" value system, this set of values has dictated generally what we call "normal" and "abnormal" behavior. It is this value system that has given rise to what has been referred to as the "medical model of mental illness."

According to this medical model, mental health problems arise when members of a culturally identifiable minority cannot or do not accept the dominant value system. There has been a tendency by the culturally naive to take the general attitude of "if those people wish to get ahead and better themselves in our society, then they must conform." This approach places the burden of responsibility of adaptability on the minority group in question, and, although it may salve the conscience of the dominant culture, it overlooks some very critical considerations. Minority groups do not control the means of getting ahead or adapting to the dominant culture. In most cases, members of the minority culture simply are not allowed to get ahead. They do not control nor can they control their acceptance into the dominant society. This initiates a vicious circle with the members of the culturally identifiable group being different, that difference being perceived and reacted against rather than celebrated. Although anthropologists and sociologists have been studying these cultural differences for numerous years, it has only been recently that psychologists have put any major effort into understanding the role these cultural differences have on patterns of behavior.

Mental Health Problems of the American Indians

At the present time there is considerable research dealing with mental health problems of ethnic minorities. However, in this chapter we will only be concerned with some of the problems of adjustment of American Indians on isolated reservations. We will restrict our discussion to this minority group for two reasons. First, other minority groups have received considerable attention for a number of years, but the problems of the Indians have only recently begun to come to the attention of the public. Second, both authors are located in regions in which we are continually exposed to the mental health problems of this particular minority group; consequently, we are particularly interested in this area.

Actually, the point must be made that the American Indians cannot be treated as a single minority group. Every tribe is culturally different as well as geographically separate. Some reservations are in essentially urban areas, whereas others are relatively isolated in sparsely populated areas. If we take the Northern Cheyenne reservation in Southeastern Montana as an example, perhaps we can gain some insight into a few of the factors affecting the mental health of the inhabitants. On this reservation there are approximately 2500 Indians living on 433,000 acres. There are three communities on the reservation, including Lame Deer (with a population of approximately 1100), Busby (with a population of around 800), and Birney community (with a population of around 300). In the village of Lame Deer, the social needs of the people are provided by one general store, two gas stations, one cafe, the tribal-council building, and a newly started library.

By way of contrast, McDonald grew up in a South Dakota town of less population than Lame Deer. Yet there were five grocery stores, two post offices, four hardware stores, three clothing stores, five cafes, seven service stations, three motels, two theatres, one public library, two pool halls, one swimming pool, one golf course, one country club, eleven churches, four automobile dealerships with garages, plus numerous small businesses, and many community activities. For most readers, this described town would also qualify as a culturally deprived community. However, in comparison to Lame Deer, the opportunity for social interaction and the development of adaptive skills was very rich.

The situation in Busby is even more acute, with 800 people being serviced by one general store/post office and one filling station. There is no other service available in the community. Is it any wonder, then, that an Indian youth who comes off the reservation to a larger town to seek work or go to school appears shy, immature, unsophisticated, bewildered, and generally unable to cope with city life? This inability to adjust gives rise to serious mental health problems.

The Primary Problem: Alcohol. Several investigators concerned with mental health problems of Indians have attempted to determine what the Indian people perceive as the most predominant mental health problems of their culture. Invariably these investigations indicate that alcoholism and the problems associated with the use of alcohol are perceived as heading the list of serious problems. This is not surprising, since the predominant stereotype of the Indian is one of a drunken Indian. Although the problem of alcoholism was discussed in detail in Chapter 16, in this chapter we will consider this problem as it relates to the Indian.

The World Health Organization (1954) defines alcoholism as "a chronic disease or disorder of behavior characterized by the repeated drinking of alcoholic beverages to an extent that exceeds customary dietary use or ordinary compliance with the social drinking customs of the community and which interferes with the drinker's health, interpersonal relations or economic functioning." If we use this definition, the vast majority of Indians who use alcohol at all must be classified problem drinkers. Mental health workers, both on and off Indian reservations, report that the Indian typically receives a paycheck and proceeds to drink until his money is gone. He usually becomes extremely inebriated, oftentimes violent, and, a very high percentage of the time, ends up in jail. Obviously, this behavior must be classified as disrupting normal family relationships and/or other social relationships, including ability to get to work.

What most members of the white culture do not take into account, however, is that there are obvious historical, legal, social, and cultural reasons for this kind of drinking, which is "abnormal" when compared to the use of alcohol in the dominant society. The Indians were restricted from developing any rational use of alcohol as a social institution. In the 1950s the Federal Government, in an outstanding act of benevolence, made it legal for Indians to purchase alcoholic beverages in bars and liquor stores off the reservation. Prior to that time it was illegal for Indians to possess, purchase, or use alcoholic beverages of any kind. Until recently, it was still illegal for Indians to possess alcoholic beverages on their reservations; although this restriction has been lifted, people do not change social habits rapidly. The point to be made is that the Indian people living on the reservation could not use alcohol in the same manner that the whites have utilized it. For example, they have been allowed for the past 15 years or so to go to an off-reservation town and drink as much as they could pay for or tolerate, but they were not free to purchase alcohol and take it to their homes. It is obvious that this creates a pattern of drinking in which overindulgence is virtually assured.

The Indian alcoholic, then, definitely does not fit the stereotype of the white alcoholic. For one thing, the Indian does not have the economic resources to continue drinking day after day. More typically, the Indian alcoholic finds part-time work, receives his pay, and then drinks until his money is gone. He usually finds himself without a job when he becomes sober, thus forcing him into a prolonged period of abstinence. If we can place any faith in the statement that "drinking stems from the desire for an antidote to unpleasant reality," then certainly unpleasant reality is to be found in abundance on the typical Indian reservation.

Mental health workers on and off the reservations are finding that these kinds of insights and awareness of the differences in alcoholism are providing better techniques for taking care of Indian alcoholics than some of the more traditional approaches. The more successful programs dealing with alcoholism are utilizing indigenous Indians to work on the reservation with other Indians. These individuals have lived on the reservations all their lives, have seen the problems, speak the language, and are accepted in the community. Thus they are capable of understanding the people and the problem.

Just as is the case with psychologists working with the deaf, with minority groups there is one basic theme that becomes most apparent: highly trained professional mental health workers that have little in common with the groups they are trying to serve find it difficult to develop an understanding and insight into the mental health problems of these special groups. For example, there are no Ph.D.-level clinical psychologists or psychiatrists that can speak the Northern Cheyenne language. There are very few psychiatrists or clinical psychologists working in rural areas who have, in fact, come from rural areas. In recognition of the problems in communication, educational level, and general lack of understanding of minority-group problems, there is a trend in the field of psychology to train indigenous workers as "go-betweens" to provide services in the mental health area to these special groups. There is considerable optimism on the part of these psychologists that this approach will be more fruitful than those we have had in the past.

MENTAL HEALTH PROBLEMS ON COLLEGE CAMPUSES

We have already considered special groups that have in common either sensory or cultural deprivation during critical stages of the development of the socialization processes. It should not be implied that only those people who are deprived in some manner develop mental health problems. For instance, as a group, college students are the least deprived socially, culturally, intellectually, and economically; however, college life can be stressful at times. This stress can, and often does, lead to mental health problems.

Most mental health professionals dealing primarily with students report that an important problem (one that is critical to students) is associated with the loss of identity. In other words, considerable anxiety, frustration, and threats are generated by the fact that, on many campuses, the students soon become

FIGURE 18-1. Many students feel they lose their identity in college or university situations. This feeling is enhanced by the emphasis on computerizing many phases of the academic process. (Photo by Sam Sprague.)

numbers or, at least, perceive themselves as such. This begins with the process of registration. On most campuses today, the first step involves obtaining a student identification number with a packet of IBM cards all appropriately punched in numerical or alphabetical order. Invariably, there are directives, warnings, and threats not to mutilate, bend, or in any way modify the cards. The thought of what would happen if this packet of cards were lost is terrifying to the freshmen. He can almost visualize an entire academic career being lost should this happen. Although this may be slightly exaggerated, being treated as if the number and IBM cards were more important than the individual does appear to threaten a large number of students.

This feeling of loss of identity is further reinforced on most modern campuses when the student goes to his first series of classes. Typically, the introductory courses are extremely large. Students report difficulty in identifying with the instructor, other students, and the purpose of the class in this kind of situation. When these factors are combined with such things as homesickness and loss of home-town friends, it takes a great deal of motivation and maturity to overcome the threats to one's identity.

In the vast majority of cases, students meet and make new friends and get involved in some kind of interaction, either extracurricular or social, that gives them some positive reinforcement and feeling of worth. Again, if a student can identify and actively participate in social activities of some kind, he becomes less threatened and more self-confident. However, some students do not make these contacts and become severely withdrawn.

Unfortunately, the majority of college campuses have inadequate mental health facilities available to the students. When these facilities are available, they are typically set up on the traditional medical-model basis. The school psychiatrist or clinical psychologist is generally available during office hours only. As you are probably aware, periods of anxiety and depression are usually most severe after five o'clock and almost always occur away from the Student Health Service or counseling center. In other words, a student must show a great deal of aggressive initiative and go to the service center if he is to receive counseling.

Recognizing the inefficiency of this system, there are several model programs proposed to put counselors in the dormitories during the evening hours, making these services available in a less imposing environment, as well as at more appropriate hours. In addition, WICHE (Western Interstate Commission on Higher Education) in the western part of the United States has initiated a series of task forces composed of psychologists, counselors, and students to work on what can be done to better improve mental health services on college campuses. It is hoped that these professional mental health workers, in combination with student assistance, will provide information that will allow mental health professionals to be of more immediate and relevant service on college campuses.

Some Other Problems: Smoking and Overeating

Obviously, in our discussions of drugs, the alcohol problem, aging, and special mental health problems, we have in no way exhausted the topics that could be included under a section dealing with intrapersonal problems. We selected these topics because of their particular relevance to our present-day society. The final problem areas to be considered—smoking and overeating—were selected not because of their impact on society (although they are a health problem) but because, to many readers, they may be quite important personally. Thus, although it is likely that relatively few of the readers of this text have a drug or alcohol problem and even fewer have an aging problem, many smoke or overeat or perhaps both.

Actually, both of these forms of behavior have been of interest to psychologists for many years, but recently there has been an upsurge of research, particularly in the area of smoking. This has been due almost entirely to the concern about the relationship between smoking and health. The conclusions reached by the Advisory Committee to the Surgeon General, called *Smoking and Health* (1964), immediately developed national interest in not only the medical and physiological aspects of smoking but also the behavioral aspects. Thus the report to the Surgeon General states that "The overwhelming evidence points to the conclusion that smoking—its beginning, habituation, and occasional discontinuation—is to a large extent psychologically and socially determined" (p. 40).

Photo by Sam Sprague.

The research approaches and the problems studied have been varied, but much of the research conducted by psychologists in this area can be classified under three main headings. (1) A number of studies have attempted to determine why individuals begin to smoke and why they may continue to do so in spite of evidence that it is harmful. Many of these kinds of investigations have also been designed to distinguish between smokers and nonsmokers on the basis of personality characteristics and other variables. (2) Other studies have been concerned with determining the effects of smoking on various aspects of behavior, such as psychomotor performance, mood, anxiety, and so forth. Finally (3), some researchers have attempted to develop and evaluate techniques aimed at preventing people from starting to smoke or getting smokers to stop.

In the area of overeating, some research has been directed at determining the dynamics of obesity. In other words, why is it that some people overeat and others do not? Recently, however, a number of investigators have become interested in ways in which overweight individuals can be made to lose weight by means of various psychological techniques and approaches. In this chapter, we will discuss some recent thinking in the area of overeating as well as some of the weight-reduction approaches and their effectiveness.

PSYCHOLOGICAL ASPECTS OF SMOKING

Although we are interested in the psychological aspects of smoking, keep in mind that with cigarette smoke we are dealing with a complex mixture of gases, uncondensed vapors, and liquid particulate matter. Actually, about 500 different compounds have been identified in cigarette smoke, and much research has been and continues to be aimed at determining the particular factors in the smoke that may be detrimental to health. Any detailed discussion of the chemical characteristics of cigarette smoke is well beyond the scope of this book, but we will briefly mention one component that has been widely studied—namely, nicotine.

Much of what we know about the effects of nicotine on physiological functions is based on studies with animals actually injected with nicotine. In these studies it has been found that nicotine has a direct effect on the nervous system, with brief excitation followed by depression or even paralysis with large enough doses. Nicotine in moderate doses causes marked increases in respiratory, blood-vessel, and stomach activity; larger doses sometimes lead to tremors and convulsions.

Smoking one or two cigarettes will cause, in most people, an increase in the resting heart rate from 15 to 25 beats per minute, a rise in blood pressure, and an increase in cardiac output of blood. There is a decrease in blood flow to the extremities, the result of which is a drop of temperature in the fingers and toes. These same types of effects have been found when nicotine alone was introduced, suggesting that the effects of smoking on the nervous system and the cardiovascular system are caused by the nicotine element of the smoke.

Basically, then, the effects of nicotine, at least in small doses, is that of a stimulant. Thus ingestion of a drug such as amphetamine will have physiological effects quite similar to those of nicotine. Keep this in mind later in this chapter, when some of the studies dealing with the effects of nicotine and smoking on psychomotor performance are considered.

As pointed out previously, research conducted by psychologists in the area of smoking and behavior falls into three broad categories. Thus a number of investigations have dealt with personality or intraindividual variables that may be connected with either the onset or continuation of smoking behavior, other studies deal with the effects of smoking on particular aspects of behavior, and, more recently, a number of studies have been dealing with techniques for effectively discontinuing smoking.

Personality and Intraindividual Variables in Smoking

Many investigators have recognized that the choice to smoke or not to smoke may be based on personality (or other variables) and have attempted, by means of various research approaches, to determine if relationships exist between these variables and smoking behavior. Typically, these approaches have involved testing groups of individuals who have been identified as smokers and groups who are nonsmokers to determine if these groups differ in any personality or other characteristics. Often, the researchers have been interested in age as a variable and have looked at differences that might be manifested between groups of adult smokers in some cases; in other instances, they were concerned with children and adolescents.

In studies with adults, several personality variables have tended to distinguish between smokers and nonsmokers. For example, there seems to be a tendency for smokers to be extroverted, whereas nonsmokers are introverted. However, in a comprehensive review of the research literature on psychological and related variables involved in smoking, Matarazzo and Saslow (1960) concluded that there was no clear-cut description of a "smoker's personality." Although a number of the investigations reviewed by these researchers revealed differences between smokers and nonsmokers on selected personality variables, no single variable was always found in one group and not in others. In a more recent review of the literature on personality and smoking, Smith (1970) was able to draw several conclusions about differences between smokers and nonsmokers. Thus he found that 22 out of 25 studies reported that smokers were significantly more extroverted than nonsmokers. Similarly, studies concerning "antisocial tendencies" were relatively clear-cut, with 27 out of 32 investigations showing smokers to be significantly more antisocial than nonsmokers. It also appears that smokers are more likely to be externally oriented: they, more than nonsmokers, will think that chance, fate, luck, and so on, rather than their own skill and effort, accounts for what happens to them. There is also some evidence that smokers are more impulsive than nonsmokers.

A number of investigations have also been aimed at determining why a person starts to smoke. Most of these investigations have involved relatively young subjects, since smoking often starts at an early age. In all of these studies, the importance of social learning is illustrated. For example, a youngster is much more likely to begin if his parents smoke. Similarly, a significant number begin to smoke because of social pressures presented by peer-group members who smoke.

McKennel and Bynner (1969) conducted a study dealing with self-concept or self-image and smoking behavior among school boys. They studied over 5000 boys between 11 and 15 years of age. One factor that tended to provide an incentive both for nonsmokers to begin smoking and for smokers to continue was the view of "toughness" that the subjects associated with the act of smoking. Interestingly enough, the one attribute the nonsmokers had that the smokers rated as being desirable was educational success.

It has become apparent from the research aimed at defining the motivational factors that cause a person to begin to smoke and to continue smoking that this is a complex topic. Logan (1970) suggests that "Initially smoking must be motivated extrinsically; youth learns to smoke to be accepted, to rebel, to reduce their feelings of inferiority, from curiosity, or the like.... In time smoking generates its own intrinsic motivation, which may make it functionally autonomous even after the initiating drives are no longer present" (p. 142). Thus a number of different motives have been suggested as being responsible for the onset of smoking behavior and for its continuation, often in spite of sustained efforts to extinguish the behavior.

Smoking and Mental Health

Under the heading of personality and intraindividual variables in smoking, it is appropriate to consider what some call a "beneficial aspect" of smoking—that is, smoking effect on mental health. Thus, in the Surgeon General's (1964) report on smoking, it is stated that "Medical perspective requires recognition of significant beneficial effects of smoking primarily in the area of mental health" (p. 356).

The relationship between smoking and mental health is, of course, difficult to establish with any degree of certainty. In the first place, the question of what is meant by "mental health" has no definitive answer. Although it is generally defined as "a relatively enduring state wherein the person is well-adjusted," there are obviously a host of factors that contribute to this state of adjustment. The fact that we can only talk in general terms about "mental health" tends to emphasize the conclusions drawn by the advisory committee on smoking and health:

But it is not an easy matter to reach a simple and reasonable conclusion concerning the mental health aspects of smoking. The purported benefits on mental health are so intangible and elusive, so intricately woven into the whole fabric of human behavior, so subject to moral interpretation and censure, so difficult of medical evaluation and so controversial in nature that few scientific groups have attempted to study the subject [p. 355].

An attempt to study the relationship between smoking and one aspect of mental health has been made in Heimstra's laboratory. We have already discussed mood as an affective state and how mood has been measured and utilized as a dependent variable in some environmental psychology studies (Chapter 2). Some think that a person's moods and how these moods fluctuate under various conditions of environmental stress are aspects of mental health. In our studies, we were interested in whether subjects who smoked under certain stressful conditions were less likely to show marked mood changes than subjects who were nonsmokers or subjects who were smokers but were not allowed to smoke.

Mood measures were routinely taken before and after subjects were exposed to a number of experimental conditions, such as sustained operation of a driving simulator and various complex psychomotor tasks. The primary purpose of these studies was to determine whether smoking had any effect on performance on the particular tasks; several of these studies will be discussed later. However, mood-change data (differences between pre- and posttest measures) were also obtained in all of these studies, and some interesting trends were revealed. In all cases, the subjects that smoked during the experiments showed less mood change (that is, change on fewer mood factors) than subjects who were nonsmokers or who were deprived of smoking. Typically, subjects in the latter groups showed the most marked mood change. The results were interpreted to mean that smoking, under certain conditions, may tend to keep a person more relaxed, less anxious, and, in general, more stable in terms of mood fluctuation (Heimstra, 1972).

Smoking and Behavior

The term *behavior* can, of course, cover a wide range of activities, and the effects of smoking on many different kinds of behavior have been studied. We will be primarily concerned with the relationship between smoking and performance on psychomotor tasks, although some mention will also be made about the effects of smoking on visual tasks.

Psychomotor Performance and Smoking.   In one of the first papers dealing with the effects of smoking on motor efficiency, Hull (1924) cited several earlier studies showing that smoking one or two cigars resulted in a decrease in precision on several tasks requiring precise motor performance. Other early studies reported that smoking had a detrimental effect on tasks such as dart throwing and cancelling certain letters in a series as rapidly and as accurately as possible, tasks requiring hand steadiness, reaction-time tasks, and so on. However, in a more recent study, Reeves and Morehouse (1950) found that the inhalation of 2.7 liters of smoke from a cigarette had no effect on performance in tests of speed, power, strength, or endurance. Since then, several other investigations have also been conducted with varying results.

Although not all studies have shown that smoking has an effect on psychomotor performance, in general it does appear that the typical initial effect of tobacco is to decrease overall motor efficiency and either increase or decrease speed and number of errors, depending on the form of tobacco used and its mode of administration.

The typical approach has been to look for detrimental effects of smoking; however, some studies have been conducted with the assumption that, under certain conditions, smoking might enhance performance. Consider, for example, an investigation conducted in Heimstra's laboratory. As part of several investigations that had been conducted dealing with the effects of fatigue on driving performance, subjects were required to complete a questionnaire related to their driving habits. One of the items was concerned with methods they utilized to "combat" fatigue on long trips; a surprising number of subjects indicated they increased their smoking consumption. Since the nicotine component of cigarette smoke is a mild stimulant, it seemed possible that smoking might actually have the effect of keeping the driver less fatigued and more alert on long trips. Consequently, it was decided to investigate this particular aspect of smoking.

In this study (Heimstra, Bancroft, & DeKock, 1967) a total of 60 subjects were assigned to three groups—a smoker group, a nonsmoker group, and a deprived smoker group. Subjects operated a driving simulator for a total of six hours without a rest pause. Those in the smoker group were allowed to smoke whenever they wished, those in the smoker-deprived group had their cigarettes removed before entering the simulator, and those in the nonsmoker group, who had indicated they had not smoked for at least a year, also did not smoke. A number of performance measures were obtained, including tracking performance, reaction time, and several measures of vigilance. The results showed that there were no significant differences in performance between the smokers and the nonsmokers, so the initial hypothesis was not borne out. However, of considerable interest was the performance of the subjects in the deprived group—that is, smokers who were not allowed to smoke during the six-hour test session. Subjects in the smoker-deprived group consistently performed poorer on all of the tasks. In addition, several of these subjects quit before completing the session, even though they had been informed that they would be paid only if the test was completed. In general, the performance data as well as the behavioral observations suggested that subjects in this group were under considerable stress.

The fact that deprived smokers tended to perform more poorly than nonsmokers or smokers who were allowed to smoke may have some practical implications. There are many types of situations in which, for various reasons, individuals are not allowed to smoke. Some of these situations require a person to perform at skilled tasks for long periods of time, and possibly, the individual's performance on these tasks when he is not permitted to smoke may suffer. "No Smoking" restrictions are often imposed with the assumption that smoking will interfere with performance, but perhaps this is not always the correct assumption; not permitting smoking may interfere more.

Smoking and Visual Tasks.   In the human, the majority of sensory input that is utilized in the execution of most tasks is visual input. Consequently, a significant amount of the research dealing with smoking and its effects on behavior has been directed toward determining how smoking affects various visual functions. Thus there have been studies conducted on the effects of smoking on sensitivity to light, visual adaptation, accommodation, convergence, flicker-fusion frequency, foveal acuity, visual-search performance, and target detection. We cannot review all of the hundreds of studies in this area, but it can be stated that, in many of the investigations, smoking has been found to have an effect on visual functions. However, the magnitude of the effect and whether an effect is obtained are very much dependent on factors such as the amount and mode of administration of the tobacco and the measures utilized. Characteristically, when effects are found, they are negative—that is, effects usually suggest that tobacco has an adverse effect on the visual function involved.

As suggested above, there are a wide range of visual functions, and many of these have been subjected to study. Recently, however, some research has been conducted in an area of visual performance previously not studied. In a study by Johnston (1965), which involved only a very small group of subjects, it was found that abstinence from smoking increased the size of the visual field of subjects and that smoking resulted in a reverse effect. Specifically, the size of the visual fields of four habitual smokers who reduced their smoking or abstained for two weeks increased 36%.

In an attempt at a more definitive study involving many more subjects and a number of experimental conditions, Krippner and Heimstra (1969) investigated the effects of smoking and abstinence from smoking on the size of the visual field. In this study, 40 subjects (30 smokers and 10 nonsmokers) were tested under various combinations of smoking, smoking deprivation, and smoking denicotinized cigarettes in order to determine how smoking affected the size of the peripheral-visual field. It was found that smoking did, in fact, decrease the size of the visual field and that, after a period of abstinence from smoking, the visual field was enlarged. After the period of abstinence, however, renewed smoking reduced the size of the field, usually within an hour after the subjects again began to smoke. The use of denicotinized cigarettes by one group showed that the effect on the visual field was probably due to the nicotine component, since the subjects in this group performed similarly to those in the group deprived of smoking.

Modifying Smoking Behavior

With the recognition that tobacco consumption constitutes a major public health problem, immediate interest developed in establishing techniques for modification of smoking behavior—that is, techniques to convince smokers they should give up smoking. These techniques have varied widely in their subtlety and in their recognition of the complex nature of smoking behavior.

Probably the least systematic of the modification procedures involved legislative action of one kind or another attempting to legislate cigarette smoking out of existence. In the United States, for example, health warnings must be printed on cigarette packages, and, recently, all television commercials for cigarette smoking were banned. Another legislative move that is often utilized is a constantly increasing tax on tobacco and tobacco products. There is no sign at present that these kinds of approaches are effective. Similarly, the various national antismoking campaigns, typically presented through the mass media, have met with very little measurable success.

A variety of different kinds of clinics have been established that employ different techniques in hopes of modifying smoking behavior. These clinics, in general, can be categorized as those using medication of some type and those not utilizing medication. In the former case, the "would-be quitter" receives information and education about smoking, an explanation of treatment techniques, and one or more drugs thought to help a person stop smoking. Clinic techniques not involving medication typically make use of some sort of therapy or education program. Research on the effectiveness of the clinics has shown that the immediate "quit rate" is relatively high; however, this rate begins to deteriorate rapidly as soon as formal clinic meetings are over. Typically, after some weeks or months, only a very small percentage of the original "quitters" are still abstaining.

It was mentioned that in one type of clinic, drugs play an important part of the treatment. Several "smoking-deterrent" drugs have been used, including anticholinergics, stimulants, and various types of nicotine substitutes. One of the most widely used substitutes is *lobeline,* whose action, like the other nicotine substitutes, will to some degree mimic the effects of nicotine. A number of studies have been conducted that, in general, have shown negative results with the use of this drug as well as others. Typically, in the well-controlled studies, there are no differences in smoking-reduction rates between groups using the drugs and control and placebo groups.

There are a wide variety of other behavior-modification techniques that have been used to attempt to bring about a change in smoking behavior. Some of these have suggested the use of alternative responses in the place of smoking, others have employed hypnosis, some techniques involve "role playing," in which smokers play the role of someone with lung cancer, and so forth. However, in recent years, interest in the use of some of the techniques that are utilized in behavior therapy, such as aversive conditioning and desensitization, has increased. For example, in aversive-conditioning studies, smoking is in some manner associated with an unpleasant stimuli (in some cases, hot air; in other studies, electric shock). The aversive stimulation is stopped when the individual puts his cigarette out. In general, however, the results of aversive-control techniques have not been encouraging.

Actually, the above sentence summarizes the status of research in the entire field of modification of smoking behavior—in other words, the results are not encouraging. In discussing the present status and directions for future research, Bernstein (1970) makes several pertinent points when he states that:

After six years of intensified research on cigarette-smoking behavior, preceded by decades of less feverish efforts, very little useful knowledge has been contributed, beyond the rather elementary observations that smoking behavior is widespread and becoming more so, that it is very probably unsafe, and that it is incredibly resistant to long-term modification. Moreover, little evidence is available at this time to indicate that the majority of workers interested in the problem are attempting to modify their own research behavior such that the cycle of relatively meaningless, though self-perpetuating "experimentation" can be broken. Attempts to refine, build upon, and apply nonvalidated techniques are still common and in turn generate most of the research that follows [pp. 39–40].

THEORIES OF HUNGER AND EATING BEHAVIOR

Over the years, a great deal of research has been conducted in the area of hunger and eating behavior, and a considerable amount of information is known about this particular topic. However, much of this research has been of a basic nature, concerned with hunger as a physiological drive. Typically, these investigations have dealt with (1) the relationship between stomach contractions or distention and hunger sensations, (2) correlations between various blood conditions and hunger and (3) central nervous system factors in hunger.

One view of hunger is that it is caused by stomach contractions, which result when the stomach is empty. Prevailing opinion, however, is that gastric contractions do not provide a total explanation for hunger, even though they may provide the basis for the sensation or the experience of feeling hungry. Thus a number of studies have attempted to establish a relationship between some blood factor and hunger contractions. Some feel that the blood-sugar level is important, but data are not available to reach a firm conclusion in this regard.

Several studies have shown that central nervous system mechanisms are involved in hunger. For example, it was demonstrated many years ago that lesions in certain areas of the brain (hypothalamus) would cause animals to overeat and become obese. Further studies have shown that two centers in the hypothalamus are important in eating behavior. It appears that one of the centers actively represses eating, and, when it is destroyed by lesions, overeating (hyperphagia) results. In other words, when the inhibitory center is destroyed by lesions, its normal function of suppressing eating is also destroyed, and the animal will overeat. Another center appears to be critical for causing eating; when it is destroyed, the animal stops eating (aphagia). Although there can be little question that these centers are important in eating behavior, just what processes are involved in their control is unclear. Several suggestions have been made about how these centers are normally controlled, but more data are required before we can be certain.

About the best conclusion that can be drawn concerning hunger and eating is that they are controlled by many variables. Although several of the variables considered most important have been listed, control of hunger is probably based on complex interactions of all of these variables, as well as others that have not been mentioned.

These theories of hunger and eating behavior do not explain a very important fact about eating. Many of us tend to overeat. It would be simple to categorize an obese individual as having a "sick hypothalamus," but this would not be supported by any data. Actually, the problem of obesity has been the subject of study for many years, and, as yet, no clear-cut causal factors are apparent. Obesity has been attributed to an enormous range of biochemical, genetic, and environmental factors, but we really do not know for sure why some people overeat and others do not. Thus, although it is common to bring in concepts like anxiety, compulsion, or even the Freudian death wish, the dynamics of obesity remain very unclear.

Although we could spend a number of pages or even chapters dealing with some of the theories of obesity, as we have indicated, these are only theories that do not have much in the way of empirical data to back them. However, recently Schachter (1971a; 1971b) has presented a new line of thinking in this area, along with some interesting experimental evidence to support his views. In the remainder of this section, we will be concerned with Schachter's hypothesis on human obesity.

External Control of Eating Behavior

The theories of hunger and eating behavior that we have very briefly outlined have a common characteristic—they assume that this behavior is brought about by internal states of the organism, such as stomach contractions and lowered blood-sugar level (hypoglycemia). It appears that gastric motility and hypoglycemia may actually trigger eating behavior in normal, nonobese people, but that different mechanisms may be involved in triggering this type of behavior in obese individuals. Rather, it appears that external food-related stimuli, such as the smell of food, the sight of other people eating, discussion of food, and so on, may trigger eating behavior in the obese. In other words, a normal individual's eating behavior is determined by internal body circumstances, whereas the obese individual's eating behavior is determined by external stimuli. Thus, as Schachter (1971a) points out:

The gist of our findings on humans is this—the eating behavior of the obese is under external, rather than internal, control. In effect, the obese seem stimulus-bound. When a food-relevant cue is present, the obese are more likely to eat and to eat a great deal than are normals. When such a cue is absent, the obese are less likely to try to eat or to complain about hunger. . . . there is evidence that, in the absence of food-relevant cues, the obese have a far easier time fasting than do normals, while in the presence of such cues, they have a harder time fasting [p. 137].

Schachter's hypothesis that eating behavior of the obese is externally rather than internally controlled is supported by some interesting research findings. For instance, if obese individuals are more stimulus-bound than normals, then it seems likely that this would hold true in situations not necessarily restricted to food-relevant stimuli. Schachter (1971a) reports several studies in which this was demonstrated. For example, subjects were asked to look at slides on which a number of objects or words were portrayed. Each slide was exposed for five seconds, and the subjects were then required to recall what they saw. Fat subjects recalled more objects than did normal subjects.

Schachter also reports a study by Rodin (1970) concerned with the effects of distraction on performance of fat and normal subjects. Rodin hypothesized that, if the stimulus-bound concept is correct, irrelevant stimuli should be more disruptive for obese subjects than for normal subjects when they are performing a task requiring concentration. The idea is that the impinging distracting stimulus is more likely to grip the attention of the stimulus-bound obese subject. In a study designed to test this hypothesis, Rodin had normal and obese subjects perform a simple proofreading task that required a high degree of concentration. In one condition, subjects corrected the proof without distraction; the level of distraction was increased in three other experimental conditions. It was found that, in the condition with no distraction, obese subjects were much better on the task than normals, but their performance seriously deteriorated as they were distracted, until, at the highest distraction condition, they were considerably worse than normals. These, as well as other studies, support the hypothesis that obese individuals are more stimulus-bound than normal individuals when outside the eating situation.

What about the evidence for external control, or the stimulus-bound nature, of eating behavior of the obese? Several lines of evidence support this view. Schachter (1971b) discusses the research of Hashim and Van Itallie (1965) at the Nutrition Clinic in St. Luke's Hospital in New York with the results of their work through 1970. In a series of experiments, these investigators restricted subjects, both normal and obese, to a bland and homogenized liquid diet similar in composition to some of the commercial diet preparations. The subjects, who were hospitalized, were allowed as much of this liquid diet as they wished. Some subjects were given a large pitcher of the material, and others were fed by a machine, which delivered a mouthful of the diet each time a button was pressed. The characteristics of the situation, then, are that the food is bland and unappealing, eating is self-determined (in that the subject eats when he wishes and as much as he wants), and the eating situation is devoid of any social stimulation.

What tended to happen in this situation was that the normal subjects ate about as much as they did before starting the experimental regime in terms of caloric intake. Typically, however, the caloric intake of the obese subjects dropped precipitously the moment they entered the experimental situation. There was a marked and persistent decrease in food consumption by the obese subjects, whereas the normal subjects consumed about their normal amount of food.

These experiments have some interesting implications, which Schachter (1971b) states:

We have a series of experiments which indicate virtually no relationship between internal state and the eating behavior of the obese subjects; on the other hand, these case studies seem to indicate a very close tie-up between the eating behavior of the obese and what might be called the circumstances of eating. When the food is uninspired and the eating situation uninteresting, the fat subject eats virtually nothing. For the normal subject, the relationships are quite the reverse—his eating behavior seems directly linked to internal state but relatively unaffected by the external circumstances surrounding the eating routine and ritual [p. 88].

There are, of course, a number of external cues that may be important in triggering eating behavior of obese persons. Sight, smell, taste, what other people are doing, and so forth, are all stimuli. Another external cue that might have an effect is the amount of time since the last meal. Thus, even if there were no internal stimuli (stomach contractions, hypoglycemia, and so on), the fact that a number of hours have passed since the last meal may be stimulus enough to trigger the eating behavior. Schachter and Gross (1968) tested this notion in an experiment. Space does not permit a description of their rather elaborate investigation, but the results showed that the passage of time had markedly stimulating effects on the amounts eaten by obese subjects and no such effects on normal subjects.

In his book dealing with obesity, Schachter (1971b) presents a number of other experiments that, taken together, offer considerable support for his view that the internal state is irrelevant for the obese and that their eating behavior is determined largely by external factors. There are a number of other theoretical views on obesity and eating behavior, but Schachter's hypothesis is one of the few that is backed up with a substantial amount of data.

Modifying Eating Behavior

A variety of techniques have been utilized in attempts to treat obesity; in general, the results have been discouraging. Attempts to modify eating behavior have, in most cases, been very similar to those utilized in attempting to modify smoking behavior. Treatments have ranged from individual and group hypnotherapy, psychoanalysis, and use of drugs for depressing the appetite to nonprofessional group activities, such as exercise clubs, yoga, and self-help organizations. More recently there has been an increased interest in the use of the behavior-therapy techniques. However, as we have indicated, results have been extremely discouraging.

If one views eating behavior in a learning-theory framework, it is not surprising that it is a difficult form of behavior to modify. For example, we know that a response positively reinforced immediately after it occurs is likely to be maintained or will become even stronger. Eating, of course, provides immediate positive reinforcement for the individual. Similarly, when there is a delay between the response and reinforcement, the response tends to become weaker. Thus, when one refrains from eating (response) in the hopes of losing weight (reinforcement), there is a long delay between the response and the positive reinforcement. In other words, overeating is likely to provide immediate positive reinforcement for the person, whereas refraining from eating in the expectation of losing weight has a long delay before any reinforcement in the way of weight loss is apparent. No wonder the data show that the type of eating leading to obesity is a form of behavior highly resistant to extinction.

part

6

PROBLEMS IN EDUCATION

What is education? Silvern (1970) states that:

It is formal maturation of the whole man to face and solve the problems of real life. It is a cradle-to-grave, womb-to-tomb continuum meeting all the learning needs of the individual. In this continuous spectrum, we see preschool education, kindergarten, elementary, secondary, college undergraduate, university graduate, and continuing education [p. 385].

Obviously, to meet these needs, the educational system of a society such as ours must be vast and complex. Because it is so vast and complex, the problems associated with a system of this type are also of major magnitude. In this section we will be concerned with some of the problems related to the educational process. Psychologists are concerned with many aspects of the educational process, and we will be able to discuss only a few of these. A number of psychologists are concerned with increasing learning efficiency for a variety of different kinds of students in a wide range of settings. In Chapter 20 we will discuss several recent innovations in education that have been developed with this purpose in mind; in Chapter 21 some of the problems associated with teaching special types of students will be considered.

chapter
20

Some New
Instructional Techniques

Within a relatively short span of years, the educational system in the United States has witnessed some rather remarkable new technological advances. Some have viewed these advances as the answer to education's problems; others have viewed them with alarm. Among the many innovations, perhaps the one with the biggest impact has been programed instruction. You have probably encountered programed instruction at least once during your education. Similarly, televised instruction has become increasingly popular in many institutions, at least from the administration's point of view, if not from the students' and teachers' points of view. Computer-assisted instruction, although not as common as programed and televised instruction, is also becoming more and more common.

Along with the development of these new techniques, questions have also arisen concerning their design, utilization, and effectiveness. A number of psychologists are actively engaged in research in this area, attempting to answer such questions as:

1. How effective are the new techniques compared to the traditional direct instruction?
2. What are the attitudes of the users of the techniques toward them?
3. What are the relative advantages and disadvantages of certain procedures associated with given techniques? For example, is a professor more effective on televised instruction than a professional communicator?
4. What sort of programs—linear or branching—are best in programed instruction?

Photo by Sam Sprague.

5. What is the best way of displaying information for a student in a computer-assisted instructional program?

These questions represent but a tiny sample of those confronting researchers in this area. Many of the investigators studying these problems are educational psychologists, but those from a variety of other psychological specialties also work in this field.

EVALUATION OF INSTRUCTIONAL TECHNIQUES

In discussing several new instructional techniques in this chapter, we will be particularly concerned with the role that psychologists are playing in the evaluation of these techniques. All too often in education and in many other areas new innovations are developed and implemented with little or no effort made to evaluate their effectiveness. This may result in the "institutionalizing" of a technique that at best may be no better than the technique it replaced and at worst may be much less effective.

The evaluation of a new technique in education is not a simple process. In the first place, the goals of a particular educational system or subsystem in which the technique is to be used must be taken into consideration in the evaluation. For example, a technique that may be effective in a program whose goal is to bring underachievers up to some minimum standard may not be effective at all in a program designed to deal with exceptionally bright children. Similarly, even when a technique is utilized with a relatively homogeneous group of students, the nature of the particular course of instruction must also be considered. Thus the technique may be less effective in a social-science subject than it is in a mathematics course. Also, studies that report favorably or unfavorably on a particular technique or innovation without comparing it against one or more other techniques of instruction are not really evaluative studies.

One of the most important aspects of an evaluative study is how the effectiveness of the new technique is measured. Even if the new technique is to be compared against several other techniques, what should be used as the measure of effectiveness? In other words, what criteria should be employed? A number of different criteria can be used, such as the length of time required to complete a particular block of material using several different techniques, the number of errors on a test, satisfaction with the course, or the retention of material over time.

An evaluation study, then, should typically involve comparing the new technique with several other techniques in programs whose educational goals are alike, with similar courses, and with criteria that are adequate to reflect any differences that might be due to the particular technique involved. As you will see when we discuss the evaluation of several of the recent innovations in educational techniques in this chapter, these requirements of evaluation studies are not always followed.

PROGRAMED INSTRUCTION

One of the major innovations in education in recent years has been the widespread introduction of "teaching machines" and other procedures for "programing" instruction. The programed-instruction movement began in the late 1950s but increased dramatically during the 1960s. The concepts on which programed instruction is based are not new; the first teaching machine was built by a psychologist (S. D. Pressey) in 1925. However, the first teaching machine developed on the basis of established learning principles was that of B. F. Skinner in the 1950s.

Basically, programed instruction provides for instruction without the presence or intervention of a human instructor. Silvern (1970), in discussing the characteristics of programed instruction, states that "It is a *learner-centered* method of instruction, which presents *subject-matter* to the trainee in *small steps* or increments, requiring *frequent responses* from him and *immediately* informing him of the *correctness* of his responses" (p. 397).

There are a variety of specific techniques utilized in programed instruction, ranging from programed textbooks to very elaborate teaching machines. These techniques have become quite commonplace in the educational system at all levels. Specific techniques may appear to be quite different, but most adhere to certain prescribed criteria or principles for programed instruction that are now generally accepted.

Principles of Programed Instruction

1. The subject matter is presented in small incremental steps or units called *frames,* which may vary in size from a short sentence to a paragraph or more. The size of the frame depends on the subject matter and the characteristics of the learner population that is involved. All the frames that are required to cover a particular subject are called a *program.*

2. As each frame is presented to the trainee, he must make a response of some sort. A response may be constructed, as is the case in a sentence-completion type frame; it may be selected from several available responses, as is the

case in multiple-choice frames; or it may be in a variety of other forms. The point is that the trainee must actively participate in the learning process.

3. The trainee is immediately informed about the correctness of his response. Immediate feedback of this type is reinforcing to the trainee, particularly when his response is correct. The fact that most programs allow for a large percentage of correct responses makes programed instruction an inherently reinforcing situation.

4. Each trainee works and learns at his own rate. He is able to complete a program as rapidly or as slowly as he wishes (within constraints that may be established in a particular course), with his progress dependent on his own motivation and abilities.

5. The sequence of lessons, which are made up of frames or units of information, is carefully planned, controlled, and consistent. The programer must analyze the learning steps involved with considerable care, and, consequently, the presentation in programed instruction is often much better "designed" than that encountered by the student in a classroom presentation.

6. Another important aspect of programed instruction is that it allows for continuous feedback to the educator as well as to the trainee. Records from teaching machines, which report the number of students missing particular frames, permit modification of the program until most trainees achieve a prescribed number of correct responses.

Programing Techniques

The key to successful programed instruction is not the elaborateness of the machine that is used to present the program but, rather, the quality of the program itself. As we have indicated, programs are the sequence of frames that together convey the required information to the trainee.

An important feature of a good program is that the trainee has a high probability of giving the correct response at each step or frame. Errors will necessarily be made, but the program should be such that, with an alert student, the errors are at an absolute minimum. This insures the maximum immediate reinforcement. Consequently, one aim of the program writer is to use methods that will ensure the correct response. One way that this is accomplished is to construct the items in such a manner that they "prompt" the correct answer. Since the material in the program should develop logically and is prepared in such a way as to prompt or "cue" the trainee about the correct answer, the trainee's response is nearly always right.

There is some question in programed instruction about the relative importance of the confirmation of the correct answer or the prompting that precedes the answer in terms of their respective value for learning. It is generally felt that the subsequent confirmation plays a less important part in the learning process than the preceding prompting, but this is still a subject to debate. More research is needed in order to determine the best amount of prompting or cueing and the most effective manner of doing it. At present, prompting takes many forms in a teaching program. Regardless of the form it takes, however, it is designed to ensure the evocation of a correct response from the student.

Types of Programs. There are two basic types of programs used in programed instruction—*linear* programs and *branching* programs. With linear programs, which were developed by Skinner and his associates, students are expected to progress through the frames in the same, fixed order. The rationale underlying linear programing is that each step or frame is dependent on those responded to previously. Thus a "teaching" machine presents one frame at a time; the student completes it and then uncovers the word or phrase that is the answer. Similar procedures are followed in programed textbooks, in which the student is requested to cover the answers or locate the answers on another page.

In the linear-, or Skinner-type, programing technique, the programer aims at designing the program in such a fashion that student errors are reduced to an absolute minimum. As Holding (1965) suggests, "An alternative course of action is to cater for a modicum of errors, using the information about the learner which a particular error reveals in order to lead him through appropriate extra material" (p. 128). In this type of program, different kinds of errors will require different kinds of remedial treatment. Thus, unlike the linear type of programed instruction, students in *branching* programs will take different routes through the program, depending on the types of errors that they make. A branching program, then, is flexible enough to handle different types of reactions to the same material.

There are different techniques for handling branching programs, but one of the most common is the so-called "scrambled" textbook. All students start on page one, but from then on, they may end up going to various other pages in the book. For example, on page one there may be a paragraph containing some factual material followed by a question with four possible answers, such as shown below.

Answer A	Page 18
Answer B	Page 25
Answer C	Page 14
Answer D	Page 39

345

Assume that answer C is correct and the student selected this answer. He would then go on to page 14, be informed that he was correct, perhaps be praised, and then continue with the next frame of the program. However, suppose he had selected answer A or one of the other incorrect answers. He would then turn to the page indicated and be told that he was not correct and what it was that was wrong. He would then go back to page one and, after rereading the material, select another answer. If he was correct, he would turn to page 14 and start the cycle again. If he was incorrect again, when he turned to the designated page, he would then be given more remedial material.

Eventually, every student will finish the book, but without having read the same number of pages or having read them in the same order, as would be the case with linear programing. The more correct responses made by a student in a branching program, the less work is involved for him.

The branching technique has some interesting variations. For example, when a student makes a particularly "bad" error at some point, he can be set back to an earlier part of the program; on the other hand, an exceptionally bright student can be "pushed forward" in the program and allowed to skip a number of frames. All in all, the branching-program approach allows for considerably more flexibility than the linear program. This is not meant to imply that the branching program is superior; both techniques have their advocates, and little research data support any statement that one is better than the other.

The Evaluation of Programed Instruction

In general, programed methods compare very favorably with the more traditional methods. Although a number of studies have shown that programed-learning techniques are no more effective than conventional techniques, more studies have shown rather striking advantages in favor of the programed instruction. For example, Buckley (1967) cites considerable evidence supporting the superiority of programed instruction as a training tool. Programed instruction has been found to be highly successful in a variety of situations with a number of different types of subject matter. By way of illustration, let us consider several evaluative studies that have been conducted with programed instruction.

Cassel and Lullum (1962) compared the effectiveness of programed instruction and traditional lecture methods in ninth- and twelfth-grade computer math classes. One group of students from each class replaced traditional instruction with three hours per week of programed instruction; the other group was taught the identical material by the traditional method at the same time. When the students were tested on identical tests, it was found that those from the programed instruction groups did far better than those from the groups that received traditional instruction.

Krimmerman and co-workers (1969), using high school seniors and college freshmen who were enrolled in philosophy courses, compared programed instruction with standard lectures. In this study, the classes were separated into two groups—one group being taught by means of the programed instruction and the other by means of the traditional instruction. When a test was administered after the course, it was found that the groups receiving the programed instruction were significantly superior to groups receiving standard instruction.

In a study by Naumann and Woods (reported by Stolurow, 1963), educable mentally handicapped children were used as subjects. These children were taught spelling by automated programed-instruction methods. Results showed that these children learned much faster with the programed-instruction technique than they did with the conventional techniques requiring rote memorization of each word.

Based on many studies such as these, it would appear that programed instruction has demonstrated its worth. However, there is need for considerable more research in this area. Comparing two methods of education is a complicated affair at best, and many of the investigations that have been conducted have not been as carefully controlled as they should have been. All too often the research was conducted by investigators with a deep interest in programed instruction, and, as Kendler (1968) points out, "It is quite possible that the amount of energy and zeal expended in making the experimental programed instruction effective has been much greater than that expended on behalf of the control (conventional) methods with which programed learning has been compared" (p. 665).

COMPUTER-ASSISTED INSTRUCTION

Programed instruction has been developing for many years, but *computer-assisted instruction* (CAI) is a relatively recent innovation. It is, however, an outgrowth of programed instruction, and many of the same principles apply. Programed instruction involves the use of programed textbooks or simple teaching machines; in CAI a computer is used instead of books or teaching machines. The computer *assists* in the instructional process, and the resulting new process is called computer-assisted or computer-aided instruction. The advantage is that the computer is a much more efficient and flexible piece of equipment than the books and teaching machines and can store tremendous amounts of organized information that can be retrieved for the use of particular students, depending on their needs. However, it is important to realize that to be a CAI system, the computer is more than just a tool for solving problems or retrieving information. As Silvern (1970) points out, "the term CAI is reserved for those particular learning situations in which a computer contains a stored instructional program designed to inform, guide, control and test the trainee until a prescribed level of proficiency is reached" (p. 398). Basically, a CAI system can be thought of as a man-machine relationship in which the man is a *learner* and the machine is a *computer*. They engage in a two-way communication process by means of a stimulus-response-feedback relationship in which the objective is human learning and retention.

The CAI System

There are several subsystems in the CAI system. One of these is the *remote-trainee console* or *terminal*, which may vary somewhat, depending on the particular system involved. However, it is at this point that the two-way communication between the learner and the computer takes place. The console has an *input* device for the transfer of information from student to computer and an *output* device for information from the computer to the student.

Probably the most popular input-output device that is currently utilized is the teletypewriter. Although this device is noisy and slow, it is relatively inexpensive when the alternatives are considered. Another popular output device is the cathode-ray tube, which looks like a television screen and on which numbers, words, symbols, and so on can be displayed to the learner. A problem with the cathode-ray tube is that the image generated may not be too clear, and reading from it for long periods of time may produce discomfort.

Audio output is also associated with the CAI system. That is, the computer selects a section of tape from a prerecorded message and has it played to the student. Similarly, slides may be utilized in conjunction with CAI systems with the computer, again, selecting slides based on the student's response.

Typically, the student makes an input to the system by means of a type-writer. However, there are also "light" pencils used, by which the student can indicate a response by touching the surface of the cathode-ray tube. Efforts being made to develop audio inputs (so that the student can ask the computer a question verbally) have not met with a great deal of success, although interest in the development of such a system remains high.

Basically, then, in a CAI system, the student sits at the console and performs two functions—he reads what is typed on the printout or displayed on the cathode-ray tube, and he responds by means of his typewriter or whatever other input device he may have available. He then receives feedback about his performance, and, depending on the feedback, can either remake the response or go on to the next step in the instructional program. The requirements of the student, then, are that he be able to read and interpret the output from the computer and be able to type at some reasonable level of proficiency in order to respond.

In a CAI system, of course, there are many other subsystems besides the input and output devices. The computer itself is the major subsystem and will include a variety of components, such as magnetic-tape units, disk storage, and communications hardware. Most large computers can be utilized for CAI, provided they have certain "memory" characteristics that are required by the CAI system.

A CAI system, then, consists of "hardware" components in the form of input and output devices and the computer itself. These are illustrated in Figure 20-1. There are also "software" components in the form of instructional programs and the computer program, which is derived from it. These software components are, of course, critical elements of the system, since, without an instructional program that is well thought-out and designed, the effectiveness of the CAI system may be reduced to a point at which it is useless. Some idea about the nature of the instructional program may be obtained when one considers the fact that often 100 hours or more of instructional-programing time may be required for every hour that a student spends at the console.

Although still a recent innovation, CAI has already been used as an instructional system in a wide variety of subject areas. It has been used to teach reading skills to relatively young children, and, with older students, mathematics, foreign languages, chemistry, pathology, and a number of other subjects. The military services have been quite interested in CAI, and have used it to train men in areas ranging from aircraft maintenance to electronics. Its use as a training technique for deaf children will be briefly discussed in the next chapter.

Research on CAI

Because CAI is still in its infancy, so to speak, a great deal more research is needed in order to fully develop the system. There are still a host of practical problems, such as communication costs, that must be solved before widespread application of CAI is feasible. Along with research aimed at improving the system itself, more research on the effectiveness of CAI compared with other instructional methods must also be emphasized.

349

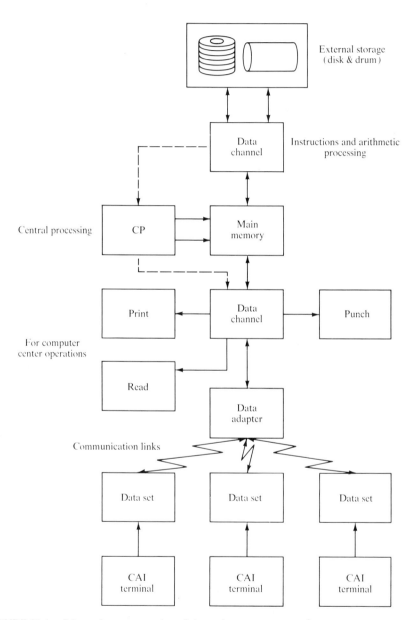

FIGURE 20-1. Schematic representation of the various components of a computer-assisted instruction (CAI) system.

Each of the components of the CAI system is being studied in attempts to improve the system. For example, research is being conducted concerning the most effective manner in which to present information to the student, although the limitations of the present systems are such that there are not too many options available. Wodtke (1967) cites studies in which identical programs were administered to students at terminals with typed printouts and to other students by means of programed textbooks. There was an increase of 25% in instructional time for the on-terminal group, with no commensurate increase in learning. In another investigation that made use of a more highly verbal program, the increase in instructional time was 75% for the on-terminal group, with no significant difference in learning when compared to the programed-text group. Wodtke suggests that the time differences are due to the slow typeout rate (120 words per minute) of the typewriter, a rate substantially slower than the normal reading speed.

Considerable research interest is being shown in developing more complex methods of evaluating and processing responses of students in CAI systems. For example, programs have typically evaluated the student's response by comparing it with a correct answer stored in the computer. The stored correct answer allowed no deviation in terms of misspelled words or grammatical error, and, if these occurred, the student's answer was incorrect and he would be required to repeat it (or do whatever else the instructional program called for). Special equipment is now developed that can evaluate the student's response and ignore spelling and grammatical errors. In other words, the student's answers do not have to "match" exactly the answers stored in the computer. This is also the case for some CAI programs in mathematics; the student's answers do not have to match the prestored answers as long as the basic steps in his computations are correct. These developments are a step forward in increasing the response-analysis complexity.

The next step in response-analysis complexity, however, will involve question-answering routines. Some systems of this kind have been built, but they are still very much in the developmental stage. When a student can ask the computer questions and receive answers, CAI will have become a much more versatile instructional device.

Effectiveness of CAI

What about the effectiveness of CAI? A limited number of studies have compared CAI with conventional procedures. Silberman (1969) points out, however, that careful experimental comparisons between conventional procedures and the various computer applications have not revealed uniformly practical differences in favor of the computer. It is interesting to speculate about the strong and persistent activity in CAI in the face of fairly limited evidence of learning benefits. Perhaps the reinforcer for the developer is the mastery of a new skill and the fun of making a novel application of the computer. It is sufficient for the developer that the instruction system works in a new fashion. Face validity may be the important factor in perpetuating many innovations that don't improve learning per unit cost over traditional methods [p. 60].

Recently, a study comparing the effectiveness of CAI with a programed-instruction text was conducted by Dick and Latta (1970). In this study, a programed-instruction text (about 30 minutes to one hour in length), which was designed to teach the concept of significant numbers to eighth graders, and a CAI version of the same material were compared in terms of their effectiveness. Students were given a pretest, which indicated they were unfamiliar with the concept of significant numbers. Students were assigned to two groups—one to be instructed by means of the CAI system and the other with the programed text. Students were given a posttest (the same as the pretest) as soon as they completed the instruction and a retention test two weeks later.

The results clearly showed that the overall performance of the students in the group that received the programed instruction was significantly better than that of the students in the CAI treatment. Students with low ability did particularly poorly in the CAI treatment. This was not the case in the programed-instruction group, in which the differences between the low- and high-ability students were not great.

It must be emphasized, however, that there is a dearth of research comparing the effectiveness of CAI with other methods of instruction, and, until there is more evidence, it is not safe to draw conclusions concerning the value of CAI as an instructional device.

INSTRUCTIONAL TELEVISION

It is safe to assume that you and every other reader of this text have, at one time or another, been exposed to instruction that has made use of television. This has become such an established part of our educational systems that most students and instructors take it for granted, although they may still question its effectiveness as a teaching tool. Actually, over the years there has been considerable controversy over the use of televised instruction, and the controversy is far from settled at the present time. The arguments have, however, generated a great deal of research aimed at establishing the effectiveness of instructional television. Most of these studies have compared television instruction with direct instruction or have made comparisons of filmed or kinescoped courses with direct instruction.

Televised or Direct Instruction?

A review of the literature dealing with research on televised instruction shows that the largest category involves "relative effectiveness" studies, in which the performance of students instructed by means of television was compared with that of other students instructed directly, or face-to-face, by the teacher in the usual fashion. These studies have included all instructional levels, ranging from elementary school to college, as well as the military services and a wide range of courses. The length of the studies has ranged from one or a few lessons to entire courses.

Nearly all of these studies have shown "no significant differences" between the measured performance of the students who were instructed by means of television and those who were instructed directly. A few investigations have shown significant differences in favor of television and a few in favor of direct instruction. Typically, however, both methods were about equally effective.

Similar findings have been reported for studies that have compared filmed or kinescoped courses with direct instruction. Usually, no significant differences are found between groups who have been taught by means of the filmed or television courses and those instructed by the direct method.

Some Problems in Experimental Design. Good experimental design involves carefully defining and manipulating independent variables, selecting a meaningful dependent variable that can be quantified, and either controlling as many "nuisance" variables as possible or making sure that all subjects are equally exposed to these kinds of variables. Studies designed to evaluate the effectiveness of television instruction have frequently suffered from the lack of good experimental design. Consequently, interpretation of the results is difficult, if not impossible.

In many studies, the main variable (television versus direct instruction) is mixed with a number of other variables. For example, several teachers may be involved in the television presentations and only one in the direct instruction or vice versa. Similarly, different teachers may present the television material and the material in the classroom, in which case it is more of an evaluation of teachers than of methods.

The importance of randomly selecting subjects has also been pointed out previously. This is rarely done in studies comparing television and direct instruction for obvious reasons. It would cause considerable disruption in most school systems to randomly assign students to various experimental conditions. However, by not doing this, there are a number of uncontrollable biasing variables, including differences in intelligence, socioeconomic background, motivation, and many others.

A number of other problems in experimental design could be listed. However, a study by Stickell (1963) summarizes the "state of the art" in television/direct-instruction comparisons. Stickell carefully examined 250 comparison studies made between television instruction and direct instruction and classified them according to whether they met certain requirements for adequate experimental design. Of the 250 comparisons, 217 were categorized as being "uninterpretable" on the basis of his criteria, whereas 23 were classified as being only "partially interpretable" because of defects in experimental design. Only 10 studies were classed as "interpretable," and, of these, none showed significant differences in learning between the subjects in the groups receiving televised instruction and those in the groups receiving direct instruction.

The Significance of Nonsignificant Differences. When we talk about "significance" in the statistical sense, we are talking about the confidence an investigator can have that the differences he found between two treatment conditions did not occur by chance. Thus, if analysis of the data shows that the difference between scores of subjects exposed to televised instruction and direct instruction is significant at the .05 level of confidence, the investigator knows this difference will occur by chance only one time in 20.

Many researchers have been disappointed at the frequency with which nonsignificant differences have occurred in learning when comparisons have been made between televised and direct instruction. There are several ways of looking at these nonsignificant findings, however. In the first place, nonsignificant results do not *prove* that differences do not exist; it is always possible that refinements in research methods and improved experimental designs will reveal that, in fact, there are differences.

Secondly, administrators and researchers feel that there is practical value in the consistent findings of nonsignificant differences between these methods. What these findings imply is that there are alternative techniques available of equal instructional merit, at least based on the types of measures that have been employed in the comparison studies. Thus an administrator may select televised instruction or direct instruction on the basis of factors other than their relative instructional merit. When these other factors are taken into consideration, there are many situations in which televised instruction has a great deal of value.

354

For example, television can extend instruction to many places simultaneously and can thus extend experienced teachers and excellent teaching resources to many more students than is possible with direct instruction. Also, televised instruction makes available courses of a highly specialized nature that might not otherwise be offered in a school or college. In many cases, there are economic advantages to televised education, and, at the present time, when all educational systems are hard-pressed financially, this is an important consideration.

Attitudes Toward Televised Instruction

Research on televised instruction has been concerned with more than just comparing the effectiveness of televised instruction with other methods. Heavy emphasis has been placed on assessing the attitudes of both students and teachers toward the use of television in the classroom.

Results of studies concerning students' attitudes toward televised instruction have ranged from overwhelmingly negative attitudes to very favorable attitudes. Many studies have found that the students do not care much one way or the other. When studies were conducted that attempted to relate attitude toward televised instruction with the actual measured learning in the course, little or no relationship was found.

Typically, faculty attitudes have been more negative than those of the students toward televised instruction. Just why this is the case is difficult to say. Perhaps it is because they feel threatened by new innovations, or perhaps many do not know enough about the technique and are "down on it because they are not up on it."

Some Other Areas of Research

The majority of studies dealing with televised instruction have involved comparisons between this method and other direct methods in terms of effectiveness and attitudes, but there have been some studies in other relevant areas. Thus there have been a few investigations dealing with production variables in instructional television programs. These studies have investigated such variables as methods of presenting material on television (lecturer, group discussion, or interviews), the use of pictures and demonstrations versus a lecture-blackboard presentation over television, and so forth. Generally, these studies have failed to find significant differences in learning due to the production variables. However, there are some important questions that need to be answered concerning these variables. For example, who makes the best television teacher—the academic specialist or the professional communicator?

Blenheim (1969) conducted an experiment involving six classes of introductory sociology, all of which were taught by televised instruction. However, three of the classes were taught by sociologists with a number of years of academic experience, and the other three classes were taught by professional communicators with at least 15 years of experience. The sociology professors each developed and delivered three lectures, which were to cover 15 basic points. Each communicator was asked to read, verbatim, the lectures that one of the three sociologists had prepared. At the end of the three lectures, students in all of the classes were tested by means of a multiple-choice test. Comparing overall scores, students in the sections taught by the professors were significantly more retentive than those in the classes taught by the professional communicators.

Blenheim's study was cited as an example of research that needs to be conducted and not as proof that a professor makes a better television teacher than a professional communicator. Much more research needs to be done to establish this. Similarly, questions concerning the most effective presentation techniques need to be answered by systematic research.

ADAPTIVE TRAINING

The instructional innovations that we have discussed so far have been used primarily in verbal learning situations. What about innovations in the area of motor learning? A procedure that has drawn considerable interest in recent years is *adaptive training*. Although this technique is not necessarily restricted to motor-skills learning, it appears to be particularly useful in that field.

According to Kelley (1969), the primary requirements of adaptive training are that (1) the performance of the trainee be continuously or repetitively measured in some way and that (2) the measurement be used to make appropriate changes in the stimulus, problem, or task. Basically, a skilled instructor attempts to do this, but it is difficult to vary the task of each student according to his performance. However, typically an instructor will assess trainee performance at particular stages during the course in order to establish the trainees' readiness to move on to a more difficult stage. Similarly, should the instructor determine that the task is too difficult for the trainee, he may "drop back" to a less difficult task. With machine-controlled adaptive training, however, there is a "feedback" loop by means of which the problem or task is automatically changed, depending on how well the student is performing. Figure 20-2 contrasts the fixed type of training with adaptive training.

In a machine-controlled adaptive-training situation, there are three essential elements. First, there must be a system for continually measuring the per-

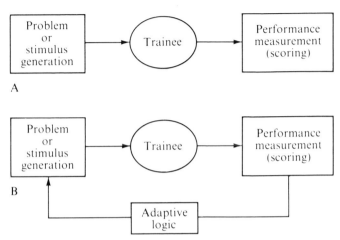

FIGURE 20-2. Schematic showing fixed (A) and adaptive-training (B) procedures. In adaptive training, by means of the adaptive logic feedback loop, the problem, stimulus, or task is changed as a result of the output (performance) of the trainee. As his performance improves, the task becomes more difficult. (From Kelley, C. R., 1969. By permission of the Human Factors Society.)

formance of the subject. Second, the task itself must be adjustable in such a way that its difficulty level can be varied, and, third, there must be a "logic" system that will automatically change the level of difficulty of the task as the trainee's level of performance changes. In other words, the task automatically gets more difficult as the subject becomes more skillful at performing the task. This feature allows for a much greater flexibility of training equipment, since the same equipment can be used with the neophyte as with the expert. As the neophyte becomes more skilled, the task becomes more difficult. As Kelley (1969) states:

Adaptive training is efficient, because it is only when training is at an appropriate level of difficulty that effective learning can take place. If a task or set of problems is too easy, a trainee learns very little by doing them. Similarly, when a task or set of problems is too difficult, the trainee may be entirely unable to cope with them. It is for this reason that a fixed program of group instruction is apt to be effective only for the more average members of the group. Fixed instruction is often too easy and proceeds too slowly for better members of the group; similarly, it is too difficult and proceeds too rapidly for the slower members [p. 548].

There has been a great deal of research with adaptive training, particularly by the military, and it has been found to be an efficient method of training. When carefully designed, an adaptive-training procedure is generally more effective than an otherwise similar procedure in which the difficulty level is held constant, or fixed, throughout the training period.

OTHER INNOVATIONS

Although possibly the most research effort is being directed at the instructional innovations discussed in this chapter, there are a variety of other technological developments in education that we have not discussed. The use of films, for example, is widespread, and considerable research has been aimed at improving the effectiveness of this particular method of presenting material. Efforts are being made in many different audio-visual areas, and one has only to glance through a few issues of *AV Communication Review,* which is a research journal devoted to studies concerned with different aspects of audio-visual instruction, to get some notion of the wide range of studies being conducted in this field. Language laboratories, which are based on the assumption that the aim in learning a language is primarily to speak it, have also become popular, and considerable research has been conducted regarding their effectiveness. Dial-access and push-button lessons, simulation and gaming, and other approaches are being tried and evaluated. There have also been many new developments in actual classroom techniques and procedures, which are beyond the scope of this book. Although our educational system may be criticized on many grounds, it certainly has not hesitated to attempt new approaches to the educational process.

chapter
21

Teaching Special Groups

Much of the research on learning and instructional techniques has involved subjects who are "normal," in that they have no particular handicaps and come into the situation without an obvious history of sensory or cultural deprivation. However, many groups are not "normal" in this sense, and psychologists and educators are frequently asked to prepare and implement a program of instruction for these types of students. Some unique problems are encountered in these situations.

There are, of course, a number of "special groups," and we cannot begin to consider all of them in this chapter. All have unique problems, and special approaches are required with all of the physically, mentally, and culturally handicapped groups, which are considered special or "exceptional" in that they do not fit the normal pattern for one reason or another.

In recent years, considerable interest has been expressed concerning the education of children from disadvantaged families. Many children experience environmental inadequacies of one kind or another and present particular problems for educators. The inadequacies often encountered in disadvantaged families may lead to progressive intellectual retardation, as well as a general inability to cope with many of the problems that exist in our complex society. Although many groups are "disadvantaged," we will be concerned with only one—the American Indian.

There are also many kinds of handicapped children who present problems to those charged with their education. Mentally retarded children, of course,

Photo by Sam Sprague.

make up a large percentage of the handicapped children; numerous educational techniques have been devised for their education. Since education programs for the mentally retarded have received so much publicity, many readers will be familiar with these programs; therefore, they will not be discussed in this chapter. Rather, we will consider two groups of physically handicapped—the blind and the deaf—and some of the more recent concepts dealing with their education.

TEACHING THE DEAF

In an attempt to determine which features of the normative model most influence the handicapped person's learning of skills, the psychologist must evaluate the existing techniques for training in skills such as reading, language development, writing, and speech. Thus a considerable amount of research compares the abilities of the deaf child with those of the hearing child. We will briefly consider some of these findings. Then we will consider some of the techniques that have been developed for training deaf children, as well as some of the arguments concerning the usefulness of these techniques.

Comparisons Between Deaf and Hearing Children

Until relatively recently, most tests designed to measure intelligence and other abilities involved, almost exclusively, the use of language. There were few tests designed, standardized, and validated that utilized other than verbal ability in obtaining IQ measures. As a consequence, these verbal tests provided very little useful data on the mental capacity or potential of the deaf.

In 1955, Hiskey developed a test of learning aptitude that was standardized on children in schools for the deaf. Since that time, several tests have been developed and utilized for description and diagnostic purposes with deaf individuals. With the increased use of performance tests, it was found that there are dimensions of intellectual ability or intelligence in which the deaf perform as well as, and sometimes better than, those with hearing. The general finding, then, was that, when measured by performance tests, deaf children filled the range of intellectual ability from genius, superior, and average to below average and mentally retarded, as did children with normal hearing.

Having demonstrated that deaf children were not inferior intellectually, many educators and psychologists became concerned about deaf children with average or above-average mental ability who did not show corresponding ability to achieve academically, especially in the area of language development.

362

Through further research it became clear that, although the deaf children did not differ quantitatively in intellectual ability from children with hearing, there were qualitative differences in their mental functioning. For example, it has been shown that deaf children fall below average on tests that require complex abstraction and reasoning processes. Similarly, it has been shown that many deaf people do not develop the ability to read beyond the level normally demonstrated at the end of the fourth grade.

Acquisition of Communication Skills in the Deaf

Communication among humans is, of course, primarily a form of verbal behavior that requires, for maximum efficiency, a functioning auditory sense. Because of the lack of this modality in the deaf, the communication process presents a number of difficulties. Considerable controversy has been generated about the most effective method of developing communication techniques for the deaf. For example, professionals in the area argue about whether the best approach is to teach the deaf to speak or to utilize sign language or both.

In the past, the philosophy of most institutions for the deaf has been to attempt to train the deaf to speak, rather than use a sign vocabulary. In fact, in an effort to force the deaf child to speak, families in which there was a deaf child were instructed not to let their deaf child "sign." Interestingly enough, children who had not previously been around other deaf children would pick up, on their own, in spite of all efforts to prohibit them, a fairly extensive working sign vocabulary during their first year at these institutions. In the last few years, many psychologists and educators working with the deaf have changed their philosophy; now they not only allow signing but, in fact, are making extensive effort to expand the working sign language.

Another area that has received a considerable amount of research effort, as well as a great deal of attention in terms of technique for application, is what is referred to as *speech reading.* Speech reading is essentially a new term for lip reading. It has been defined as a process of comprehending the words of the speaker by associating meaning with the movements of his lips. When audition is not available and the verbal language system is the goal, a substitute sensory channel must be utilized.

Although there have been some reports of moderate success using the sensory modality of touch, the visual modality is the system that has proved more effective. Proponents of this technique consider that speech reading is a form of verbal behavior. In other words, they propose that the subject can symbolize the meaning of the speaker's lip movements visually just as he symbolizes the meanings of words using the auditory channels. There are other cues and functions involved, but this process primarily involves the ability to retain lip movements mentally while the speaker is speaking, to sequentialize group movements, and, finally, to associate these movements with past experience.

Investigators have made some effort to correlate speech-reading ability, or lack of it, with tests of intelligence. Speech-reading ability has been found to be correlated with some dimensions of intelligence and unrelated to other dimensions. Although this is no great surprise, in most cases of speech-reading comparison, one factor is somewhat surprising and, as of yet, unexplained. Males of all ages (at comparable levels of intelligence) that reside in institutions consistently are better speech readers than students living at home attending these schools during the day. It is possible that resident students outside of the classroom practice speech reading with each other, consciously or unconsciously, more than students returning home every night. In addition, success in speech reading is also related to the ability to use other aspects of language, such as written language, reading, and manual-sign language.

FIGURE 21-1. Special techniques are required for teaching deaf children. Often these techniques require much more personal attention on the part of the teacher than is required with hearing children. (Photo courtesy of *Volante*, the student newspaper of The University of South Dakota.)

The teaching of accurate speech reading is extremely difficult and, at most institutions for the deaf, the students spend a great deal of time and effort developing this complex skill. At the present time the philosophy of psychologists and educators is that the effort is worthwhile for several reasons. First, most students who develop the skills typically become very accurate, thus providing them with another means of communication. The second reason is that, since speech reading is positively correlated with other means of communication such as reading, writing, and sign language, it is assumed that associations will be made more readily, given this additional input. In other words, the more opportunity for acquiring verbal associations, the more easily the student will go beyond this level of learning and advance to the more complex kind.

Although the ultimate goal of developing speech and "hearing" is communication, it is very difficult to teach deaf children to speak. Yet this has been the goal and dream of parents, educators, many psychologists, and administrators since the history of the psychology of the deaf. Most practicing professionals concerned with learning in the deaf do not really have any hope of developing speech to the degree necessary for its utilization as an expressive language. On the other hand, there is some evidence that speech reading and written language, as well as signing, are facilitated when students can be taught to produce speech sounds, even though they can attach little meaning to these sounds. This is an extremely difficult training task to accomplish. On the other hand, short answers, statements, and short questions can be developed adequately in some students. An interesting new feedback approach might facilitate this.

One of the most important dynamics in any learning situation is feedback. The student always needs immediate feedback if he is to progress very rapidly. It is very apparent that children with no hearing have no feedback for direct sounds when uttered, making the task of producing correct speech sounds extremely difficult. Some studies have been conducted using artificial feedback of one kind or another. Thus in one study a system was designed to provide visual feedback to the student when making speech movements. With the use of some sophisticated electronic techniques, including a glossal transducer for conversion of tongue motions (which were then transmitted to an oscilloscope), it was possible to provide immediate visual feedback of the motor act involved in speaking. In essence, a word would be spoken by the investigator and a line tracing would appear on the oscilloscope. The deaf student could then practice his production of that word until it matched the oscilloscope tracing of the investigator. Although there are many complex factors yet to be teased out of this technique and other similar techniques, it is an area that holds a great deal of promise.

365

In conclusion, it should be pointed out that several investigators have found that it makes little difference what kind of communication process is used or what particular type of language modality a child develops as long as he develops some kind. If this communicative ability can be developed prior to or during the critical period for conceptualization and verbal associations, then the later efforts to teach symbolization, abstraction, generalization, and complex problem solving should be greatly facilitated. Although much research needs to be done to demonstrate the efficacy of this approach, it is certainly one of the most exciting challenges facing the psychologists working in this area.

Computer-Aided Instruction for the Deaf

A variety of specific techniques have been developed and utilized for teaching particular subject areas to deaf students. Some of the approaches discussed in the previous chapter have been used with mixed success. By way of illustration, we will consider the use of one special technique—computer-aided instruction.

In an article dealing with computer-assisted instruction for the deaf (Jacobs, 1971) the success of programs in several different schools using the CAI technique is discussed. In 1963 at Stanford University, Drs. Suppes and Atkinson developed a mathematics program for hearing children. Each student is pretested to determine at what level he should start. Once he has been started at his proper level and as long as he is capable of solving problems in the program, he automatically moves forward. The first attempt to use the CAI program with deaf children was tried at the Kendell School in Washington, D. C.

The teachers in this experiment have reported that the reaction of the students to the CAI program has been highly enthusiastic. They seem to respond with interest and increased efficiency through the kind of individualized instruction CAI offers to each student. In addition, teachers have reported that 64% of the students participating in the first mathematics program had completed the full year's work at the end of five months. Although this program is set up for the instruction of mathematics in grades one through eight only, it is hoped that this kind of generalization and problem-solving ability necessary for lower-grade mathematics will be built into future programs dealing with more sophisticated mathematics. In addition to the mathematics program, language development is presently being attempted for grades seven through nine. Whether or not these programs will be as effective as the mathematics program remains to be seen. However, with the continual accumulation of knowledge and understanding of CAI programming, as well as a number of other techniques, the future looks more optimistic for deaf students than it has in the past.

VISUALLY HANDICAPPED STUDENTS

Visually handicapped students range from those who are totally blind to those who are only partially blind. Because the educational process depends so much on the sense of vision, special adaptations to the process must be made for the visually handicapped. In this section we will be concerned with some of these adaptations.

Characteristics of the Blind Student

As was the case with the deaf student, a considerable amount of research has been conducted in an effort to determine whether or not blind children differ from nonblind children in characteristics other than those associated with vision. Studies have shown that there are no differences in the general health, height-weight ratio, intelligence, and educational achievement of blind children, compared to those with normal vision.

Differences do appear to exist, however, in the area of motor coordination, with research showing quite clearly that the blind and paritally sighted are usually somewhat inferior to normals. There also appear to be some problems in terms of personal adjustment on the part of the blind student, which may be due in large part to the attitudes of others toward the blind (or the manner in which the blind perceive the attitudes of others). Speech development differs between blind and normals, with the blind tending to show less vocal variety, lack of modulation, and less lip movement. Similarly, language development may be somewhat different in the case of the blind, although it can be concluded that the language of blind children is not deficient if concepts that require vision are excluded.

Education of the Blind Student

As we have indicated, education of the blind requires special adaptation of the educational process. As Kirk (1972) points out:

Most of the adaptations necessary for visually handicapped children stem from an effort to provide comparable experiences which do not involve the use of sight or which utilize the limited vision available. That is, the children must be given tactual experiences and verbal explanations. The visually handicapped child's ability to listen and relate and remember must be developed to its fullest. He must learn efficiency and conservation of time because the techniques he must use to acquire the same information or accomplish the same task are sometimes more cumbersome and time consuming [p. 333].

What are some of the adaptations necessary in teaching blind children? Lowenfeld (1952) has suggested several. For instance, much more individual attention is required in instructing the blind child. Consequently, class size must be considerably smaller. The blind child must be presented with numerous concrete objects that he can touch and manipulate in order to gain an understanding of the world around him. Instruction must be "unified," in that blind children may only understand parts of a situation without grasping the whole, unless care is taken by the teacher. Whenever possible, the blind student should be exposed to additional stimulation. This stimulation is obtained by systematically exposing the child to as wide a range of activities and different environmental conditions as possible. Adaptations such as these are necessary if the blind child is to obtain maximum benefit from his educational experience.

There are, of course, certain skills that blind students must master that are not necessary for seeing children. Braille reading and writing are two of these. Similarly, it is necessary for blind children to learn to use a standard-print typewriter at an early age, because acquisition of handwriting skill is difficult for the blind. Thus the typewriter has virtually replaced the devices once used to help teach handwriting.

Kirk (1972) points out that teaching command of the environment is of special importance to the blind child, since both his social and physical independence are involved. Command of the environment involves training the child in skills needed to move about with ease, to find objects and places, and to orient himself in all kinds of new and strange situations. Increasing effort is being directed toward training the blind to become more mobile. Thus efforts are being made to teach specific skills to young blind children to make them form habits of independent travel. Also, physical education, which was once thought to be dangerous for the blind, is now stressed in many training programs.

In addition to the special educational areas that must be stressed because of their blindness, these students must also master the traditional academic areas to which normal children are exposed. Obviously, however, the same techniques used to instruct the normal child in these subjects may not be applicable with blind children. Many books have been produced in Braille, and "talking" books and audio tapes are available in numerous areas. Highly specialized aids have also been developed for use in teaching the blind, and much has been accomplished in this area in recent years.

Some New Approaches

Because the blind have lost the use of one sensory modality, it would appear that some compensation for this loss might be achieved through systematic development of the use of other modalities. Blind children, for example, are trained in "listening" skills and are more proficient than seeing children in this regard.

In recent years, considerable research has been conducted dealing with the feasibility of using the cutaneous or "skin" sense as a modality for communication. Much of this research has not been concerned specifically with the blind; rather, it has been directed at determining the most effective techniques and the variables of importance for presenting an individual with information cutaneously. For example, how should this information be presented? Many of the studies have used vibratory devices of one kind or another, which were located on different regions of the body. Information is coded in terms of duration and intensity of vibratory patterns. More recently, investigators have made use of painless electrocutaneous stimulation to present information.

How the data obtained from research of this type can be applied to the blind is shown in the development of the device called the Optacon. This particular device, which is still being developed at Stanford University, scans print and transfers it onto 144 tactile pins. These pins will produce a vibratory image of the letter on the finger of the blind person. Preliminary work with this device shows that a person can read with it at 60 or 70 words per minute. The value of a device of this type is that a blind person using it can read regular books and other printed material that have not been converted into Braille.

CULTURALLY DEPRIVED STUDENTS

For many years, educators as well as psychologists have been concerned that students coming from the very low socioeconomic levels have had difficulty achieving academically. More recently, the expressions "culturally deprived" and "socially disadvantaged" have been used a great deal to describe these students. The basic philosophy behind the use of these terms, as related to academic settings, is that, generally, children growing up in the slum, ghetto, or Indian reservation have not been exposed to the rich and varied environment normally encountered by children from more affluent circumstances and that this affects their academic achievement.

Although there is some controversy concerning this philosophy, educators have demonstrated that there is a relationship between these so-called culturally deprived students and success in the early grades. These students find it very difficult to learn the skills required. Numerous techniques have been proposed to counteract the effects of this deprivation. For example, programs such as Head Start have been initiated in an attempt to improve on the reading readiness of children entering schools. Other schools have initiated "nursery" and "kindergarten" programs, as well as special preparation classes for these slow learners.

Unfortunately, at the present time it is extremely difficult to evaluate the success of these programs. The Head Start programs have come under extreme criticism nationally, the primary argument being that the whole idea of cultural deprivation is questionable. For example, it has been suggested that this philosophy be labeled a "vacuum ideology." This vacuum ideology emphasizes the disposition of teachers and administrators to establish and support programs and special classes for the culturally deprived, again suggesting that these students are meager, empty, and lacking in experience, whereas it is possible that the opposite is true. For example, by the time any child starts to school, he has acquired a considerable body of knowledge, attitudes, values, and skills. These attributes or sources of information may not immediately support the kinds of skills and knowledge necessary for academic progress in the typical school setting. Some psychologists are attempting to evaluate and assess the kinds of information the culturally deprived child does bring to the school situation in an effort to see if these experiences can be capitalized on in a meaningful way. Nevertheless, it remains to be seen whether these enrichment programs will, in fact, help to alleviate the problem of under-achievement in academic endeavors.

The Crossover Phenomenon

A very interesting phenomenon that occurs with some cultural minorities is referred to as the crossover phenomenon. Basically, this refers to the observed fact that these children initially do as well as nonminority children both in terms of the acquisition rate of new knowledge as well as the total amount. This process continues with no discriminable difference between the two groups until approximately the middle of the fourth grade. At that time, the cultural-minority students begin doing more poorly and continue to fall behind their classmates throughout the rest of their academic career. We shall look at this phenomenon rather briefly and will use as our example the cultural minority, the American Indian.

There is little history of intelligence or achievement testing of Indians until around 1940. Since that time, no aspect of Indian education has received more attention than achievement and intelligence testing. Every kind of possible comparison has been made. Indians with whites, full bloods with mixed, boys with girls, tribe with tribe, one type of school with another, English-speaking with non-English-speaking, Indians with state, local, and national norms, achievement in one subject matter with another, and aculturated versus nona-culturated are just a few of the many comparisons that have been made. With few exceptions, the results indicate that, in the first several years of school, there are no differences in ability or achievement. It is after the fourth grade that the achievement begins to decline very noticeably. Psychologists working with this problem have approached it in a variety of manners and have offered a number of explanations. In the remainder of this section, we will be concerned with some of these approaches and explanations.

Personality Conflicts.　One approach has been to identify the relationship between scholastic failure and personality conflict. A number of people, including Bryde (1970), suggest that, as the Indian child reaches the level of understanding that he is Indian, he becomes withdrawn, anxious, and has feelings of rejection. Bryde reports that the concept of alienation, including most of the dynamics such as depression and rejection, is the central integrating pattern explaining the behavior of the Indian student. If this is the case, then the obvious first step to the solution of the problem is to initiate and maintain intensive psychotherapeutic service to combat these extreme feelings of alienation. The Bureau of Indian Affairs and the Indian Health Service have responded by greatly increasing the number of positions for mental health workers in their systems.

Home Environment.　A second approach assumes that the problem is based on the home environment. Certainly, any child's success in school depends in part on the help and encouragement he receives from his family. There has been very little research reported on relationships between Indian parents' attitudes and their children's academic achievement. However, the most common report is that parents are typically "apathetic" (or some other synonym of the word). Thus the common complaint of teachers in Indian schools is that the parents are indifferent, apathetic, or uncooperative. The apparent lack of enthusiasm and projected encouragement on the part of Indian parents is not unexpected when we consider the alienation of students in the present schools. Since the school structure seldom takes into account the desires or problems of the Indian parents, little participation and cooperation is possible. In addition, it is difficult for parents to generate any real enthusiasm for the child's achievement when they are very much aware that the results of education will probably not benefit the child in any immediate or direct way. Finally, with an average annual family income across most reservations of less than $700 per year, the more primitive needs of the family for food, warmth, and clothing are of far more concern than the achievement levels reached by the children. Whether or not the home environment is the primary cause of the lack of achievement in Indian students is still controversial. However, psychologists are developing comprehensive programs that include family factors in their efforts to alleviate the poor achievement by these students.

Health Factors. An area closely related to the family problem concerns itself less with attitudinal causes and attributes the lack of achievement to the general physiological state of the student. There is no question that the Indians on our reservations have extremely poor health in comparison with the national norms. Tuberculosis on Indian reservations is over ten times as high as in the white population. Starvation is still prevalent on many reservations. Internal parasites, various ear and eye infections, vitamin deficiencies, and many other physical ailments contribute to the chronically poor physical state of the Indians. The proponents of this position maintain that one cannot expect physically sick children to be interested or enthusiastic toward their school work. Although the reasoning or logic of this point of view is acceptable, one must question why the crossover phenomenon occurs so consistently. Certainly a particular child is not sick throughout his entire academic career. Psychologists that go along with this point of view are attacking the problem directly by attempting to make maximum use of available foods, mental and health facilities, and general education of the family toward the health needs of the children.

Language Problems. Still others suspect that the explanation lies in the fact that a very high percentage of the students speak their native tongue. In fact, it has been estimated that 10% of the children living on the reservation come to school speaking no English. Another 60% speak minimal English, but the native language is the one used in the home. Less than 10% of the Indian children from the reservation speak only English. It has been suggested that bilingual people have essentially two language systems. One is composed of words used in speaking, and the other is the language of recognition and comprehension. The material typically used in the lower grades is primarily that of a talking vocabulary. For example, you probably remember the Dick and Jane, Spot, Father and Mother reading primers from your own past experience. However, at about the fourth-grade level, the vocabulary used in the school system beings to be more comprehensive. It has been suggested that even those students speaking some English use English as their talking vocabulary but maintain their native tongue as their comprehensive language. This means that material presented to the student must be translated to the native language, producing a very difficult problem.

The problem is that, for the most part, there is a very limited correlation and overlap between English and most of the Indian languages. In other words, the student is presented with a stimulus word, is capable of learning various presented relationships of that word, yet does not comprehend the implications and meaning of the term. Several projects are now underway that involve the use of teacher aides who speak the language of the students to help eliminate this problem. In addition to using the technique of translating information, there are several demonstration projects in which the test material is presented completely in both languages. Again, these projects are recent and, as of now, no conclusions can be drawn about their efficacy in eliminating underachievement.

Teachers' Attitudes.   Teachers and their attitudes toward Indian students have been the focus of researchers attempting to solve this complex learning problem. Thus Berry (1968) states that:

If teachers and other members of the dominant group are convinced that the Indian is innately inferior and incapable of learning, such attitudes will be conveyed in various and subtle ways. A child will come to think of himself in that negative way and set for himself lower standards of effort, achievement, and ambition. Thus, the teacher's expectation and prediction that her Indian pupils will do poorly in school and in later life become major factors and guarantee the accuracy of her prediction [p. 34].

Although not concerned with Indian children, an interesting experiment by Rosenthal and Jacobson (1968) lends a great deal of support for this theory that teachers' expectations play an important part in determining how well a student will do. The investigators administered a new test they called "The Test of Inflected Acquisition," with which teachers were not familiar. They then tested a number of elementary-school pupils and in a casual, indirect manner gave the teachers the misinformation that certain of their pupils proved to be what they called potential spurters. They suggested that these spurters, before the end of the term, would suddenly increase at a much faster rate than the rest of the class. In actuality, about five students in each class had been selected randomly, without regard to any results from any tests.

At the end of the academic year, numerous tests were given. The results indicated that those students from which the teachers expected greater gain did, in fact, show these gains. More interestingly, when teachers were asked to describe the classroom behavior of the spurters, they were described as more interesting, better adjusted, affectionate, happier, more curious, and having better prospects of success as adults. The teachers were then asked to describe the behavior of other students, and, of course, these descriptions were much less favorable. The implication of this research is that the attitudes and expectations the teacher has toward these students definitely affects the actual achievement and success of the students.

Numerous researchers have undertaken the task of attempting to modify teacher attitudes toward their students. In addition, the behavior-modification techniques are being applied in teacher training to help teachers control and modify the numerous kinds of subtle reinforcement that students pick up, such as voice inflection, facial expression, and general body gestures.

A New Approach

Another approach has come from a team of researchers from Florida Atlantic University. The team includes clinical psychologists, educational psychologists, speech pathologists, psychometricians, and reading specialists. It is designed to serve Seminole Indian children on the Big Cypress Reservation deep in the Everglades. As on many other Indian reservations, the testing program demonstrated that the Seminole children showed a range of intellectual ability not deviant from the average and that the achievement level of these children was below that of the national norm. The purpose of the program was to develop a remedial and compensatory program of learning, which would hopefully reverse the scholastic regression trend. The approach was to utilize peer-to-peer interactions as a teaching device, including peer-developed materials. In addition, a system was used called VACT (Visual Auditory Chemithetic Tactile) using multi-modality presentations in an effort to draw as many relationships among reading lessons as possible. Again, the tutors are fellow students that have mastered a particular program, producing six advantages.

1. Because there are plenty of peers in any given group, this technique is economically feasible where the use of a teacher for each child would not be logistically possible.
2. The children are closer in age, and often a child can reach another child who is having difficulty when an adult cannot.

374

3. The slow-learning child does not compare his skills as unfavorably with others when he is not being taught by a teacher.
4. Youngsters feel reassured because, when they need help, they can ask a fellow student and therefore avoid feeling stupid or dumb.
5. The student tutors often offer more realistic modes of behavior for the child and do not have unrealistic expectations about his performance.
6. A real growth of self-confidence and self-worth develops, both within the student tutor and his teams.

In the preparation of materials, the first step was to motivate the children to create and develop their own reading materials using their own personal experiences and stories. These stories were then illustrated by the children, and the selected materials prepared for the library. As the class progresses, it is planned that the children will develop stories of more complexity and sophistication. It would appear that getting materials relevant to the experience, age, and level of sophistication of the students might make a great deal more sense than to continue using materials designed and prepared by teachers. Although there is some question about whether this will work for content-type courses, it certainly has a great deal of potential for the teaching of reading and language skills.

references

American Automobile Association. Driver education reduces accidents and violations. Washington, D. C.: Author, 1964.

Bandura, A., & Walters, R. H. *Social learning and personality development.* New York: Holt, Rinehart & Winston, 1963.

Barker, R. G. Explorations in ecological psychology. *American Psychologist,* 1965, **20,** 1–14.

Baron, R. A. Effects of presence of an audience and level of prior anger arousal on adult aggressive behavior. Paper presented at the 79th Annual Convention of the American Psychological Association, Washington, D. C., September, 1971.

Bartz, W. R. While psychologists doze on. *American Psychologist,* 1970, **25**(6), 500–503.

Bechtel, R. B. Hodometer research in architecture. *Milieu,* 1967, **2,** 1–9.

Berkowitz, L. *Aggression: A social psychological analysis.* New York: McGraw-Hill, 1962.

Berkowitz, L. Simple views on aggression. *American Scientist,* 1969, **57**(3), 372–383.

Bernstein, D. A. The modification of smoking behavior: An evaluative review. In W. A. Hunt (Ed.), *Learning mechanisms in smoking.* Chicago: Aldine, 1970.

Berry, B. The education of American Indians: A survey of the literature. Washington, D. C.: Report prepared for the Special Subcommittee on Indian Education of the Committee on Labor and Public Welfare, United States Senate, 1968.

Bevan, W. Behavior in unusual environments. In H. Helson and W. Bevan (Eds.), *Contemporary approaches to psychology.* Princeton, N. J.: Van Nostrand, 1967.

Bexton, W. H., Heron, W., & Scott, T. H. Effects of decreased variation in the sensory environment. *Canadian Journal of Psychology,* 1954, **8,** 70–76.

Birren, J. E. *The psychology of aging.* Englewood Cliffs, N. J.: Prentice-Hall, 1964.

Birren, J. E. Increments and decrements in the intellectual status of the aged. *Psychiatric Research Reports,* 1968, **23,** 207–214.

Birren, J. E. Toward an experimental psychology of aging. *American Psychologist,* 1970, **25**(2), 124–135.

377

Bishop, R. W. Evaluating simulator instruction for accomplishing driver education objectives. *Traffic Safety Research Review,* 1967, **11**(1), 12–17.

Blenheim, L. C. Television teaching by professional performers? *AV Communication Review,* 1969, **17,** 322–326.

Blum, M. L., & Naylor, J. C. *Industrial psychology: Its theoretical and social foundations.* New York: Harper & Row, 1968.

Borkenstein, R. F., Crowther, R. F., Shumate, R. P., Ziel, W. B., and Zylman, R. (Dale, A., Ed.) *The role of the drinking driver in traffic accidents.* Department of Police Administration, Indiana University, 1964.

Bowen, H. M. Diver performance and the effects of cold. *Human Factors,* 1968, **10,** 445–463.

Bowen, H. M., Anderson, B., & Promisel, D. Studies of divers' performance during the SEALAB II project. *Human Factors,* 1966, **8,** 183–199.

Boyer, R., & McAvoy, G. Scheduling big issue in driver education. *Traffic Safety,* 1968, **68**(9), 23–24, 36–37.

Brunschwig, L. A study of some personality aspects of deaf children. *Contributions to education #687.* New York: Columbia University Press, 1936.

Bryde, J. F. *The Indian student.* Vermillion: University of South Dakota Press, 1970.

Buckhout, R. Toward a two-child norm: Changing family planning attitudes. *American Psychologist,* 1972, **27**(1), 16–26.

Buckley, J. W. Programmed instruction in industrial training. *California Management Review,* 1967, **10,** 71–79.

Burg, A. An investigation of some relationships between dynamic visual acuity, static visual acuity and driving record. *Technical Report,* Department of Engineering, University of California, Los Angeles, 1964.

Burkett, S. Youth, violence and alcohol. Paper presented at the Joint Conference on Alcohol Abuse and Alcoholism, College Park, Md., February, 1972.

Buss, A. H. *The psychology of aggression.* New York: Wiley, 1961.

Calhoun, J. B. Population density and social pathology. *Scientific American,* 1962, **206**(2), 139–148.

Calhoun, J. B. Population. In A. Allison (Ed.), *Population control.* Baltimore: Penguin Books, 1970. Pp. 110–130.

Campbell, B. J. The effects of driver improvement actions on driving behavior. *Traffic Safety Research Review,* 1959, **3**(3), 19–31.

Canter, D. *The measurement of meaning in architecture.* Unpublished report, University of Strathclyde, 1968.

Carpenter, J. A. Effects of alcohol on some psychological processes: A critical review with special reference to automobile driving skill. *Quarterly Journal of Studies on Alcohol,* 1962, **23**(2), 274–314.

Cassel, R. N., & Lullom, W. A preliminary evaluation of P. I. with students of high ability. *Psychological Reports,* 1962, **10,** 223–228.

Cautela, J. R. Covert sensitization. *Psychological Reports,* 1967, **20,** 459–468.

Chapanis, A. *Man-machine engineering.* Monterey, Calif.: Brooks/Cole, 1966.

Chasdi, E. H., & Lawrence, M. S. Some antecedents of aggression and effects of frustration in doll play. In D. McClelland (Ed.), *Studies in motivation.* New York: Appleton-Century-Crofts, 1955.

Christian, J. J. Effect of population size on the adrenal glands and reproductive organs of male white mice. *American Journal of Physiology,* 1955, **181,** 477–480.

378

REFERENCES

Christian, J. J., & Davis, D. E. The relationship between adrenal weight and population status of urban Norway rats. *Journal of Mammalogy*, 1956, **37**, 475–486.

Clough, G. C. Lemmings and population problems. *American Scientist*, 1965, **53**, 199–212.

Coleman, J. C. *Abnormal psychology and modern life.* (3rd ed.) Chicago: Scott, Foresman, 1964.

Conger, J. J., Miller, W. C., & Rainey, R. V. Effects of driver education: The role of motivation, intelligence, social class, and exposure. *Traffic Safety Research Review*, 1966, **10**(3), 67–71.

Connecticut Department of Motor Vehicles. *Driver education study.* February, 1964.

Craik, F. I. M. Short-term memory and the aging process. In G. A. Talland (Ed.), *Human aging and behavior.* New York: Academic Press, 1968.

Craik, K. H. Environmental psychology. In K. H. Craik et al., *New directions in psychology four.* New York: Holt, Rinehart & Winston, 1970.

Crancer, A., Dille, J. M., Delay, J. C., Wallace, J. E., & Haykin, M. D. The effects of marijuana and alcohol on simulated driving performance. *Science*, 1969, **164**(3881), 851–854.

Crawford, A. Fatigue and driving. *Ergonomics*, 1961, **4**, 143–154.

Cudrin, J. M. Self-concepts of prison inmates. *Journal of Religion and Health*, 1970, **9**(1), 60–70.

Damkot, D. K. A comparison of auditory, visual, and electrocutaneous displays in a vigilance task. Unpublished doctoral dissertation, University of South Dakota, 1969.

Davis, G. C., & Brehm, M. L. Juvenile prisoners: Motivational factors in drug use. Paper presented at the 79th Annual Convention of the American Psychological Association, Washington, D. C., September, 1971.

Dick, W., & Latta, R. Comparative effects of ability and presentation mode in computer-assisted instruction and programed instruction. *AV Communication Review*, 1970, **18**, 33–45.

Dole, V. P., Nyswander, M. E., & Warner, A. Successful treatment of 750 criminal addicts. *Journal of the American Medical Association*, 1968, **206**(12), 2708–2711.

Dollard, J., Doob, L., Miller, N., Mowrer, O., & Sears, R. *Frustration and aggression.* New Haven, Conn.: Yale University Press, 1939.

Dubos, R. *Man adapting.* New Haven, Conn.: Yale University Press, 1965.

Dudycha, A., & Naylor, J. C. The effect of variations in the cue R matrix upon the obtained policy equations of judges. *Educational and Psychological Measurement*, 1966, **26**, 583–604.

Ellingstad, V. S. A factor analytic approach to the driving task. *Behavioral Research in Highway Safety*, 1970a, **1**, 115–126.

Ellingstad, V. S. A driving task analysis. In N. W. Heimstra, (Ed.), *Injury control in traffic safety.* Springfield, Ill.: Charles C. Thomas, 1970b. Pp. 176–200.

Ellingstad, V. S., Hagen, R. E., & Kimball, K. A. An investigation of the acquisition of driving skill. *Technical Report 11*, Human Factors Laboratory, University of South Dakota, 1970.

Ellingstad, V. S., & Heimstra, N. W. Performance changes during the sustained operation of a complex psychomotor task. *Ergonomics*, 1970, **13**(6), 693–705.

Ellingston, J. R. *Protecting our children from criminal careers.* New York: Prentice-Hall, 1948.

379

Empey, L. T. Contemporary programs for convicted juvenile offenders: Problems of theory, practice, and research. In D. J. Mulvihill, M. M. Tumin, and L. A. Curtis, *Crimes of violence.* A staff report to the National Commission on the Causes and Prevention of Violence, U. S. Government Printing Office, Washington, D. C., 1969. Pp. 1377–1426.

Eriksson, K. Factors affecting voluntary alcohol consumption in the albino rat. *Annual Zoology Fennicae,* 1969, **6,** 227–265.

Fenton, R. E. Automatic vehicle guidance and control—A state of the art survey. *Vehicular Technology,* 1970, **19**(1), 153–161.

Fitts, P. M. Engineering psychology and equipment design. In S. S. Stevens (Ed.), *Handbook of experimental psychology.* New York: Wiley, 1951.

Fitts, P. M., & Jones, R. H. Analysis of factors contributing to 460 "pilot-error" experiences in operating aircraft controls. In H. W. Sinaiko (Ed.), *Selected papers on human factors in the design and use of control systems.* New York: Dover, 1961.

Fournet, G. P., Distefano, M. K., & Pryer, M. W. Job satisfaction: Issues and problems. *Personnel Psychology,* 1966, **19,** 165–183.

Garver, N. What violence is. *The Nation,* June 24, 1968.

Gilligan, J. P. (Ed.) *Wilderness and recreation.* (Study report #3.) Washington, D. C.: Outdoor Recreation Resources Review Commission, 1962.

Glueck, S., & Glueck, E. T. *Unraveling juvenile delinquency.* Cambridge, Mass.: Harvard University Press, 1950.

Goffard, S. J., Heimstra, N. W., Beecroft, R. S., & Openshaw, J. W. Basic electronics for minimally qualified men: An experimental evaluation of a method of presentation. *Technical Report No. 61,* Washington, D. C.: Human Resources Research Office, 1960.

Greenshields, B. D., & Platt, F. N. The development of a method of predicting high accident and high violation drivers. *Journal of Applied Psychology,* 1967, **51,** 205–210.

Grether, W. F. Vibration and human performance. *Human Factors,* 1971, **13,** 203–216.

Griffith, W., & Veitch, R. Hot and crowded: Influences of population density and temperature on interpersonal affective behavior. *Journal of Personality and Social Psychology,* 1971, **17,** 92–98.

Grossman, J. C., Goldstein, R., & Eisenman, R. Openness to experience and marijuana use: An initial investigation. Paper presented at the 79th Annual Convention of the American Psychological Association, Washington, D. C., 1971.

Guttmacher, M. S. *The mind of the murderer.* New York: Farrar, Straus, & Giroux, 1960.

Haddon, W., Suchman, E., & Klein, D. *Accident research.* New York: Harper & Row, 1964.

Hall, E. T. *The hidden dimension.* New York: Doubleday, 1966.

Harlow, H. F. The nature of love. *American Psychologist,* 1958, **13,** 673–685.

Harlow, H. F., & Harlow, M. K. Social deprivation in monkeys. *Scientific American,* 1962, **207,** 136–146.

Hashim, S. A., & Van Itallie, T. B. Studies in normal and obese subjects with a monitored food dispensing device. *Annals of the New York Academy of Sciences,* 1965, **131,** 654–661.

Hathaway, S. R., & Monachesi, E. D. The personalities of predelinquent boys. *Journal of Criminal Law, Criminology and Police Science,* 1957, **48,** 149–163.

Heimstra, N. W. The effects of "stress fatigue" on performance in a simulated driving situation. *Ergonomics,* 1970, **13**(2), 209–218.

REFERENCES

Heimstra, N. W. The effects of smoking on mood change. Paper presented at the Conference on Motivation in Cigarette Smoking, St. Martin Island, French-Netherlands Antilles, January, 1972.

Heimstra, N. W., Bancroft, N. R., & DeKock, A. R. Effects of smoking upon sustained performance in a simulated driving task. *Annals of the New York Academy of Science*, 1967, **142**, 295–307.

Heimstra, N. W., Ellingstad, V. S., & DeKock, A. R. Effects of operator mood on performance in a simulated driving task. *Perceptual and Motor Skills*, 1967, **25**, 729–735.

Heimstra, N. W., & McDonald, A. L. Social influences on the response to drugs. III. Response to amphetamine sulfate as a function of age. *Psychopharmacologia*, 1962a, **3**, 212–228.

Heimstra, N. W., & McDonald, A. L. Social influences on the response to drugs. IV. Stimulus factors. *Psychological Record*, 1962b, **12**, 383–386.

Heimstra, N. W., Nichols, J., & Martin, G. An experimental methodology for analysis of child pedestrian behavior. *Pediatrics*, 1969, **44**(5, part II), 832–838.

Helson, H. *Adaptation level theory*. New York: Harper & Row, 1964.

Herzberg, G., Mausner, B., & Snyderman, B. B. *The motivation to work*. New York: Wiley, 1959.

Hofmann, M. A., & Heimstra, N. W. Tracking performance with visual, auditory, or electrocutaneous displays. *Human Factors*, 1972, **14**(2), 127–134.

Hogan, R., Mankin, D., Conway, J., & Fox, S. Personality correlates of undergraduate marijuana users. *Journal of Consulting and Clinical Psychology*, 1970, **35**, 58–63.

Holding, D. H. *Principles of training*. New York: Pergamon Press, 1965.

Hollister, L. E. *Chemical psychoses*. Springfield, Ill.: Charles C. Thomas, 1968.

Hoover, J. E. *Crime in the United States*. Washington, D. C.: Federal Bureau of Investigation, U. S. Department of Justice, 1971.

Hulbert, S. Human factors and traffic engineering. *Traffic Engineering*, 1968, **38**(12), 16.

Hulbert, S., & Burg, A. Human factors in transportation systems. In K. B. DeGreene (Ed.), *Systems psychology*. New York: McGraw-Hill, 1970.

Hull, C. L. The influence of tobacco smoking on mental and motor efficiency: An experimental evaluation. *Psychological Monographs*, 1924, **33**, 1–161.

Human Resources Research Organization. Development of driver education objectives. A driving task analysis. Alexandria, Va.: Author, 1969.

Hurley, W., & Monahan, T. M. Arson: The criminal and the crime. *British Journal of Criminology*, 1969, **9**(1), 4–21.

Hurst, P. M., Radlow, R., & Bagley, S. K. The effect of d-amphetamine and chlordiazepoxide upon strength and estimated strength. *Ergonomics*, 1968, **11**(1), 47–52.

Ilfeld, F. W. Overview of the causes and prevention of violence. *Archives of General Psychiatry*, 1969, **20**, 675–689.

Ittleson, W. H. Environmental psychology of the psychiatric ward. In C. W. Taylor, R. Bailey, and C. H. H. Branch (Eds.), *Second national conference on architectural psychology*. Salt Lake City: University of Utah Press, 1967. Pp. 2-1-2-21.

Jacobs, L. The computer assisted program for the deaf. *The Deaf American*, June, 1971, 3–5.

Jellinek, E. M. Phases of alcohol addiction. *Quarterly Journal of Studies of Alcohol*, 1952, **13**, 673–678.

Jellinek, E. M. *The disease concept of alcoholism.* New Haven, Conn.: Yale Center for Alcohol Studies, 1960.

Johnston, D. M. A preliminary report of the effect of smoking on size of visual fields. *Life Sciences,* 1965, **4,** 2215–2221.

Jones, H. E. Problems of aging in perceptual and intellective functions. In J. E. Anderson (Ed.), *Psychological aspects of aging.* Washington, D. C.: American Psychological Association, 1956.

Jones, H. V., & Heimstra, N. W. Ability of drivers to make critical passing judgments. *Journal of Engineering Psychology,* 1964, **3,** 117–122.

Kaestner, N. F., Warmoth, E., & Syring, E. Oregon study of advisory letters: The effectiveness of warning letters in driver improvement. *Traffic Safety Research Review,* 1967, **11**(3), 67–72.

Kaplan, S. The challenge of environmental psychology: A proposal for a new functionalism. *American Psychologist,* 1972, **27**(2), 140–143.

Kasmar, J. V., & Vidulich, R. N. A factor analytic study of environmental description. Unpublished manuscript, University of California Medical Center, Los Angeles, 1968.

Kates, R. W. Perceptual regions and regional perception in flood plain management. *Papers and Proceedings of the Regional Science Association,* 1963, **11,** 217–228.

Kelley, C. R. What is adaptive training? *Human Factors,* 1969, **11,** 547–556.

Kendler, H. H. *Basic psychology.* (2nd ed.) New York: Appleton-Century-Crofts, 1968.

Kibrick, E., & Smart, R. G. Psychotropic drug use and driving risk: A review and analysis. *Journal of Safety Research,* 1970, **2**(2), 73–84.

Kirk, S. A. Educating exceptional children. Boston: Houghton Mifflin, 1972.

Kolansky, H., & Moore, W. T. Effects of marihuana on adolescents and young adults. *Journal of the American Medical Association,* 1971, **216**(3), 486–492.

Korman, A. K. *Industrial and organizational psychology.* Englewood Cliffs, N. J.: Prentice-Hall, 1971.

Krimmerman, L. I., Elder, S. T., Cieutat, V. J., & Kennedy, B. F. Teaching effectiveness of traditional logic and the ven diagram: A programed introduction. *Psychological Reports,* 1969, **24,** 587 589.

Krippner, R. A., & Heimstra, N. W. Effects of smoking on peripheral visual acuity. Technical Report, Human Factors Laboratory, University of South Dakota, 1969.

Kryter, K. D. *The effects of noise on man.* New York: Academic Press, 1970.

Langdon, F. J. The social and physical environment: A social scientist's view. *Journal of the Royal Institute of British Architects,* 1966, **73,** 460–464.

Latané, B., & Darley, J. M. Bystander "apathy." *American Scientist,* 1969, **57**(2), 244–268.

Leake, C. D., & Silverman, M. *Alcoholic beverages in clinical medicine.* Chicago: Year Book Medical Publishers, 1966.

Lemere, F. The nature and significance of brain damage from alcoholism. *American Journal of Psychiatry,* 1956, **133,** 361–362.

Lemere, F., Voegtlin, W. L., Broz, W. R., O'Hallaren, P., & Tupper, W. E. Conditioned-reflex treatment of chronic alcoholism. XII: Technique. *Diseases of the Nervous System,* 1942, **3,** 243–247.

Lester, D. Self-selection of alcohol by animals, human variation and the etiology of alcoholism. *Quarterly Journal of Studies on Alcohol,* 1966, **27,** 395–438.

Lilly, J. C. Mental effects of reduction of ordinary levels of physical stimuli on intact, healthy persons. *Psychiatric Research Reports,* 1956, **5,** 1–28.

REFERENCES

Lindner, H. The psychology of the adult criminal. In G. Dudycha (Ed.), *Psychology for law enforcement officers*. Springfield, Ill.: Charles C. Thomas, 1955.

Locke, E. A. Toward a theory of task motivation and incentives. *Organizational Behavior and Human Performance*, 1968, **3**, 157–189.

Locke, E. A., & Bryan, J. F. Performance goals as determinants of level of performance and boredom. *Journal of Applied Psychology*, 1967, **51**, 120–130.

Locke, E. A., & Bryan, J. F. The directing function of goals in task performance. *Organizational Behavior and Human Performance*, 1969, **4**, 35–42.

Logan, F. A. The smoking habit. In W. A. Hunt (Ed.), *Learning mechanisms and smoking*. Chicago: Aldine, 1970.

Lorenz, K. *On aggression*. New York: Harcourt Brace Jovanovich, 1966.

Lowenfeld, B. The child who is blind. *Journal of Exceptional Children*, 1952, **19**, 96–102.

Lucas, R. L. Attitudes, personal characteristics, and driver behavior. In N. W. Heimstra (Ed.), *Injury control in traffic safety*. Springfield, Ill.: Charles C. Thomas, 1970. Pp. 129–153.

Lynch, K. *The image of the city*. Cambridge, Mass.: M. I. T. Press, 1960.

Malinovsky, M. R., & Barry, J. R. Determinants of work attitudes. *Journal of Applied Psychology*, 1965, **49**, 446–451.

Mann, L. The social psychology of waiting lines. *American Scientist*, 1970, **58**, 390–398.

Markiewicz, D., & Brennenstuhl, W. Zimiamy neuropathologiczne w alkoholizme z objawami psychodegeneracji. *Problems Alkzmu*, 1969, **17**, 1–3.

Martin, G. L. Alcohol and driving: An overview. In N. W. Heimstra (Ed.), *Injury control in traffic safety*. Springfield, Ill.: Charles C. Thomas, 1970. Pp. 108–128.

Martin, G. L. The effects of small doses of alcohol on a simulated driving task. *Journal of Safety Research*, 1971, **3**, 21–27.

Martin, G. L., & Heimstra, N. W. Perception of hazard by children. Technical Report, Human Factors Laboratory, University of South Dakota, 1970.

Maslow, A. H. A theory of human motivation. *Psychological Review*, 1943, **50**, 370–396.

Mast, T. M., & Heimstra, N. W. Prior social experience and amphetamine toxicity in mice. *Psychological Reports*, 1962, **11**, 809–812.

Matarazzo, J. D., & Saslow, G. Psychological and related characteristics of smokers and nonsmokers. *Psychological Bulletin*, 1960, **57**, 493–513.

McCormick, E. J. *Human factors engineering*. (3rd ed.) New York: McGraw-Hill, 1970.

McDonald, A. L., & Clark, N. Evaluation of the interpretive program for Yellowstone National Park. Technical Report prepared for National Park Service, 1968.

McDonald, A. L., & Heimstra, N. W. Social influences on the response to drugs. V. Modification of behavior of nondrugged rats by drugged. *Psychopharmacologia*, 1965, **8**, 174–180.

McDonald, A. L., Heimstra, N. W., & Damkot, D. K. Social modification of agonistic behaviour in fish. *Animal Behavior*, 1968, **16**, 437–441.

McEachern, A. W., & Taylor, E. M. The effects of probation. Los Angeles: University of Southern California Youth Studies Center, 1967.

McGuire, F. L., & Kersh, R. An evaluation of driver education. Berkeley: University of California Press, 1969.

McKennel, A. C., & Bynner, J. M. Self images and smoking behaviour among school boys. *British Journal of Educational Psychology*, 1969, **39**(1), 27–39.

Milgram, S. The experience of living in cities. *Science*, 1970, **167**(3924), 1461–1468.

Moran, M. J. Reduced-gravity human factors research with aircraft. *Human Factors,* 1969, **11**(5), 463–472.

Morgan, C. T., Cook, J. S., III, Chapanis, A., & Lund, M. W. *Human engineering guide to equipment design.* New York: McGraw-Hill, 1963.

Mortimer, R. G., & Olsen, P. L. Variables influencing the attention getting quality of automobile front turn signals. *Traffic Safety Research Review,* 1966, **10**(3), 83–88.

Mosel, J. N., & Goheen, H. W. The validity of the employment recommendation questionnaire in personnel selection. *Personnel Psychology,* 1958, **2**, 481–490.

Mosel, J. N., & Goheen, H. W. The employment recommendation questionnaire: III. Validity of different types of references. *Personnel Psychology,* 1959, **12**, 469–477.

Mulvihill, D. J., Tumin, M. M., & Curtis, L. A. *Crimes of violence.* A staff report to the National Commission on the Causes and Prevention of Violence, U. S. Government Printing Office, Washington, D. C., 1969.

Myklebust, H. R. *The psychology of deafness.* New York: Grune & Stratton, 1964.

National Safety Council. 1968 Metropolitan Life awards for research in accident prevention. *Traffic Safety Research Review,* 1968, **12**(4), 122.

National Safety Council. *Accident Facts.* Washington, D. C.: Author, 1971.

Neville, J. N., Eagles, J. A., Samson, G., & Olson, R. E. Nutritional status of alcoholics. *American Journal of Clinical Nutrition,* 1968, **21**, 1329–1340.

New York Department of Motor Vehicles. An evaluation of the driving records of high school driver education students in New York State. Albany, N. Y.: 1964.

Newton, J. R., & Stein, L. I. Alcohol addicts. *Science News,* 1971, **100,** 809.

Nichols, J. I. The effects of redundant multisensory information displays on the reduction of operator error in a compensatory tracking task. Unpublished doctoral dissertation, University of South Dakota, 1970.

Nichols, J. L. Driver education and improvement programs. In N. W. Heimstra (Ed.), *Injury control in traffic safety.* Springfield, Ill.: Charles C. Thomas, 1970. Pp. 49–87.

Nichols, J. L. *Drug use and highway safety: A review of the literature.* National Highway Traffic Agency, DOT. Washington, D. C.: U. S. Government Printing Office (#50003-0050), 1971.

Nowlis, V. Research with the mood adjective check list. In S. S. Tomkins and C. E. Izard (Eds.), *Affect, cognition and personality.* New York: Springer, 1965.

Osgood, C. E., Suci, G., & Tannenbaum, P. H. *The measurement of meaning.* Urbana, Ill.: University of Illinois Press, 1957.

Osmond, H. Function as a basis of psychiatric ward design. *Mental Hospitals,* 1957, **8,** 23–29.

Panton, J. H. The response of prison inmates to seven new MMPI scales. *Journal of Clinical Psychology,* 1959, **15**(2), 196–197.

Payne, D. E., & Barmack, J. E. An experimental field test of the Smith-Cummings-Sherman driver training system. *Traffic Safety Research Review,* 1963, **7**(1), 10–14.

Pease, K., & Preston, B. Road safety education for young children. *British Journal of Educational Psychology,* 1967, **37**(3), 305–313.

Peters, D. L., & Bentzen, W. R. Human ecology: Planned human adaptation for a crowded future. Paper presented at the 79th Annual Convention of the American Psychological Association, Washington, D. C., September, 1971.

Proshansky, H. M., Ittelson, W. H., & Rivlin, L. (Eds.) *Theory and research in environmental psychology.* New York: Holt, Rinehart and Winston, 1970.

Rainey, R. V., Conger, J. J., Gaskill, H. S., Glad, D. D., Sawrey, W. L., Turrell, E. S., Walsmith, C. R., & Keller, L. An investigation of the role of psychological factors in motor vehicle accidents. *Highway Research Board Bulletin* No. 212. Washington, 1959.

Reeves, W. E., & Morehouse, L. E. The acute effect of smoking upon the physical performance of habitual smokers. *Research Quarterly of the American Association of Health,* 1950, **21,** 245–248.

Rodin, J. Effects of distraction on performance of obese and normal subjects. Unpublished doctoral dissertation, Columbia University, 1970.

Roethlisberger, F. J., & Dickson, W. J. Management and the worker—An account of a research program conducted by the Western Electric Company, Hawthorne Works, Chicago. Cambridge, Mass.: Harvard University Press, 1939.

Rosenthal, R., & Jacobson, L. Teacher expectations for the disadvantaged. *Scientific American,* 1968, **4,** 19–23.

Safford, R. R., & Rockwell, T. H. Performance decrement in twenty-four hour driving. Presented at the 45th Annual Meeting of the Highway Research Board, Washington, D. C., January, 1966.

Schachter, S. Some extraordinary facts about obese humans and rats. *American Psychologist,* 1971a, **26**(2), 129–144.

Schachter, S. *Emotion, obesity, and crime.* New York: Academic Press, 1971b.

Schachter, S., & Gross, L. Manipulated time and eating behavior. *Journal of Personality and Social Psychology,* 1968, **10,** 96–106.

Schori, T. R. A comparison of visual, auditory, and cutaneous tracking displays when divided attention is required to a cross-adaptive loading task. Unpublished doctoral dissertation, University of South Dakota, 1970a.

Schori, T. R. Experimental approaches and hardware for driving research. In N. W. Heimstra (Ed.), *Injury control in traffic safety.* Springfield, Ill.: Charles C. Thomas, 1970b. Pp. 154–175.

Schultz, D. P. *Psychology and industry.* New York: Macmillan, 1970.

Schuster, D. H. Follow-up evaluation of the performance of driver improvement classes for problem drivers. *Journal of Safety Research,* 1969, **1,** 80–87.

Schuster, D. H., & Guilford, J. P. The psychometric prediction of problem drivers. *Human Factors,* 1964, **6,** 393–421.

Scott, J. P., & Langston, M. V. Critical periods affecting the development of normal and maladjusted social behavior of puppies. *Journal of Genetic Psychology,* 1950, **77,** 25–60.

Seminara, J. L., & Shavelson, R. J. Lunar simulation. *Human Factors,* 1969, **11,** 451–462.

Silberman, H. F. Application of computers in education. In R. C. Atkinson and H. A. Wilson (Eds.), *Computer-assisted instruction.* New York: Academic Press, 1969.

Silver, C. A. Performance criteria—direct or indirect. *Highway Research Record No. 55.* Washington, D. C.: Highway Research Board, 1964.

Silvern, L. C. Training: Men-man and man-machine communications. In K. B. DeGreene (Ed.), *Systems psychology.* New York: McGraw-Hill, 1970.

Smart, R. G., Schmidt, W., & Bateman, K. Psychoactive drugs and traffic accidents. *Journal of Safety Research,* 1969, **1**(2), 67–73.

Smith, G. M. Personality and smoking: A review of the empirical literature. In W. A. Hunt (Ed.), *Learning mechanisms and smoking.* Chicago: Aldine, 1970.

Smith, M. B. Ethical implications of population policies: A psychologist's view. *American Psychologist,* 1972, **27**(1), 11–15.

Smoking and health. Report of the Advisory Committee to the Surgeon General. Washington, D. C.: U. S. Department of Health, Education, and Welfare, 1964.

Spady, A. A., Jr. Prototype of a new lunar-gravity simulator for astronaut mobility studies. *Human Factors*, 1969, **11**(5), 441–450.

Spiegel, J. P. Psychosocial factors in riots—old and new. *American Journal of Psychiatry*, 1968, **125**, 281–285.

Srivastava, R. K., & Peel, T. S. *Human movement as a function of color stimulation.* Topeka, Kans.: Environmental Research Foundation, 1968.

State of California Highway Patrol. Report on alcohol, drugs and organic factors in fatal single vehicle traffic accidents. Final report, 1967.

Stickell, D. W. A critical review of the methodology and results of research comparing televised and face-to-face instruction. Unpublished doctoral dissertation, Pennsylvania State University, 1963.

Stolurow, L. Programed instruction and the mentally retarded. *Review of Education Research*, 1963, **33**(1), 126–136.

Suchman, E. A. A conceptual analysis of the accident phenomenon. In *Behavioral approaches to accident research.* New York: Association for the Aid of Crippled Children, 1961.

Super, D. E., & Bohn, M. J., Jr. *Occupational psychology.* Belmont, Calif.: Wadsworth, 1970.

Talland, G. A. Age and the span of immediate recall. In G. A. Talland (Ed.), *Human behavior and aging.* New York: Academic Press, 1968.

Tranel, N. Rural program development. In H. Grunebaum (Ed.), *A practice of community mental health.* Boston: Little, Brown, 1970.

U. S. Surgeon General's Scientific Advisory Committee on Television and Social Behavior. *Television and growing up: The impact of televised violence.* U. S. Government Printing Office, Washington, D. C., 1972.

Vedder, C. B. *Juvenile offenders.* Springfield, Ill.: Charles C. Thomas, 1963.

Verdy, M., & Brouillet, J. Alcohol and adrenocortical function: Negative effect of ACTH reserve in man by metyrapone. *Quarterly Journal of Studies on Alcohol*, 1970, **31**, 545–549.

Ward, W. S., & Grant, D. P. Potentials for collaboration between human factors and architecture. *Human Factors Society Bulletin*, 1970, **13**(2), 1–3.

Warner, H. D. The effects of intermittent noise on human target detection. *Human Factors*, 1969, **11**, 245–250.

Warner, H. D. Methodological issues in traffic safety research. In N. W. Heimstra (Ed.), *Injury control in traffic safety.* Springfield, Ill.: Charles C. Thomas, 1970. Pp. 201–224.

Warner, H. D., & Heimstra, N. W. Effects of intermittent noise on visual search tasks of varying complexity. *Perceptual and Motor Skills*, 1971, **32**, 219–226.

Warner, H. D., & Heimstra, N. W. Effects of noise intensity on visual target-detection performance. *Human Factors*, 1972, **14**(2), 177–181.

Weiss, D. J., & Dawis, R. V. An objective validation of factual interview data. *Journal of Applied Psychology*, 1960, **44**, 381–385.

Welford, A. T. *Ageing and human skill.* London: Oxford University Press, 1958.

Wernimont, P. F. Intrinsic and extrinsic factors in job satisfaction. *Journal of Applied Psychology*, 1966, **50**, 41–50.

Wilson, D. P. *My six convicts.* New York: Holt, Rinehart & Winston, 1951.

Wodtke, K. Educational requirements for a student-subject matter interface. University Park, Pa.: Pennsylvania State University, The Computer-Assisted Instruction Laboratory, March, 1967.

REFERENCES

Wohlwill, J. F. The emerging discipline of environmental psychology. *American Psychologist,* 1970, **25**(4), 303–312.

Wolfgang, M. E. Violence and human behavior. In F. F. Korten, S. W. Cook, and J. I. Lacey (Eds.), *Psychology and the problems of society.* Washington, D. C.: American Psychological Association, 1970. Pp. 309–326.

Wolfgang, M. E., & Ferracuti, F. *Subculture of violence.* London: Tavistok, 1967.

World Health Organization, Expert Committee on Alcohol. *First Report* (W. H. O. Technical Report Series #84), Geneva, 1954.

World Health Organization. Report of an Expert Committee on Alcohol. (W. H. O. Technical Report Series #94), Geneva, 1955.

Zell, J. K., Rockwell, T. H., & Mourant, R. R. Visual search in driving as a function of experience. Paper presented at the annual meeting of the Human Factors Society, Philadelphia, October, 1969.

Zimbardo, P. G. The human choices: Individuation, reason, and order versus deindividuation, impulse, and chaos. In W. J. Arnold and D. Levine (Eds.), *Nebraska symposium on motivation.* Lincoln: University of Nebraska Press, 1969. Pp. 237–307.

index